Guerrilla Radios in Southern Africa

Africa: Past, Present & Prospects

Series Editor: Toyin Falola (the University of Texas at Austin) and Olajumoke Yacob-Haliso (Babcock University)

This series collates and curates studies of Africa in its multivalent local, regional, and global contexts. It aims fundamentally to capture in one series historical, contemporary, and multidisciplinary studies that analyze the dynamics of the African predicament from deeply theoretical perspectives while marshaling empirical data to describe, explain, and predict trends in continuities and change in Africa and in African studies.

The books published in this series represent the multiplicity of voices, local and global, in relation to African futures. It not only represents diversity, but also provides a platform for convergence of outstanding research that will enliven debates about the future of Africa, while also advancing theory and informing policy making. Preference is given to studies that deliberately link the past with the present and advance knowledge about various African nations by extending the range, breadth, depth, types, and sources of data and information existing and emerging about these countries.

The platform created proceeds from the assumption that there is no singular "African experience," nor is it possible to, in any way, homogenize the identities, histories, spaces, and lives of African people.

Titles in the Series

Ghanaian Politics and Political Communication, Edited by Samuel Gyasi Obeng and Emmanuel Debrah

Beyond History: African Agency in Development, Diplomacy and Conflict Resolution, Edited by Elijah Nyaga Munyi, David Mwambari and Aleksi Ylönen

Reflections on Leadership and Institutions in Africa, Edited by Kenneth Kalu and Toyin Falola

Imagining Vernacular Histories: Essays in Honour of Toyin Falola, Edited by Mobolanla Ebunoluwa Sotunsa and Abikal Borah

Insights into Policies and Practices on the Right to Development, Edited by Serges Djoyou Kamga and Carol C. Ngang

Guerrilla Radios in Southern Africa: Broadcasters, Technology, Propaganda Wars, and the Armed Struggle, Edited by Sekibakiba Peter Lekgoathi, Tshepo Moloi, and Alda Romão Saúte Saíde

Guerrilla Radios in Southern Africa

*Broadcasters, Technology,
Propaganda Wars, and the
Armed Struggle*

Edited by Sekibakiba Peter Lekgoathi,
Tshepo Moloi, and Alda Romão Saúte Saíde

ROWMAN & LITTLEFIELD
Lanham • Boulder • New York • London

Published by Rowman & Littlefield
An imprint of The Rowman & Littlefield Publishing Group, Inc.
4501 Forbes Boulevard, Suite 200, Lanham, Maryland 20706
www.rowman.com

6 Tinworth Street, London SE11 5AL, United Kingdom

British Library Cataloguing in Publication Data
A catalogue record for this book is available from the British Library

ISBN: HB 978-1-78661-560-2

Library of Congress Cataloging-in-Publication Data

Names: Lekgoathi, Sekibakiba Peter, editor.
Title: Guerrilla radios in southern Africa : broadcasters, technology, propaganda wars, and the armed struggle / edited by Sekibakiba Peter Lekgoathi.
Other titles: Africa: past, present & prospects.
Description: Lanham, Maryland : Rowman & Littlefield, 2020. | Series: Africa: past, present & prospects | Includes bibliographical references and index. | Summary: "This collection brings together essays on the role that radio played in political resistance against oppressive regimes during the period of the armed struggle in the region"—Provided by publisher.
Identifiers: LCCN 2020026533 (print) | LCCN 2020026534 (ebook) | ISBN 9781786615602 (cloth) | ISBN 9781786615619 (epub) | ISBN 9781538148440 (pbk)
Subjects: LCSH: Radio broadcasting—Africa, Southern. | Radio broadcasting and war—Africa, Southern. | Radio in propaganda—Africa, Southern. | Government, Resistance to—Africa, Southern.
Classification: LCC HE8699.A356 G73 2020 (print) | LCC HE8699.A356 (ebook) | DDC 384.540968—dc23
LC record available at https://lccn.loc.gov/2020026533
LC ebook record available at https://lccn.loc.gov/2020026534

Contents

Abbreviations and Acronyms

AABN	Dutch Anti-Apartheid Movement
AAC	African Affairs Centre
AIM	Mozambique News Agency
ANC	African National Congress
AFP	Agence France Presse
APLA	Azanian People's Liberation Army
APRP	African People's Revolutionary Party
AU	African Union
AWA	African Writers Association
AZANYU	Azanian National Youth Unity
BBC	British Broadcasting Corporation
BCM	Black Consciousness Movement
BSAP	British South Africa Police
CIA	Central Intelligence Agency
CPSU	Communist Party of the Soviet Union
DGS	General Department of Security
DIP	Department of Information and Publicity
FBC	Federal Broadcasting Corporation
FM	Frequency Modulation
FNLA	National Liberation Front of Angola

FNV	Federatie Nederlandse Vakbeweging
FRELIMO	Mozambique Liberation Front
GDR	German Democratic Republic
MANU	Mozambique African National Union
MK	uMkhonto we Sizwe
MPLA	People's Movement for the Liberation of Angola
NACTU	National Council of Trade Unions
NAHECS	National Heritage and Cultural Studies Centre
NAZ	National Archives of Zimbabwe
NDP	National Democratic Party
NEC	National Executive Committee
NGO	Nongovernmental Organization
NP	National Party
NUSAS	National Union of South African Students
OAU	Organization of African Unity
OvRF	Omroep voor Radio Freedom
PAC	Pan Africanist Congress
PAIGC	The African Party for the Independence of Guinea and Cape Verde
PAYM	Pan African Youth Movement
PIDE	International and State Defense Police
PLAN	People's Liberation Army of Namibia
PSYOP	Psychological Operations Unit
RBC	Rhodesian Broadcasting Corporation
RNTC	Radio Netherlands Training Centre
RSA	Republic of South Africa
SAAF	South African Air Force
SABC	South African Broadcasting Corporation
SACP	South African Communist Party
SACTU	South African Congress of Trade Unions
SADCC	Southern African Development Coordination Conference

SADET	South African Democracy Education Trust
SADF	South African Defense Force
SASO	South African Student Organization
SASM	South African Student Movement
SCCIA	Centralization and Coordination of Information Service of Angola
SCCIM	Mozambique Information Coordination and Centralization Service
SEK	Swedish Krona
SIDA	Swedish International Development Authority
SOMAFCO	Solomon Mahlangu Freedom College
SRC	Students Representative Council
SWB	Summary of World Broadcasts
SWAPO	South West African People's Organization
TBC	Tanzania Broadcast Corporation
UDENAMO	The National Democratic Union of Mozambique
UDI	Unilateral Declaration of Independence
UFH	University of Fort Hare
UK	United Kingdom
UNESCO	United Nations Educational, Scientific and Cultural Organisation
UNIN	United Nations Institute of Namibia
UNIP	United National Independence Party
Unisa	University of South Africa
UNITA	The National Union for the Total Independence of Angola
USSR	Union of Soviet Socialist Republics
UWC	University of the Western Cape
VoN	Voice of Namibia
VOR	Voice of the Revolution
VOZ	Voice of Zimbabwe
WFDY	World Federation of Democratic Youth
WIDF	Women's International Democratic Federation

ZANLA	Zimbabwe African National Liberation Army
ZANU	Zimbabwe African National Union
ZAPU	Zimbabwe African People's Union
ZBS	Zambia Broadcasting Services
ZIPRA	Zimbabwe People's Revolutionary Army
ZTV	Zimbabwean Television

Acknowledgments

This book draws inspiration from the two workshops held at the University of the Witwatersrand in Johannesburg and at Pedagogic University in Maputo in February and November 2017, respectively, under the title "Liberation War Radios in Southern Africa, 1960–early 1990s." In 2016, Sekibakiba Lekgoathi took the initiative by submitting an application for funding from the National Institute for the Humanities and Social Sciences' (NIHSS) Catalytic Research Project. Lekgoathi, together with Tshepo Moloi, Alda Romão Saúte Saíde, and Eléusio Viegas Filipe, coordinated the workshops and saw to the successful execution of this initiative. The team is grateful for the generous financial support for the Liberation War Radios project received from the NIHSS.

These workshops attracted like-minded researchers and scholars based mostly at universities in southern Africa, and whose projects explored guerrilla radios and the role they played in the liberation struggle in the southern African region. We would like to thank the contributors to the February and November 2017 workshops who revised and sharpened their original papers for publication in this volume.

The book project arose from the realization that despite the proliferation of research on liberation struggles in southern Africa, there remained a dearth of studies on the media that the liberation movements employed, particularly radio. Guerrilla radios served as a source of alternative information and counter-propaganda, spending a considerable amount of time dispelling the messages propagated through the media of the white minority regimes. By looking at case studies of guerrilla radios from the region, the project sought to contribute toward advancing regional scholarship on the histories of these radios and their contestation of the colonial/apartheid states' monopoly of the airwaves.

We received a great deal of support and encouragement from colleagues at the University of the Witwatersrand and Pedagogic University. Most notably, we would like to thank Professor Mucha Musemwa, head of the School of Social Sciences, who opened the February 2017 workshop, as well as Professor Noor Nieftagodien for his unstinting endorsement from the conceptual stage of this project and for the insightful comments made throughout the two days of the first workshop. These workshops would have not happened had it not been for the sterling work of Antonette Gouws, the senior administrator for both the SARChi Program in "Local Histories and Present Realities" and the History Workshop who dealt with the financial aspects and logistics of the organizing, from the booking of accommodations, flights, and shuttles through to catering arrangements. Mphako Machete was very helpful in transcribing some of the interviews used in the book.

On the Mozambican side, our appreciation goes out to the dean of the faculty of Social Sciences and Philosophical Science, Professor Bento Rupia; the director of International Relation Offices, Professor Sarita Monjane Henriksen, and the director of the Central Library, Dr. Aissa Issak for making it possible for the workshop to be accommodated at the university. We thank the secretary of the Maputo Municipal Council, Ms. Susana Laíce, for the small tokens of appreciation given to the participants of the workshop.

This book would have not been complete had it not been for the willingness and patience of staff at various archives in the region and overseas. In particular, we are indebted to Mosoabuli Ike Maamoe, the archivist at the National Heritage and Cultural Studies Centre at the University of Fort Hare, whose outstanding knowledge of the ANC and PAC collections made the search of documents less cumbersome. The archives staff at Robben Island Museum and Mayibuye Centre were very helpful in facilitating access to Radio Freedom's sound collection—in particular, we thank Lebohang Sekholomi and Stanley Sello. We also note staff at the Wits Historical Papers. We thank also the former broadcasters, managers, and listeners of the guerrilla radios from the whole southern African region who graciously gave up valuable time from their busy schedules to share invaluable memories about these radios.

Our thanks go out as well to the publisher of this edited volume, Rowman & Littlefield International, the reviewers, as well as the copy editor, Monica Seeber.

Sekibakiba Peter Lekgoathi, Tshepo Moloi, Alda Romão Saúte Saíde
October 2020

Chapter One

Radios of the Liberation Struggle in Southern Africa

Sekibakiba Peter Lekgoathi, Tshepo Moloi, and
Alda Romão Saúte Saíde

Since the 1950s radio has been the predominant medium of mass communication in Africa. Not only was radio broadcasting employed by the colonial states in the service of empire, but the liberation forces also appropriated it as a weapon in the struggle for independence. With the turn to the armed struggle and movement into exile in the early 1960s, access to a radio station became a top priority for the nationalist movements in southern Africa. Through radio, the guerrilla movements sought to maintain a sonic presence among their supporters at home. It was a means through which they could shape their supporters' political views and behavior—and more especially their activities in resisting white rule.[1]

The liberation movements also, of course, used other media (particularly print), but radio occupied a very special place in the struggle for independence in southern Africa. Sound had the most appeal. Through radio, the liberation movements could address their supporters instantly and directly behind enemy lines. They could maintain their presence at home without being physically present. The appropriation of radio by the nationalist movements nevertheless caused severe nervousness on the part of the white minority regimes in the region, unwilling to surrender their monopoly over the airwaves.

Radio first came to Africa as a tool of empire. This was true of radio throughout southern Africa, where this modern technology was inaugurated, as Mhoze Chikowero writes in chapter 4 of this volume, "as an instrument of contending European imperial propaganda wars against each other and on colonized Africans." Radio symbolized a European presence.

1

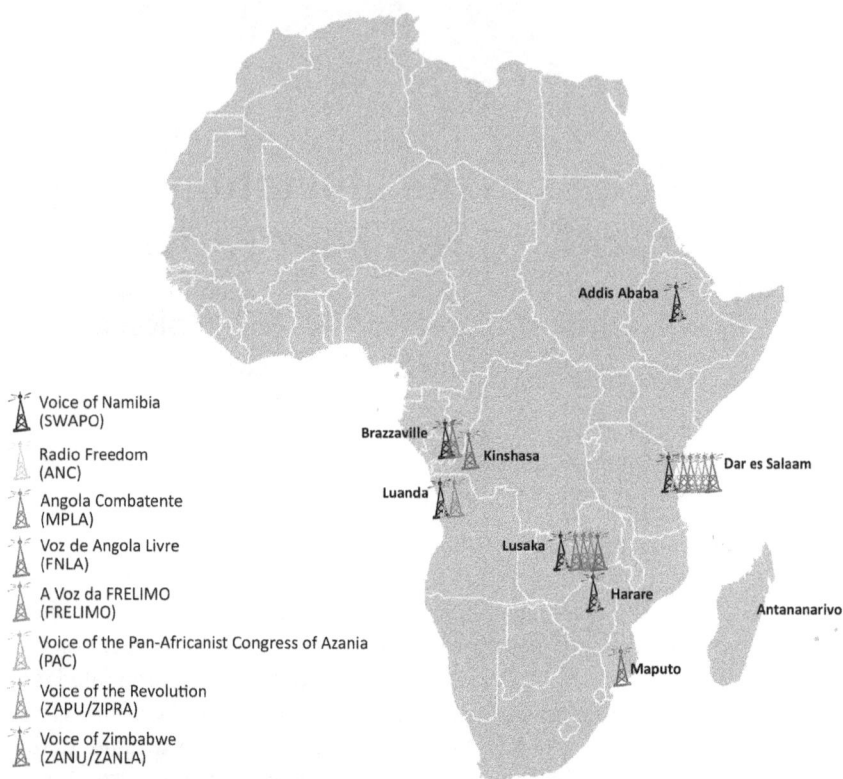

Figure 1. Map of Africa illustrating the independent countries in south, central and east Arica which hosted the various southern African guerrilla radios.
Source: **Robert Heinze.**

The first broadcasting stations were mainly in European languages and directed primarily at white audiences in the colonies. The first propaganda radio that made a concerted effort to influence political opinion in southern Africa was the Nazi station Radio Zeesen. Broadcasting in Afrikaans in the 1930s, before the Second World War, this radio was aimed at certain elements in Namibia and South Africa that were sympathetic to the Nazi cause.[2] Radio broadcasting in African languages was first established in the early 1940s, against the backdrop of growing interracial mistrust during the war. There were growing fears among the white rulers at the time that Africans would scupper the war effort unless they received regular war communiques, in their own languages, that urged support for the war. Those who championed radio broadcasting in African languages saw it as the most effective tool for educating the masses and instilling loyalty to the empire.

In South Africa during the apartheid era, as Sekibakiba Lekgoathi argues, the South African Broadcasting Corporation (SABC) introduced African-language radio stations that were ethnically divided. Collectively named Radio Bantu, radio in African languages was introduced to reinforce the bantustan policy of ethnic separatism.[3] Radio "became a critical tool of modern technology for achieving the ambitions of those who were determined to govern the black population by domination rather than consent."[4] It was in the interest of those in power to control and contain African access to radio, and when African nationalist movements flipped the script and adopted radio as a means for contesting colonial domination and attaining liberation, a protracted warfare of the airwaves ensued.

Radio played an inimitable role in the liberation struggle in southern Africa, particularly after the turn to the armed struggle. It became a tool for pushing the liberation struggle propaganda and galvanizing opposition against white minority rule. Yet no substantial work has been conducted that has made an effort to situate guerrilla radios within a broader regional context—apart from some cursory hints in the voluminous body of essays, memoirs, biographies, and autobiographies of former activists and political leaders in southern Africa about the role that radio played in the liberation struggle. Most of the works produced tend to be parochial in approach, analyzing each guerrilla radio within the framework of the nation-state. There has been very little sustained research to provide historical and social analyses of the use of sound in the liberation struggle in the region as a whole. We know very little about *how* the nationalist movements were able to engage in a war of the airwaves against the white minority regimes, or to capture the hearts and minds of the people from their bases in exile. We know even less about content production and reception of the messages broadcast on these radio stations.

Guerrilla Radios in Southern Africa is a collection of chapters on the histories of the radios attached to the armed wings of the liberation movements in the region. It is about the experiences of the broadcasters and listeners during the era of the armed struggle. Using archival sources such as sound recordings of the guerrilla radio stations, together with interviews conducted with former broadcasters and listeners, the chapters contained in this volume ask complex questions about the social histories of these stations. They explore the workings of propaganda and counter-propaganda and probe the effects the radios had on the activists and supporters of the liberation movements—and, on the other hand, on the colonial counter-insurgency projects. The chapters also examine the relationships that these radios forged at their multiple sites of operation in host countries, and look at international solidarity and support, specifically for radio broadcasting initiatives. In the end, this book pushes the frontiers of knowledge production beyond exploration of broadcast content toward a more nuanced conception of radio as a medium formed by social and political processes.

Guerrilla radio broadcasting, we argue, became a very powerful technology for disseminating insurgent propaganda messages of the liberation movements and for mobilizing African workers, peasants, students, and youth in the struggle against white minority domination in the entire region. From Angola to Mozambique, and from Zimbabwe to Namibia through to South Africa, the modern technology of radio provided the liberation movements in exile with a platform for an aural or sonic presence among the followers of the liberation movements back home. It became an effective instrument for propagating the ideologies of the liberation movements and for countering the propaganda messages of the oppressive white minority regimes.

The cheapest and most direct medium of communication, guerrilla radios transcended boundaries and were widely listened to, albeit illegally. These radio stations existed, according to Marissa Moorman, "beyond the jurisdiction of colonial law but within the broadcast range of the colonial state and the territory it claimed."[5] Their public and legal operation behind enemy lines and outside the reach of the colonial or apartheid laws, coupled with the reality that many people within the colonial territories tuned in, caused severe anxiety on the part of the state. We borrow the concept of the nervous condition of the colonial state from Mhoze Chikowero (in this volume), who in turn coined the term from Nancy Rose Hunt's work on the condition of the Belgian colonial state in the Congo.[6] Because of the invisibility and transience of sound and the insecurity of the authorities, the police and the military were put on the defensive. As Moorman shows in chapter 3 of this volume, the colonial state listened in to the guerrilla radios and transcribed the broadcast messages—and arrested and prosecuted anyone caught listening. Quite commonly, as Sifiso Mxolisi Ndlovu illustrates in chapter 9, the white minority regimes sought to counter guerrilla radio propaganda with their own propaganda disseminated through state channels such as Radio Republic of South Africa (Radio RSA). Simultaneously, surveillance was put on guerrilla radios and their frequencies were jammed.

The support that the independent African countries (Egypt, Algeria, Ethiopia, Ghana, Tanzania, Zambia, Congo-Brazzaville, Congo-Kinshasa, and Angola, among others) and other international solidarity groups and governments gave to the southern African liberation movements in exile was immense. Yet the existing studies on the liberation struggles only provide perfunctory hints, at best, of this. Very few historical works have uncovered the multi-layered histories of these radios and analyzed the dynamics of the relationships fostered at the points of operation in exile. The paucity of regional scholarship on the liberation struggle generally, and on broadcasting in particular, is unfortunate given the region's shared experiences of white minority rule, the continental initiatives to fight against it, and the growing significance of radio as a medium of mass communication in the era after the Second World War.

In his chapter in this volume Lekgoathi shows that substantial financial and logistical support was advanced to the African National Congress's (ANC's) Radio Freedom by governments, solidarity groups, and civil society organizations in eastern and western Europe (the Soviet Union, the German Democratic Republic, the Nordic countries, the Netherlands, and others). While the fight against the injustices of the apartheid system was important, these countries and support groups also had other underlying motivations. During the Cold War, the communist bloc supported the liberation movements in order to expand their ideological influence in Africa. The Scandinavian countries and the Netherlands saw support for Radio Freedom as part of a larger struggle against state monopoly of the airwaves and the promotion of media pluralism and democracy. Informed by their pan-Africanist outlook and commitment to a decolonized Africa, sovereign African countries such as Egypt, Ethiopia, Tanzania, and Zambia (despite their own struggling economies and sociopolitical challenges) accommodated these radios on the external services of their national broadcasters. The sacrifices they made were significant. Some endured spates of military incursions and air bombardment by the South African military that destabilized the entire region. Radio Freedom, Voice of the Pan Africanist Congress, Voice of Namibia, A Voz da Frelimo, Voice of the Revolution, Voice of Zimbabwe and others benefited greatly from such magnanimity by the frontline states.

THE SONIC ARCHIVE AND LIBERATION IN SOUTHERN AFRICA

Despite the key role that radio played in the struggle for independence on the African continent, the nationalist historians studying the liberation movements in the period from the 1960s to the 1980s had been reluctant to venture beyond documentary materials in their quest for sources of historical evidence. Their obsession with documents resulted in a failure to comprehend the mechanics through which the liberation movements communicated their messages.[7] Besides the dismal state of the sonic and documentary archives of the liberation movements themselves, the ephemerality of radio, the invisibility of sound, and the transience of intimacies created by this technology have all made it burdensome to undertake research on it.[8] Nevertheless, much has changed in the last three decades, and since the early 2000s African radio histories have begun to flourish. The new works have examined some of the ways in which the liberation movements tapped into this modern technology of mass communication, the use of propaganda, listenership, and the effects of the radio messages on the listeners and supporters of the liberation movements—and the states' counter-insurgency projects.[9] The chapters in this volume are indicative of this turn in the fortunes of radio scholarship.

Even so, very few of the guerrilla radios discussed here have left substantial sonic and documentary archival remnants to make it possible to paint a fuller picture of their histories. This is in part a consequence of the reality that underground political operatives did not keep journals or diaries. Those operating clandestinely within the territories under white rule invariably took a conscious decision not to keep written records of meetings. It was deliberate. They were being cautious about retaining any records that might be confiscated during the frequent police raids and lead to the exposure of their comrades. The white minority regimes constantly monitored anyone suspected of involvement in nationalist activities and to avoid implicating themselves political activists got rid of records of their activities or links to banned organizations.

Compounding the problem of record keeping was the precarious existence of the liberation movements in exile. Survival depended on financial donations and logistical support from international solidarity groups and governments—mostly from the communist bloc—as well as from sovereign African countries. In most cases the resources at the disposal of the liberation movements could barely cover their basic needs. The guerrilla radios relied heavily on the generosity of the host countries for airtime on the external services of their national radios—which precluded any long-term plans for systematic archiving. The audio reels and cassettes required for recording the radio programs were often in short supply, so recycling became a common practice, resulting in loss of valuable sound archives. The consequence is that, perhaps with the notable exception of South Africa, there are very few sound recordings of guerrilla radio programs for the period from the 1960s to 1970s.

Regarding the particular situation of archives of the armed liberation movements in the former Portuguese territories, record keeping was not a priority during the transition period between the military coup in Portugal in April 1974 and independence the following year. As the returning exiled movements pushed for political dominance, archiving became the last thing on their minds and "sound reels and [the] few written transcripts that existed were lost, damaged, reused, or simply forgotten."[10] This is the case even for the victorious People's Movement for the Liberation of Angola (MPLA) in Angola and Mozambique Liberation Front (FRELIMO) in Mozambique. Conducting research on the histories of guerrilla radios (including listenership, not only in the Portuguese colonies but also in Namibia, South Africa, and colonial Zimbabwe) is challenging because of their status as illegal radios. Whereas they operated above ground from their studios in the frontline states, listeners in their target countries had to tune in in secret. The white minority rulers tuned in as well but did not conduct any scientific surveys to measure listenership patterns, program preference, and the impact of these radios on the people. Fear of losing control was the main factor motivating them to clamp down on listenership.

Notwithstanding these limitations, the Portuguese colonial state produced and kept a voluminous archive of broadcast transcripts and memos regarding listenership to guerrilla radios in Angola and in Mozambique. The agents of the International and State Defense Police (PIDE) and later the military and Centralization and Coordination of Information Service of Angola (SCCIA) agents diligently listened, recorded, transcribed, and categorized the broadcasts of the banned liberation movements as dangerous, "anti-Portuguese," and "enemy" propaganda. In the eyes of the authorities, listening to the banned radios implied endorsement and, at the very least, aroused suspicion.[11] Massive volumes running into thousands of pages of broadcast transcripts were generated. They have been deposited in the PIDE files of the Portuguese National Archives and the Military History Archive in Lisbon. These documents are not impartial. After all, they were generated by officials who feared losing power. Moorman suggests that scholars should listen to these documents and pick up their "acoustic registers," as the words in the PIDE reports have a tone and timbre. "It is not the tone and timbre of the broadcast voice (much of which disappeared with the recordings though some is captured in the text); instead, it is one that quivers and shouts in response to it, one that registers its effects."[12]

The state of the archives of the liberation movement in Zimbabwe also deserves some reflection. There are some transcripts of the broadcasts of the two guerrilla radios (ZAPU's Voice of the Revolution and ZANU's Voice of Zimbabwe), as well as some documents and newspaper reports that have been deposited at the National Archives of Zimbabwe (NAZ). Selected sound recordings of the Zimbabwean liberation movements which broadcast from Radio Mozambique in Maputo have been deposited at the national archives. There is also a massive collection of documentary and visual recordings at the national broadcaster Zimbabwean Television (ZTV). It should, however, be pointed out that after independence in 1980, the postcolonial ZANU government confiscated the records owned by ZAPU's armed wing, ZIPRA.[13] This was part of an attempt to achieve political hegemony. There was a concerted effort to obliterate the contribution made by ZAPU and ZIPRA from even the archives, and to rewrite the history of the liberation struggle in Zimbabwe from the perspective of ZANU and its armed wing, the Zimbabwe African National Liberation Army (ZANLA)—what is often referred to as the "Zanu-fication" of the liberation struggle narrative in Zimbabwe.

The sources used in the chapter on the Namibian liberation radio are varied and interesting, suggesting other spaces where scholars can find very useful data on the programs and contents of guerrilla radios. These include the special collections such as the Katjavivi Collection in the SWAPO Party Archives and Research Centre at the University of Namibia Archives and the Swapo Collection at Basler Afrika Bibliographien in Switzerland, as well as documents collected by foreign broadcasters, based on information they gleaned from monitoring and listening to particular radios. The BBC's radio archives are an important resource, as well as the US-based Foreign Broadcast Information Service (FBIS), an online archival service that is a repository of transcripts of radio broadcasts from all over the world.

Compensating for evidentiary gaps in archival material, the authors of the chapters contained in this book have relied on a substantial body of oral interviews conducted (mostly by the researchers themselves) with former broadcasters, managers, and listeners. Using this oral history material, the contributors have been able to weave highly textured and rich accounts that fill major gaps in historical scholarship on radio.

The South African liberation movements have some archival collections on guerrilla radios that are relatively substantial (particularly for the 1970s and 1980s) compared to those of the country's neighbors. While the communist bloc had been a major source of material support in the 1960s and early 1970s, more support started flowing in from other parts of the world in the aftermath of the June 16, 1976 Soweto students' uprising. The ANC was actually the major beneficiary, receiving funding and equipment from other parts of the world, including western Europe. Most came from the Nordic countries and from solidarity groups in Europe and other parts of the world. Although there is some material on the PAC, incessant internecine power struggles paralyzed the PAC and made it difficult for the organization to function properly from the beginning. Brutal state repression following the killing of whites and of black collaborators by the Poqo fighters in the 1960s rendered the PAC dysfunctional and made it hard for the organization to keep proper archives, especially the sound clips of its guerrilla radio. While we have an abundance of audio recordings of Radio Freedom at the Mayibuye Centre in Cape Town, hardly any sound recording has been preserved in any of the archives in South Africa that gives an auditory sense of the Voice of the PAC.

The magnanimous support from the international community enabled the ANC in exile to accumulate a sizable volume of sonic and documentary archival materials unmatched by other liberation movements in southern Africa. It would appear that, post-1976, some consciousness about the importance of archiving had been aroused within the ANC, which perhaps accounts for the richness of their existing collections. Once political organizations were unbanned in 1990, the ANC was able to ship large quantities of this material back home from its exile missions. Most of these resources have been deposited at the Robben Island Museum and the Mayibuye Archives Centre at the University of the Western Cape and the "Liberation Archives" at the National Heritage and Cultural Studies Centre (NAHECS) at the University of Fort Hare at Alice in the Eastern Cape. This archive houses the reports, memoranda, internal propaganda files (including scripts of the radio programs), complete collections of *Sechaba, Mayibuye, African Communist*, and other journals of the liberation movement, other documents from its external missions, as well as the publications of the PAC and other organizations. More than 70 percent of the documents in this archive belong to the ANC; the rest was received from the PAC, AZAPO, and other organizations.[14]

The second major archive is the Robben Island Museum-Mayibuye Archive (hereafter the Mayibuye Archive) at the University of the Western Cape, which houses the Radio Freedom Collection. This collection comprises hundreds of recordings of programs and the vinyl music records that were played on the station from the frontline states. The recordings are available on audiocassettes only and not in the form of transcripts.

The Dr. Karel Roskam Collection, also deposited in the same archive, constitutes the third important source of information on Radio Freedom. It comprises interviews with some prominent anti-apartheid activists and the Radio Freedom broadcasters that Dr. Roskam himself conducted and aired on Vara, a progressive radio station in the Netherlands. Dr. Roskam was a Dutch anti-apartheid activist and radio journalist associated with Omroep voor Radio Freedom (Broadcasting for Radio Freedom), which supported the broadcasting efforts of the nationalist movement. He also drafted a few papers on the liberation movement and the role of the Dutch anti-apartheid movement, copies of which he donated to the Mayibuye Archive in the early 1990s. In addition, oral interviews have been conducted since 2009 with some of the former political activists who had tuned in to Radio Freedom in the 1970s and 1980s, as well as with the workers of this radio station. Finally, the National Archives of South Africa in Pretoria is an important repository of the primary sources on the apartheid state's Department of Information.

AFRICAN LIBERATION
HISTORIOGRAPHY AND THE SONIC ARCHIVE

Even though radio has been a very popular medium of communication on the African continent for more than half a century, it is only recently that scholars have started giving it serious scholarly consideration. The earliest works have examined larger issues of political economy and the use of radio by ruling parties for purposes of political control but have left little room for discussions of human agency.[15] Later works have delved into "broadcast cultures," state monopoly over broadcasting, the multiplying of community and local radios, politics, democracy, the use of African languages, globalization, and so forth, that characterized the continent in the early 1990s.[16] A number of innovative studies have been produced on radio and popular culture, music, radio drama, subversion, the creation of communities and ethnic identities, as well as on the use of radio by the liberation movements.[17] While most of the literature is specifically on radio in South Africa, Marcus Power's work has looked at the historical landscape of radio broadcasting in colonial Mozambique and examined its role in promoting the Portuguese "civilizing mission,"[18] Mhoze Chikowero has explored the introduction of radio broadcasting for Africans in colonial Zambia, Zimbabwe, and Malawi as part of imperial propaganda, to persuade the Africans to support the imperial war effort during the Second World War.[19]

The most groundbreaking study of radio is an edited volume by Liz Gunner, Dina Ligaga, and Dumisani Moyo that examines the multiple roles of radio in the lives of listeners across sub-Saharan Africa.[20] It brings together essays that deal with the role of radio in the culture and politics of countries, language, gender, religion, the creation of communities, and new publics. Some of the essays discuss the current role of radio and the significance of talk shows in creating listening communities that radically transform the nature of the public sphere; others turn to the history of radio in terms of its various manifestations in different countries.[21]

Globally, historical literature on radio propaganda is only now beginning to receive serious scholarly consideration. The major propaganda stations of the Cold War era such as Radio Moscow, Radio Liberty, and Radio Free Europe have received some attention over the past few years.[22] Of the three, work on Radio Moscow has been quite challenging because the research materials remain classified and the Russian archives are virtually inaccessible to researchers.[23] For scholars of radio in Africa this is very unfortunate considering Radio Moscow's importance to listeners on the continent and the hard work that the station put into influencing African audiences. Without access to the Russian archives it is difficult to uncover information about the forms of support given to the guerrilla radios of southern Africa and to determine their significance for audiences in the region. However, the biggest shortcoming of studies about radio propaganda during the era of the Cold War is that they tend to look at the war from the perspectives of the superpowers.[24]

On the African continent, some work has appeared recently that looks at the liberation movements and international propaganda radio. Radio Cairo certainly played a leading role as a major anti-colonial radio, offering airtime to guerrilla movements on its frequencies. It was followed by Radio Tanzania in Dar es Salaam (1964) and Radio Lusaka in Zambia (1968).[25] Some work has been done on the role that the guerrilla radios played as conduits of the liberation movements' propaganda. This includes Julie Frederikse's documentary collection on the liberation war in Zimbabwe.[26] In 1994, an exploratory study by Lebona Mosia, Charles Riddle, and Jim Zaffiro made a comparative analysis of four stations in southern Africa, although its conclusion regarding their actual impact was rather indeterminate.[27] Very recently, Stephen Davis and Sekibakiba Lekgoathi have explored aspects of the history of the ANC's Radio Freedom, focusing mainly on the relationship between the ANC and South African Communist Party (SACP), the political position of the radio station in relation to the liberation movement, as well as on listenership and the music played.[28] In Angola, Marissa Moorman has examined the use of radio programs by the liberation forces to communicate information employed as a weapon in the struggle against Portuguese colonialism.

In most of the historical analyses that exist, the focus is usually on either the political status of a given station in the movement in exile or on its reception by audiences back home. In his recent article on the history of the Voice of Namibia, SWAPO's clandestine radio that mobilized resistance, Robert Heinze has looked at both the connections and interactions between the different levels of politics, production, media content, and reception.[29] One of the major shortcomings of the existing literature on radio is that it does not tell us much about the day-to-day experiences of the radios and their broadcasters in host countries. We do not know much about the specific nature of support that the host radio stations provided to guerrilla radios and the relationships that developed between and among the guerrilla radios in the region. This book attempts to address this deficiency by looking at the guerrilla radios not just from the reception side of their broadcasts but also from their operational or production sites in the frontline states.

ARCHITECTURE OF THE BOOK

The book consists of eleven key chapters roughly divided into four sections, each of which focuses on guerrilla radio(s) targeting particular colonial territories. The chapters are also arranged chronologically according to the years in which each country attained independence. Chapters 2 and 3 look at the Portuguese colonial territories of Mozambique and Angola, which also happen to be the first two colonies in southern Africa to attain independence in 1975, following a protracted period of armed struggle starting in the 1960s. The second part (chapters 4–7) is about guerrilla radios in Rhodesia (colonial Zimbabwe), while the eighth chapter is the only one looking at SWAPO's Voice of Namibia. The last four chapters of the book (chapters 9–12) discuss guerrilla radios in South Africa.

The role of radio as a propaganda tool for the liberation movements in southern Africa is a central theme in the majority of chapters in this volume. Virtually all the chapters explore the role of guerrilla radios in the region as an important medium through which the liberation movements, based in exile and broadcasting from the stations of sovereign African states but well within the earshot of the white minority rulers, could address the masses of their supporters at home. As Alda Romão Saúte Saíde shows in her chapter, *A Voz da FRELIMO* proved effective in bringing a new dimension to the struggle—the battle of the airwaves. Guerrilla radio, she argues, complemented the armed struggle that was already under way, and "was no less dangerous than the armed struggle." It served as a conduit for Frelimo propaganda messages and mobilized underground political activists in Mozambique during the 1960s and 1970s. The Portuguese government, in attempting to counter A Voz da Frelimo, on the one hand, created the psychosocial radio service "A Voz de Moçambique" broadcast from Lourenço Marques, Nampula, Zambezia, Cabo Delgado, and Dondo. This colonial government radio used Mozambican languages, namely Ronga, Shangana, Macua-Meto, Swahili, Nyanja, Sena, Ajaua, and Maconde. The programs featured political, anti-FRELIMO propaganda, especially the *Hora da Verdade* (Hour of Truth), as well as commercial and recreational productions. On the other hand, the manufacturers produced more affordable radio receivers so that large numbers of audiences could tune in to colonial government radios away from the military theaters.

The point about guerrilla radios as a channel of the liberation movements' propaganda messages finds strong articulation in most of the chapters in the book, especially those by Moorman, Ndlovu, Mushonga et al., and Ali Khangela Hlongwane. What is also common across the region is that despite severe penalties for listening to these guerrilla radios, political activists and followers tuned in anyway and were influenced by the messages they received. These radios succeeded not only in radicalizing the masses; they also subverted the power of the state.

Marissa Moorman employs the concept of the "unnerved colonial state" in her analysis of the guerrilla radios of two of the Angolan liberation movements. Angola Combatente of the People's Movement for the Liberation of Angola (MPLA) operated from Brazzaville, while A Voz Livre de Angola of the National Liberation Front of Angola (FNLA) broadcast from Kinshasa. The broadcasts of these radios allowed the liberation movements to maintain an auditory and aural presence in the Angolan territory from their bases in exile and to be involved in a war of the airwaves with the Portuguese colonial state with whom they were fighting a ground war. The chapter analyzes the influence of these rebel broadcasts on the listeners, state and nonstate. Moorman shows how these stations were tools of mobilization of popular anticolonial sentiment, utilized to harass the colonial government and army and to persuade enemy soldiers (both African and Portuguese) to abscond. Her main argument revolves around the specificities of radio technology and broadcasting—its invisibility, ephemerality, and intimacy—that expose the limitations of the colonial counter-insurgency program.

Mhoze Chikowero takes us into the second part of the book with his chapter on guerrilla broadcasting in colonial Zimbabwe. He looks at how Africans used radio broadcasting that was intended to serve as a tool for turning them into useful, loyal, subjects of empire. The project to politically engineer African minds via radio broadcasting was inaugurated in colonial Zambia, Zimbabwe, and Malawi in 1939 as part of the colonial war effort, effectively a war effort waged not simply against Nazism but also on "the native mind." However, Africans had in place their own systems of information production, processing, and dissemination, which dispatched the colonial propaganda press that came before radio. These African systems took the oral, aural, and visual shapes and worked through complicated linguistic and cultural registers that similarly paralyzed both radio and cinema, and sowed the seeds of guerrilla broadcasting right there in the colonial broadcasting studio by the 1950s. Chikowero's chapter shows how, through guerrilla radio, Africans effectively wrested control of this new medium and redeployed it as a technology of state crafting and self-liberation. They were able to do so because they were already technologically equipped in systems of knowledge and information management and dissemination. In trying to understand technologies of self-liberation in Africa, the chapter argues, the focus should not be so much on the gadgets as on the agency of the subject in the deeper African historical context.

As does Chikowero, Dumisani Moyo and Cris Chinaka focus on the two guerrilla radios in Zimbabwe. Their main emphasis, however, is on propaganda, persuasion, and mass mobilization. They critically analyze the connection between spirit mediums and guerrilla radios in the strategies of communication utilized by ZANU and ZAPU. In order to legitimize their broadcast messages, guerrilla broadcasters often invoked spirit mediums to the masses of audiences. Moyo and Chinaka argue that despite the constraints of operating from exile and the counter-propaganda of the colonial state, the two movements effectively used sophisticated communication strategies that combined oral tradition, spirituality, song, and modern technology in the form of radio and face-to-face communication with villagers, through evening meetings, to mobilize support for the struggle.

The next two chapters are coauthored by Munyaradzi Mushonga, Munyaradzi Nyakudya, and Lloyd Hazvineyi. In chapter 6 the authors look at the effects of ZAPU's Voice of the Revolution (VOR) in the radicalization of the nationalist struggle in Zimbabwe during the period of the Smith regime (1965–1980). Through political radio programs and news broadcasts in Shona, Ndebele, and English, they argue, ZAPU launched a new wave of nationalism that sought not only to agitate for militancy and insurgency against the Rhodesian government but also to represent it as a fetish that could be ridiculed, thus subverting its power. The insurgency and the violence that began to be experienced following the Smith regime's Unilateral Declaration of

Independence (UDI) in 1965 were not a coincidence but, rather, a consequence of the broadcasts by the guerrilla radios, in this case VOR.

In chapter 7, the same authors deal with the biographies of three guerrilla
radio broadcasters, Jane Lungile Ngwenya (VOR) and Sobusa Gula-Ndebele
and Nyasha Donald Musiiwa (VOZ), outlining their experiences of colonialism and liberation war radio broadcasting. Jane's narrative dispels the myth
that women were passive in the liberation struggle while Sobusa and Nyasha's stories both reveal students' political activism. The reminiscences of
these broadcasters bring to light some major differences between VOR and
VOZ in terms of their approaches, content, and style in war radio broadcasting—for example, VOZ's preference for educated broadcasters with battlefield experience and use of noms de guerre, as opposed to VOR's flexibility
on levels of education and openness about broadcasters' real identities.

Chapter 8 takes us to Namibia, where Robert Heinze explores SWAPO's
Voice of Namibia as an instrument of diplomacy. The chapter looks at the
Voice of Namibia (VoN) first as an instrument of mass communication that
enabled Swapo to have a sonic presence in Namibia. It was through this radio
that the people could receive information about the progress of the war in
Angola and about the anti-apartheid struggle in Namibia despite the South
African media curfew. Second, this guerrilla radio addressed international
audiences. It intervened in international public discourse in order to counter
Radio RSA, the propaganda radio of the South African government, and to
bring international public opinion onto Swapo's side. More importantly, the
chapter demonstrated the role the United Nations played in establishing and
supporting this guerrilla radio to galvanize the struggle against apartheid and
to educate journalists for an independent Namibia.

The use of propaganda radio by the South African regime in the war over
the airwaves is taken up by Sifiso Mxolisi Ndlovu in chapter 9, which centers
on propaganda and counter-propaganda. The chapter investigates the tough
battle over the hearts and minds of the international community between the
ANC's Department of Information and Publicity (DIP) and the apartheid
regime's Department of Information. It looks at the apartheid regime's use of
its sophisticated propaganda radio, Radio RSA, to champion the country's
foreign policy in Africa, which was labeled "outward looking policy" and
"détente." Sympathetic foreign media based in South Africa followed the
lead of Radio RSA and produced exaggerated reports about worsening divisions within the Organization of African Unity (OAU), on détente and on
holding dialogue with the apartheid regime. To counter the regime's propaganda radio, Ndlovu asserts that the DIP was charged with fostering an
understanding of ANC policies and objectives among elements outside the
country that normally supported apartheid South Africa, with the intention of
eventually winning their hearts and minds. The ANC was striving to nullify
the apartheid regime's formidable propaganda machine, diminish its credibil-

ity, and counter its efforts to foster disunity and isolate the ANC so that its support from the international community and the OAU dried up. The DIP adopted multimedia communication strategies to counter the apartheid regime's offensive. Among these strategies was the establishment of Radio Freedom.

Chapter 10 by Tshepo Moloi focuses on the role Radio Freedom played in influencing members and supporters of the Black Consciousness Movement (BCM) to make a political shift to Congress politics within South Africa. While BCM and ANC politics differed, the Black Consciousness activists nonetheless tuned in to the ANC's Radio Freedom and listened to its programs—and in this way many were inspired and converted to ANC politics. Post-1976, the majority fled the country into exile, where they joined the ANC.

Sekibakiba Lekgoathi, in chapter 11, explores the history of Radio Freedom with specific reference to the support it received from solidarity groups and allies in Europe and on the African continent. Like other guerrilla radios in the region, Radio Freedom operated from several independent African countries and was supported by the international community in Europe. Lekgoathi demonstrates that through airtime and accommodation on the external services of the national radios of the host African countries, Radio Freedom was able to have a sonic presence at home. Equipment, finances, and other forms of logistical support, as well as the training given to broadcasters and other media workers by governments and solidarity groups in both Eastern and Western blocs, enabled Radio Freedom to connect with listeners inside South Africa. The radio station was able to mobilize the masses, to influence political developments inside the country, and to counter the white minority regime's propaganda messages.

The final chapter, chapter 12, by Ali Khangela Hlongwane, reports on the Pan Africanist Congress of Azania's Voice of the PAC (the most underresearched of all the guerrilla radios covered in the book). The Voice of the PAC is the most marginalized liberation radio in the region. Not a single chronicler has yet ventured into the PAC's space to look at how this organization used radio as a weapon of liberation. Yet there are scattered fragments of evidence from archival and oral history sources and from unpublished manuscripts that show footprints of the PAC in radio in countries in North Africa, western Africa, eastern Africa, and central Africa from the early 1960s. The chapter demonstrates that, like other liberation movements, the PAC established working relationships with sovereign African countries and its radio was given airtime on the national radios of Ghana, Egypt, Algeria, the Congo, and Tanzania. Thus, the PAC was able to counter the apartheid government's propaganda and to project its own voice to international communities and to its supporters back home.

To sum up, *Guerrilla Radios in Southern Africa*, unlike previous studies, provides a more comprehensive coverage of the main radios of the liberation movements that operated in the region during the era of the armed struggle. Where, previously, scholarship tended to provide narrow nationalist or country-specific analyses of liberation war radios, this book is transnational in orientation, exploring the workings of these radios from their areas of broadcast in exile, as well as the counter-insurgency measures employed by the settler colonial states to keep guerrilla radios in check.

NOTES

1. For more on why and how the liberation movements launched guerrilla radio stations, see, for example, Lebona Mosia, Charles Riddle, and Jim Zaffiro, "From Revolutionary to Regime Radio: Three Decades of Nationalist Broadcasting in Southern Africa," *Africa Media Review* 8, no. 1 (1994): 1–24; Stephen R. Davis, "The African National Congress, Its Radio, Its Allies and Exile," *Journal of Southern African Studies* 35, no. 2 (June 2009): 349–73; Sekibakiba P. Lekgoathi, "The African National Congress's Radio Freedom and Its Audiences in Apartheid South Africa, 1963–1991," *Journal of African Media Studies* 2, no. 2 (2010): 139–53.

2. Mosia, Riddle, and Zaffiro, "From Revolutionary to Regime Radio," 4.

3. Sekibakiba P. Lekgoathi, "Bantustan Identity, Censorship and Subversion on North Sotho Radio, 1960–1994," in *Radio in Africa: Publics, Cultures, Communities* ed. Liz Gunner, Dina Ligaga, and Dumisani Moyo, 117–33 (Johannesburg, Wits University Press, 2011); "'You are Listening to Radio Lebowa of the South African Broadcasting Corporation': Vernacular Radio, Bantustan Identity, and Listenership, 1960–1994," *Journal of Southern African Studies* 35, no. 3 (2009): 575–94; "Ethnic Separatism or Cultural Preservation? Ndebele Radio under Apartheid, 1983–1994," *South African Historical Journal* 64, no. 1 (March 2012): 59–80.

4. Liz Gunner, *Radio Soundings: South Africa and the Black Modern* (Johannesburg: Wits University Press, 2019), 6.

5. Marissa Moorman, "Guerrilla Broadcasters and the Unnerved Colonial State in Angola (1961–74)," *Journal of African History* 59, no. 2 (2018): 260.

6. Nancy R. Hunt, "An Acoustic Register, Tenacious Images, and Congolese Scenes of Rape and Repetition," *Cultural Anthropology* 23, no. 2 (2008): 220–45.

7. James M. Kushner, "African Liberation Broadcasting," *Journal of Broadcasting* 18, no. 3 (1974): 299, cited in Moorman, "Guerrilla Broadcasters," 244.

8. Moorman, "Guerrilla Broadcasters," 244.

9. Mhoze Chikowero, "Is Propaganda Modernity? Press and Radio 'for Africans' in Zambia, Zimbabwe and Malawi during World War II and its Aftermath," in *Modernization as Spectacle in Africa*, ed. Peter J. Bloom, Stephan Miescher, and Takyiwaa Manuh (Bloomington and Indianapolis: Indiana University Press, 2014); Lekgoathi, "African National Congress's Radio Freedom"; Robert Heinze, "'It Recharged Our Batteries': Writing the History of the Voice of Namibia," *Journal of Namibian Studies* 15 (2014): 25–62.

10. Moorman, "Guerrilla Broadcasters," 244.

11. Ibid., 246.

12. Ibid.

13. Njabulo B. Khumalo, "ZPRA this, ZPRA that! Where are the Records to Prove ZPRA's Role in the Liberation Struggle in Zimbabwe?" *Oral History Journal of South Africa* 6, no. 7 (2018): 1–10.

14. Personal conversation with Luvuyo Wotshela, director of NAHECS, University of Fort Hare, at Southern African Historical Society (SAHS) Biennial Conference, Makhanda, Eastern Cape, June 25, 2019.

15. Keyan Tomaselli, Johan Muller, and Ruth Tomaselli, eds., *Currents of Power: State Broadcasting in South Africa (Addressing the Nation)* (Bellville: Anthropos Publishers, 1989); J. M. Phelan, *Apartheid Media: Disinformation and Dissent in South Africa* (Westport, CT: Lawrence Hill, 1987); G. Hayman and Ruth Tomaselli, "Introduction," in *Addressing the Nation*, ed. Tomaselli et al.; Richard Carver and A. Naughton, eds., *Who Rules the Airwaves? Broadcasting in Africa* (London: Index on Censorship, 1995).

16. Richard Fardon and Graham Furniss eds., *African Broadcast Culture: Radio in Transition* (Westport, CT: Praeger, 2000); J. Minnie, "The Growth of Independent Broadcasting in South Africa: Lessons for Africa?" in *African Broadcast Cultures*, 174–79.

17. Mosia, Riddle, and Zaffiro, "From Revolutionary to Regime Radio," 1–24; K. M. Gqibitole, "Contestations of Tradition in Xhosa Radio Drama under Apartheid," English Studies in Africa 45, no. 2 (2002): 33–45; Liz Gunner, "Wrestling with the Present, Beckoning to the Past: Contemporary Zulu Radio Drama," Journal of Southern African Studies 26, no. 2 (2000): 223–37; Liz Gunner, "Resistant Medium: The Voices of Zulu Radio Drama in the 1970s," Theatre Research International 27, no. 3 (2002): 259–74; Liz Gunner, "Supping with the Devil: Zulu Radio Drama under Apartheid—The Case of Alexius Buthelezi," Social Identities 11, no. 2 (2005): 161–69; Liz Gunner, "Zulu Choral Music: Performing Identities in a New State," Research in African Literatures 37, no. 2 (2006): 83–97; Davis, " African National Congress"; Lekgoathi, "You are Listening to Radio Lebowa"; "Bantustan Identity, Censorship and Subversion"; "African National Congress's Radio Freedom."

18. Marcus Power, "*Aqui Lourenço Marques!!* Radio Colonization and Cultural Identity in Colonial Mozambique, 1932–74," *Journal of Historical Geography*, 26, no. 4 (2000): 605–28.

19. Mhoze Chikowero, "Is Propaganda Modernity? World War II and Post-War 'Radio for Africans' in Zambia, Zimbabwe and Malawi, 1939–1950s," in *Modernization as Spectacle in Africa*, ed. S. Miescher, P. Bloom, and T. Manuh (Bloomington and Indianapolis: Indiana University Press, 2014).

20. Liz Gunner, Dina Ligaga, and Dumisani Moyo, eds., *Radio in Africa: Publics, Cultures, Communities* (Johannesburg: Wits University Press, 2011).

21. See for example Davis, "African National Congress"; Lekgoathi, "Bantustan Identity."

22. Most of the existing literature on Radio Free Europe and Radio Liberty tends to be contemporary and autobiographical in orientation. See, for example, A. Ross Johnson, *Radio Free Europe and Radio Liberty: The CIA Years and Beyond* (Washington, DC: Woodrow Wilson Center Press, 2010); A. Ross Johnson and Eugene Parta, eds., *Cold War Broadcasting: Impact on the Soviet Union and Eastern Europe. A Collection of Studies and Documents* (Budapest, New York: Central European University Press, 2010); Alexander W. Badenoch, Andreas W. Fickers, and Christian Henrich-Franke, eds., *Airy Curtains in the European Ether: Broadcasting and the Cold War* (Baden-Baden: Nomos, 2013).

23. S. Mikkonen, "To Control the Information Flows—Soviet Cold War Broadcasting," in *Airy Curtains in the European Ether*, ed. Alexander W. Badenoch, Andreas W. Fickers, and Christian Henrich-Franke (Baden-Baden: Nomos, 2013).

24. Heinze, "'It Recharged Our Batteries.'"

25. James Brennan, "Radio Cairo and the Decolonization of East Africa, 1953–1964," in *Making a World After Empire: The Bandung Moment and Its Political Afterlives*, ed. Christopher J. Lee (Athens: Ohio University Press, 2010); Davis, "African National Congress"; Lekgoathi, "African National Congress's Radio Freedom."

26. Julie Frederikse, *None but Ourselves: Masses vs. Media in the Making of Zimbabwe* (Johannesburg: Ravan, 1982).

27. Mosia, Riddle, and Zaffiro, "From Revolutionary to Regime Radio," 1–24.

28. For a discussion of the relationship between the ANC and SACP vis-à-vis Radio Freedom, see Davis, "African National Congress." For a discussion of the political position of the radio station in relation to the liberation movement, listenership, and the music played on the station, see Sekibakiba P. Lekgoathi, "The African National Congress's Radio Freedom, Its Audiences and the Struggle against Apartheid in South Africa, 1963–1991," in *The Road to Democracy*, Vol. 5: The 1990s. Part 1, South African Democracy Education Trust (Pretoria: Unisa Press, 2013), 548–87; Sekibakiba P. Lekgoathi, "Radio Freedom, Songs of Freedom and the Liberation Struggle in South Africa under Apartheid," in *Soundtrack of Conflict: The Role*

of Music in Radio Broadcasting in Wartime and in Conflict Situations, ed. M. J. Grant and Ferdia J. Stone-Davis, 111–29 (Hildesheim Zurich and New York: Olms Verlag, 2013).
    29. Heinze, "'It Recharged Our Batteries.'"

Chapter Two

A Voz da Frelimo and the Liberation of Mozambique

Alda Romão Saúte Saíde

The new international situation after the Second World War favored self-determination and allowed a remarkable radicalization of global nationalist movements that culminated in the independence of scores of countries under colonial rule in Africa. In Mozambique, however, the Portuguese reacted to this wind of change by intensifying the exploitation of African human and material resources, reinforced by even more repressive colonial legislation, particularly of the African resistance that it considered subversive.

To prevent political subversion, the Portuguese regime initiated a series of repressive measures in the metropole and colonies. In 1949 they established the Council of Public Security (Conselho de Segurança Pública) with specific, vigilant, and rigorous rules against lawbreakers; in 1954 they created the International and State Defense Police (Polícia Internacional de Defesa do Estado [PIDE]), which assumed authority over many branches of law; and in 1960 institutionalized penal sanctions to control individuals and subversive groups.

Marking this hardening of the colonial counter-insurgent state, on June 16, 1960 Portuguese policemen shot and killed hundreds of Mozambican peasants and wounded hundreds of others who had gathered in Mueda, Cabo Delgado, in the northern part of Mozambique, to demand independence. They imprisoned the subversive leaders in the Fort of Ibo, Sommerschield, and Machava prisons. Among the many prisoners were leaders Faustino Vanomba, Kiribiti Diwane, and Modesta, arrested in the Porto Amélia jail (now Pemba); later Vanomba was driven to the Machava jail and Modesta was imprisoned at the Fortress of Ibo.[1]

As in Mozambique, Angolans rose up and were similarly repressed, particularly in 1961. This colonial repression forced the nationalist movements to regroup abroad, out of immediate reach of PIDE. The National Democratic Union of Mozambique (UDENAMO) was created in 1960 in Southern Rhodesia (now Zimbabwe), the Mozambique African National Union (MANU) was formed in 1961 in Tanganyika (now Tanzania), and the National African Union of Independent Mozambique (UNAMI) was established in Nyasaland (now Malawi) in 1961. With Tanganyika's independence in 1961, the three nationalist movements opened separate offices in Dar es Salaam and, later, merged and formed the Front for the Liberation of Mozambique (FRELIMO) on June 25, 1962, under the leadership of Eduardo Mondlane.

It was in response to brutal state repression and the refusal by the Portuguese colonial authorities to enter into dialogue with the colonized that FRELIMO decided to turn its back on negotiations and embark on armed struggle as a strategy for bringing independence and the end of the Portuguese fascist regime. The turn to armed struggle demanded the establishment of systems and structures for information management in order to mobilize and drum up support from the broader liberation support community. This is how the radio A Voz da Frelimo was born in Tanzania (later also transmitted from Zambia). The key objectives of the radio A Voz da Frelimo were to serve as the main means of mobilization, of the recruitment of guerrillas, as the core source of information on the progress of the struggle and the work that was being carried out in the liberated zones, to counter the Portuguese regime's propaganda, and as the major instrument for the articulation of an alternative vision for African nation-building through the liberation struggle. Its broadcasts were in Portuguese and Mozambican languages to reach as many listeners as possible.

Studies on radio broadcasting, particularly on liberation war radios in Mozambique, are scanty and far between. The book *História da Rádio Clube de Moçambique*[2] described the origins, development, and programs of radio broadcasting in colonial Mozambique with an emphasis on the relationship between Radio Clube de Moçambique and the colonial state. The article "Notas para a história da radiodifusão em Moçambique: O caso do Rádio Clube de Moçambique, 1933–1973" describes the context of the emergence of radio broadcasting:[3] Rádio Clube de Moçambique; the objectives; the target audience; the evolution of the programs; developments in the country; listeners in the countries neighboring Mozambique. Particularly important was the "Native time/Voice of Mozambique" program introduced in 1958 for colonized indigenous Mozambicans and transmitted entirely in their languages: Ronga, Shangana, Xi-sena, Xi-Nhungué, Xi-nyanja, Kijaua, Ki-Swahili, Ki-maconde, E-macua, and Xi-chuabo.

Deepening the study on broadcasting in Mozambique, the book *A Radiodifusão em Moçambique: O caso da Rádio Clube de Moçambique,*

1932–1974,[4] in addition to describing the general evolution of Rádio Clube de Moçambique in the different periods of its existence, critically analyzes the relationship between it and the Portuguese state. It also covers the use of broadcasts in English and Afrikaans and in Mozambican languages, a very important component for the promotion of anti-Frelimo radio advertising. Taken as a whole, the three books demonstrate how white Portuguese and the Portuguese state were concerned with the "portugalization" of the colonized through the promotion of the Portuguese language, culture, and civic education. The programs were intended to infuse the colonized with the colonizers' linguistic and cultural elements as part of assimilation, to divert Mozambicans from listening to anti-colonial propaganda broadcast from Radios Moscow, Peking, Conakry, and the BBC and later from Tanzania and Zambia as well as to counter international pressure against colonialism. Since 2000, a significant number of autobiographies, biographies, and other books have been written on the liberation struggle in Mozambique, emphasizing military and diplomatic action.[5] Little research, however, has been conducted on the role of the radio broadcasts employed in the struggle against the Portuguese fascist regime.

By using a combination of written sources, audio footage, and oral accounts, this chapter seeks to examine the content transmitted by A Voz da Frelimo and its effect on the underground political activities and mobilization of Mozambicans to support or engage in the armed struggle led by Frelimo from the 1960s to 1970s. Some questions explored are:

How did A Voz da Frelimo, operating from Dar es Salaam and Lusaka, connect with their listeners inside Mozambique where listening to it was illegal?

Who were the audiences for A Voz da Frelimo?

What kind of news and messages were conveyed through A Voz da Frelimo?

To what extent did such messages inspire the underground political activists and Mozambicans in general to support and join Frelimo?

POLITICAL SITUATION OF
MOZAMBIQUE IN THE LATE 1950s

In the late 1950s Mozambique was bordered to the west by South Africa, Southern Rhodesia (Zimbabwe), Northern Rhodesia (Zambia), and Nyasaland (Malawi), to the south by Swaziland and South Africa, to the east by the Indian Ocean, and to the north by Tanganyika (Tanzania). Apart from South Africa, governed by the apartheid regime, the countries were British colonies in which African political activities were legal and Mozambican migrant workers participated in those activities. In Mozambique they were illegal, and political activity had to resort to techniques of underground action, secrecy, and exile.

Nevertheless, in the late 1950s and early 1960s, Mozambique experienced a growth of nationalist consciousness, political experience, and the development of organized groups, associated in part from reading newspapers (the *Tribune*, *Notícias*, *Star*, *Guardian*) and listening to radio broadcasting (Radio Moscow, BBC radio, Mozambique radio club) that addressed African politics of self-determination and independence in neighboring countries. For instance, between 1957 and 1958, Amaral Matos (a radio-telegraph operator in the navy) and his brother and friends met regularly to discuss and exchange information on politics and decolonization. Their sources of information were Moscow and BBC radios and newspapers. Similarly, in the dormitories of Miguel Bombarda Hospital (now Maputo Central Hospital), Albino Maheche (a male nurse trainee) and his classmates on the nurse practitioner course (for blacks) gathered to read newspapers and listen to Mozambique radio club and to discuss the situation in the Portuguese colonies and other African colonies, as well as Mozambique's "indigenous" policy.[6]

In September 1958, a group of peasants from Guijá district, Gaza province, led by Gabriel Makavi, organized a protest in front of the Portuguese colonial administration. They were protesting the use of violence in cotton production, the intensification of labor force recruitment, the increase of land expropriation, and the supply of resources to increasing numbers of white Portuguese settlers, particularly the sole use of the dam water resources for their cattle and small stock.[7] By the end of 1950, the political situation of Mozambique was explosive. On the one hand, the Portuguese colonial regime intensified repression, violence, imprisonment, censorship, and strengthening of the PIDE secret police, and on the other hand they established cooperative agreements with the South African, Southern Rhodesian, and Malawian regimes to ensure police support in the pursuit and prosecution of Mozambican nationalist militants in exile.

A VOZ DA FRELIMO AND THE LIBERATION STRUGGLE

FRELIMO was not alone in the region in using radio as a means towards liberation. FRELIMO drew upon international experience of the political use of radio by nationalist movements[8] for whom radio was one of several tools of political education and awakening of the people. Radio allowed the movements to put forth their ideological goals and communicate the changing conditions of struggle to their followers. It was also a way of explaining the plight and the suffering of the Mozambican people under the burden of colonialism, of mobilizing public opinion and gaining support from friendly countries, organizations, and individuals, and of recruitment and military communication.

THE INSTITUTIONAL SETUP OF
A VOZ DA FRELIMO STATIONS

The government of Tanzania saw the promotion of nationalist movements in southern Africa as one of its foreign policy objectives. The use of the station by nationalist movements was boosted in 1968 with the creation of Tanzania's External Service Radio, which supported the liberation of Africa. In the same year, 1968, nationalist movements including FRELIMO, ANC, SWAPO, ZAPU, ZANU, and MPLA used Radio Tanzania, which became the bastion of the African liberation movements. In 1970–1971, Radio Zambia also began broadcasting A Voz da Frelimo on its external services. Thus, Tanzania and Zambia played an important role in helping Frelimo and other southern African movements to mobilize, train, and equip, as well as giving them broadcasting time to disseminate their ideologies, to communicate with their militants and ordinary citizens in their own countries, and to talk back to the enemy.

A Voz da Frelimo was part of the Department of Information and Propaganda of FRELIMO (DIP). The DIP was made up of three sections: radio, a combination of photography and cinema, and the press. The department was led by a secretary who was part of the cabinet of the central office of FRELIMO. It was located within and had financial support from the Mozambican Institute. Jorge Rebelo, the secretary of DIP, was responsible for the planning, production, and dissemination of information, in collaboration with Joaquim Chissano, the secretary of the Department of Security. They focused on the Mozambican population, guerrillas, and FRELIMO militants, whereas Marcelino dos Santos, the secretary of the Department of Foreign Affairs, focused on relations with foreign governments. Moreover, the secretary of the DIP discussed communications overall, including elements of design and art production, with the other three section heads.[9]

The two stations consisted of between three and five broadcasters under the direction of a supervisor. The head of the radio section, Rafael Maguni, held the task of programming and broadcasting in Portuguese and the Maconde languages, and José Sebastião and Morais Mabyeca were broadcasters in the Nyanja and Ronga languages.[10] Rafael Maguni, interviewed in the late 1970s, stated that A Voz da Frelimo in Dar es Salaam had broadcasters such as José Sebastião António (Maconde), Smart Katawala (Nyanja), and himself (Portuguese and Maconde). In May 1973, Maguni was moved to Lusaka, where he was joined by the broadcasters Rosária Tembe (Shangana), José

Aguiape (Sena), and Lázaro Avunazi (Xinhungue). Alberto Cassimo was the first broadcaster in Zambia.[11]

Jorge Rebelo, the secretary of the DIP, was the one who received information from the interior of Mozambique (battle fronts and liberated zones) and abroad and then produced the content to be transmitted on the radio. Frequently (fortnightly or monthly), Jorge Rebelo went to the war zones to collect material (photographs, reports, and testimonies about battles) in order to feed the information organs of FRELIMO. Information from the interior was received through the communiqués of war from the greater state of operation in Nachinguea, whereas that from outside came from the Conference of the Nationalist Organizations of the Portuguese Colonies (CONCEP), the representation of FRELIMO in Algeria, and sympathizers to the cause of liberation of Mozambique scattered in several countries.[12] However, in time, and with the expansion of the radio to Zambia, the selection and production of the content became the responsibility of the broadcasters. For example, Rosária Tembe remembered vividly as a broadcaster in Zambia:

> The content was a selection of material received from the Information and Propaganda Office in Dar es Salaam, mainly war reports, some recreation and revolutionary songs. These materials were written in Portuguese and the broadcaster read in Portuguese, English and then translated into other Mozambican languages. In my case, I translated the contents to Shangana/Ronga.[13]

Every broadcaster had to be able to translate content and commentary. Requests often went out for persons with specific language skills. For instance, Smart Katawala stated that he was selected from the Nachinguea military camp to become a broadcaster because he was fluent in Nyanja.[14] Similarly, Rosária Tembe said that she was assigned to be a broadcaster because she spoke very well Shangana.[15] However, from the duties performed by these broadcasters, and looking at their education portfolios, it is clear that they were literate (at least with secondary schooling), knowledgeable in the Mozambican languages, and politically conscious.

In the case of A Voz da Frelimo, the broadcasters were thrown into the job without any preparation. Much of the training was done on the spot and squeezed in between daily tasks. Rafael Maguni, one of the initiators of A Voz da Frelimo in Dar es Salaam, vividly recalled:

> After four years on the battle fields in the interior of Mozambique, I started to work on the program A Voz da Frelimo at the Dar es Salaam radio station. There were three broadcasters namely: José Sebastião António, Smart Katawala and I. In the beginning, we [the team of broadcasters] faced various difficulties: one, we did not have enough proficiency in English but we were required to translate the news of Radio Tanzania into Portuguese; two, we did not have training or experience of broadcasting work. We knew little about writing

commentaries and news. These difficulties were overcome with the help and guidance of Jorge Rebelo and the collaboration of Tanzanian broadcasters; three, lack of quick communications with the interior of Mozambique which delayed the information on time of the war communiqués. Unfortunately, the process of data collection, processing and sending to the DIP and then to the radio was so tedious that a war communiqué from August would only be transmitted in September or October! [16]

Similarly, Rosária Tembe ended up working for A Voz da Frelimo as a broadcaster in Portuguese and Shangana/Ronga-Tsonga without any training. In her own words:

> Due to an order from Samora, I started as a broadcaster in Dar es Salaam at the A Voz da Frelimo in 1968. Late in 1971, I received an order to go to Zambia and work for A Voz da Frelimo. I have never had training in broadcasting in my life, but I was required to fulfill the task. With encouragement and support from my colleagues I quickly mastered the microphone and started running the programs. Rafael Maguni was smart and solved my concerns. [17]

Corroborating Rafael Maguni's and Rosária's testimonies, Smart Katawala stated:

> In Dar es Salaam, Jorge Rebelo told me you have been chosen to work in A Voz da Frelimo, and immediately I just said ok because it was the way we were working in the organization. I began talking to the microphone without any training. I had never worked with radio equipment. [18]

Training was one of the most urgent and important jobs for A Voz da Frelimo but was not addressed throughout the existence of the radio. Much of the training was on the spot.

PROGRAMS AND CONTENTS OF A VOZ DA FRELIMO

A Voz da Frelimo ran a vast array of programs that included news, communiqués of war, interviews, commentaries (including the appeal for support), recreation, and revolutionary songs. In general, the transmissions followed a set pattern. The program opened with the song XiPalapala, followed by greetings to the listeners, the outline of the program of the day, a musical interlude, and then news, a musical interlude, war communiqués or interviews, another musical interlude, commentaries, and another musical interlude. It closed with the song XiPalapala, [19] a very popular Mozambican song, sung in the Shangana language by musician Gabriel Chiau. It speaks of the women of Chamanculo, one of the most populous neighborhoods in the city of Lourenço Marques (Maputo) and mostly inhabited by "uncivilized" black people whose daytime witchcraft was denounced by blowing Palapala horns.

It was one of the most popular songs in Mozambican languages at the time, recorded and broadcast on "Hora Nativa/Voz de Moçambique" programs in the colonial context promoting "Mozambican folklore."[20] Probably, FRELIMO used this song so that its broadcasts would go unnoticed by the colonial government, and to attract the ordinary population to tune in and listen to FRELIMO news, especially in the southern part of Mozambique far away from the theater of war.

The A Voz da Frelimo was transmitted on Radio Tanzania external services on Mondays, Wednesdays, and Fridays from eight to half past eight in the evenings, in a wavelength of 19.44m, frequency of 15435 kilohertz and also in a wavelength of 59.4m and frequency of 5050 kilohertz. Later, in the early 1970s, the program was extended to an hour because there were more broadcasters and more available material.[21]

The news and commentaries consisted of information about the objectives of the FRELIMO struggle, appeals for support from inside the country and abroad, and the violence of the Portuguese regime. For example, in an attempt to portray the reasons for the adoption of armed struggle, a commentary transmitted in Ronga on A Voz da Frelimo, on October 10, 1972, addressed Mozambican listeners as follows:

> Good evening listeners. Who is our enemy? . . . Our enemies are the Portuguese settlers, their government, their soldiers, their *Cipaios* and all the equipment that they employ to govern our people . . . for our people to live in poverty, without unity. . . . The objective of Frelimo is to finish the Portuguese government and its bad action . . . That is, we are not fighting with the ambition to expel the Portuguese, replacing them by Africans. . . . Our struggle is not against the white man; our subversive war is a struggle against the Portuguese settlers and does not reach other populations who live in our land. . . . It is necessary that our people know the following: we do not identify our enemy by the colour of his skin; our enemy is everybody who refuses to collaborate for our independence, our friend is the one who is on our side, who supports our struggle, who make an effort for the people to live free in their land. . . . Brothers, the struggle continues! Independence or death, we shall win![22]

This clearly defined the enemy of FRELIMO and the Mozambican population, stated the objectives of FRELIMO's struggle, and mobilized the Mozambican people to the struggle. Trying to gain the "hearts and minds" of the Mozambicans, the broadcaster Smart Katawala appealed: "We are in war against the Portuguese because the negotiations were refused by the Portuguese. Remember the Mueda Massacre in Cabo Delgado. We have only one way left, which is to fight. Brothers and sisters, awake, it is time to fight for freedom."[23]

The radio message also targeted those white Portuguese and African soldiers who hardened their hearts against their own people, asking them to reconsider. This broadcast reveals how Frelimo spoke to white Portuguese soldiers who served colonial interests:

> Portuguese soldier, as usual, this is the day that we [Frelimo] have time to talk to you, Portuguese soldier, who is compulsorily in Mozambique to accomplish the criminal mandates of your colonial, fascist Portuguese government against our people. . . . Our program is to make you understand that our struggle is not a racist war and that you have a benefit, when you desert from the Portuguese colonial army, to be sheltered by Frelimo. . . . In 1967 [the compulsory military service] was extended to four years, and now [1972] the Portuguese government wants to extend it to six years. . . . This news brings you great discontent, you Portuguese soldiers who are listening to us. . . . Your desertion to Frelimo will save you from the six years of military service ordered by your officials. These [officials] never go to the bush. They never put their bodies into harm's way. . . . Portuguese soldiers who are listening to us, this war does not belong to you. This war belongs to the capitalists who never gave you any of the wealth they exploited from Mozambique. . . . This war does not belong to the Portuguese people. The Portuguese population is discontent and demoralized by the death of their innocent sons. . . . Come, come quickly and know that Frelimo will receive you as allies. The war continues! Independence or death, we shall win! [24]

The broadcast transmitted a message to those who knew that soldiers were dying in battle, that their officers were giving orders without going into battle, and that the war took them far away from their homeland. This message was to raise questions, to target the soldiers' frustration and loss of morale, and to raise their awareness of anti-Portuguese war sentiment. To the Mozambicans in the Portuguese army, A Voz da Frelimo made the following appeal: "You are a son of Mozambique, why are you continuing to obey and fulfill the Portuguese colonialist orders? Run away and join your comrades who have already escaped and are with Frelimo." [25]

The revolutionary songs sung in Mozambican languages and transmitted along with the news, commentaries, and interviews were also meant to give the people the opportunity to know about FRELIMO ideology, war, and the enemy. They were recorded in the camps (in contrast to the Zimbabweans and South Africans, who not only recorded songs by guerrillas but also songs by regular artists, and others adapted from religious songs). [26] This difference was perhaps related to FRELIMO's guiding principles: formation of a new society and creation of a "new man" free from the backward aspects of Mozambican "traditional" society, free from Portuguese oppression, religion, and exploitation—a society inspired by technical-scientific ideals of historical materialism. It is in this context that one can understand FRELIMO's radicalism in not being inspired by religious songs or popular musicians. For instance, one of the revolutionary songs:

First verse: We trust you, Frelimo, our guide in the struggle. Our struggle, comrades, continues and shall succeed. (repeat twice)

Second verse: In the 70s, Arriaga was deceived by the struggle in Mozambique, Caetano was mistaken. (repeat twice)

Third verse: He was smashed, trampled, and went back bleeding (repeat twice)

Fourth verse: Our force united, always firm defending our honor, bravery unique (repeat twice)

Fifth verse: We will always be aggressive people for the national cause (repeat twice)

Sixth verse: Our country immortal, we are always defending ourselves from the slavery of Portuguese governance (repeat twice)

Seventh verse: Our blood will be shed on the national flag (repeat twice)[27]

The message of A Voz da Frelimo was attuned to persuade and to strike resonance, rather than to awe and intimidate. It tended to appeal to enemies, rather than threaten them.

Through the communiqués of war, the broadcasters were also giving the people information about guerrilla activities, particularly battles, in order to counter the misinformation of the Portuguese and demonstrate that FRELIMO was fighting a successful war. One communiqué of war stated, "Recent events at the battlefront should leave no one in doubt. For example, in Cabo Delgado alone, in a little over two months—from 7 August to 21 October 1969—our fighters were engaged in no less than 33 successful operations, killing 167 Portuguese soldiers and destroying 31 military vehicles."[28]

Another Frelimo communiqué covering military activities in Tete for the period of September 1969 and January 1970 reported:

18 December, Frelimo guerrillas attacked the post of Oliveira. Two houses were destroyed and eight soldiers killed.

22 January 1970, the bridge over the Mutandezi river was destroyed. It was 12 meters long and 4.50 meters wide.

22 January 1970, the bridge over Kalila river—15 meters long and 5 meters wide—was destroyed.

After the destruction of these two bridges the road connection between Zumbo and Fingoe, and Zumbo and Malawere (Portuguese military headquarters) was cut. The only possible connection is now by air.[29]

These communiqués of war were very important for the morale of the FRELIMO guerrillas, militants, and sympathizers because it contradicted the Portuguese anti-Frelimo propaganda that spread the message that FRELIMO was in deep crisis and that the guerrilla war that at first was difficult to counteract was already in the possession and knowledge of the Portuguese soldiers who everywhere discovered the camps, captured weapons, arrested the surrendering "terrorists," and eliminated those who offered resistance. Yet the war communiqués showed that FRELIMO military actions were aimed at targets of the colonial Portuguese government and not against the population.

Indeed, Rafael Maguni and other broadcasters located in Zambia wrote an open letter to His Excellency General Arriaga, exposing his shame when going back to Lisbon without defeating FRELIMO while he had claimed to defeat it in three days through the Gordian Knot military campaign. He had completed three commissions but without a victory![30]

In sum, the testimonies of the three broadcasters, voice recordings (1969–1974) and PIDE sources demonstrate how broadcasting was a weapon that should not be underestimated; it was a powerful instrument of conscience awareness, recruitment, and mobilization. The radio A Voz da Frelimo addressed a very broad population such as men and women, old and young, urban and rural, Mozambicans and Europeans, soldiers and guerrillas, regional and international sympathizers, or supporters and enemies. Therefore, this radio had a stronger impact in the people's lives.

The radio, by using the language of brotherhood (comrades, brothers and sisters), addressed people's grievances and emphasized popular participation at various levels in the collective process of the construction of a new nation-state. It was a unifying tool, an instrument of contending the Portuguese colonial propaganda war against the colonized Mozambicans.

LISTENERS TO A VOZ DA FRELIMO

A Voz da Frelimo was so widely known that no one could forget its name, even if that name was too dangerous to speak in the late colonial period. If PIDE caught individuals or groups of people listening or suspected of listening to the broadcasts of A Voz da Frelimo, they would be arrested, interrogated, or imprisoned. In fact, PIDE had an absolute power with attributions of prevention and repression of political crimes; the power to arrest and the power to instruct processes; and relations with foreign police for reciprocal exchange of information. It was an institution that did not need the courts, a juridical entity responsible for judging, imposing prison sentences, or issuing security measures. PIDE has arrested and held hundreds, even thousands of Mozambicans in political jails without organizing any trial or length of sentence. There were very few political judgments of Mozambicans in the colonial period. Two examples to cite, in 1961: Amaral Matos, together with his brother Alexandre Matos, Nuno Caliano da Silva, Youssuf Bin Abubakar, Lopes Lapiseiro Baúle, Daniel Henriques, Abdul Carimo Varzina, Agueda Ceita, Luisa Ceita, Matsombe, Ibrahimo Manguço, Vírgilio Lemos (the only white person in the group), Luisa and Águeda's aunt, Dumande, Mário Mondlane, and the Régulo de Magude were arrested on charges of spreading the message about the Mueda—Cabo Delgado massacre in June 1960. They were questioned, tried, and acquitted.[31] In 1964, those responsible for the IV Frelimo Military Region were arrested, tried, and convicted, namely Joel dos Santos Monteiro (Maduna Xinana), Mathias Thomas Khumaio (Matata Bombarda Tembe), Lameque Michangula, Daniel Sebastião Manguele (Mahlayeye), Justino Saul Mucal (Saul Tomo), André José Munjoro, and Alexandre Jossefate Machel. They also arrested militants of the clandestine political network such as Luís Bernardo Honwana, Afonso André Uchoane, Daniel Tomé Magaia, Abner Sansão Muthemba, Rogério Jauana, José Gomes Junior, José Craverinha, Julio Sigaúque, Malangatana Ngwenya, João dos Reis, Francisco Rui Barreto (Rui Nogar), Armando Pedro Muiuane, Ebenizário Guambe, and Domingos Arouca, who remained in prison for a long time.[32]

With the advance of the armed struggle, PIDE/DGS was structured and sophisticated as an autonomous state defense police, above all authority, served by a whistleblower at all levels of colonial society, namely ordinary people, *régulos*, *cipaios*, civil servants, employers, doctors, clergy, engineers, finally civilians, military, and paramilitary in addition to the common police, for this case, the Polícia de Segurança Pública—PSP (Public Security Police) and Serviço de Coordenação e Centralização da Informação de Moçambique—SCCIM (Mozambique Information Coordination and Centralization Service). Political activities, particularly support of FRELIMO, was extremely dangerous.

The broadcasting of A Voz da Frelimo was transmitted from exile (Dar es Salaam and Lusaka), and listening within the borders of Mozambique was practiced in secret, under blankets, behind closed doors, and in the bushes (according to the interviewees below). Despite the colonial state repression and imprisonment of Mozambican nationalists, FRELIMO adopted the "exile space as a transcendental playgrounds to boost the nationalism and root for the creation of the nation state."[33]

There is evidence that political activists, sympathizers, and ordinary people both in urban and rural areas tuned in to A Voz da Frelimo from the beginning of its broadcasting. Aurélio Valente Langa, former political prisoner who was part of the underground political work in Lourenço Marques (now Maputo) in the 1960s recalled:

> We listened to the radio A Voz da Frelimo and followed the guidelines that said "we must continue organizing in all fronts; the armed struggle of FRELI-MO is a prolonged struggle for all the Mozambican people; FRELIMO had support from the international community; FRELIMO was recognized in the United Nations and its armed struggle was just. Our broadcasters finished the transmissions with the following words: Independence or death. We shall win!" Then, the broadcasters said their names. I remember Artur Vilanculos, Jorge Rebelo, Rosária Tembe (magnificent broadcaster!), Adelino Gwambe (speaking in national languages), Betuel Matavele and later on, Rafael Magu-ni. They did not speak always in Portuguese, they spoke in Maconde, Shanga-na, Nyungwe, Yawo . . . all national languages and also in English. [34]

Similarly, Muheti Mbazima, a former political prisoner who was part of the underground political work in Lourenço Marques (now Maputo) in the 1960s, stated that it was in 1963 when he started to listen about FRELIMO in a broadcasting from Radio Tanzania and using Portuguese and other national languages. [35] Juvenália Muthemba, former political prisoner who was part of the underground political work in João Belo (now Xai-Xai) in the 1960s, said that her father, uncle Mateus, and Lucas Mula [friend] oftentimes stayed together at night to listen to the FRELIMO programs from Radio Tanzania [A Voz da Frelimo]. They did not allow her to be nearby. Later, she ended up listening to this radio through her colleagues of the Nucleus of the Secondary Students of Mozambique—NESAM. [36]

Other individuals recalled that A Voz da Frelimo, and Radio Ghana, and Radio Moscow were critical to their political awakening. Simione Samabane Chivite, former underground political activist and political prisoner, stated that before 1963–1964, he listened to Radio Ghana or Radio Moscow at night talking of the independence of Ghana, Zambia, the process of Congo-Leopoldville, and the war in Algeria. However, it was in 1963–1964 when he and other friends listening to A Voz da Frelimo decided to prepare them-selves to go there [to join FRELIMO in Tanzania]. [37]

Fernando André Fazenda Mbeve, former underground political activist and political prisoner, said that they gathered in small groups (cells) in a secret place and listened to the broadcast of A Voz da Frelimo and Radio Moscow. They listened in this manner because they feared the PIDE infor-mants. For Mbeve, listening to A Voz da Frelimo took place even before they had any contact with the guerrillas. [38] Indeed, Radio Moscow and other inter-national radio broadcasts were important in the awakening of the conscience of the colonized, particularly in Africa. For instance, in October 1964, Radio Moscow transmitted a message to the Mozambican people from Urias Si-mango, vice president of FRELIMO, as follows:

Since the arrival of the Portuguese colonialists, slavery and exploitation continues: Endless suffering! Until today, according to the agreement between the
Portuguese government and the government of South Africa, Mozambicans
are sold to work in the mines. The Portuguese make millions of pounds a year
from this business. . . . Faced with this abominable situation, we had no other
way than to form a gigantic Movement, called: Frente de Libertação de
Moçambique (Frelimo) as the only way to solve this national problem. Now
this Movement, known and supported by all Mozambicans, works first, for a
very clear purpose, total independence for our country . . . to dispose the fate
of the country in the hands of the people, now considered as savage and
uncivilized. . . . I do not make this appeal to the Mozambican people in the first
place because I am Frelimo Vice-President, but Mozambican, who suffers the
same oppression, who now dedicates himself to the national work and wishes
to see Mozambique free. To the companions, both female and male: in prisons,
in the valleys, in the mountains, in the cities, in the villages and in the countryside of Mozambique, there will never be a better time to get rid of this Portuguese colonial burden than we have now. . . . We are bravely to face the
enemy! Frelimo will command. DIFFICULTIES OR DESTRUCTION WE
WILL ALWAYS WIN! INDEPENDENCE OR DEATH! COME OUR
FIGHT![39]

The content of the message was an appeal compelling all Mozambicans to
join FRELIMO and support the struggle as the only way to attain their
independence. In order to attract the listeners, Simango addressed the Mozambicans as companions who suffered the same plight as he did.

Portuguese soldiers listened to A Voz da Frelimo. Alberto Estevão Canjuela, a former Portuguese soldier in Tete and Chicualacuala, described A
Voz da Frelimo as a wakeup call to action, but a potential "death certificate,"
if one was caught listening. He vividly recalls,

I started listening to the broadcasting A Voz da Frelimo in 1968 at night living
at Vila Cabral (now Lichinga). As a bachelor and living alone, I listened at
home in bed under the blankets in the dark. The following day I would chat
carefully with my friends Joaquim Bonamara, Eduardo, Motinho, and
Mário. . . . In Tete—Changara as a Portuguese soldier continued listening to
the broadcasting A Voz da Frelimo in my barracks in the bed under blankets. I
remember listening to Rafael Maguni addressing the Mozambican soldiers in
the Portuguese army: "Why are you African soldiers selling and killing your
people? You are our children . . . you, soldiers if it is true, you are children of
Mozambique, why do you continue following and serving the Portuguese colonialists?" Speaking to Portuguese soldiers, he stated: "Portuguese soldiers,
you are doing an unjust war. Mozambique is not Portugal. This war does not
belong to you! This war belongs to the Portuguese fascist government . . .
Portuguese soldier, wake up and desert to FRELIMO." In Changara, I continued doing political activity. I would rather do it in my free time amongst
comrades while taking beer. Some colleagues thought that I was drunk and
talking no sense, but others knew that I was not and they paid attention. . . .

The result of this political work was the desertion of Taela, a Mozambican soldier, with his weapon from the camp and my "sudden" transfer to Chicuala-cuala![40]

Corroborating Canjuela's testimony, Eldorado Dabula, a former Portuguese soldier with the rank of private first class, recalled that in 1969–1970 in the fulfillment of his military service, he worked in the offices of the Vila Cabral barracks (now Lichinga). Although he was not one of the soldiers in the battle zone, he knew—through the movement of the Portuguese military columns, helicopter movements, and conversations with returning combatants—that the war was serious in that region. It was at the barracks that he began to listen to A Voz da Frelimo, concealing it from his fellow soldiers Maximiano, Ngomane, and David Manhiça. Smiling, Eldorado remembered the songs and messages transmitted by A Voz da Frelimo:

> The FRELIMO war aims to end Portuguese domination and exploitation. The fight we have is only against Portuguese settlers. . . . Announcements of the "operations" carried out by their guerrillas in Cabo Delgado and Eastern Niassa: during the past months our liberation struggle has intensified with our great victories, as evidenced every day by the service of information of the Portuguese armed forces announcing the death of Portuguese soldiers in combat. Our struggle therefore continues victoriously. . . . Brothers, the fight goes on! Independence or death, we will win![41]

Eldorado further said that his father, a broadcaster at Radio Clube de Moçambique of the program A Voz de Moçambique, transmitted in the Ronga language, also listened to A Voz da Frelimo. To avoid being discovered by the PIDE, his father only placed the antenna on the roof of the house in the evening and when the time came to listen in he sent his wife and children outside. "At mealtimes, dad used to say that things on the other side were moving forward. Guebuza was there. When we children asked how he knew, he just smiled."[42]

In a similar vein, Smart Katawala stated that he had heard about FRELIMO in 1963, through Chiteta, who told him that Radio Tanzania was "inviting Mozambican youth to go there to study." This information circulated from mouth to mouth among the students at the Technical School of Vila Cabral. It was this message, on the radio, about the harshness of the Portuguese regime, that made up his mind to run away and join FRELIMO in late 1963.[43]

PIDE files corroborate the accounts of these three witnesses to the messages disseminated by A Voz da Frelimo and the impact among Mozambicans in the country and abroad.

Given the illegality of FRELIMO and its radio A Voz da Frelimo, as well as the mass arrest of the guerrillas of the fourth military region of FRELIMO and members of the underground network of southern Mozambique in 1964 and 1965 by PIDE/DGS, it was dangerous and difficult to develop a listenership group that would discuss the content of broadcasts. Although listening was an individual activity, these listeners were also transmitters because, after secretly listening to the radio, they shared the information with close relatives and friends, away from the eyes of strangers. From testimonies we can infer that A Voz da Frelimo transformed the conscience of many Mozambicans. They hated the Portuguese settlers and the fascist Portuguese regime. In fact, A Voz da Frelimo was no less dangerous than the armed struggle. Radio was an instrument through which the Mozambican liberation movement challenged the Portuguese regime and its allies.

COLONIAL STATE COUNTER-SUBVERSION PROGRAMS AGAINST A VOZ DA FRELIMO

Open and direct fascist colonial repression was central to the regime's policy and the PIDE political police were instrumental in achieving effective exploitation of Mozambique's human and natural resources. Harmful laws and regulations that denied the exercise of political and civil rights were enacted for the vast majority of Mozambicans. Among other repressive measures to prevent political "subversion," the Portuguese established the Council of Public Security, with rigorous rules applied to those considered lawbreakers. The PIDE was established in all Portuguese colonies. In 1960, the PIDE institutionalized the use of prisons to control individuals and "subversive" groups and created the General Directorate of Security (DGS) with the aim of collecting, searching, centralizing, coordinating, and studying security information, as well as maintaining reciprocal relations with national and foreign police to exchange intelligence.[44]

With the upsurge in clandestine anti-colonial activity and the formation of political movements in exile (UDENAMO, UNAMI, MANU, and their subsequent merger into FRELIMO), and the beginning of the armed struggle for the liberation of Mozambique in the north, the Portuguese government began to worry about the type of information available to the public in the metropole and especially in the colonies. In 1961, the Psychosocial Action Service was set up in Mozambique, with the responsibility to shape the thinking and opinion of the colonized peoples of Mozambique in favor of the cause of Portuguese fascism—and to demoralize FRELIMO, reduce their desire to fight, and instill a sense of insecurity, impotence, and doubt—to undercut their determination to achieve the objectives of their struggle. Therefore, the Portuguese government structured the services of the Psychological Action Unit for the Portuguese army, for the Mozambican population and the political prisoners.[45]

The operations of A Voz da Frelimo therefore troubled the PIDE, army officers, and informants, as well as members of the government. The PIDE, the military, and Portuguese citizens also listened to A Voz da Frelimo. The PIDE transcribed the programs, with translations into Shangana/Ronga, Nyanja, Maconde, and Nhungwe. They titled and filed those transcriptions as "subversive broadcasts" or "clandestine radio," although they were hardly secret. Transcriptions of broadcasts from Radio Moscow, Radio Peking, and Radio Conakry were similarly filed. But there was nothing secret or illegal about those either. The PIDE might have liked them to be clandestine, but they were not. Everyone knew. Many listened. Based in exile and broadcasting from the stations of sovereign foreign states, these stations existed beyond the jurisdiction of Portuguese colonial law but well within the state's earshot.

In an interview with the *Star* newspaper in Johannesburg, PIDE Chief Inspector Fernando Vaz stated that by 1964 Frelimo had launched a propaganda campaign through the use of radio and pamphlets to recruit its militants by promising scholarships and diplomas in a short time.[46] One PIDE officer from the GDS in Mozambique wrote a letter claiming that A Voz da Frelimo transmitting from Zambia was having an impact on the Mozambican migrant miners in South Africa. Significant numbers of Mozambican miners were joining FRELIMO. Alberto Mathavele, António Dias Sitoe, Américo Afonso, João Seti Macuacua, and J. C. I. Mune were among them. The broadcaster Rosária Tembe was an effective inspirational voice in radio propaganda, motivating the listeners to the point of their writing letters asking for additional information![47]

This confidential information was used by PIDE and the government (metropole and colony) to develop programs against such "subversion," and repressive measures against individuals and communities. The Portuguese government considered the conquest to win over the hearts and minds of the Mozambican population to be fundamental throughout the course of the liberation struggle directed by FRELIMO. It recognized that without popular support FRELIMO's guerrilla war would be condemned to fail. One tactic that PIDE (and other military and civil services) employed was the use of FRELIMO dissidents. For instance, Lázaro Kavandame, a member of the Central Committee of FRELIMO and chief of the Cabo Delgado zone, was presented publicly as a dissident on April 3, 1969. In that presentation he said that he voluntarily rebelled against his co-religionists in FRELIMO and turned himself in to the Portuguese authorities, claiming that only under the shadow of the Portuguese flag could all ethnicities enjoy social welfare and have the foundations of development that would allow them to face the future with confidence.[48] In June 1969, the editor of the newspaper *Ressurgimento* interviewed an African soldier, Eduardo Chacha, who had deserted from FRELIMO to the Portuguese army. Chacha claimed that FRELIMO only brought misery, hunger, and massacre but the Portuguese government treated Mozambicans with friendship, and only wanted us to live in peace— and that FRELIMO, which claimed to represent the will of the Mozambican people, was merely an advance guard for Chinese communism.[49]

From the Portuguese perspective, these public presentations of FRELI- MO dissidents helped to mobilize the population in their favor. They hoped this would contribute to psychological action to encourage more dissent within FRELIMO, demoralize the guerrillas, and discredit the movement. The Psychological Action Unit developed posters, pamphlets, and news- papers, and broadcast in Mozambican languages to target FRELIMO and to discredit it. Later, the Psychological Action Unit also scheduled regular meetings (*banjas*) with village populations and discussed self-defense ac- tions, further setting communities against FRELIMO.

However, PIDE itself admitted that, despite desertions and pamphlets circulating about them, FRELIMO had a stronger-than-ever leadership at that time, and it had "terrorists" in high positions who were mentally and morally equipped as military leaders and who enjoyed ever increasing external sup- port.[50] PIDE recognized a formidable threat that pervaded the colony, includ- ing among the soldiers of the Portuguese military.

With the rise of anti-colonial radio advertising from foreign broadcasters (Radio Ghana, the Voice of Cairo, Radio Peking, Radio Moscow, and Radio Tanzania) since the early 1960s, the Portuguese government created the psychosocial radio service "A Voz de Moçambique," which first aired on March 1, 1962. In 1963, A Voz de Moçambique broadcasts from Lourenço Marques were daily, in the Ronga and Shangana languages, as well as in Macua and Chuabo through the Nampula and Zambezia regional broadcast- ers. From the Cabo Delgado regional broadcaster, the emissions were bi- weekly and in the Macua-Meto language. In 1967, A Voz de Moçambique was also issued in Swahili and Nyanja from the Nampula regional broadcast- er, and in 1969 in Ronga, Shangana, Sena, Nyanja, Ajaua, Swahili, and Maconde. In 1970, the Voice of Mozambique was issued from the broadcast- ing center of Dondo, which, as the war progressed, became the main radio axis of psychosocial warfare.[51]

The programs featured political, anti-FRELIMO propaganda, especially the *Hora da Verdade* (Hour of Truth), as well as commercial and recreational productions such as *Hora de recreio* (Recreational Time), *Sorte grande* (Great Luck), *programa do Emigrante* (Program for emigrants), *Músicas pedidas* (Music Requests), *Relatos de futebol* (Football Reports) and new talent contests.[52]

In order to attract high audience levels, especially in the southern Save/ Southern Mozambique region away from the military theaters, radio receiver assembly lines (mainly producing transporters manufacturing batteries) were installed and sold at affordable prices. In the villages created by the Portuguese army, collective listening radio stations were set up, especially in Cabo Delgado, to ensure the broadcasts of A Voz de Moçambique would be heard.[53] In the perception of the Portuguese government, conditions were created to prevent listening to A Voz da Frelimo, but Mozambicans used these devices for listening to A Voz da Frelimo and other anti-colonial propaganda radio.

Indeed, radio was an important instrument used by both the Portuguese government and FRELIMO, not only to win the hearts and minds of the exploited and suffering Mozambican population, but also to score ideological points.

CONCLUSION

This study fills an important gap in the literature about the war radio broadcasts in the history of nationalism in Mozambique that remain largely untold and unknown. Radio brought a new dimension to the struggle, the battle of the airwaves, to complement the armed and the diplomatic contest already happening. A Voz da Frelimo was no less dangerous than the armed struggle.

It is true that, following the adoption of the armed struggle by FRELIMO, and conscious of the Portuguese repression, violence, and censorship, it was important to use radio broadcasting as an alternative source of information for the military and the community that supported the liberation struggle. Although listening to A Voz da Frelimo was illegal, and there were severe measures if one were caught, that did not deter political activists and followers of FRELIMO from tuning in. This radio was successful not only in radicalizing the masses, but also in "creating a panic and nervousness on the part of the state, thus subverting the state's power."[54] A Voz da Frelimo transformed the conscience of many Mozambicans.

NOTES

1. Alda Saúte Saíde, "As mulheres e a luta de libertação Nacional," in *História da Luta de Libertação Nacional*, coord. Joel das Neves Tembe, vol. 1. (Maputo: Ministério dos Combatentes, 2014), 560; Eduardo Mondlane, *Lutar por Moçambique* (Lisboa: Sá da Costa, 1976), 125–26; *Mozambican Revolution* 25 (1966): 3.

2. *História da Rádio Clube de Moçambique* (Gazeta do Sul, Montijo, 1959).

3. Pedro Roque, "Notas para a história da radiodifusão em Moçambique, 1933–1973," Arquivo, Maputo 3 (April 1988): 47–60.

4. Ernesto Barbosa, *A radiodifusão em Moçambique: O caso da Rádio Clube de Moçambique* (Maputo: Promédia, 2000).

5. Some examples of the literature on the liberation struggle in Mozambique: Teresa Cruz e Silva, *A Rede Clandestina da FRELIMO em Lourenço Marques (1960–1974)*, Licenciatura thesis, Maputo, UEM, 1986; Aurélio Valente Langa, *Memórias de um combatente da causa* (Maputo: JV Editores, 2011); Dalila Cabrita Mateus, *Memórias do Colonialismo e da Guerra* (ASA, Lisboa, 2006); Alda Romão Saúte Saíde e Joel das Neves Tembe, "Moçambique e a luta de libertação na África Austral," in *SADC Hashim Mbita Project, Southern African Liberation*

38 *Alda Romão Saúte Saíde*

Struggles, Contemporary Documents 1960–1994, vol. 2 (Tanzania: Mkuki na Nyota Publishers Ltd., 2014), 211–303; Joel das Neves Tembe, coord., *História da Luta de Libertação Nacional*, vol. 1. (Maputo: Ministério dos Combatentes, 2014).
   6. Interview by Alda Saúte Saíde, Albino Maheche, Maputo, March 29, 2016.
   7. D. Hedges and A. Chilundo, "A Contestação da Situação Colonial, 1945–1961," in *História de Moçambique: Moçambique no auge do colonialismo, 1930–1961*, coord. D. Hedges (Maputo: Imprensa Universitária, 1993), 212–13.
   8. After World War II, the major international powers did not stay out of Africa for long and the continent was soon dragged into the Cold War. In 1958 Radio Moscow began a regular broadcast to Africa; Prague Radio, Radio Peking, and the Voice of America began regular African transmissions in 1959. In 1960, East Germany, Poland, Rumania, and Bulgaria started broadcasting to the continent. L. Mosia, C. Riddle, and J. Zaffiro, "From Revolutionary to Regime Radio: Three Decades from Nationalist Broadcasting in Southern Africa," *Africa Media Review* 8, no. 1 (1994): 4.
   9. ANTT—PT/TT/PIDE/D-A/1/2826-7, Direcção Geral de Segurança—Delegação de Moçambique, October 21, 1972, 2–5.
   10. Ibid.
   11. Rádio Moçambique, interview, Rafael Maguni, Maputo, late 1970.
   12. Rádio Moçambique, interview, Rafael Maguni, Maputo, late 1970; Mateus, *Memórias*, 395.
   13. Interview, Rosária Tembe, Maputo, September 6, 2007, by Alda Saúte Saíde.
   14. Interview, Smart Katawala, Metangula, June 25, 2019, by Alda Saúte Saíde.
   15. Interview, Rosária Tembe, Maputo, September 6, 2007, by Alda Saúte Saíde.
   16. Rádio Moçambique, interview, Rafael Maguni, Maputo, late 1970s.
   17. Interview, Rosália Tembe, Maputo, September 6, 2007.
   18. Interview, Smart Katawala, Metangula, June 25, 2019.
   19. Rádio Moçambique, interview, Rafael Maguni, Maputo, late 1970s; interview, Rosária Tembe, Maputo, September, 6, 2007; interview, Smart Katawala, Metangula, June 25, 2019; AHM 2443; AHM 2444; AHM 2472; AHM 2660 and AHM 2697.
   20. Interview, Lindo Lhongo, Maputo, June 8, 2016, by Alda Saúte Saíde; Roque, "Notas para a história da radiodifusão em Moçambique, 1933–1973," 58–59.
   21. AHM 2660; Frelimo, *A Voz da Revolução*, #7, Janeiro 1967; Radio Moçambique, interview, Rafael Maguni, Maputo, late 1970s.
   22. ANTT—PT/TT/PIDE/D-A/1/2826-7, Direcção Geral de Segurança—Delegação em Moçambique, 20 November 1972, 1–3.
   23. Interview, Smart Katawala, Metangula, June 25, 2019.
   24. ANTT, PT/TT/PIDE/D-A/1/2826-7, Direcção Geral de Segurança—Delegação em Moçambique, 20.11.1972: 1–4.
   25. ANTT, PT/TT/PIDE/D-A/1/2826-7, Direcção Geral de Segurança—Delegação em Moçambique, 17.11.72: 2.
   26. For more information, read Mhoze Chikowero, *African Music, Power and Being in Colonial Zimbabwe* (Bloomington: Indiana University Press, 2015) and Sekibakiba Peter Lekgoathi, "The African National Congress's *Radio Freedom* and Its Audiences in Apartheid South Africa 1963–1991," *Journal of African Media Studies* 2, no. 2 (2010): 139–53.
   27. AHM 2443.
   28. AHM 2660.
   29. AHM 2697.
   30. Rádio Moçambique, interview, Rafael Maguni, Maputo, late 1970s.
   31. Mateus, *Memórias*, 67–71.
   32. Interview, Armando Pedro Muiuane, Maputo, January 8 and 12, 2016, by Alda Saúte Saíde.
   33. Mhoze Chikowero, "Guerrilla Radio: Liberation Broadcasting, Engineering the Post-Colonial African Nation State," 3 (paper presented at workshop on Liberation War Radio, Johannesburg, February 2017).
   34. Langa, *Memórias*, 144.
   35. Mateus, *Memórias*, 526.

36. A. B. Mussanhane, *Protagonistas da Luta de Libertação Nacional* (Maputo: Marimbique, 2012), 504.

37. Mateus, *Memórias*, 601.

38. Interview, Fernando André Fazenda Mbeve, Maputo, May 10, 1916, by Alda Saúte Saíde.

39. JSTOR, Duialumibnto Propaganda, Radio Moscow, October 1964.

40. Interview, Alberto Estevão Canjuela, Maputo, November 20, 2017, by Alda Saúte Saíde.

41. Interview, Eldobrado Dabula, Maputo, July 5, 2018, by Alda Saúte Saíde.

42. Ibid.

43. I nterview, Smart Katawala, Metangula, June 25, 2019.

44. Dalila Cabrita Mateus, *A PIDE/DGS na guerra colonial, 1961–1974* (Lisboa: Terramar, 2004), 23–24 and 41–43.

45. Diploma Legislativo Ministerial #28, de 19 Outubro de 1961. *Boletim Oficial de Moçambique*, 1ª série, #45(5° suplemento): 1360–1361; Amélia Neves de Souto, *Caetano e o ocaso do "Império": Administração e Guerra colonial em Moçambique durante o Marcelismo, 1968–1974* (Porto: Edições Afrontamento, 2007), 188–202.

46. ANTT, PT/PIDE/D-A /1/2826-1.

47. ANTT, PT/TT/PIDE/D-A/1/2826-10.

48. *Notícias*, Lourenço Marques, ano XLIII, # 14318, 4 April 1969: 1; *Ressurgimento*, Machava, #11, May 31, 1969, 1–2.

49. *Ressurgimento*, Machava, #11, June 30, 1969, 9.

50. Aquino Bragança and Immanuel Wallerstein, *Quem é o inimigo* (II) (Lisboa: Iniciativas Editoriais, 1978), 176–77.

51. Roque, "Notas para a história da radiodifusão em Moçambique, 1933–1973," 58–59; Barbosa, *A radiodifusão em Moçambique*, 90–93.

52. Barbosa, *A radiodifusão em Moçambique*, 94–95.

53. Ibid.

54. Marisa J. Moorman, "Guerrilla Broadcasters and Unnerved Colonial State in Angola, 1961–1974," 28–29 (paper presented at workshop on Liberation Radios in Southern Africa, Maputo, November 2017).

Chapter Three

Guerrilla Broadcasters and the Unnerved Colonial State in Angola, 1961–1974

Marissa J. Moorman

Luanda's urban space is twice marked with the history of liberation radio. The brutalist modernist edifice of what is today *Rádio Nacional de Angola* (RNA—Angolan National Radio) (figure 2), the former colonial broadcaster, built to counter the disturbing broadcasts of the liberation movement radios, is still at the center of the country's communications network. A block away, a modest, well-maintained, representation of the *Movimento Popular para a Libertação de Angola's* (People's Movement for the Liberation of Angola, MPLA) radio *Angola Combatente* (Fighting Angola) is part of a mural (figure 3) on the walls surrounding the military hospital. This work of public art recounts the history of the MPLA's struggle and triumph against Portuguese colonialism. The modernist radio station is the product of late colonial counter-insurgency infrastructure and the mural the result of a postcolonial socialist popular art mobilization and official public history. The former bespeaks the colonial state's nervousness, the latter the new MPLA state's need to project a sense of certainty about history and memory.

This chapter explores how the MPLA and the FNLA, via Angola Combatente (AC) and Voz de Angola Livre (VAL), used broadcasting to maintain a sonic presence in the Angolan territory from exile and to engage in a war of the airwaves with the Portuguese colonial state with whom they were fighting a ground war. First and foremost, it analyzes the effects of these rebel broadcasts on listeners, be they state or nonstate actors. A reading of the state secret police and military archives exposes the colonial state's nervousness and weakness even as it was winning the war. Portugal was fighting a war on three fronts: Angola, Mozambique, and Guinea-Bissau. Guinea-Bissau and

Mozambique presented military challenges to the Portuguese military. Angola, with three national liberation movements often fighting one another, proved an easier front.[1] So why did rebel broadcasting make the Portuguese so nervous if they had the military situation under control? How did radio level the playing field? I argue that by understanding radio's specificity as a technology (the immateriality and intimacy of sound and the process of transduction) we gain insight into this nervousness and into the power of radio.

THE ARCHIVE AND READING FOR SOUND

Angola Combatente and Voz de Angola Livre have left few sonic and documentary archival traces. In 1974 *Voice of America* and United States Information Agency researcher James M. Kushner, in an article on African liberation radios, worried that studies ignored *how* liberation movements communicated their messages.[2] He found work of the period too focused on print. Much has changed in the intervening forty-plus years. African radio studies thrive. Historical work on the radio is growing. The recent spate of scholarly work on African liberation radios is generating a conversation about sources, propaganda, and listenership.[3] This new work points to the difficulty of locating and/or accessing reliable archival material. This has to do, in part, with the particularity of radio as a medium and the state of the archives.[4] Radio's ephemerality, the invisibility of sound, and its fleeting intimacies, along with the generally dismal state of sound and documentary archives of liberation movements, usually hinder research.[5]

This too is the case for the Angolan armed liberation movements. The pressures on returning exiled movements jostling for hegemony in the period of transition between the coup by the Portuguese Armed Forces on April 25, 1974 and independence on November 11, 1975, muddied further by foreign intervention, relegated the urgency of paper keeping and put a premium on the recycling of reel. Sound reels and the few written transcripts that existed were lost, damaged, reused, or simply forgotten.[6] This is true even for the triumphant MPLA.

Under such circumstances, discerning the basics of what and how they broadcast is difficult. Accessing listenership for any once clandestine radio is even more so. S. P. Lekgoathi, writing about audience and the African National Congress's (ANC) Radio Freedom, noted: "it was unlawful to listen to it within the country and logically it would have been illegal if not downright impossible to conduct research on the phenomenon."[7] Finding systematic studies is close to impossible. In this regard, the situation in the Portuguese colonies was no different.

Yet a substantial archive of transcribed broadcasts and memos regarding listening in Angola does exist. The colonial state listened in and classified the broadcasts of the stations of the banned liberation movements dangerous, "anti-Portuguese," and "enemy" propaganda. Listening denoted support or, at the very least, inspired suspicion. It was illegal. But the PIDE, *Polícia pela Defesa do Estado* (Police for State Defense/secret police) listened diligently. They recorded and transcribed broadcasts. Later the military and the *Serviço de Centralização e Coordenação de Informações de Angola* (Centralization and Coordination of Information Service of Angola, SCCIA) undertook this labor. The result is thousands of pages of transcribed radio broadcasts of *Angola Combatente*, and to a lesser extent Voz de Angola Livre, in the PIDE section of the Portuguese National Archives/Torre de Tombo and in the *Arquivo Histórico Militar* (Historical Military Archive) in Lisbon. These are not systematic, scientific studies. What we know of the broadcasts, and of their reception, is filtered through the interests and concerns of police chiefs, surveillance officers, soldiers, and informers.

These state agents recorded broadcasts and then transcribed them. The original recordings and many transcriptions scheduled for destruction before the fall of the Portuguese regime, in April 1974, no longer exist.[8] Transcriptions collected before 1969, namely those done between 1966 and 1968, are still available.[9] But none of the files for the years 1969 to 1973 remain. The ears of the PIDE and military listened in on, and their equipment recorded not only Angola Combatente and Voz de Angola Livre but also any other stations broadcasting material with an "anti-Portuguese character" (1966–1968) and later described as "enemy broadcasts" (1973–1974). This included the liberation movement radios as well as Radio Moscow, the Voice of Nigeria, Radio Hanoi, and sometimes the BBC.

The Torre do Tombo and military archives in Lisbon hold the transcriptions but no extant recordings. How, then, do we read these documents? Transcriptions written in all capital letters tell us more about the desire to foster legibility than about inflection. The voice is lost. While transcriptions tell us something about the broadcast content and transmission quality, they tell us more about the preoccupations of their transcribers. Accompanied by commentaries about the conditions of transmission, the perceived danger of the content, and/or the range of the message from the PIDE officer or local informer, the documents tremble with concern. SCCIA grids subordinate nerves to organization: they dissect the broadcasts by theme, substantive content, target audience, and additional commentary, quantifying conclusions. In noting that they "ignore" disturbing content in African languages, these reports betray their nerves, suppressing sounds they cannot decipher.[10] Their maps plot the targets of sounds' waves. We need to learn to listen to these documents, to hear what Nancy Rose Hunt calls their "acoustic register," as much as parse their language for the subjects of broadcasts and harvest them for data.[11] This is true when we read all archival documents but it is more urgent when analyzing the effects and work of radio. These words have a tone and timbre. It is not the tone and timbre of the broadcast voice (much of which disappeared with the recordings, although some is captured in the text); instead, it is one that quivers and shouts in response to it, one that registers its effects.

I follow Mhoze Chikowero in mining the colonial radio archive to destabilize the solidity of the state's story about its own project.[12] Here, he says, in response to concerns about broadcasting and how Africans read the press, we can locate the "nervous condition of colonial authority."[13] Nancy Rose Hunt's theorization of the Belgian colonial state in the Congo as "A Nervous State" is likewise key. A nervous state is not merely anxious. It is "taut, a nervous wreck"; that is, on edge, on the verge, unstable. In Hunt's telling this develops around therapeutic insurgencies, on the one hand, and the enumerating, modernist visibilizing practices of the bio-political state (health clinics promoting pro-natalist policies to correct colonial destruction billed as uneducated "native" health behaviors), on the other.[14] In particular, she scours the archives for sonic traces of violence to loosen the grip of the visual on how the Congo Free State and the Belgian Congo are framed and imagined. In that space, it becomes possible to think the nervous state. For Hunt, laughter destabilizes and unsettles the routine violence of the state. Attending to sound in the PIDE and military archives on AC and VAL broadcasts means thinking at the interface of sound, nervousness, and nationalist insurgency (real and imagined). We can hear that although the Portuguese were winning the ground war—a narrative repeated in news reports in the Portuguese press—the archives disclose their insecurity and nervousness. Guerrilla radio, I argue, produced this.

ANTI-COLONIAL WAR

Radio in Angola got its start in the hands of hobbyists. Radio clubs spread across the territory connecting white settlements by the mid-1940s. The state got involved in broadcasting belatedly. The anti-colonial war and the need to defend its position motivated its move to the airwaves. Nationalist organizers were squelched in 1959 and many were jailed in Luanda while others were sent to Tarrafal Prison in Cape Verde in the *Processo de 50* (Trial of 50). This brought the PIDE to Angola.[15] But it did not stop insurgency.

In early January 1961, cotton workers in Malanje went on strike to protest forced labor and taxation. They mobilized around a prophetic movement that announced the arrival of a woman named Maria, delivering freedom from Portuguese oppression. António Mariano, originally from the region of Malanje but recently returned from the Congo (newly independent), galvanized a following preaching Maria's return, in what became known as "Maria's War."[16] Historian Aida Freudenthal called this an "anti-colonial revolt permeated by an ethno-nationalist ferment," although it lacked a nationalist or even any clear political program.[17] The movement evidenced, if not prefigured, a robust, cross-border, and inter-world (spiritual and material) communications network well before the advent of guerrilla broadcasting.[18] Aharon de Grassi argues for a revisionist reading of the revolt that sees it as part of nationalist mobilization that connected Luanda, small and large towns in Malanje, and Congo-Kinshasa, through migration, activism, and contract labor.[19] Malanje was a "crossroads of nationalism."[20] The mobilization surfaced processes that were territorial and not just local.[21] African residents of the Angolan territory pursued and nurtured ties of language, cultural practice, and commerce across the colony and region. If the colonial state and Portuguese settlers had been largely deaf to African discontent, this clamor finally perforated that veil of silence.[22]

In the face of strikes, the Portuguese colonial state sent in the army, police, and air force to bomb villages with napalm in the Baixa de Kassanje between February and March. Estimates of the dead range between the hundreds and 30,000.[23] More conservative projections suggest that thousands were killed and many more thousands fled to the Congo, seeking shelter from the bombings and continued Portuguese repression.[24]

In the midst of this, although disconnected from it, on February 4, 1961, a group of activists attacked two prisons in Luanda, hoping to free some of the political prisoners jailed in the Trial of 50. Organized in part by the Catholic Canon Manuel das Neves, in coordination with the *União de Populações de Angola* (Union of Angolan People, UPA, the predecessor of the FNLA), this action also met with extreme state repression. In Luanda, Portuguese civilians received arms and meted out a reckless violence on urban elites they imagined were associated with the revolt.[25] And on March 15, 1961, five hundred armed men from UPA crossed the border from the Congo into northern Angola and invaded numerous villages and coffee plantations, brutally killing owners and migrant workers from the country's south. The colonial state and military responded with unprecedented violence: decapitating Africans and posting their heads on stakes to terrorize the local populations. Historian David Birmingham described it in this manner:

> The chain reaction which followed the shooting of wage demonstrators on a coffee estate created the largest colonial uprising to be experienced in any part of tropical Africa during the whole of the colonial period. The closest parallel was the Mau Mau war in Kenya, but the scale of killing of both settlers and insurgents was ten times greater in northern Angola.[26]

Feeling under siege, unwilling to negotiate, the Portuguese colonial state again reacted with violence.[27] This would be war.[28]

The three attacks, uncoordinated one from the other, nonetheless brought to the surface systems of coordination and communication at work that the Portuguese colonial state had neither glimpsed nor heard. The jailings of nationalist agitators in the Trial of 50 temporarily squelched anti-colonial politics.[29] While it heightened surveillance and security, the events of 1961 exposed desires illegible to the Portuguese state even as their police scoured the land for signs of communist infiltration. They might have had more success had they listened.

Already in the territory since 1959, the PIDE followed radio broadcasts in the region. Primarily concerned with the Portuguese opposition, when Angola Combatente began broadcasting in 1964, they were tuned in (while Voz de Angola Livre began broadcasting consistently in 1965, the PIDE did not begin systematically recording and transcribing it until 1966).[30]

GUERRILLA RADIOS AND THE WAR

The events of 1961 demanded the nationalist movements consolidate themselves in exile. Based outside the Angolan territory, they needed a way to communicate with militants in the territory and to spread their message. The external services of newly independent countries offered airtime to nationalist movements fighting the white settler redoubts of southern Africa.[31] This was how the MPLA and FNLA accessed the international airwaves. Intermittent broadcasts came from Ghana. Consistent transmission occurred only after the MPLA settled in Brazzaville and the FNLA, already based in Kinshasa, established a relationship with the broadcaster.

AC's program A began broadcasting from Brazzaville in 1964.[32] Program B broadcast from Dar es Salaam from 1968, but without great audition quality.[33] Program C broadcast from the MPLA base camp *Vitória é Certa* (Victory is Certain) in Lusaka started in 1972 in order to cover the eastern areas of Angola in that region's languages (Luvalu, Tchokwe, Umbundu, and Portuguese).[34] An outgrowth of the movement's Department of Information and Propaganda, *Angola Combatente* was the bailiwick of party intellectuals (in Brazzaville, Aníbel de Melo and Deolinda Rodrigues, later Adolfo Maria; in Lusaka, Paulo Jorge, Mbeto Traça, and Ilda Carreira).[35] None had previous radio experience. Some had worked in journalism; others were committed militants with more education than average cadres and, therefore, the skills to have them placed writing broadcasts, newsletters, and pamphlets, and producing photos, film clips, and news releases. Propaganda work often took place in coordination with foreign journalists.[36]

Program A broadcast from the Radio Voice of the Congolese Revolution in Brazzaville, a well-used and -guarded inheritance from De Gaulle's Free France in World War II. This station had the strongest transmitter on the continent. The independent government of the Republic of the Congo maintained and expanded the station's technical capacity. Like many other newly independent African states, the Republic of the Congo supported the liberation movements of those still under colonial rule and put its broadcast power at the service of the MPLA.[37]

> Speaking to you from Brazzaville this is the revolutionary program of the Movement for the Popular Liberation of Angola in the struggle to overthrow Portuguese colonial tyranny. On the Voice of the Congolese Revolution this program is a manifestation of solidarity dispensed by the Republic of the Congo Brazzaville to the struggle of the Angolan people.[38]

The PIDE agent who transcribed this broadcast closed by reporting sound interference, likely atmospheric. Reliant on the ionosphere to bounce electromagnetic waves to faraway places, what shortwave gains in distance it often loses in quality. But as the many files of broadcast transcriptions attest, plenty of broadcasts came through loud and clear.

The FNLA broadcast from the Voice of Zaire in Kinshasa and Lubumbashi, in the name of the GRAE, the Revolutionary Government of Angola in Exile. I can say much less about the Voz de Angola Livre. I interviewed FNLA President Holden Roberto in 2005, although his health and memory were failing. Other party members never returned my calls or were unavailable to meet. What I can say derives from PIDE, SCCIA, and military documentation and what Roberto told me.[39] According to Roberto, the FNLA began broadcasting as soon as they arrived in Kinshasa in 1961 and ended in 1974. PIDE transcriptions of the program date to 1966, although the documentary film *Independência* (*Independence*, 2015) includes a broadcast from 1963, a 1964 PIDE report from Malanje mentions the broadcasts, and the PIDE had been listening to regional airwaves since the late 1950s.[40] The mid-1960s emerge as the consensus date.

Two men ran the FNLA's radio service.[41] Both received training in radio at Zaire's National Radio Station. Like AC, broadcasts pushed back against Portuguese propaganda, addressed Portuguese soldiers and encouraged them to desert, followed the EOA closely, sent news of battlefront gains and losses, reported on Roberto's diplomatic travels, and communicated messages to Angolans in the interior.[42] Much more of VAL programming, than that of Angola Combatente, addressed Angolans in exile in Zaire and announced or reported on local community events. In what would later take on an ironic ring, one VAL broadcast even attacked American imperialism.[43]

The PIDE and military archives contain greater numbers of transcribed AC programs than those of VAL. From what can be pieced together of their programming, the MPLA broadcast more regularly. Comments in PIDE and military documents emphasize the MPLA's investment in propaganda, particularly the radio. For example, a military report on psychosocial action from late October 1968 mentioned "among the EN [enemy] psychological activities for the period, the MPLA continues to distinguish itself for having best undertaken them, especially in radio broadcasting."[44]

The military mounted a surveillance operation as part of its counter-insurgency strategy. This strategy was largely reactive and it emphasized what the military called "psychosocial action," centered on the soldier and his interactions with the local population.[45] In the wake of the Baixa de Kassanje attack, a working group composed of military, PIDE, and civilian elements proposed the formation of the SCCIA to draw together information collected by the various surveilling agencies. Political in-fighting between the secret police, military, and SCCIA hindered coordination.[46] But, by the same token, communication was frequent and in Angola (more than Mozambique or Guinea) the military drew on support from the PIDE and its various investigative arms.[47] Surveillance proved effective enough that by the late 1960s, the PIDE had dismantled urban-based MPLA-, FNLA-, and UNITA-affiliated cells.[48]

Radio surveillance fell to both the PIDE and SCCIA. Transcriptions of radio broadcasts from these two bodies were forwarded to the military, which also had its own radio listening unit (Chefia de Reconhecimento das Transmissões/Broadcast Reconnaissance Command, CHERET). PIDE focused on transcriptions while SCCIA included both transcriptions and, by the late 1960s, maps that offered a graphic of broadcast reception and quality included in monthly situation reports. Here we can see a duplication, if not triplication, of labor, an inefficient need to record. The PIDE followed listening practices in the territory, while SCCIA focused more tightly on broadcast content. But the military also worried, in a general sense, about the fact of listening and the impact of what they called "enemy propaganda" on soldiers, the white population, and Africans.[49]

CLANDESTINE LISTENING:
THE INTERSECTION OF MEMORY AND ARCHIVE

Listening to Angola Combatente remains a proud, vivid memory in official and popular discourse of the liberation struggle in exile. Commemorated in the public history mural on the Military Hospital in central Luanda, the image of the radio with two listeners next to a man reading the MPLA's paper *Vitória ou Morte* (*Victory or Death*)/Brazzaville/*Último Comunicado da Guerra* (*Latest War News*), is a key part of the MPLA's official narrative of the national liberation struggle. While the current MPLA regime and new businesses raze other artifacts of the early days of independence (signs, marks to denote building occupations, monuments), painters refresh this mural, maintaining visual narrative certainty against street-level dust and the to-and-fro of daily life in Luanda. Radio broadcasting, as the newspaper in the mural suggests, played its part in a propaganda strategy that involved information broadly cast: pamphlets, an international network of connections with socialist political movements, international journalists, and exiled centers of study.

Three lines joined in the upper corner denote an interior listening scene, reminding viewers that people hid their listening. A memo from the *Comissão Orientadora de Radio em Angola* (Corangola, or the Steering Committee on Radio in Angola) in 1968 to the PIDE confirmed this. Informers encountered a rumored, duplicitous listening practice in the *musseques* (Luanda's informal neighborhood predominantly populated by Africans): "many radio owners have two apparatuses: one located in the entry room tuned to a Luanda broadcaster and another, located in the back of the home, tuned to Brazzaville."[50] Memory and archive intersect.

People often hid in much more extreme ways to listen to Angola Combatente and Voz de Angola Livre (or these are the memories they recount), and while the broadcasters were out of sight (located in exile), and the exiled movements of which they were a part were largely invisible to those inside the country, the broadcasts themselves were not a secret. That, in fact, would have undermined the broadcast's utility. Visibility, or rather invisibility, counted relative to listening practice, not to content. One hid to listen. Militants and interested listeners dissimulated in order to tune in.[51] Some people later met secretly to pass along what they had heard. Liberation movement sympathizers, and their opponents, participated in networks of communication in which guerrilla radio broadcasts constituted one node. Transmission of messages from the radio sometimes became visible, the immaterial, material. Historian Marcelo Bittencourt tells us that echoing the messages broadcast on AC, "in 1966 slogans and words of support for the MPLA started appearing posted or painted in public places."[52]

Individuals recall the guerrilla stations as critical to their political awakening. Rodeth Gil said that it was through the exiled broadcasters that she heard that a war against the colonialists and in favor of the Angolans had started.[53] Based in exile, radio waves could perforate the silence created by Portuguese state censorship of the colonial press.[54] Ruth Mendes remembered hearing about the liberation movements and tuning in as a twelve-year-old girl: "then we started listening to Angola Combatente without the adults knowing."[55] Young people hid listening from the PIDE and their elders.[56] Lote Sachikwenda recalled young boys in groups of four or five gathering

around the radio to listen to the broadcasts of the movements discussing their
work in exile. This, she said, is how we learned about them, before ever
having any contact with a guerrilla.[57] Radio sparked political awakening.

Scenes of secret or semi-secret listening, shrouded in fear, often anchor
memories of guerrilla radio. Lekgoathi notes the similar development of
"listening cultures" in South Africa where listeners met secretly, under cover
of night, to avoid detection by police and informants, and later debated issues
from the ANC's Radio Freedom broadcasts.[58] Manuel Faria, owner of a
recreational club in the *musseque* Sambizanga, recalled driving to a soccer
field, turning off the car's engine, and tuning in on a transistor inside the dark
car in the field's empty expanse. The composer and musician Xabanu listened with his political cell and Alberto Jaime, among the directors of the
recreational Clube Maxinde, described Angola Combatente as a wake-up call
to action, but a potential "death certificate" if you were caught listening.[59]

In a somewhat uncharacteristic scene (for the size of the radio and the
inversion of location), in Zeze Gamboa's 2013 film *O Grande Kilapy* (*The
Great Swindle*), the playboy protagonist and nationalist Joãozinho comes
home late one night and startles his father, who he finds with his ear close to
the family's large table radio, following the Angola Combatente broadcast. A
similar tale of the masculinist and paternalist construction of nationalism is
offered by Jardo Muekalia, today a senior member in UNITA. In it he
contrasts the memory of his father's pleasure in listening to the official news
and discussing it with friends and colleagues to his solitary listening of
Angola Combatente and the attendant dangers. Vibrant conversations endured for hours outside on the patio under the trees, always in the company
of the radio. But one night in 1968 nine-year-old Jardo found his father alone
and listening to the radio at low volume. Approaching, he hears the call sign
from Brazzaville. When his father realizes Jardo is near, he turns off the
radio immediately, asks him to repeat what he heard, and cautions him to
never say anything about it to anyone lest he endanger the family's well-
being. Noticing his father had not changed the frequency, Jardo returns to
listen:

> they continued to talk about the MPLA and colonialism. In any case, it was all
> Chinese to me. All I knew was that it was a dangerous broadcaster. From then
> on, I listened now and then to the dangerous broadcaster, accompanied by my
> brother Tiago, until one day my father caught me. I had never seen him so
> angry.[60]

Weeks later the PIDE arrested his father, a Methodist minister raising funds
for the local mission. He was accused of supporting the "*turras*," Portuguese
slang for terrorists and a general reference to the nationalist movements.

Material from the PIDE archives underscores the trope of hidden listening, if not the sense of fear. Semi-clandestine better describes the listening practices police and informers encountered. In their reports, police informants noted with disdain the moxie of listeners. In Luanda in 1967, informants expressed exasperation at public displays of listening to radio from the independent Congos and reported enthusiasm in the *musseques* for AC, accompanied in domestic space:

> Enough of the shamelessness of natives who walk around with transistors in hand in the middle of the musseque, listening to broadcasts from the Congos—Kinshasa and Brazza. As for the MPLA broadcasts, they are listened to inside the home. The influence among natives is great, increasing their euphoria in favor of independence.[61]

This is a rare, direct reference to independence by a PIDE informer. More typically "insurgency" or "terrorism" or the "enemy broadcasts" are the words chosen to describe the desires of Angolans for independence. In other words, they usually did not take on the content directly (even as they transcribed it) but thought it through a predetermined ideological frame.

In the *musseques*, one officer reported in 1967 that the PIDE commonly "surprise whole families grouped around the radio listening devotedly as if it were a religious cult."[62] PIDE officers often spoke of the population of the *musseques* as a whole, as if they were a kind of horde, one indistinguishable from the next. For example, six months later, a different informant reported that "almost the whole population of the *musseques* can't stop listening to the Brazza broadcasts."[63] Lumping together *musseque* residents and all programming from the station, the informant equates listening with "insurgency." In Sambizanga, "in various backyards, it was noted that avid subversives were found, listening to Brazza, and in one, there were five individuals with a radio inside a basket, listening to the broadcast in religious silence."[64] Some committed political activists, at least, cultivated a sense of religious devotion around their listening.[65] Whether this was true for the average *musseque* listener, or whether it was the projection of those recording the act, is harder to know. But people did gather at a regular time, although often in different places, to listen quietly and with focus. The association between radio broadcasting, listening, and religion or spirituality is a tight one, as scholars have noted. Aside from the widespread use of radio by religious organizations worldwide, the communications scholar John Durham Peters observed the mutual exchange between early radio enthusiasts and spiritualists in the late nineteenth century.[66]

Overall, the memories of Angolans and the documents in the PIDE archive emphasize the occlusion, not invisibility, and the muffling, not total silencing, of acts of listening. Faria listened openly, but in the dark. Muekalia

Senior listened outside but at low volume. And listeners shared the contents of the broadcasts, relishing and debating details. They passed along the coded names of friends, or friends of friends or contacts, who had managed to make it to exile, or news of victories in international diplomacy. Muekalia's reminiscence points to youthful curiosity and the attraction of danger, in what sounded like a foreign language, in the MPLA's alternative interpretation of lived reality. He too stresses, like Jaime, the tremendous risk nationalist sympathizers—or those just curious about other points of view—faced and the fear of the PIDE with which many lived in the late colonial period. Transgressing the law, even when impelled by a sense of righteousness, or curiosity, still involved fear.

Indeed, listening *could* get you arrested. Take this example from 1967 in the central Angolan village of Mungo near the city of Nova Lisboa (later the stronghold of UNITA). A local administrator reported the story to the local PIDE office, which then transmitted it to the head office in Luanda.[67] Around 7:00 p.m. one August night, the administrator walked into a bar to buy cigarettes. As he entered, the bar man, Timoteo Chingualulo, turned down the volume on the radio and then his friend, a microscope nurse from the local Health Delegation, António Francisco da Silva "Baião," changed the station. After he left, they tuned back in to the original station: Radio Brazzaville broadcasting the MPLA's program. The administrator could hear it from his veranda. They knew they were wrong, the officer reported. And they played the program, initially, at full volume for a bar with ten to fifteen "Africans." The local police detained both men and the offending radio (property of the bar owner, one José Texeira). While

> it has not been concluded that they are part of any cells of that or any other "subversive movement," it is inferred that the accused are partisans of an independent Angola, who, for now, are trying to satisfy their ambition by sending out the Brazzaville broadcasts publicly.[68]

Here too, listening marked one as a subversive.

Press censorship and PIDE surveillance made radio listening a risk. Angolans feared the PIDE. The fear and perceived danger involved in listening to the guerrilla stations means that former listeners sometimes recall having listened as a mode of participation in the struggle for liberation. They offer the memory of listening as a symbol of having been a part of or aligned with the exiled movements, but particularly that of the MPLA, where service in exile is a significant marker of party membership status.[69] Some people thus proffer listening as a badge of longstanding loyalty to the ruling party. At a book launch for a novel by an Angolan author in Lisbon, Portugal, in April 2016, one attendee exclaimed, "I am from the MPLA. We listened to Angola Combatente!" Here the speaker collapses party affiliation, if not militancy, and listening. If listening generated real fears, and listeners ran risks that some feel demand recognition or recompense, PIDE officers and informers had their own affective responses.

THE COLONIAL STATE UNNERVED

The PIDE sometimes arrested listeners, but not always. A nurse working in Luanda was found rejoicing over news he heard on Angola Combatente in 1964. Passed along by an informer, this seemed not to have had immediate repercussions, although he was likely then surveilled.[70] As the arrest of Chingualulo and Baião demonstrates, PIDE files offer evidence that the practice of listening extended beyond the politically conscious and engaged activists of urban areas. Even a cursory reading of the many thousands of pages of documents of broadcast transcriptions, interrupted listening séances, decrees about how to handle the new broadcasts, and reports of rumored listening brought to the PIDE (all jumbled together in their archives), amplifies the trope and complicates our understanding of the meaning of listening.

It is difficult to know precisely how many people listened and how widely. PIDE transcriptions come from nearly all provinces—but not necessarily accounts of Africans tuning in. In a study of broadcasting in the Portuguese colonies, Alexander F. Toogood reported low radio density in Angola:

> Considering that in 1971 there were only about 95,000 receivers in the country, one-third concentrated in the Luanda district and mostly in the hands of Europeans, it seems doubtful that broadcasts by the nationalist movements could have a widespread impact. . . . It may be a measure of Portugal's insecurity that it nevertheless tried strenuously to counter the propaganda broadcasts by increasing Radio Angola's provincial coverage and giving financial support to private stations.[71]

If memories of listening seem amplified relative to the actual numbers of radios in homes (even if one radio set served many ears), so too does Portuguese insecurity.[72] In Toogood's account this paranoia motivated action.

When the PIDE began receiving consistent reports about VAL in 1966, those reports described it as similar to the MPLA's broadcast, that is, "of a subversive character." They recommended that steps be taken to jam the program, as they were attempting to do with AC.[73] Often issued from the Luanda delegation, it is not clear from these documents where reception occurred, although an entire file of nearly one thousand pages of transcriptions of both AC and VAL from 1966–1968, when the transcription service began, includes nearly a third from two posts in other areas: Dundo-Portugalia in the Lunda region of eastern Angola (the base of Diamang) and Lobito, a port city, in the central southern area. [74] The sound came from all around and was widely received, in other words.

Memos relating to radio all crossed the desk of the PIDE's head of office, Jaime Oliveira. He received and signed off on nearly every report of listening. He drafted memos and circulars that resound with what Chikowero calls the "nervous condition of colonial authority." In May 1966 he reported on listenership securing the very trope that dominates in memory: "In the most complete silence and isolation, uniting all the possible and imaginable precautions, the middle class, that is, administrative functionaries and servants and others, in an incredibly large number, listen to Radio Brazzaville on Sundays (the Program of the subversive broadcasts)." More prudent than "civilized" or elite listeners, these middle-class listeners, he surmised, were difficult to count. [75] He continued, "These broadcasts inspire them and give them ideas and oblige us to think, to judge that these [broadcasts] are no less dangerous than the armed war." Add to them seven "civilized" listeners that Oliveira listed by name, a laughable number, he noted, given the sizable total number of listeners including "a large number of white sympathizers." [76]

Propaganda, the war of words, of hearts and minds, captured the attention of large swathes of colonial society. Not even whites could be trusted not to listen. [77] Broadcasts encouraging soldiers, particularly Portuguese soldiers, appealed to listeners and troubled the PIDE. In a series of reports from across the territory, from Pereira d'Eça in the far south, to Cuanza Norte and Luanda in the center, the PIDE registered anticipation about and chatter around interviews with deserters in the late 1960s. [78] One officer noted the effect on soldiers from the metropole who suddenly "realize that they are defending someone else's cause, that of the capitalists, without any compensation to justify their sacrifice." [79] Two months later another report claimed that an AC broadcast encouraging soldiers to desert because "the army doesn't defend the Nation but the capitalism of 'Diamang,' of Oil and a half-dozen wealthy individuals because the people of Angola live in misery" had wide repercussions in Luandan public opinion. [80] An AC interview of African soldiers who deserted the Portuguese army was "listened to attentively" and one man was overheard repeating it nearly "word for word" to a friend. [81]

In December 1966 Oliveira issued Secret Circular 52/66. It went to all delegations and sub-delegations of the PIDE from the Luanda office. This circular noted the growth in anti-Portuguese radio propaganda, especially that of the MPLA. Commenting on reception:

> This activity of the En ["In," short for inimigo, enemy] aims at the subversion of the Angolan populations, whose programs reach the Province with the best conditions for listening, giving the sensation that we are hearing a local broadcast, and a large part of the population, even the Europeans, listens closely. [82]

He went on to solicit help from local post and telegraph offices and radio clubs in jamming Angola Combatente. At this point, he did not know if it would be effective or even possible. Caught out both technologically and in the propaganda game, the PIDE scrambled to take the upper hand, calling on local expertise and trying to centralize information and skills in a disarticulated colonial world, whose coherence lay only in violence. [83]

But the PIDE had been following foreign-based broadcasters since the late 1950s. They already knew of the MPLA's and the FNLA's broadcasts well before 1966 even if they were not yet following them systematically. Attempts and requests to interfere with Brazzaville's signal were not new. Neither was the nervousness. It was a nettling, destabilizing force that would not go away. A report from the PIDE sub-delegation in Malanje from late 1964—brimming with colonial stereotypes—requested that Luanda insist with Lisbon on "the interference of Brazzaville communications." [84] The body of the report concerned "strange facts" apparent in the "life of natives" in certain Malanje towns in the preceding month. Among them: a rumor that people should not work on Saturdays and Mondays, aimed at "damaging the economy of the Province and as some kind of protest of something that is not yet clear." The head of the PIDE delegation put the blame on local African priests, pastors, and catechists, Catholic and Protestant. He associated it with a state of unrest and rumors that circulated in 1961 when colonial military were first stationed in the area, following the uprisings against forced cotton production and the resultant massacre by the Portuguese military in January that year in the Baixa de Kassange.

The head of the delegation stacked up evidence and fueled agitation. He described the residents of these Malanje villages as "arrogant, insolent, and daring" in their interactions with whites. Residents have been told they should all have a guitar to play and sing "the anthem of independence." Thus the "native masses" wandered around with homemade guitars. This "animates the idea of latent agitation noted and confirms the state of subversion observed all around." Added to this is the conspiratorial plan of those engaged in healing and witchcraft "who work clandestinely to achieve their ends." Finally, the last link in the chain,

> in mixed commercial establishments and those which sell electrical articles, it's common to see natives, some of whom we are surveilling, buying portable radios and this is due, without a doubt, to the reception conditions of Radio Brazzaville, via which the directors of the MPLA, incite the mass [*sic*] to rebellion, in all manner of conspiratorial ways. [85]

If we remove the charged terms, the chief of the Malanje PIDE office reported absenteeism from work on Saturdays and Mondays, the increased appearance of artisanal guitars, healing rituals, and radio sales. He linked these phenomena, which he could see, to what he could not see: rumor, clandestine (his word) witches and healers, and the MPLA on Radio Brazzaville. He read "strange behavior" as indexical of clandestine political activity. Where there is smoke, there is fire.

This document evokes many associations typically attributed to Africans interacting with new technologies, like radios or cinema or medical devices.[86] Africans, colonial administrators insist, see magic in machines (so of course do most first-time users anywhere), use rumor as a form of communication, and are naturally inclined to musical recreation. Here the PIDE chief incorrectly divines a single cause: the MPLA broadcast. You can just hear the MPLA leadership tittering with delight if you listen closely enough.

RADIO TECHNOLOGY AND NERVOUSNESS

The PIDE officer evinces nervousness in the face of what he calls "strange behavior." To quell his tremulousness, he writes. In the act of writing he knits visible symptoms with a causality he locates in the invisible voice of the MPLA broadcast. The solution? Jamming. Scramble the sound, interfere with transmission, block reception, calm the nerves. But his blunt diagnosis and such definitive action rest on shaky evidence. The uprising in the region in 1961, not linked with any organized political movement, had some ties to Congo-Kinshasa where its founder had worked, and had been touched by the Congolese politics of independence.[87] De Grassi reminds us that protestors chanted Lumumba's name.[88]

The officer clutches for causal certainty to counter his edgy state. But what precisely is the source of the nervousness? Hunt argues that "the Belgian colonial state was born from nervousness and the Congo became a nervous state."[89] She finds its beginnings in the "tense, aggressive Free state, fierce Stanley, taut officers, wrathful inebriated concession agents, and armed sentries."[90] For Chikowero the colonial archive on radio bespeaks the "nervous condition" of the colonial state by exposing its fear that radio would inspire nationalist insurgency that undermined its authority, a sentiment vibrating through this document.[91] While the Portuguese colonial state in Angola, thickened in reiterated acts of violence, strewn across the difficulties of metropolitan and territorial politics and identities, certainly was a nervous state, this officer's nervousness, and that of Jaime Oliveira and the PIDE and military, also derived from the specificity of radio technology.

Immateriality, intimacy, and transduction characterize the radio. Sound waves travel through the ether, diminish distance, banish time. Michele Hilmes describes the unifying ambitions of broadcasting in the early-twentieth-century United States: "the basic technical qualities of radio would unite the nation physically, across geographic space, connecting remote regions with centers of civilization and culture, tying the country together over the invisible waves of ether."[92] Radio broadcasting can connect across an empire despite miles and time differences or stitch together white settlements in a far-flung colonial territory, as member-based radio clubs did in Angola. But those invisible sound waves could be used to create intimacies of a different stripe as well. Guerrilla stations, based in exile in sovereign foreign states, existed beyond the jurisdiction of colonial law but within the state's and territory's earshot. Herein lies the power of radio's immateriality, short-wave in particular, to disrupt, to unnerve. It is unruly, does not respect borders, runs roughshod over the sense of inviolable national territory. Broadcasting anti-colonial propaganda, the MPLA's and FNLA's stations put the colonial state and its police and military on edge and on the defensive.

Salazar's lack of interest in radio broadcasting meant that guerrilla broadcasters caught the state off-guard. If even *musseque* dwellers owned radios, and PIDE officers nervously repeated rumors that some homes had two (one in the front tuned to the state broadcaster, one in the back tuned to Brazzaville), surely hidden listening in and outside the home was rife. And plenty of Europeans and black civil servants listened in the isolation of the private home. This was the transgressive downside of unity and intimacy, overcoming the isolation of distance, created seclusion in intimate listening space.[93]

PIDE and military officers found a diverse set of listeners huddled around radios, alone or in groups, attentive to the nationalist movements' news, critiques, and exhortations. One military report noted the MPLA programs' "electrifying" effects.[94] Here the intimacy of radio, the fact of broadcasting into the private space of the home, into the ear and head of the listener, set the minds of PIDE officers reeling. They were unsettled, jumpy, and reactive.

Radios are transducers. They change sound energetically as the waves move across and through them.[95] Perhaps what made the PIDE officers and informers so nervous was this transformation and potential transubstantiation. Bodies close to radios, ears penetrated by that energy, might be transduced and changed. Officers nervously opined that radio listening made subversives of listeners or that listening equated to subversion. Perhaps it was the apprehension of how radios work on sound and bodies, the fear that this transformation was less about content and ideas than about how machines affect bodies that made officers and informants and Oliveira himself so very nervous. The technical operations of radio troubled the minds of PIDE officers and informants and the bodies of listeners.

CONCLUSION

Today's RNA, once the EOA, sits not far from the MPLA mural of the Angola Combatente broadcast. It allows for a slippage from guerrilla broadcasting to national radio that forgets the complexities of radio and the anti-colonial war, among other dynamics. A close reading of PIDE archive documents on the guerrilla stations and foreign broadcasting with an ear to the operations of radio technology adds new tones to our understanding of the colonial state and the newly independent state. They sound less sure than they once did. The immaterial world of sound production and reception and how state and nonstate actors understood it, matter. This can help us see differently too. The buildings and walls of urban space, carefully maintained, appear now more as fragments rather than the seemingly complete stories of this past.

NOTES

1. The *União Nacional de Independência Total de Angola* (National Union for the Total Independence of Angola, UNITA) joined the war in 1966 when Jonas Savimbi broke from the FNLA to form this movement. Joseph Sanches Cervelló, "Caso Angola," in *Guerra Colonial*, ed. Aniceto Afonso and Carlos de Matos Gomes (Lisbon: Editorial Notícias, 2000), 74 and *The Decolonization of Portuguese Africa: Metropolitan Revolution and the Dissolution of Empire* (New York: Longman, 1997), 35–36.
   2. James M. Kushner, "African Liberation Broadcasting," *Journal of Broadcasting* 18, no. 3 (1974): 299.
   3. Stephen R. Davis, "The African National Congress, Its Radio, Its Allies and Exile," *Journal of Southern African Studies* 35, no. 2 (2009): 349–73; Robert Heinze, "'It Recharged Our Batteries': Writing the History of the Voice of Namibia," *Journal of Namibian Studies* 15 (2015): 30. The ANC's Radio Freedom debuted in 1967 in Lusaka, Zambia (after an aborted start at Lilliesleaf Farm in 1963). See Sekibakiba P. Lekgoathi, "The African National Congress's Radio Freedom and Its Audiences in Apartheid South Africa, 1963–1991," *Journal of African Media Studies* 2, no. 2 (2010): 141. Dumisani Moyo and Cris Chinaka discuss ZANU's Voice of Zimbabwe broadcasts from Mozambique and ZAPU's Voice of the Revolution from Zambia in "Persuasion, Propaganda and Mass Mobilisation Through Underground Radio in the Zimbabwe War of Liberation: A Comparative Study of Radio Voice of the People and Voice of the Revolution" (paper circulated at the Wits Workshop on Liberation Radios in Southern Africa, University of the Witwatersrand, February 2017). For work on the Voz da Frelimo that broadcast from Tanzania and Zambia, see Eléusio dos Prazeres Viegas Filipe, "Voice of FRE-LIMO Insurrection against the Voice of Mozambique: Waging Propaganda War against Portuguese Colonialism and Building a National Consciousness, 1960s–1975" and Alda Romão Saúte Saíde, "A Voz da Frelimo and the Struggle for the Liberation of Mozambique, 1960s to 1970s" (papers circulated at the Wits Workshop on Liberation Radios in Southern Africa, University of the Witwatersrand, February 2017). Saíde dates broadcasts to 1962 from Tanzania.
   4. John Mowitt, in *Radio: Essays in Bad Reception* (Berkeley: University of California Press, 2011), notes the sense of radio as a forgotten, understudied technology in the field of radio studies.
   5. Heinze, "'It Recharged Our Batteries,'" 4. Work on radio off the continent emphasizes the tension between work on a sound technology and the necessity of relying on documentary archives because there are few recordings. See, for example, Susan Douglas, *Listening In: Radio and the American Imagination* (Minneapolis: University of Minnesota Press, 1999), 3 and 9; and Michele Hilmes, *Radio Voices: American Broadcasting, 1922–1952* (Minneapolis: University of Minnesota Press, 1997), xvi.
   6. Radio Nacional de Angola (Angolan National Radio, RNA) has one recording of *Angola Combatente* from its Brazzaville and Lusaka years. The Associação Tchiweka de Documentação (Tchiweka Association Documentation Center, the private archive of MPLA

leader Lúcio Lara) has 15–20 transcriptions of radio broadcasts from Brazzaville and Dar es Salaam translated from Portuguese to English by Marga Holness and kept with her records. General Mbeto Traça, director of the Lusaka station, and Guilherme Mogas, the second director of RNA, both recalled trying to recover materials from the exiled stations in Brazzaville and Lusaka but said they had been lost over the course of the 1980s. They may yet appear. Interview with Guilherme Mogas, May 11, 2011, Luanda and interview with General Mbeto Traça, May 9, 2011, Luanda.

7. Lekgoathi, "African National Congress's Radio Freedom," 144.

8. For example, see PIDE/DGS Del. Angola, P Inf. 11.08.E, U.I. 1818, ff. 1–474 and 11.08.F, U. I. 1817, ff. 1–950. These transcriptions were collected by CHERET, the Chefia de Reconhecimento das Transmissões (Broadcast Reconnaissance Command) and published in their Boletim Periódico de Escuta de Rádio/Perbolrad (Period Bulletin of Radio Listening) circulated to military and police with a certain class of security clearance. Earlier transcriptions from the years 1964 through 1968 were collected by the PIDE, under different rules, which did not mandate the disposal of the documents.

9. See, for example, the documents in PIDE/DGS, Del. Angola, P. Inf. 14.17.A, U. I. 2044, all of which are from this period.

10. See, for example, PT AHM/7B/13/4/273/40, Sit. Rep 339, September 1968, p. 6 of 6, in which the head of SCCIA, instead of just reporting that the African language broadcast was ignored (the usual practice), notes that doing so ignores its danger and weakens potential counter-propaganda.

11. Nancy Rose Hunt, "An Acoustic Register: Rape and Repetition in the Congo," in *Imperial Debris: On Ruins and Ruination*, ed. Ann Laura Stoler (Durham, NC: Duke University Press, 2013), 39–66.

12. Mhoze Chikowero, "Is Propaganda Modernity? Press and Radio for 'Africans' in Zambia, Zimbabwe, and Malawi during World War II and Its Aftermath," in *Modernization as Spectacle in Africa*, ed. Peter J. Bloom, Stephan F. Miescher, and Takyiwaa Manuh (Bloomington: Indiana University Press, 2014), 113 and 132.

13. Chikowero, "Is Propaganda Modernity?" 114.

14. Nancy Rose Hunt, *A Nervous State* (Durham, NC: Duke University Press, 2016).

15. Dalila C. Mateus, *A PIDE/DGS na Guerra Colonial 1961–1974* (Lisbon: Terramar, 2004), 227.

16. Aida Freudenthal, "A Baixa de Cassanje: algodão e revolta," *Revista Internacional de Estudos Africanos* no. 18–22 (1995–1999), 245–83. Freudenthal analyzes then newly released documents to revise the historical reading of this until then little-known peasant revolt. She notes, for example, how the Portuguese colonial administration not only responded violently but then acted to disappear and downplay the events to both cover over their violence and obscure the causes (a pitiless forced labor regime by the state-sanctioned concessionary Cotonang) of the revolt, claiming it was motivated by outside agitators. See, for example, 250–51 and 270–71.

17. Freudenthal, "A Baixa de Cassanje," 274.

18. Jason Loviglio points out the association between radio's invisible voices and the supernatural in the 1920s, radio's earliest days of broadcasting. Jason Loviglio, *Radio's Intimate Public: Network Broadcasting and Mass-Mediated Democracy* (Minneapolis: University of Minnesota Press, 2005), xviii.

19. Aharon De Grassi, "Rethinking the 1961 Baixa de Kassanje Revolt: Towards a Relational Geo-History of Angola," *Mulemba—Revista Angolana de Ciências Sociais* 10 (2015): 29–109.

20. De Grassi, "Rethinking," 93. Pointing to the resurgence of interest in and debates around this historical event in Angola, de Grassi argues that "the discussion over the character of the revolt is also a proxy for other debates, including about moral claims to a dignity and a share of national development," 41.

21. De Grassi, "Rethinking," 67–70. Here de Grassi points beyond the movements of labor and road construction to villagization, a process he documents across the twentieth century and not just as a counter-insurgency strategy.

22. The arrests, trials, and jailings of nationalists in 1959 and 1960 demonstrate the Portuguese colonial state's disinterest in negotiated political rights. They simply acted to squelch Angolan political organizing and refused to engage it. John Marcum, *The Angolan Revolution* Vol. I: *The Anatomy of an Explosion* (Cambridge, MA: MIT Press, 1969), 33–34 and Douglas Wheeler and Réné Pélissier, *Angola* (New York: Praeger, 1971), 162–66.

23. De Grassi, "Rethinking," 35; Freudenthal, "A Baixa de Cassanje," 252; Marcum, *Angolan Revolution*, Vol. I, 125; and Wheeler and Pélissier, *Angola*, 174.

24. Freudenthal, "A Baixa de Cassanje," 276. Gerald J. Bender, *Angola Under the Portuguese: The Myth and the Reality* Berkeley: University of California Press, 1978), 158 and 165.

25. Marcum, *Angolan Revolution*, Vol. I, 129; Wheeler and Pélissier, *Angola*, 175–76.

26. David Birmingham, *Frontline Nationalism in Angola and Mozambique* (Trenton, NJ: Africa World Press, 1992), 42.

27. The uncoordinated response by the Portuguese state exacerbated tensions between white settlers and the state. They pressured Salazar to make reforms that gave settlers more representation and encouraged foreign investment. See Fernando Pimenta, "O Estado Novo português e a reforma do Estado colonial em Angola: o comportamento político das elites brancas (1961–1962)," *História* 33, no. 2 (2014): 250–72.

28. The war began in earnest in May 1961 with the reoccupation of the north of the country undertaken by forces arriving from Portugal. See Aniceto Afonso and Carlos de Matos Gomes, *Guerra Colonial* (Lisbon: Editorial Notícias, 2000), 38–41.

29. The Processo de 50 marked the opening of the nationalist struggle. Fifty-six nationalist activists were arrested and tried in three trials that named three different organizations: ELA (Exército de Libertação de Angola), MIA (Movimento para a Independência de Angola), and MLA (Movimento para a Libertação de Angola) although numerous other small groups were involved. See, for example, Anabela Cunha, "'Processo dos 50': memórias de luta clandestina pela independência de Angola," *Revista Angolana de Sociologia* 8 (2011): 87–96.

30. They were concerned with an Angolan settled Portuguese citizen living in Brazzaville who was aligned with the Portuguese opposition. I detail this story in chapter 3 of my forthcoming book, *Powerful Frequencies*.

31. James R. Brennan, "Communications and Media in African History," chapter 26 in *The Oxford Handbook of Modern African History*, ed. John Parker and Richard Reid (Oxford: Oxford University Press, 2013), 501–2 and Heinze, "'It Recharged Our Batteries,'" 30.

32. This was the first consistent broadcasting. The MPLA broadcast briefly and inconsistently from Ghana in the early 1960s. Kushner, "African Liberation Broadcasting," 301–3.

33. See Stephen R. Davis on the ANC's Freedom Radio that likewise broadcast from Dar es Salaam and later Lusaka. Davis, "The African National Congress," 379.

34. Interview with General Mbeto Traça, May 9, 2011, Luanda.

35. Marcelo Bittencourt, *"Estamos Juntos!" O MPLA e a luta anticolonial (1961–1974)*, Vol. I (Luanda, 2008), 272.

36. See, for example, Don Barnett, "Liberation Support Movement Interview: Sixth Region Commander, Seta Likambuila, Movimento Popular de Libertação de Angola" (Vancouver, 1971); Don Barnett, "Liberation Support Movement Interview: Member of MPLA Comité Director Daniel Chipenda, Movimento Popular de Libertação de Angola" (Vancouver, 1972); Augusta Conchiglia, *Guerra di popolo in Angola* (Rome, 1969); and Basil Davidson, *In the Eye of the Storm: Angola's People* (New York: Doubleday, 1972). Lekgoathi notes that in the case of the ANC, radio journalism provided an easy route for foreign solidarity given the polarizing rhetoric of the Cold War. Lekgoathi, "African National Congress's Radio Freedom," 142.

37. Heinze mentions support first from Radio Cairo in the 1950s, then Radio Ghana, and Tanzania. Heinze, "'It Recharged Our Batteries,'" 30. See also James R. Brennan, "Radio Cairo and the Decolonization of East Africa, 1953–1964," in *Making a World After Empire: the Bandung Moment and its Political Afterlives*, ed. Christopher J. Lee (Athens: Ohio University Press, 2010), 173–95.

38. Institute of National Archives/Torre do Tombo, Lisbon, PIDE/DGS, Delegação de Angola, Processo de Informação 14.17.A, f915.

39. I tried several times during different visits to contact Ngola Kabangu and the head offices of the FNLA, leaving my number and card, but I was never able to set up a meeting. I

had hoped to interview Hendrik Vaal Neto, now a member of the MPLA, but during the late colonial period a member of the FNLA. He is serving as ambassador to Egypt and so I was unable to meet him in Angola.

40. *Independência* (Luanda, 2015). Historian Marcelo Bittencourt also notes that the PIDE archive contains fewer transcriptions of VAL than AC broadcasts.

41. Roberto indicated a Sr. Campos and the other was Hendrik Vaal Neto, recently the Angolan Ambassador to Egypt and someone who left the FNLA for the MPLA in the 1980s. Interview with Holden Roberto, August 9, 2005, Luanda.

42. All citations from the following file: INA/TT, PIDE/DGS, Delegação de Angola, PInf. 11.08. E, U.I. 1818. Examples include battlefront victories, ff. 927–29; addressing Portuguese soldiers, ff. 912–13, and "Portuguese oppressed by the Caetano regime," ff. 930–33; Roberto's visit to Bucharest, f800 and to China, ff. 927–29; and sending greetings to family and asking particular people to show up at the delegation headquarters, f911.

43. INA/TT, PIDE/DGS, Delegação de Angola, PInf. 11.08. E, U.I. 1818, ff. 912–13.

44. PT/AHM/FO/007/B/38, SSR 4- Angola, 1961970, 7/B 38/4 cx 360, pasta 18, rel tri APsic 4/68 1 Out a 31 dez 68, 1. See too PT/AHM/7B/13/4/273/40, Sit. Rep. 334 p. 2 of 3 and Sit. Rep. 339, p. 6 of 6.

45. Gomes and Matos, *Guerra Colonial*, 67; and John P. Cann, *Counterinsurgency in Africa: The Portuguese Way of War* (Pinetown, UK: Praeger, 2012), chapters 3 and 6. These writers all emphasize that even more than in counter-insurgency wars in general, the Portuguese approach focused on soldiers and their work with local populations. Matos and Gomes, former soldiers, attribute the overreliance on psychosocial action to the weak presence of the colonial administration, its low-cost relative to other military operations (like combat), and the poor conditions in which most of the local population lived (meaning that development projects and appeals to their aspirations could prove compelling).

46. Mateus, *A PIDE/DGS na Guerra Colonial*, 376–78.

47. Ibid., 381–82.

48. Ibid., 187–93.

49. PT/AHM/7B/38/4/360, 1962 and PT/AHM/7B/13/4/306, the "Orgânica da Contra-Subversão," April 15, 1970.

50. This item received an F6 classification, which meant it was considered not trustworthy but deserving of further investigation. It also noted that in a study done by a commercial outfit, the program Kussungila (on *Voz de Angola*) was the most popular in Luanda *musseques*. Torre de Tombo, PIDE/DGS, Delegação de Angola, PInf. 15.33.A, U.I. 2099, f275.

51. Lekgoathi reports similar listening practices in 1970s and 1980s in South Africa by listeners of the ANC's Radio Freedom. Lekgoathi, "African National Congress's Radio Freedom," 143–45.

52. Bittencourt, *"Estamos Juntos!"*, 273.

53. *Independência* (Luanda: Geração 80, 2015).

54. Censorship was not absolute. José Filipe Pinto and Angolan journalists argue it was more intense in the metropole than in the African colonies (radialist Sebastião Coelho played songs banned in the metropole in Angola, for example). A Censorship Commission and a Reading Council followed print materials closely. Anything they determined to be Marxist-Leninist, to promote *Angolanidade* (Angolanness), or situated from an Angolan perspective, they then banned. They listened to radio but generally censored after the fact. See José Filipe Pinto, "A censura em Angola durante a Guerra Colonial" and interviews with "Diamantino Pereira Monteiro" and "David Borges" in *O Jornalismo Português e a Guerra Colonial*, ed. Sílvia Torres (Lisbon: Editora Guerra & Paz, 2016), 121–27 and 173–94.

55. *Independência* (Luanda, 2015).

56. Interview with Albina Assis, January 22, 2002, Luanda.

57. *Independência* (Luanda, 2015).

58. Lekgoathi, "African National Congress's Radio Freedom," 151. He also notes the recording and circulation of broadcasts, particularly Tambo's speeches, 145 and 151. This did not happen in Angola since the broadcasts predated cassette recording technology.

59. Interview with Alberto Jaime, December 4, 2001, Luanda.

60. Jardo Muekalia, *Angola A Segunda Revolução: Memórias da luta pela Democracia* (Lisbon: Sextante Editora, 2010), 16.

61. INA/TT, PIDE/DGS, Delegação de Angola, PInf. 14.17.A, U.I. 2044, f. 266. The exasperation may suggest that this was not a trained police officer but a neighborhood informant, given that the level of security confidence accorded the report is middling (C3 on a scale of A1-3–F1-3, most to least trustworthy). Or it may be frustration with the genuine inability of the PIDE to control information in the territory and further evidence of the sense of nervousness that independence in neighboring countries produced in the PIDE officers.

62. INA/TT, PIDE/DGS, Delegação de Angola, PInf. 14.17.A, U.I. 2044, f. 332, July 14, 1967.

63. INA/TT, PIDE/DGS, Delegação de Angola, PInf. 14.17.A, U.I. 2044, f. 101, February 26, 1968.

64. INA/TT, PIDE/DGS, Delegação de Angola, PInf. 14.17.A, U.I. 2044, f. 101.

65. See Marissa J. Moorman, *Intonations: A Social and Cultural History of Nation, Luanda, Angola, 1945—Recent Times* (Athens: Ohio University Press, 2008), 151. Albina Assis discusses how she and her female friends dissimulated listening by saying they were going to *bençon*, a special gathering in the Catholic church, and a word that means "blessing."

66. Paul Apostolidis, *Stations of the Cross: Adorno and Christian Right Radio* (Durham, NC: Duke University Press, 2000); and John D. Peters, *Speaking into the Air: A History of the Idea of Communication* (Chicago: University of Chicago Press, 2000); see chapter "The History of an Error: the Spiritualist Tradition." With reference to African broadcasting, see, for example, Dorothea E. Schulze, "Equivocal Resonances: Islamic Revival and Female Radio 'Preachers' in Urban Mali," in *Radio in Africa: Publics, Cultures, Communities*, ed. Liz Gunner, Dina Ligaga, and Dumisani Moyo (Johannesburg: Wits University Press, 2011), 63–80.

67. INA/TT, PIDE/DGS, Delegação de Angola, PInf. 14.17.A, U.I. 2044, ff. 279–81.

68. INA/TT, PIDE/DGS, Delegação de Angola, PInf. 14.17.A, U.I. 2044, f. 281.

69. Jean-Michel M. Tali, *O MPLA Perante Si Próprio: Dissidências e Poder de Estado (1962–1977)*, Vol. I (Luanda, 2001), 209–20; see especially the chart on 219 with the composition of the Central Committee and the Political Bureau emerging from the Inter-Regional Conference of the MPLA in 1974. Of the thirty-four members only five came from clandestine work or the prisons; all others were active in the exiled guerrilla struggle.

70. INA/TT, Lisbon, PIDE/DGS, Delegação de Angola, Processo de Informação 15.28.A, f1076.

71. Alexander F. Toogood, "Portuguese Dependencies," in *Broadcasting in Africa: a Continental Survey of Radio and Television*, ed. Sydney Head (Philadelphia: Temple University Press, 1974), 163.

72. See Lekgoathi on group listening in South Africa, 144. For two examples of group listening in non-clandestine situations, see Harri Englund, *Human Rights and African Airwaves: Mediating Equality on Chicewa Radio* (Bloomington: Indiana University Press, 2011), 176–79 and Debra Spitulnik, "Documenting Radio Culture as Lived Experience: Reception Studies and the Mobile Machine in Zambia," in *African Broadcast Cultures: Radio in Transition*, ed. Richard Fardon and Graham Furniss, 152–55 (London: Praeger, 2000). Englund and Spitulnik discuss not only group listening but the need to take a "socio-centric" approach to understanding interpretation in such a context.

73. INA/TT, Lisbon, PIDE/DGS, Delegação de Angola, Processo de Informação 14.17.A, f814.

74. INA/TT, PIDE/DGS, Delegação de Angola, PInf. 14.17.A, U.I. 2044.

75. By this he meant former *assimilados*. The state abolished the indigenato, which divided the African population into *assimilados* (assimilated or civilized) and *indígenas* (indigenous) after the uprisings of 1961 but class and cultural cleavages continued.

76. INA/TT, Lisbon, PIDE/DGS, Delegação de Angola, Processo de Informação 15.28.A, f1051. The military was concerned with the impact of "enemy" propaganda on the white population too. In PT/AHM/7B/38/4/360, 1962, pp. 1–4, the Regional Military Commander for Angola region reported to the Military Chief of Staff in Lisbon that the white population, which "theoretically and erroneously considered a priori pro-national, finds itself perplexed and disillusioned or already contaminated by the insinuating propaganda of the En."

77. David Borges remembered tuning in to *Angola Combatente* in Cunene but only becoming "politically conscious" after the Portuguese coup of April 25, 1974. Interview with "David Borges" in Torres, ed., *O Jornalismo Português*, 187. José Oliveira remembers tuning in when serving in the colonial army in the late 1960s. When at home, he recalled his mother leaning against his door at night at 7:00 p.m., nervously listening to hear if he was following the *Angola Combatente* broadcast. Interview with José Oliveira, December 14, 2015, Luanda.

78. INA/TT, PIDE/DGS, Delegação de Angola, PInf. 14.17.A, U.I. 2044, ff. 183–184, 234, and 191.

79. INA/TT, PIDE/DGS, Delegação de Angola, PInf. 14.17.A, U.I. 2044, f. 191, December 1, 1967.

80. INA/TT, PIDE/DGS, Delegação de Angola, PInf. 14.17.A, U.I. 2044, f. 113, February, 12, 1968.

81. INA/TT, PIDE/DGS, Delegação de Angola, PInf. 14.17.A, U.I. 2044, f. 339. The transcriber noted that the soldiers did not speak Portuguese well, a suggestion they had been recruited from areas of thinnest Portuguese presence.

82. INA/TT, Lisbon, PIDE/DGS, Delegação de Angola, Processo de Informação 14.17.A, f885.

83. See Bender, *Angola Under the Portuguese*. On Mozambique see Allen Isaacman and Barbara Isaacman, *Dams, Displacement, and the Delusion of Development: Cahora Bassa and Its Legacies in Mozambique, 1965–2007* (Athens, OH: Heinemann, 2013); *Mozambique from Colonialism to Revolution, 1900–1982* (Boulder: Westview, 1993); and Allen Isaacman, *Cotton Is the Mother of Poverty* (Portsmouth, NH): Heinemann, 1996.

84. INA/TT, Lisbon, PIDE/DGS, Delegação de Angola, Processo de Informação 15.28.A, ff 1065–7 and DGS report on Malange, 1964, f38.

85. All preceeding citations from INA/TT, Lisbon, PIDE/DGS, Delegação de Angola, Processo de Informação 15.28.A, ff 1065–7.

86. Brian Larkin, *Signal and Noise: Media, Infrastructure, and Urban Culture in Nigeria* (Durham, NC: Duke University Press, 2008), 40, 85 and Luise White, *Speaking with Vampires: Rumor and History in Colonial Africa* (Berkeley: University of California Press, 2000), 142–47. Both point out that these European representations of African responses tell us more about European projects and ideas than about Africans.

87. On the politics of independence and their relation to the Congo see Marcum, *Angolan Revolution*, Vol. I, 60–64, 70–76, and 83–88. On Congolese independence see Ch. Didier Gondola, *The History of the Congo* (Westport, CT: Greenwood, 2002); Georges Nzongola-Ntalaja, *Congo: from Leopold to Kabila, a People's History* (New York: Zed Books, 2002); and Crawford Young, *Politics in the Congo: Decolonization and Independence* (Princeton, NJ: Princeton University Press, 1965).

88. De Grassi, "Re-Thinking the Baixa de Kassanje," 57.

89. Hunt, *A Nervous State*, 1.

90. Hunt, *A Nervous State*, 8.

91. Chikowero, "Is Propaganda Modernity?" 114.

92. Hilmes, *Radio Voices*, 14.

93. Hilmes, *Radio Voices*, 14.

94. PT/AHM/FO/007/B/38, SSR 4, Angola 1962–1970, 7/B 38/4 cx 360, pasta 18, relatório trimestral APsic 4-68, 1 Out a 31 Dez 68, 2.

95. Stefan Helmreich, "Transduction," in *Keywords in Sound*, ed. David Novak and Matt Sakakeeny, 222–31 (Durham, NC: Duke University Press, 2015).

Chapter Four

Broadcasting Chimurenga — Engineering a Postcolonial Zimbabwe

Mhoze Chikowero

In the aftermath of the collapse of their propaganda press for Africans, British proponents of radio broadcasting to Africans contended that radio was the most effective tool for educating the masses of Africans into useful and loyal subjects of empire.

The project to politically engineer African minds through radio took off in colonial Zambia, Zimbabwe, and Malawi in 1939 as part of the colonial war effort. It was effectively a war effort waged not simply against Nazism but, more importantly, on "the native mind." But the so-called native mind was not a blank slate; Africans had in place their own systems of information production, processing, and dissemination, systems that quickly killed the colonial propaganda press that had preceded radio. Mostly taking the oral, aural, and visual formats, these systems were short-handed and criminalized as pernicious rumors in the colonial counter-insurgency discourse. As I have shown in my work on early colonial radio, these African modes worked through complicated linguistic and cultural registers that similarly paralyzed both radio and cinema, and sowed the seeds of guerrilla broadcasting right there in the colonial broadcasting studio by the 1950s.

This chapter demonstrates that Africans were able to effectively appropriate and redeploy radio as a technology of state crafting and self-liberation because they were already technologically equipped in systems of knowledge and information management and dissemination, both inside and outside the colonial labs of radio broadcasting. It is my argument, then, that in trying to understand technologies of self-liberation in Africa the focus should be less on the gadgets than on the agency of the subject that utilized whatever tools became available in the program of African self-liberation.

BEFORE GUERRILLA RADIO, HIS MASTER'S VOICE

Radio broadcasting emerged in Africa by the Second World War as an instrument of contending European imperial propaganda wars against each other and on the colonized Africans. By the middle of the twentieth century, African broadcasters and listeners had appropriated the medium, rendering broadcasting an even messier domain of "propaganda wars of the air."[1] African listeners in southern and central Africa welcomed with critical minds the advent of African voices hired to market anew British propaganda radio in the aftermath of its failure during the war.[2] In the 1950s and 1960s, for instance, African broadcasters based at the Lusaka Station of the Federal Broadcasting Corporation (FBC) were perplexed when African listeners attacked them in letters threatening them with death through arson, branding them *banyama* (vampire-men) for wishing them "death" (preaching the hated Federation) and when they vandalized field recording equipment in the villages in an era that almost dealt a deathblow to colonial radio in the federated territories (colonial Zambia, Zimbabwe, and Malawi). At the same time, broadcasters like Andreya Masiye employed the power of African languages to subvert the medium by clandestinely propagating pro-nationalist sentiments in the stories, plays, songs, and news that they broadcast.[3]

These were the seeds of guerrilla radio, which blossomed with the independence of Ghana, Tanzania, Zambia, and, later, Mozambique, allowing the extension of pan-African broadcasting beyond Ethiopia and Egypt, which had run anti-colonial broadcasts to Africa since the 1940s. Together with their South African and Namibian counterparts, the Zimbabwe African People's Union (Zapu) and the Zimbabwe African National Union (Zanu) perfected guerrilla broadcasting as a crucial technology to destroy the recalcitrant Rhodesian state and craft a new nation-state. This chapter is a preliminary effort to map the constitution and operation of guerrilla radio broadcasting in the struggle for self-liberation in southern Africa, and principally in colonial Zambia, Zimbabwe, and Malawi. It is part of my larger research program on technologies of state making.[4]

CONCEPTUALIZING GUERRILLA RADIO AND TECHNOLOGICAL STATE CRAFTING

Radio has largely been studied through an evolutionary anthropological lens of modernity,[5] with scholars explicating the various ways in which the medium helped Africans to cultivate new identities and self-representations, a perspective that often remains entrapped by the foundational colonial agenda that radio would help Africans evolve socially and suppress independent thought and the feared prospect of political revolution. This chapter is interested in the ways that Africans utilized guerrilla broadcasting to effect political revolution, overthrow the colonial state, and craft the postcolonial nation-state. Conceptually, the idea of guerrilla broadcasting trains our focus on the significance of purveying information in unconventional ways and its consumption in equally unconventional spaces with the objective of outranging brutalizing state power. Guerrilla broadcasting was enabled by a transcendental space—exile—and guerrilla listening was practiced within secret and intimate spaces under blankets, behind closed doors, and out in the bush, from where reverse flows—feedback, encouragement, and other forms of informational transactions—emanated. Whereas the colonial state had employed exile (together with the jail, the concentration camp, and the restriction and detention camps) as a device to politically immobilize Africans, the guerrilla movement embraced the space as a transcendental pan-African commons to engineer the nation-state.

This process necessarily makes the African postcolonial nation-state a relational entity. The broader argument, therefore, is that the African nation-state was not born individually and of discrete processes; it came as part of a critical collective. It was crafted by the collective efforts within the pan-African and transnational neighborhood of support that drew its rationale from broadly shared historical, cultural, and political backgrounds and outlooks. The radio, a technology of communication, operating within an assemblage of other technologies such as the gun (a technology of force) furnished a crucial instrumentality in the making of the nation-state, particularly because of this contextualization. Exile enabled the deployment of the radio, the cached gun, and the guerrilla mystique toward the engineering of the nation-state (from) beyond the colonial line. This is how Africans redeployed the radio as a technology of political engineering on their own terms.

The fight for the independence of the southern African settler colonies was the originary rationale of the Organization of African Unity (OAU) and other transnational support movements. Rededicating itself to that mandate, Radio Tanzania established an external service section in 1968, with the purpose of supporting the liberation of Africa, African unity, the fostering of good neighborliness, and the positive portrayal of Tanzania's image outside its borders.[6] Tanzania became the bastion of African liberation movements. Not only did it help to mobilize, train, equip, and deploy these movements, but it also gave them broadcasting time to articulate their ideologies, communicate with their people back in their own countries, with each other on the front and with their supporters, and to talk back at the enemy. ZAPU and ZANU (the Patriotic Front after 1975) enjoyed the same facilities in Zambia, Mozambique, Madagascar, Ethiopia, the USSR, and East Germany, from where they broadcast as the Voice of Zimbabwe, the Voice of the Revolution, and the Revolutionary Voice of Zimbabwe.

Some of the key cadres of guerrilla broadcasting, such as Grey Tichatonga (Mark Marongwe), Webster Shamu, and John Chifamba, had learned
radio craft at the Rhodesian Broadcasting Corporation (RBC), whose fare
was the denunciation of nationalists as terrorists and the suppression of songs
that demanded African freedom. Thus pre-equipped, they crossed the line to
invade the airwaves with banned Chimurenga music, counter-propaganda,
and popular African views sent on postcards and letters by listeners who
variously prosecuted the war as differently armed combatants from within
the country. This reciprocal guerrilla communication system enabled
Africans not only to counter the colonial state's story, but also, and more
importantly, to imagine, engineer, and collectively produce a new nation
from both inside and outside the country.

This look at guerrilla radio utilizes oral history in the form of published
and new interviews with former broadcasters, listeners, and propaganda operatives, and archived broadcasts to illustrate how radio helped the engineering of Zimbabwe from exile.

PORTRAIT OF A GUERRILLA
BROADCASTER, GUERRILLA LISTENER

Zimbabwean nationalist radio was an intervention against the colonial media's shutting out of independent African voices from the public domain in a
spirited attempt to maintain Rhodesia as a white man's country "for at least a
thousand years," in the words of its last prime minister, Ian Douglas Smith.
When Smith subverted imminent African majority rule by unilaterally declaring Rhodesia independent of British overlordship in those infamous
words, Africans saw their future robbed at the moment of delivery and became convinced of the military imperative. It is not surprising, then, that
youngsters from varied backgrounds like Victor Mhizha Murira, Sobusa
(Gazi) Gula Ndebele, Charles Ndlovu, and women like Jane Lungile Ngwenya slipped out of Rhodesia to wield the gun and the microphone. Many
abandoned the trappings of what had promised to be relatively comfortable
futures for "middle class" Africans under Rhodesian apartheid; others had
become utterly disillusioned and abandoned school, and many carried the
scars of political imprisonment, torture, and everyday colonial violence. This
chapter tells these stories primarily from the former guerrilla's mouth while
at the same time redefining "guerrilla" to show that this was a broad, more
inclusive category than often allowed in narrow, self-serving latter-day nationalist discourses.

Victor Mhizha Murira shied away from university by a school term after
he abandoned his Advanced Level studies at St. Augustine's Mission School
in Penhalonga to join the Zimbabwe African National Liberation Army (Zan-

la) in Mozambique in July 1975 with seven other teenage boys.[7] He was convinced that he would have enjoyed a "very bright future in Rhodesia" if he stayed to finish his high school and enroll to study medicine or engineering at the University of Rhodesia, but he swapped school science education for the science of war, going through political and military instruction at Wampoa and Chitepo Political Academies after serving a year on the front. He was then thrust into Zanu's Information and Publicity Department, where he was involved in the publication of party magazines such as *Chimurenga* before the secretary of that department, Rugare Gumbo, moved him on to radio in Maputo in 1977. He remembers this formative moment very clearly:

> I found myself in broadcasting by default. I had gone to Maputo to work as a print journalist, but they did not have enough broadcasters at the Voice of Zimbabwe. I was good at writing; I had come from school where I had been doing Upper Sixth Form in Biology, Physics, Chemistry, and Maths, so I was very articulate compared to the average guy in the liberation war. I mean I could communicate well, especially in writing. But at the same time I could not speak very well because I had a lisp.[8]

With encouragement and support from Gumbo—who listened to his broadcasts every night—Dzingai Mutumbuka, fellow broadcasters John Chifamba, Grey Tichatonga, and Webster Shamu the "Master Blaster," Murira quickly mastered the microphone and started running a vast array of programs that included writing and reading daily commentaries, news, and analysis and the popular Chimurenga Requests where he read listeners' letters and played their requested liberation songs.

Murira's lisp, immortalized in the film *Portrait of a Terrorist*, which captures him on the microphone opening a Voice of Zimbabwe program on Radio Mozambique, did not impede him. In the film, distant, emotive guerrilla chorales and the unmistakable thudding of Afrosonic ngoma echo through his bold declamation of the staple sloganeering to imbue a triumphalist aural environment that blurs the studio and the warfront:

> Forward with Chimurenga; forward with the war; forward with the masses of Zimbabwe; down with imperialism; down with neocolonialism; down with Ian Smith; down with Ndabaningi Sithole; down with Abel Muzorewa. Aluta continua. The Patriotic Front is now broadcasting your program through Radio Mozambique. The people of Zimbabwe, victory is certain![9]

Like Murira, Sobusa Gazi also abandoned the classroom for the uncharted forests. He was one of the few African students admitted at the University of Rhodesia when he decided to hit the trail to Mozambique with five other boys.[10] He underwent military training at Mgagao in Tanzania before serving at the front. Gazi found himself in the Chimurenga studio by way of a transit military camp in Tanzania. Shamu and other military leaders intercepted him on his way to Yugoslavia for further military training, asking him to write commentaries for radio:

> I did that and I think they liked it. They asked the overseers of the camp if I could be attached to the Voice of Zimbabwe for the duration of my stay at the transit camp, writing commentaries for radio. It was for a month or so; then we left. And when we came back everybody on the radio wanted me to be part of them instead of being redeployed to the front.

His colleagues, including Grey Tichatonga, were also called from the front.

Unlike these young men, Jane Lungile Ngwenya was already a "mother of the revolution" before she skipped the country in 1970. Ngwenya's political activism dated to the years of the reformist Southern Rhodesia African National Congress, before she was elected into the National Council of the National Democratic Party (NDP), a party she cofounded in 1960. She went in and out of prison, after the 1959 NDP-led riots and after ZAPU was banned in 1964. She was banished to Gonakudzingwa together with other prominent leaders of the movement, and later detained without trial at Wha-wha. She then sneaked out to Zambia in 1970, a year after her release. She received inside information that her name topped a list of people to be "dis-appeared," and she immediately beat her way out.[11] In Zambia, Ngwenya was involved in the reorganization of ZAPU after the split with Zanu and the Frolizi debacle had badly damaged the party. She also started recruitment campaigns on the Voice of the Revolution, which piggybacked on Radio Zambia, encouraging "sons and daughters of the soil" to join their compatri-ots in fighting the colonizers. She also trained younger broadcasters.

This sketch of select broadcasters' profiles makes clear the point that the guerrilla broadcaster was someone who was literate and politically con-scious, of any gender and background, who crossed into exile with the con-viction to fight for the liberation of the country. Military training and experi-ence on the front were key attributes not only to ensure that the broadcasters were talking about what was familiar to them, but also to appreciate the psychological and security implications of what they were broadcasting. In-formation management was a high-security endeavor and almost all the guer-rilla broadcasters canvassed their identities behind noms de guerre. As Sobu-sa Gazi—whose name was a declaration that "We shall rule through blood"—explained, this was to protect family back home from the inevitable harassment by the Rhodesian regime.[12] Almost all, that is, except spitfire Ngwenya, who was a former detainee and well-known, state-branded "terror-ist," having led the NDP and ZAPU before each was banned in turn.

Ngwenya thinks there was danger in anonymous or pseudonymous broad-casting. "What if people were called out by the enemy? Some used pseudonyms but I did not use one because I was not a secret politician. It did not matter that the enemy could identify me. Also, we were in a free country, and we were protected by our hosts."[13] Yet this exposed her aged mother and sister to constant police harassment. For prominent individuals like Ngwenya, boldly declaring their identities was also an apparent recruitment device because, as she reminisced, "After consistently hearing that voice and name, we saw boys coming from South Africa, leaving whatever belongings and jobs they had there—coming to join the liberation struggle. And this was the time when we were also working with Umkhonto we Sizwe to help our people join the front from both countries."[14] Ngwenya announced her name at the beginning and end of each broadcast.

IMAGINING THE AUDIENCES

To whom did these guerrilla broadcasters broadcast? According to Gula Ndebele, "Our audiences were largely imagined. Having come from the front, we could easily talk to the guerrillas at the front. But we also targeted youths in the urban and rural areas, those who supported the war, but also enemy forces."[15] Even fully made nation-states remain imagined communities, let alone those in the process of formation.[16] Thus, guerrilla radio had a clear mission: to recruit, mobilize, and rally an "imagined community" to reinforce the struggle, and to assault, demoralize, and counter the enemy's propaganda programs. Guerrilla radio was a mouthpiece for explaining the war, its rationale and objectives, and communicating the liberation movement's ideologies. Successful recruitment also depended on boosting the morale of the fighters and those who supported the war. All this also entailed countering the commanding colonial discourse.

When she got to Zambia, Ngwenya found herself shouldering this crucial mandate. The Zambian Broadcasting Corporation gave them radio time hourly. Ngwenya was an influential broadcaster who appealed to Africans' common travails under colonialism and their duty to free themselves. For example, in 1976, Sotsha Moyo, a rural Plumtree boy, "failed to see any purpose in pursuing school" and crossed with his five teenage friends into Botswana on a tortuous journey that took them into the Zambian refugee camps. Like Albert Nyathi, Obbie Xaba and crowds of other youngsters who were adjudged too young to fight upon reaching Zambia, Moyo found solace in Black Umfolosi, an acapella singing group he cofounded to stoke the war spirit in the painful camps.[17] Moyo felt impelled after listening to Ngwenya's incessant calls on his family's shortwave radio urging youngsters to come for military training. He felt Ngwenya was talking directly to him.

> Look here, please come and take up your own gun and fight for our country.
> The country is waiting for you. The war will not be won without your input;

but even if others win it while you just sit there, what are you going to say you
did for the fatherland, which was taken by the Boers?[18]

Ngwenya was quite conscious of the psychological essence of her words
because she was addressing her people, whose plight and desires she shared.
She knew she touched her people's hearts when she spoke to them in the
multiple languages of Zimbabwe that included Sotho, Shona, Ndebele, and
English. Ngwenya knew she was talking to people like Sotsha Moyo.

> You are telling this to someone who knows that their cattle were taken while
> they watched; their homes were destroyed so that their fowls were abandoned
> to become wild birds while young and old men were foot-bound and kid-
> napped for *chibharo* (forced labor). You don't tell him twice.[19]

The broadcasters were quite didactic, targeting also "those Africans who
hardened their hearts against their own people" by fighting on the side of the
colonizers. The broadcasts constituted psychological games, hoping to demoralize these Africans into reconsidering their stance. Murira remembered
particularly well how he chipped at the *askaris'* conscience. He targeted his
messaging to named regiments in specific locations, decrying their known
acts of outrage.

> Brother, what are you doing there? Have you ever thought about your own
> future after Zimbabwe has become independent? I am talking to you, the
> member of the African police based in Gwelo. Listen to us; we are talking
> about African liberation. It is inevitable. And the African Regiments of Smith,
> your notoriety with the NATO; what is it doing? Killing your own brothers
> and sisters. The best you can do is walk over; the worst is to fire in confronta-
> tions.[20]

Defectors and captives provided a golden opportunity for propaganda
through recorded interviews.[21]

Most imagined listeners at home constituted (potential) support communities—"parents," "brothers," and "sisters." Many of them were already listening to the RBC. And now there was a new voice on the airwaves, albeit
one that the state criminalized and tried to silence—and bringing excitement
to the whole experience of listening to radio. As always, the colonial crimi-
nalization of the African voice piqued Africans' curiosity; now they could
tune into both the RBC and the "pirate" radios, compare the stories and draw
their own conclusions in light of their daily experiences.

Simon Pashoma Ncube was a student at Gokomere High School in the
1970s, and he and his friends saw themselves as heroes for defying the
government's ban on listening to the guerrilla broadcasts. They risked being
jailed if caught, so they had to be very tactical. With a small group of trusted

friends, Pashoma Ncube climbed into the local hills to engage in guerrilla listening:

> What really drew us to nationalist radio were the explanations about the libera-tion war. We also used to listen to RBC and read newspapers, and so we would compare what we heard from these white sources . . . and you would, for instance, question where all these thousands of guerrillas were coming from if, as the newspapers and the RBC were claiming, the war was favoring the whites. It then became very clear that this was propaganda. We thus ques-tioned the official view and got more substance for our discussions from nationalist radio. We called ourselves *magamba* [heroes]; you know, we also read war novels like Kutonhodzwa KwaChauruka and we saw ourselves as some of Jane Lungile Ngwenya's heroic characters in those books. [22]

Defying the colonial state and its psychological propaganda weapons and threats became acts of heroism.

Samuel Mkhithika was one young radio enthusiast who would later work for the RBC. A curious mind, he habitually tuned into Radio Moscow, Radio Zambia, and Radio Mozambique to hear what the nationalists were saying after his parents retired to bed. [23] Thomas Mapfumo, a guitar guerrilla whose Chimurenga hits caused him harassment and imprisonment, recounted a typi-cal guerrilla scenario at home, and the attendant deep sense of insecurity:

> The brother to my father had a small radio. I had my own radio but it couldn't just catch Mozambique; it was disturbed by those funny sounds [jamming by the state]. You could [try to tune in] very carefully, otherwise if they caught you doing that they could put you behind bars. . . . We would have to lock the doors and sit down with the whole of the family and you open the radio and everyone is quiet. You turn that radio so low that the man outside can't hear anything. [24]

This organized group and individualized guerrilla listening and political edu-cation during *pungwes* (night vigils) shaped the political consciousness of students across the country, destabilizing schools and leading to a massive exodus of students for training camps. Such acts often attracted merciless reprisals from Rhodesian forces, as happened at Manama Mission in Gwanda in January 1977, when soldiers ambushed and massacred students en route to Botswana. The broadcasters credited radio for the floods of recruitment, which overwhelmed them by 1978, forcing them to urge new would-be re-cruits to stay at home and engage the enemy from there with the aid of combatants already deployed in the country. [25]

The devices of insurgent immobilization—exile, "keeps" (concentration camps), restriction, detention, and imprisonment—were meant to punish, dis-cipline, and demoralize the colonized. But even in these constricted spaces Africans conversed with each other through radio, songs, letters, and an

intricate system of coded signs and symbols that defied the watchman, high
walls, and razor wire. Moreover, many prison guards were sympathetic to, or
clandestinely worked for, the nationalist movement from within the system.
These crucial operatives provided African political prisoners, restrictees, and
detainees with inside information and conduits to smuggle contraband such
as radio sets and letters. At both Gonakudzingwa and Whawha, for instance,
Ngwenya and her colleagues had access to radio sets that could tune into
short- and medium-wave frequencies.

Radio sets were precious possessions in jail, and prisoners made sure that
they would not be found out listening to them or sold out by informers
planted in their midst. Ngwenya and her colleagues utilized guerrilla tactics
to listen to the radio for news.

> We assigned one person, or at the most two people, to listen to the wireless to
> prevent plants from discovering our sources of information. Then in the eve-
> ning we would sit outside the cells in the yards, singing and getting updates on
> radio news. Then the plants would be surprised how we knew what was trans-
> piring outside. We would flush out some of them; many tended to pretend to
> be zealots, ultimate sons and daughters of the soil. And some we converted by
> the time they were "released." And because we also had our own plants within
> the system, we were able to pass news in and out, or around the cells on
> scribbled toilet paper and on our palms.[26]

Guerrilla listening in the colonial prison gave inmates no scope to listen to
Chimurenga music, but only news. When they wanted music, they sang the
songs themselves. Otherwise radio music was for those outside prison walls.
For those outside, one specialized Chimurenga music program that became
synonymous with Zanla was Chimurenga Requests.

"*NZIRA DZEMASOJA*": CHIMURENGA REQUESTS

Chimurenga songs punctuated nationalist radio programs, which opened with
sounds of rattling gunfire, drumming, and background singing, and typically
closed with the song "*Kune nzira dzemasoja*" (Guerrilla Code of Conduct),
reminding combatants to be disciplined fighters.[27] Chimurenga Requests was
a program dedicated primarily to musical requests by guerrilla listeners at
home. Broadcasters read listeners' letters and played them the songs they had
requested. Victor Mhizha Murira hosted this program, which ran for thirty
minutes every Saturday. The RBC ran its own along similar lines: Forces
Requests, produced by Sally Donaldson, the "sweetheart of the Rhodesian
Forces." Murira regarded Forces Requests as "one of the Rhodesians' most
lethal programs . . . it was a serious morale booster."[28]

Song was a mainstay of propaganda radio. Anthropological wisdom had taught the colonists that the power of African music could be exploited to cultivate African subjectivity.[29] With the advent of the "saucepan special" in the late 1940s, for instance, the director of the Central African Broadcasting Services in Lusaka, Harry Franklin, argued that providing Africans with radio listening facilities (saucepan specials and street loudspeakers) would ensure their "happiness" and avert communist-inspired "mischief." "The African loves music, plays, rhetoric, argument—all the things that radio can put across so well," and he declared, "Let him have them!"[30] Similarly, in 1960, E. A. Smart, a radio and advertising merchant, sought a government tender by suggesting that Africans could be entrapped in a propaganda vortex through repeated radio music:

> Africans like repetition in the music that is supplied and, if an effective advertising message is prepared, [they] appear to look for it as an old friend when traveling on the bus. . . . An advertisement containing a simple 30 second jingle in the vernacular becomes a "hit" tune in Salisbury after only being played for two days.[31]

From the late 1950s, Africans were seized with freedom songs while the state broadcaster continued to foist on them what it considered apolitical music.[32] It censored songs with political sensibilities that seemed to challenge colonial authority. In line with colonial cultural policy, therefore, radio sought to de-emphasize the politics of African music.[33] Needless to say, the power of African music resides in its contextual usage.

In contrast to the music programs on the RBC, Chimurenga Requests churned out the raw militancy in the songs that Africans were producing in the 1960s and 1970s. In other words, guerrilla radio helped to elaborate Chimurenga songs and to reinforce the ideological rationale behind the war, as Mapfumo noted of Radio Mozambique.

> It wasn't only just talking; they would sing Chimurenga songs before Comrade Mugabe's speech. I liked best that Chimurenga Requests program because it was for the people and it gave the people what [they] wanted. . . . So each time we could open Mozambique and listen to Comrade Mugabe and that music, and afterwards we were pleased and we could close our radios and then listen to the rest of the rubbish on the Rhodesia radio.[34]

One Sister Clara of Berejena Mission remembers writing to the program— and how it helped to recruit more fighters: "We used to write letters to Maputo and give them to the comrades, and the comrades passed them on . . . encouraging the comrades to hurry with the war. I encouraged many boys to join."[35] Ordinary old women without apparent political profiles also carried these letters on trains and buses for ZAPU and ZANU.[36] Chimurenga Re-

quests was aimed at audiences in Zimbabwe, whom the broadcasters addressed as comrades, parents, brothers, and sisters, such as in the following
excerpt quoted by Julie Frederikse:

> (Music . . . sounds of gunfire: rat-a-tat-tat). Good evening, sons and daughters
> of Zimbabwe, from the Zambezi to the Limpopo. Your Chimurenga Requests
> programme is on the air once again. Our first letter this evening comes from
> Gatooma. Comrade Z, you would like to join the struggle but you don't know
> how. Brother, it's not difficult. The freedom fighters are now operating
> throughout the country. Make any effort—you will find them. If you don't,
> they will find you. . . . (Rat-a-tat-tat). . . . Now we have a letter from racist
> South Africa, from Orlando, Soweto. You say, "Coming to South Africa, I
> thought things would be different, but to my surprise, I went from the frying
> pan into the fire. I am labouring for nothing in the black holes of South Africa,
> working for the slave masters of Wenela. Brothers, I am badly in need of a
> bazooka or an AK-47. The traitors who are selling our birthright must be
> smashed. Away with the murderer Ian Smith!" That's from one of our many
> patriots in apartheid-ruled South Africa.[37]

Zimbabweans and other southern Africans had historically invaded the mines
of South Africa (willingly, and by both brute force and the force of circumstances), often accruing relatively better means of survival for their families.
These mobilities mapped critical itineraries and networks for mobilizing resources, intelligence, and manpower for the guerrilla wars in later decades.
Radios (and bicycles) marked out the status of the families privileged to have
such adventurous men (and, less often, women). Not only did these self-
acquired radios network channels for communication, but the sets also became available to the fighters whenever called upon, complete with village
technicians to service them. "Hero" Pashoma Ncube, who had remained
behind because of a disability when some of his fellow Gokomere students
crossed into Mozambique and Zambia, learned to repair radios, opened a
small workshop at home and turned himself into a supplier of radios to
guerrillas, a purveyor of letters, and a recruiter.[38] This collective effort is the
reason, as Gula Ndebele observed, that fighters at the front had to worry only
about munitions, because things like radios, clothes, and food were always
available from the people.[39] The collective efforts instilled a sense of popular
ownership of the struggle among those who were behind the cause, which
guerrilla radio effusively fostered.

Requested songs, usually dedicated to "our brothers and sisters on the
front," to "the masses supporting the war," and to "the leaders of the struggle" were interspaced with letters and other forms of feedback from listeners.
The Chimurenga discography was wide, covering those songs recorded within the country by artists such as Zexie Manatsa, Thomas Mapfumo, and
Oliver Mtukudzi, which the RBC censored, and those recorded in the camps

by the guerrilla choirs, such as the Zanla's Leopold Takawira Choir, and the popular *Ikwaya KaMdala* (the old man [Joshua Nkomo]'s choir), Zipra's Light Machine Gun, and others. Songs like *"Tumirai Vana Kuhondo"* (Send Your Children to the War) by Mapfumo, and *"Maruza Vapambepfumi"* (You Have Lost the War Now, Plunderers) by guitar guerrilla and Takawira Choir composer the late Comrade Chinx, drove recruitment.

> I taught the choir the song [*"Maruza Vapambepfumi"*] during *mapungwe* and we kept polishing it, hitting it until people went crazy, and we then sent it over to Maputo, where every one of my new compositions was requested for recording and radio play. And man, what recruitment that song inspired back home![40]

Mapfumo's *"Tumirai Vana Kuhondo"* directly called on youths to cross for guerrilla training, unlike most of his other caustic songs that speared from behind a heavy linguistic veil in a vain attempt to beat the censors. It caused a headache for the state and for Teal Records. Here is how Tony Rivet, a Teal official, remembered it:

> Thomas's music! Whew! If you knew what the words were before—we had to change some of the words, to a certain extent, and let the meaning be understood through innuendo, though everybody knew what was going on. We had to change the words so the songs could be acceptable to the government. I remember they came along to me at one time and said, "the *terrs* are getting all the tribespeople to sing *gook* songs." The one they really didn't like was *"Tumirai Vana Kuhondo."* I told them it was a bloody RAR marching song, an old military marching song.[41]

Rhodesian intelligence operatives listened in to these programs. David Brooks was a Rhodesian Air Force operative. This is what he thought about Chimurenga Requests:

> Sure, I heard that radio broadcast from Maputo. A lot of it was silly, broadcasts of victories that you couldn't believe. But that "Chimurenga Requests" program! It was very effective propaganda, because of the songs and emotion put into it. I felt, hell, this was it; damn Rhodesia, up Zimbabwe, after some broadcasts. It was totally different from our "Forces Requests" program. That was just morale-boosting whereas "Chimurenga Requests" gave a really rousing, spiritual feeling. It had everyone singing. I've come across Africans in the bush, sitting around the radio, singing.[42]

Radio elaborated the power of song, employing music to cultivate emotionalism without which nationalism becomes hollow. Guerrilla radio created and moderated, transnationally, a popular engagement with matters that affected Zimbabweans, at home, displaced, or deployed. The semantic devices such as "sons and daughters of the soil," the language of brotherhood, emphasized

popular participation at various levels in the collective crafting of a new
nation-state and reinforced the foundational nationalist discourse of self-
legitimation that put paid to claims that guerrillas were *magandanga*, wild
animals that savaged the innocent and brought nothing but disease.

TIRI MUVANHU: WE ARE EVERYWHERE

Subtly dismissing the epithet of wildness in the ascription *magandanga*, the
guerrillas declared that they were *in* and *among* the people, as implied in the
program of the same name: *Tiri Muvanhu/Sise Bantwini* (We Are Among the
People). This program, introduced in the late 1970s, showcased the rapport
between the guerrillas and the noncombatant populations with increasingly
closer interaction promoted via the "liberated zones." Interviews with villagers began to take prominence on radio with the introduction of this program,
villagers contributing their views on the progress of the war and what should
be done to escalate it in the remaining settler strongholds, particularly the
urban areas. Similarly, such conversations also purportedly took place even
in the "keeps," the concentration camps into which the Rhodesian regime
interned villagers to separate them from the guerrillas. Radio then enabled
and portrayed Africans transgressing and blurring the distinctions between
guerrilla broadcasters and guerrilla listeners on the one hand, and armed
combatants and differently armed populations on the other—a key strategy in
guerrilla warcraft. This meant that, in effect, the guerrillas were everywhere.

   Toward the end of the 1970s, Rhodesia was fighting to keep the front of
war away from the towns and the wholesale "contamination" of villagers by
"terrorist" influence. As an arsenal of warcraft, guerrilla radio played on
these fears. For example, when asked in one Tiri Muvanhu episode what she
thought should be done about the settler retreat to the towns, Comrade Ku-
rauone Magamba urged Africans in the towns to beat back the tide of white
retreat:

> It is the time for urban dwellers to stand up and draw the weapon. At the
> beginning of the war we hit the enemy until he abandoned the farming areas to
> seek refuge in the cities. So city dwellers must now hit him very hard there so
> that he can run away again. They must also stop putting their money into the
> banks, or patronising white recreational places otherwise they are giving mon-
> ey to the enemy to buy more weapons. Or they can all leave the cities and go to
> the rural areas so that we can overrun the towns without putting our own
> people at risk.[43]

One very loud statement in this encroaching urban front was the bombing of
the Shell oil depot in Salisbury, which cost the country millions of dollars
and drove white anxieties high. There is a suggestion that some episodes of

Tiri Muvanhu, including the many interviews with "villagers" inside the "keeps" were actually recorded in the camps in Mozambique, [44] but the point is that no one would pick this up from listening to the recordings. The effectiveness of the programs depended on their credibility and psychological impact on the listeners, friends and foes. Equally important, they had to have resonance with the experiences of the targeted audiences.

Guerrilla radio vied for the Africans' hearts and minds against rabid state anti-nationalist programs and campaigns of intimidation and counter-insurgency. The Ministry of Internal Affairs (the former Native Affairs Department) collaborated with the Ministry of Information and the security sector to run propaganda blitzes through newspapers such as the *African Times*, raining leaflets and flyers from airplanes portraying nationalists as terrorists and, as the publications showed, their alleged gruesome savaging of villagers. They also dangled dead bodies of collaborators and captured guerrillas from helicopters to drive fear into the hearts of Africans. Ben Musoni, a Ministry of Information operative, broadcaster, and African face of the Rhodesian propaganda machinery, produced what, in retrospect, he called a "most terrible propaganda program," *Padare* ("African Village Court") which derided as ludicrous the whole idea of Africans imagining that they could ever fight whites, defeat them, and rule the country. [45] Johan Meiring worked for the Psychological Operations Unit, and he thinks their propaganda failed because it was too advanced for the "savage tribesman's mind."

> As we became more skilled in the art of communication with the tribesmen, we became possibly a little too slick, a little too polished, and we earned their distrust—nas was borne out by the net result. They simply didn't believe us. But bear in mind, Psychological Operations was directed by whites. We were on a different wavelength with the tribesmen. I'd say, "Hey, I'm a highly paid and highly-skilled star copywriter. If I can write copy for Air Rhodesia or Barclays Bank, I can talk to an ignorant black savage." If that copy was as great as I thought it was, Mugabe wouldn't have won a landslide in the end. [46]

Clearly, the apparatchiks did not know the people whom they condescendingly regarded as ignorant, simple "tribesmen." But settler ignorance alone does not fully explain the success by the nationalists. Africans faced the challenge squarely with their own guerrilla radio, newsletters, and other modes of unconventional communication.

War communiqués were a critical form of information packaging and dissemination on both sides. The Rhodesian Combined Forces Command issued these communiqués daily, announcing tallies of "terrorists" killed, their own losses, civilians killed in the all-too-common "cross-fires," and related information. The guerrillas, on the other hand, lacked the infrastructures to gather such data and issue their own communiqués as frequently. One tactic they employed, then, was to listen to every Rhodesian war communiqué, news bulletin, and piece of propaganda, and invert them into raw materials for their own counter-propaganda. Recalled Gula Ndebele:

> We benefited a lot from Rhodesian radio for our own information, because ours wouldn't come regularly because we lacked similar communication lines. . . . In their daily communiqués, the Rhodesians would indicate that today one member of the security forces has been killed. Tomorrow they would say two have been killed, et cetera. We would compile those statistics and add them for the month, or two months, then announce: "Over the past month (or two) our forces have killed so many dozens of Rhodesian forces." We would also tally their daily statistics of civilians (collaborators, as they called them) killed, and after a month what do we have? A massacre! And during the 1970s, the Rhodesians were massacring dozens a day, and we would announce that to the people, scandalizing them with their own information. [47]

While Rhodesian media thrived on demonizing, denigrating, and threatening, guerrilla broadcasters did not lose the point that they were trying to build a new society based on an alternative moral order. This was a lesson from their pan-African mentors and hosts that they took to heart. Rafael Maguni was one of the Radio Mozambique initiators of anti-colonial radio broadcasts to the last bastions of white settlerdom:

> We considered that broadcasting was a weapon that should not be underestimated, so after we attained our independence, we started broadcasting a programme about the war to the Zimbabwean masses, starting on the day that Mozambique closed the border with the UDI rebel government [in 1965]. Then we invited the Patriotic Front comrades to take over the programme, because we knew from our own years of experience that it's very important to use radio to mobilise the people and explain the objectives of the war. [48]

The Mozambicans advised their Zimbabwean counterparts that "the broadcasts of a liberation movement should be impeccable, above the rubbish language that the Rhodesian station was using against them." [49] Murira considered himself to have been one of the best propagandists in the movement because of a combination of this cardinal tenet of liberation broadcasting and his own personal values that drove him to the warfront: "freedom, choice, and tolerance." [50] The philosophy was broadly reflected in both ZANU and ZAPU broadcasts. It required that the guerrilla broadcasters address themselves in proper relational registers to parents, sisters, and brothers where Rhodesians talked at "tribesmen" and "savages." Similarly, they tended to appeal to, rather than threaten, their enemies. The propaganda seemed mostly subtle and sophisticated and attuned to persuade and strike resonance, rather than to intimidate and abuse.

Again, this was a strategic approach grounded in African cultural ethos and the understanding that winning the war was not an end in itself but a basis for nation building. Nathan Shamuyarira expressed a self-aggrandizing investment into this imagined future. He told me that he decided to use his own birth name rather than a nom de guerre on radio "because I wanted people to remember me as that guy who spoke to you on radio, and vote for me."[51] Mugabe regarded Shamuyarira—who would become his most loyal propaganda czar after independence—as not only self-aggrandizing, but also dangerous.[52]

GUERRILLA RADIO AND POWER

Among other punitive measures, the colonial state had banished Africans who challenged it into exile, removing them from fertilizing discontent in the territories they controlled. But in the age of radio mass communication technology, Africans embraced exile, withdrawing from the brutalization of the colonial state and employing that transcendental space to organize and fight for self-liberation across the lines. Exile positioned them within broader transnational collectivities of support, from where they harnessed radio technology to communicate across physical geographies of control and challenge official narratives. Guerrilla broadcasting necessitated popular dialogue in the creation of the postcolonial African nation-state. Radio elaborated and cross-fertilized the shared imaginations of fighters and supporters, guerrilla broadcasters and guerrilla listeners, and letter writers. Both Zanu and Zapu quickly realized the power of radio in the struggle for self-liberation, and utilized it optimally with the help of frontline and other friendly states. Most former guerrillas believe that Zimbabwe's liberation war could have turned out very differently had they not used radio. Comrade Mutero argued that radio was perhaps the most important technology, after the gun, in the fight for Zimbabwe.[53] To Gula Ndebele, the nationalist movement felt the critical importance of communication technology "because they did not have it."[54] For this reason, they optimized what little they had.

NOTES

1. Rosalynde Ainslie, *The Press in Africa* (London: Gollancz, 1966), 152.
2. Mhoze Chikowero, "Is Propaganda Modernity? Press and Radio 'for Africans' in Zambia, Zimbabwe and Malawi during World War II and its Aftermath," in *Modernization as Spectacle in Africa*, ed. Peter J. Bloom, Stephan Miesc, and Takyiwaa Manuh (Bloomington: Indiana University Press, 2014).
3. Andreya Masiye, *Singing for Freedom: Zambia's Struggle for African Government* (Lusaka: Oxford University Press, 1977); Andreya Masiye, interview, July 2016, Lusaka; Peter Fraenkel, *Wayaleshi* (London: George Weidenfeld & Nicolson Ltd., 1959). Masiye would run UNIP radio in Tanzania and Malawi in the early 1960s.

4. Mhoze Chikowero, *African Music, Power and Being in Colonial Zimbabwe* (Blooming-ton: Indiana University Press, 2015); Mhoze Chikowero, *Tools of Empire, Technologies of Self-Liberation: Radio Broadcasting in Colonial Zambia, Zimbabwe and Malawi* (work-in-progress).

5. Hortense Powdermaker, *Copper Town: Changing Africa; The Human Situation on the Rhodesian Copperbelt* (New York: Harper & Row), 1962; Dina Ligaga, Dumi Moyo and Liz Gunner, eds., *Radio in Africa* (Johannesburg: Witwatersrand University Press, 2011).

6. David Wakati, "Radio Tanzania Dar Es Salaam," in *Making Broadcasting Useful: The African Experience*, ed. George Wedell, 213 (Manchester, UK: Manchester University Press, 1986).

7. Interview with Victor Mhizha Murira, June 2011, Harare.

8. Ibid.

9. Portrait of a Terrorist, https://ia600709.us.archive.org/4/items/TheLionOfZimbabwe RobertMugabe/the%20lion%20of%20zimbabwe%20robert%20mugabe.mp4 .

10. Interview with Gula Ndebele, July 2011, Harare.

11. Interview with Lungile Ngwenya, July 2011, Esigodini.

12. Interview with Gula Ndebele.

13. Interview with Lungile Ngwenya.

14. Ibid.

15. Interview with Gula Ndebele.

16. Benedict Anderson, *Imagined Communities: Reflections on the Origin and Spread of Nationalism* (London: Verso, 1990).

17. Interview with Lungile Ngwenya; interview with Sotsha Moyo, July 2011, Bulawayo; interview with Albert Nyathi, July 2011, Harare; interview with Juliet Xaba, July 2011, Bulaw-ayo. Xaba's revolutionary choir, LMG, was the official Zapu musical troupe in Zambia.

18. Interview with Sotsha Moyo, July 2011, Bulawayo.

19. Interview with Lungile Ngwenya.

20. Interview with Victor Mhizha Murira.

21. NAZ, VOZ tape collection.

22. Interview with Simon Pashoma Ncube, July 2011, Harare. Kutonhodzwa KwaChauruka roughly translates to The Silencing of Chauruka, a legendary warrior.

23. Interview with Samuel Mkhithika, Harare, June 2011.

24. Thomas Mapfumo, quoted in Julie Frederikse, *None But Ourselves: Masses vs. Media in the Making of Zimbabwe* (Vancouver: OTAZI and Anvil Press, 1982).

25. Interview with Victor Mhizha Murira.

26. Interview with Lungile Ngwenya.

27. See http://www.youtube.com/watch?v=L5MAF1t7_-Y.

28. Interview with Victor Mhizha Murira.

29. Chikowero, *African Music*.

30. Harry Franklin, "Report on the Development of Broadcasting to Africans in Central Africa, 1949," Government Printer, p.15.

31. NAZ, F121/H3/53, Letter from E. A. Smart, Director Ready Music (Pvt) Ltd. to the Secretary of Home Affairs, 25/05/1960.

32. Mhoze Chikowero, "The Zimbabwe Music Industry" (Hons diss., University of Zimbab-we, 2001).

33. See Masiye, *Singing for Freedom*.

34. Mapfumo, in Frederikse, *None But Ourselves*, 103.

35. Sister Clara, Berejena Mission, Chibi, in Frederikse, *None But Ourselves*,103.

36. Interview with Lungile Ngwenya.

37. Voice of Zimbabwe, June 3, 1978, in Frederikse, *None But Ourselves*, 104.

38. Interview with Simon Pashoma Ncube, July 2011, Harare.

39. Interview with Sobusa Gula Ndebele.

40. Interview with Cde Chinx, December 2006, Chitungwiza.

41. Tony Rivet, Teal Recording Company, quoted in Frederikse, *None But Ourselves*, 108.

42. David Brooks, in Frederikse, *None But Ourselves*, 105.

43. NAZ, ATR 62/VOZ, Chimurenga Music, Tiri Muvanhu, Internal Settlement.

44. Interview with Comrades Mukaro, Maposa, Chitera, et al., July 2011, Harare.
45. Interview with Ben Musoni, July 2011, Harare.
46. Quoted in Frederikse, *None But Ourselves*, 123.
47. Interview with Sobusa Gula Ndebele, 2.
48. Rafael Maguni, Radio Mozambique, quoted in Frederikse, *None But Ourselves*, 100.
49. Ibid.
50. Interview with Victor Mhizha Murira.
51. Interview with Nathan Shamuyarira, July 2011, Harare.
52. Edgar 2-Boy Zivanai Tekere, *A Lifetime of Struggle* (Harare: SAPES Books, 2007).
53. Interview with Comrade Mutero et al.
54. Interview with Gula Gazi Ndebele.

Chapter Five

Spirit Mediums and Guerrilla Radio in the Zimbabwe War of Liberation

Dumisani Moyo and Cris Chinaka

In almost every African country where military struggle for independence was waged, underground radio became a critical communication tool for guerrilla movements; it enabled connection between the movements and their support bases. In Zimbabwe, the split in the liberation movement into two leading contending forces (the Zimbabwe African National Union [ZANU] and the Zimbabwe African People's Union [ZAPU]) in 1963 resulted in the formation of two distinct external broadcasting channels that championed the cause of each of these movements. This study critically analyzes the nexus between spirit mediums and underground radio in the communication strategies used by these two liberation movements. More specifically, it seeks to address the *what* and *how* questions regarding the persuasion and propaganda strategies used by the two movements to mobilize support from the "masses" in a war that has often been described as a battle over the hearts and minds between the liberation movements and the Rhodesian government forces. The chapter explores various theories relating to political persuasion, propaganda, and mass mobilization; through archival research and historical analysis it explores the tactics used by these two liberation movements to engage with the publics in a context where alternative forms of communication were severely restricted. It argues that despite limitations of being "stateless" and having to operate from exile, the two movements effectively used sophisticated communication strategies that combined oral tradition, spirituality, song, and modern technology in the form of underground radio and face-to-face communication with villagers through evening gatherings to mobilize support for the struggle.

MEDIATING RESISTANCE BEFORE THE RADIO AGE

While Zimbabwe's protracted civil war has been documented from multiple perspectives, little has been written on the communication strategies used by the two leading guerrilla movements, ZANU and ZAPU. Undoubtedly the most influential work in this regard to date is Julie Frederikse's 1982 book *None But Ourselves*, which chronicles the role of the mass media in the struggle for liberation. Written in an unconventional manner with lots of interviews with key actors in Zimbabwe's liberation struggle, interwoven with powerful visuals (including photographs, cartoons, newspaper cuttings, text extracted from broadcasts, campaign posters, and confidential letters), songs, and poetry, Frederikse's book provides some rare data and insights on the communication strategies used by both the Rhodesian government and the liberation movements. It is a book about the agency of the ordinary people in the making of Zimbabwe, and hence merits special mention in this study.

From March 1976, ZANU's main broadcasting was hosted by Radio Mozambique on its external service between eight and eight-thirty at night on six shortwave bands and on medium wave. The program was extended to an hour in mid-1977 as the war intensified in Zimbabwe. The Voice of Zimbabwe (VOZ) also broadcast its programs on shortwave bands from the external radio services of Ethiopia and Madagascar, at the same times, from 1978 until independence in 1980.

In Tanzania, President Julius Nyerere forced ZANU and ZAPU to broadcast on the Radio Tanzania External Service between 1978 and 1980 as he pushed the two movements to consolidate unity under the umbrella of the Patriotic Front.

In response to the pan-African drive by Ghana's Kwame Nkrumah and Egypt's Abdul Nasser, the Zimbabwe liberation movement also used radio stations in Accra and Cairo respectively for their propaganda. Both became unavailable after changes in government.

ZAPU's main broadcasting center was in Lusaka, where the Zambia National Broadcasting Services had set thirty minutes (in the morning) for English, Shona, and Ndebele programs by Voice of the Revolution (VOR). ZAPU also used Radio Moscow intermittently from 1968, but Angola more regularly from 1978. However, it is the Mozambique and Zambia broadcasts for the two respective parties that were most significant toward the end of the war, and this chapter lays more emphasis on broadcasts from these two locations.

Operating from two bordering countries, Mozambique (for ZANU) and Zambia (for ZAPU), the two movements had to overcome numerous hurdles that limited their ability to communicate, with their guerrillas on the ground and with the mass population that formed their support bases inside Zimbabwe. Underground radio broadcasts via short-wave from the two neighboring countries therefore offered a noteworthy opportunity, despite the limited availability of receivers and batteries to power them on one hand, and the clampdown by the Rhodesian forces on possession of these gadgets on the other.

While this study is primarily about the two guerrilla radio stations during Zimbabwe's war of liberation in the 1960s and 1970s, Voice of the People (ZANU) and Voice of the Revolution (ZAPU), it would be important to journey back in history and draw some critical links between this liberation struggle and earlier resistance at the onset of colonialism in the 1890s in terms of communication "mediums" and strategies. Although radio was non-existent during that period, we argue that some key elements of the communication and mass mobilization strategies that we discuss about the two radio stations can be traced back to the First Chimurenga.[1] Mediation of the message was a critical element right from the start—not through technologies such as radio, however, but through human and superhuman agents, the "spirit mediums"—the *svikiros* or *mhondoros*, as they are known in Shona.[2] During the First Chimurenga, leaders of the resistance, notably the iconic national spirit mediums, Nehanda and Kaguvi, used prophecy as their major persuasive tool to mobilize the masses to fight the invaders.[3]

Historical accounts of this early resistance invariably put these spirit mediums at the center of the struggle, both as mobilizing agents and instigators of the resistance.[4] In the absence of modern technology, the spirit mediums used oral tradition, village gatherings, and traditional courts to disseminate information about the political situation and mobilize for resistance. A clear distinction has to be made, however, between the modern technologies of mass communication, which fit within what Foucault called technologies of production (technologies that allow us "to produce, transform, or manipulate things") and the spirit mediums, which we could view in Foucauldian terms as technologies of the sign systems (technologies that allow us to "use signs, meanings, symbols and signification").[5] By conceptualizing technology as multidimensional, Foucault allows us to move away from a fixed view of technology and technological innovation as inherently Western and as hardware, to seeing innovative practices and agency among supposedly backward African communities as essentially technological. In other words, the signification created by the spirit mediums is technology. We argue that as technologies based on use of sign systems, the spirit mediums were influential in shaping discourses that informed and leveraged the resistance to colonial occupation.

Back then, spirit mediums were very powerful and played a significant role in the sociopolitical life of the community, as various historical accounts testify. They occupied a revered position among Africans, who regarded them as intercessors between the living and the dead, with the dead connecting the living to the supreme deity (*Musikavanhu or Mwari* in chiShona, and *uNkulunkulu* in isiNdebele). To the living, the spirit mediums were both the message and messenger who brought together "absence and presence,"[6] and carried the weight and will of the dead with incontestable prophetic messages. By combining human and "spiritual" agency in the messaging of resistance politics, this, we argue, also extends the meaning of Marshall McLuhan's adage that "the medium is the message" in the sense that the performance of the spirit mediums in the delivery of the message (which was often in a trance) considerably enhanced the legitimacy and power of the message; it resonated among a community that had a shared belief system.

As we argue below, the mobilizing power of spirit mediums was reinvoked in the mass mobilization strategies of the Second Chimurenga (Zimbabwe Liberation Struggle, 1966–1980), where their renewed call for taking up arms against colonial occupation became a rallying cry for the new offensive, connecting past and present struggles, the "departed" and the living in a common cause. The settlers were quick to appreciate the power of these mediums and sought to appropriate them in an attempt to legitimize their occupation and delegitimize the liberation movement. As David Lan has noted, "Tape recordings of mediums denouncing the guerrillas while, supposedly, in trance were broadcast from aeroplanes." In one of the propaganda leaflets dropped over operational areas and addressed to "All the People of the Land," the Rhodesian administration lamented that

> Some of you have been helping terrorists who came to cause disturbances to you and your families. Your spirits have told your spirit mediums that they are disappointed because of your action. Mhondoro, your tribal spirit, has sent a message to say that your ancestral spirits are very dissatisfied with you. As a result of this there has been no rain. It is only the government which can help you, but you have to realise your obligation to help the government also.[7]

At the same time, attempts were made to "capture" these mediums (both physically and metaphorically), as part of a strategy to weaken the resistance movement on one side while strengthening the regime cause on the other. As Jimmy Tambaoga, a ZANLA combatant who operated in ZANU's east and southeastern Gaza military province and a reporter for the VOZ argued,

> A number of spirit mediums were killed by the Rhodesians for supporting the liberation struggle, in Chipinge, Chiredzi, Chimanimani, Gutu, Bikita, Zaka. The Rhodesians also tried to win the support of the spirit mediums because they knew their propaganda value. Some of the spirit mediums were compromised by the Rhodesians, but a majority remained solidly behind the liberation movement.[8]

These attempts to "capture" traditional (spiritual) mediums and "convert" them into expressing the message of the colonizer through modern mass media (mainly the regime-controlled radio) was meant to create some form of "cognitive dissonance" among the recipient African population, considering the strong resistance of spirit mediums to anything modern (most of these mediums would not wear Western clothing or use modern transport, for instance). It was therefore inevitable that regime broadcasts that attempted to appropriate the spirit mediums were never as effective as intended.

PROPAGANDA, PERSUASION AND MASS MOBILIZATION: SOME THEORETICAL REFLECTIONS

The three theoretical concepts underpinning this study (propaganda, persuasion, and mass mobilization) are, to a great degree, closely interlinked in the sense that they denote forms of communication aimed at influencing target populations for specific ends. Of these three, propaganda is undoubtedly the most contested, not least because of its usage in Nazi Germany, where it earned notoriety. Prior usage of the term did not carry as much pejorative connotations as is the case today. In this chapter, we view propaganda in the manner it has been defined by David Welch as "the deliberate attempt to influence public opinion through the transmission of ideas and values for a specific persuasive purpose that has been consciously devised to serve the self-interest of the propagandist, either directly or indirectly."[9] In this context of the battle over hearts and minds, propaganda was deployed from either side, with varied assumptions about the level of sophistication of the intended receivers.[10] The concepts of "mass" and "mobilization" can also be viewed as having earned negative connotations over time. In the perception of the liberation movements, however, "the masses" or "our masses" were terms used with fondness for the people who formed their support bases. Similarly, the idea of "mobilization" had positive meaning among the freedom fighters, as an act of rallying together and readying the masses for war, contrary to the general perceptions of an act of bringing together irrational and uncontrollable "mobs" often attached to it.

While this study is not about the effects and efficacy of propaganda and persuasion on the "masses," it is important to highlight that we do not subscribe to the perception of propaganda as all-powerful—in the "hypodermic needle" or "magic bullet" sense proposed by Harold Lasswell many years ago.[11] Rather, we agree with the notion that people's beliefs and behaviors are influenced by numerous factors, and that, as several writers have argued, propaganda "confirms rather than converts—or at least is more effective when the message is in line with existing opinions and beliefs."[12] In the context of Zimbabwe's liberation struggle, the "freedom fighters" or the "comrades," as they were known, were preaching to the converted, as it were; their messages played on the lived realities of the masses—including grievances over critical issues such as land dispossession, discrimination, forced labor, oppression meted out by the white settlers. Their reliance on the memory of prophesies passed over time by generations of spirit mediums only served to enhance the credibility of their message and cause.

REGIME PROPAGANDA AND
GUERRILLA COUNTER-PROPAGANDA

The colonial government went to extremes in its use of a combination of newspapers such as the *African Times*, flyers, and booklets as propaganda tools to delegitimize the liberation movements, who were invariably depicted as "terrorists" and "cowards" who murdered innocent villagers.[13] In his recent article "Reverberations of Rhodesian Propaganda in Narratives of Zimbabwe's Liberation War," Jephias Dzimbanhete highlights four thematic areas around which settler propaganda was centered: the framing of the liberation movements as responsible for killing innocent civilians; murdering white missionaries; killing African rural businessmen; and being "spineless forces bent on attacking soft targets."[14] These perceptions were routinely peddled on various media platforms, and often accompanied by grisly images, either of dead bodies of "terrorists" killed by Rhodesian forces or dead bodies of "victims" of the "terrorist menace." This strategy was buttressed by the Rhodesian Selous Scouts, a counter-insurgency unit that often masqueraded as ZANLA or ZIPRA forces in what were called "pseudo operations," and committed atrocities that were blamed on the two liberation movements. As Dzimbanhete argues,

> Cutting off of lips, jaws, ears and goring out eyes were some of the atrocities that visited members of the rural populace. The media that was used to disseminate Rhodesian propaganda quickly reported such atrocities and also hastily blamed ZANLA forces. The horrendous pictures that appeared in the Rhodesian Ministry of Information booklet, *Anatomy of Terror*, were reported on the radio, television and in the newspapers in Rhodesia.[15]

All this was deliberately calculated to cause fear and resentment of the guerrillas among rural communities. Another prominent Rhodesian propaganda booklet, *Massacre of Innocents*, also routinely carried pictures of victims of "terrorism" as part of dissuading villagers from supporting the guerrilla movements.[16] It was a strategy that backfired, however, in most instances; the African public saw through the propaganda and maintained support for the liberation movements.

The use of propaganda and counter-propaganda became a key feature of the war on both sides. The Rhodesian government was armed with sophisticated media (radio, newspapers, television, fliers dropped from the air, and, sometimes, announcements made directly from hovering helicopters). The liberation movements relied on lean, seemingly unsophisticated but nimble tools that included networks of informers (*mujibhas* and *chimbwidos*), "underground" radio that was susceptible to jamming from time to time, and the *pungwes* (the rallies bringing together members of the community under cover of darkness to propound the cause of the war). Political messages delivered at these *pungwes* covered the socioeconomic and political grievances of the Africans and how these were rooted in colonial domination and, therefore, the need to abolish the system altogether. The songs were based on both traditional tunes and Christian hymns, while the messages were designed to drum home the evils of colonialism, the importance of the party/movement and its leadership, and the role of the armed struggle in the dismantling of oppression and exploitation.[17] In other words, the songs served to cultivate political awareness and also to strengthen the spirit of resistance among the people. Each guerrilla unit had a political commissar whose role was to articulate the principles underpinning the liberation struggle. As Agrippah Mutambara pointed out,

> Our Political Commissars were skillfully trained to walk the cadres through the intricate maze of grievances against the settler regime that constituted the propelling reason for their decision to join the revolutionary armed struggle. . . . The cadres learnt how through pieces of legislation and brute force the black majority were dispossessed of their land, denied access to areas reserved for whites, barred from a universal right to vote, and allowed limited access to educational opportunities, just enough to serve their interests.[18]

According to Black Moses, a former ZIPRA commander and political commissar, ZAPU's operational and mass mobilization criteria included an ability to organize an information and intelligence gathering and share courier service; the capacity to operate as a guerrilla for at least six months without being known by the enemy; the establishment of a trustworthy relationship with the community; the ability to identify and use underground ZAPU structures for support services; familiarity with operational terrain, including escape routes; and the conversion of locals in operational area into informers, transporters, reserves, or complements to the ZIPRA forces.[19]

THE SPIRIT MEDIUMS, RADIO,
AND MOBILIZING FOR THE WAR EFFORT

Endorsement of the war effort by the spirit mediums in the areas where ZANLA and ZIPRA guerrillas operated was critical for them to get the support they needed from local communities. Rino Zhuwarara, a university lecturer and director of the Zimbabwe Film School, views the spirit medium as a critical "institution" in the liberation struggle:

> As an institution, the *svikiros* are an inexhaustible source of knowledge, self-knowledge and self-identity. During the war it was a resource institution with capacity to promote and protect the fighter by accepting them in a district and therefore legitimizing their cause. The *svikiros* could also be regarded as communal libraries who had access to the past and the present on the basis of which they could predict how the war would turn out. Their role was not limited. They acted as guardians of the moral order of society. They were important for securing political legitimacy, food, clothing and they generated confidence for both the community and freedom fighters. The fighter is dislocated from home, from the comfort of the familiar, and needed the spirit mediums to regain confidence and to help create a secure operating environment. The spirit mediums helped create a homely and secure environment for the fighters.[20]

This was corroborated by the ZANLA former combatant Tambaoga, who stressed that the endorsement of the liberation war by spirit mediums was critical to mass mobilization:

> Our command was clear that we had to win the support of spirit mediums in the areas that we were operating because in our African culture, these mediums are respected as the people's link with the ancestral world. The spirit mediums are consulted for guidance on how to deal with traditional protocol issues, social problems, leadership disputes. They are consulted by troubled families and communities. Their guidance is widely sought over issues of general communal welfare. During the war, we paid homage to spirit mediums, sought their blessings and made sure that the masses knew that the spirit mediums, and, by extension, our Zimbabwean ancestors were backing the war.[21]

Some freedom fighters went beyond merely securing the symbolic support needed for mass mobilization by "engaging the spirit mediums to give them charms to strengthen or protect them during the war." Linking the radio broadcasts with spirit mediums was also essential in these efforts, as Tambaoga further said:

> For our mass mobilization, we also made sure the Voice of Zimbabwe broadcast of the liberation war enjoyed unqualified support of spirit mediums and

Zimbabwe's spirit world. This was consistent with the role of spirit mediums in the First Chimurenga where Mukwati, Nehanda and Kaguvi, who were spirit mediums, led the first revolutionary war against white colonialism.[22]

Thomas Mandigora, another ZANLA war veteran and VOZ broadcaster, also highlighted the role that spirit mediums played:

> Their support emboldened both the masses and the freedom fighters. But it also undermined the confidence of black soldiers in the Rhodesian army who were coming from a culture that places a premium on the role of the spirit world. Many people believe that if you don't have the backing of your ancestral spirits, your fate is sealed.[23]

There was slight divergence when it came to the "use" of spirit mediums on the ZAPU side, where pragmatism and science were emphasized. Andrew Moyo, a ZIPRA combatant who operated in Gokwe district, ZIPRA's Northern Front-2, highlighted that ZAPU cadres knew the value of securing the support of spirit mediums, but balanced that with the scientific reality of the war. As he put it,

> There was obvious propaganda value in ensuring all people, including the valuable traditional structures of spirit mediums, were accommodated in the freedom train. The one common theme for the liberation movement was that we were fighting a people's war. But ZAPU and ZIPRA discouraged fighters from actively seeking or relying on the guidance of spirit mediums in waging the war. The war was and had to be fought on the science and art of war.[24]

Saul Gwaku Ndlovu, a former VOR broadcaster, says that while taking a scientific approach, ZAPU and the Zimbabwe liberation movement as a whole benefited from active or indirect association with spirit mediums, pointing out that "both the spirit mediums and the people believed the war was just and blessed by our forebears."[25]

The role of spirit mediums in Zimbabwean everyday life, and in the liberation struggle in particular, has also been captured in several literary works, and hence subjected to much scholarly discussion.[26] The lead character in journalist Angus Shaw's 1993 novel on the Zimbabwe independence war, *Kandaya: Another Time, Another Place*, is a mystic guerrilla fighter with "a particularly unpleasant spirit medium" who is given to appearing from nowhere for battles. "It is this *n'anga* (medium) who has got the *povo* (masses) shitting in their pants." Rhodesian war history also acknowledges this. The pseudo guerrilla unit, the Selous Scouts brigade, recorded this from close range. "The terrorists were playing heavily on the African people's superstitious—particularly their belief that messages purporting to come from their spiritual tribal forefathers through the mouths of entranced *sviki-*

ros—spirit mediums. The *svikiros* on the side of ZANLA terrorists were calling for support of the Chimurenga War."[27]

Kumurai Jeke, a Zanla war collaborator, now seventy-eight, says there were several spirit mediums in his home district of Chiweshe, seventy kilometers north of Harare, who worked closely with guerrillas, providing spiritual support and "mystic medication" that sharpened the bush fighters' survival instincts. "There was Chimbikiza, and there was Gweshe. Both men were clearly genuine mediums from our great past. They could cast spells on enemy soldiers to get lost in mysterious mist, and they could organize mystical birds to lead the comrades to safety."[28]

While bravery and skilled fighting still counts for the survivors of the heroic war, many ex-combatants say that things "stranger than fiction" happened at the war front, including miraculous escapes and victories. "Forty years later, I am still not comfortable getting into details about some of those spiritual things," said Justice Dhliwayo, a former ZANLA combatant and post-independence broadcaster.

For many liberation war veterans, radio was the catalyst in their decision to join the struggle. Tambaoga and Chipoyera's separate testimonies below are repeated by many.

> We lived in Highfield [township] in Harare. My father was hooked to Voice of Zimbabwe. Every night we listened to news and music from Mozambique. I found the political messages very persuasive. One day I confided in a friend about Voice of Zimbabwe and was shocked to realize he was also a listener. . . . In May 1977, five of us abandoned school and went for military training in Mozambique.[29]

Parker Chipoyera (born Bernard Manyadza), a former ZANLA combatant, said,

> I used to listen to Radio Moscow and Radio Tanzania External Service, which were broadcasting news on African politics and liberation struggles. I was very active in the student movement, but those broadcasts formed a foundation of my political consciousness that motivated me to join the war in 1973.[30]

A more systematic study of liberation war radio listening cultures and patterns would be essential to understand influences, especially on decision making for would-be freedom fighters. However, it is evident that radio played a significant role.

GUERRILLA RADIO, SONG,
DANCE, AND CODED LANGUAGE

One of the earliest lessons at the start of the liberation struggle was that the war could not be sustained without support from ordinary people, the peasants and structures that would provide combatants with intelligence and information as well as shelter, food, clothing, and, sometimes, transport. ZANU and ZAPU and their military wings seized on the reach of radio from external bases to propagate the aims of the struggle, to raise morale and rally support around their party leaders. Most importantly, radio became the key instrument for persuading and mobilizing young people to join the armed struggle. Both VOR and VOZ mainly broadcast news, commentary, letters, and revolutionary song requests. Several letters read out on VOZ in the late 1970s were from young men and women who confirmed that they were inspired by the broadcasts and needed information on how they could cross the border to join the struggle and carry their own bazooka or AK-47 to fight the settler regime. Letters to the VOZ in 1977, obtained from the National Archives, attest to this.[31] They range from young people asking the freedom fighters to come and take them across the border, to moral support for the "comrades," to denouncing "sell-outs" (especially the leaders who had entered an internal settlement with the Smith regime, Abel Muzorewa, Ndabaningi Sithole, and Chief Chirau). Invariably, they ended with a slogan (forward with the struggle), and a song request. These letters came from both inside and outside Zimbabwe, quite a number coming from Zimbabweans working in South Africa under the Wenela program.[32]

Radio's ability to break through all literacy levels became a critical tool in the propaganda war—articulating black grievances and mapping the vision of a free, majority-ruled, united, and prosperous Zimbabwe. The history of this critical aspect of the Zimbabwe liberation struggle remains largely unrecorded, with most information held in fragmented form in individual collections or in trusts formed for archiving after independence. Until recently, in the absence of a formal organized effort to record the history of the liberation struggle, very few former combatants from the Zimbabwe independence war have published their memoirs. This is in stark contrast to dozens of books published by those who fought under the Rhodesian Front flag.

For the nationalists, three features of the 1893–1896 war endured to play a prominent role in mobilization, propaganda, and persuasion in the Second Chimurenga: song, dance, and the coded language. At rallies and public meetings in the 1960s, the long hissing sound or whisper of "zhii, . . . zhii!" became a popular coded message to herald danger, or to indicate presence or allegiance to a group or a call to action. Many war songs from the First Chimurenga, including some celebrating the bravery of the combatants and the spirit mediums who led the resistance movement, became popular on the battlefield and the liberation war radios broadcasting into Zimbabwe from exile. Sung by mass choirs on these liberation radio stations, these songs inspired and galvanized many to cross the border and join the liberation struggle. As Everette Ndlovu pointed out:

> Through radio ZAPU appealed directly to able-bodied Zimbabweans from the southern region to abandon all they were doing, as the country then had no future for them. Through VOR, ZAPU enticed them to cross the border to Zambia to train as freedom fighters so that they could liberate the country in which they would live with full honour and dignity. It was radio that made many revolutionaries understand that there was no dignity in gaining education to be a slave of the colonial master in the land of their birth. [33]

Ngwabi Bhebhe recounts that by 1977 the two liberation war radio stations were playing a critical role in urging young Zimbabweans to take up arms to fight the colonial regime. "The propaganda and inspiring liberation songs from these stations won the hearts of young men and women so much so that they needed little prompting to cross the Mozambique and Botswana borders."[34] The compulsory call-up to draft youths into national service in the Rhodesian army only intensified the recruitment of young people by both liberation movements. Similarly, Eddison Zvobgo, one of ZANU's leading propagandists, recounted the centrality of radio broadcasting in the propaganda war:

> We would give full accounts of various battles that had taken place in the country, which was very encouraging to the people. They could listen to what the regime could say, that they had killed terrorists and they had only killed those civilians who were caught in the crossfire, and then we would give an account of how the regime's forces entered a village, asked no questions and simply shot at unarmed women and children. Since that would have been what happened, the local population would then identify with us more than with the enemy. [35]

Such accounts also helped liberation movements raise support from the international community; the battle over hearts and minds had to be fought on both domestic and international platforms.

FRAMING THE NEWS ON GUERRILLA RADIO

Both ZANU's Voice of Zimbabwe, and ZAPU's Voice of the Revolution radio broadcasts used largely standard production formats to frame news bulletins and war communiques between song and slogans. The typical hour of Voice of Zimbabwe broadcasts from Maputo started with a liberation song, followed by the sound of staccato gunshots, then a booming and authoritative battle cry, "The People of Zimbabwe, Victory is certain!" This was followed by the news bulletin or communique highlighting that the war was spreading and the liberation fighters were winning. Often, this was followed by more war songs interspaced by letters from the listeners—many signed off in assumed Chimurenga names—asserting the revolution was enjoying popular support and that ordinary people were divesting themselves of their imposed Christian names (for example one would sign off as Sekuru Mabhunu Muchapera (translated as "we will wipe out the colonialists"). This ended with a signature tune and the slogan *"Pamberi neChimurenga"* (Forward with the Revolutionary War).

ZAPU broadcasts opened with the roar of a lion, followed by gunfire, then a ZIPRA song, "ZIPRA is Invincible."[36] Quoting ZAPU publicity chief Willie Musarurwa, Mosia, Riddle, and Zaffiro pointed out that "Lusaka transmissions were intended to provide reliable information on the military aspects of the struggle to combat the misinformation of the Smith regime," and to "project the role of ZAPU as the leading and first party in the struggle, via its leadership in the fighting."[37]

The propaganda and persuasion strategy of the liberation movements was built around mobilizing popular support, recruiting military cadres, articulating the national grievance and the vision of a free, united, and prosperous Zimbabwe. The radio broadcasts would also express support for the party leaders in song and slogans, celebrate landmark victories on the battlefront, and decry the inhuman acts of the enemy. Through these songs, both parties were able to package their ideologies of Maoist-Communism and Marxist-Leninism in very simplified forms that appealed to their followers.

Both ZANU and ZAPU radio broadcasts extensively exploited the rocket attacks that set Rhodesia's oil tanks on fire and left the country without fuel for weeks, and the downing of a passenger plane in Kariba that left the white settler regime and population in a sense of shock in September 1978, to project the movement as invincible and marching to victory. On the other hand, their coverage of the Rhodesian army's cross-border bombing campaigns in Zambia and Mozambique, in which thousands of ZANU and ZAPU refugees perished, was designed to highlight to the world the cruelty and inhumanity of the colonial regime. "The tragic slaughter of unarmed innocent civilians, including women and children, gave us irrefutable evidence that we were dealing with a racist, oppressive and brutal regime. We used this to highlight this point," says ZAPU's Saul Ndlovu. Both the Voice of Zimbabwe and the Voice of the Revolution also routinely used big military battles and notable successes by the guerrilla fighters to project an image of an unstoppable liberation force. As Eddison Zvobgo said in 1980, after the war, "Our war was a people's war, and our information strategy was to underline the depth of our national grievance, the justness of our cause and the invincible position we occupied."[38]

Above all, the two radio stations focused on building an "imagined community" in the post-independence era. They boldly spoke to, and about, a future nation, Zimbabwe. That imagining was a critical part of the language of persuasion used to win hearts and minds, and guerrilla radio played a significant role in its construction. Unlike the then Rhodesia, which was characterized by oppression and white dominance, Zimbabwe symbolized freedom, equality, and opportunity, and was likened to the biblical promised land of Canaan. Alongside the liberation war radio stations, both ZANU and ZAPU also published monthly magazines abroad—*Zimbabwe News* and *Zimbabwe Review* respectively—to advance their agenda and aid the "construction" of the new nation.

IDEOLOGICAL INFLUENCES IN THE ZANLA
AND ZIPRA GUERRILLA RADIOS

A number of factors distinguished the two movements and their respective radio stations. While the two movements shared common objectives in terms of liberating the country from colonial rule and building a new nation, they came from slightly different ideological persuasions and hence had different approaches to the way they engaged with the masses and executed the struggle. As in many other African countries, socialism had a great appeal to both movements. The ZANLA guerrillas were largely influenced by Maoist communism and received much support from China, while ZIPRA, with their close ties with Russia, were more inclined toward Marxist-Leninism. This, we argue, had implications for the political cultures within these movements as well as the approaches to persuasion and mass mobilization in their respective radio stations. The stations broadcast in English, Shona, and Ndebele to appeal to as many people as possible.

Voice of Zimbabwe and Voice of the Revolution also had a few things in common, both institutionally and in terms of the range of programs they produced. At the institutional level, both stations used broadcasting time "donated" to them by their host countries—Zambia in the case of ZAPU, and Mozambique in the case of ZANU. It is important to note that earlier, the two movements had shared the same platform in Tanzania. In 1978 they were forced by the Nyerere government into joint broadcasting from Tanzania under the umbrella of the Patriotic Front, building upon years of separate and intermittent programming since 1968. The two nationalist movements had also, between 1963 and 1966, broadcast programs from Ghana, the first African country to gain independence in 1957, after being given a slot by Kwame Nkrumah's government.[39] Ghana had become a leading champion in the struggle for the liberation of Africa from colonial rule and the pursuit of a continental political program, which led to the founding of the Organization of African Unity (OAU), renamed African Union (AU) in 2002. The Zimbabwe Liberation Radio program in Ghana was closed when Nkrumah was deposed in a military coup in 1966. Alongside Ghana, Radio Cairo had also given liberation movements slots to broadcast their program from the 1950s. Agrippah Mutambara, a ZANLA commander whose guerrilla name was Dragon Patiripakashata, says in his biography that ZANU recognized the "essentiality of a people-driven and politically sanitised revolution" that infused political orientation into every phase and structure of the party and this element was "definitely identified as the engine or soul without which the armed struggle would fail."[40] He goes on to say,

> Different approaches used to deliver the political message included slogans, songs and political orientation classes. These were complemented by codes of discipline every comrade was expected to uphold and project. Through the instrument of slogans we acclaimed our President, venerated those leaders who solidly supported our armed struggle, chastised our enemies and expressed our hopes and aspirations.[41]

Mutambara contends that The Voice of Zimbabwe's broadcast from Maputo was surreptitiously tuned into and proved immensely popular among the Zimbabwean masses. The broadcast, he says, through songs and commentaries highlighted the iniquities of the Rhodesian regime and projected a favorable picture of the armed struggle and what it sought to achieve.

REGIME RESPONSES TO GUERRILLA RADIO PROPAGANDA

As highlighted above, the Rhodesian regime responded to the guerrilla radio broadcasts by intensifying their counter-propaganda campaign, calculated to highlight the "communist/terrorist menace" and alienate the liberation fighters from the "masses." Seizure of shortwave radio receivers (a feature that was later to arise in the post-independence era with the emergence of so-called pirate radio)[42] and placement of people in concentration camps (the infamous "keeps") where they were "insulated" from the "terrorists," were some of the tactics. Strict censorship of the press became the order of the day. In addition, the Rhodesian regime introduced the Psychological Operations Unit (the PSYOP) in 1977 as part of its counter-offensive strategy against the liberation movements.[43] The main objective of the PSYOP was "to gain, preserve and strengthen civilian support for the government" through "planned use of communications through words, symbols and actions to influence behaviour of selected target audiences in order to promote the achievement of national objectives."[44] Leaving nothing to chance, the Rhodesian authorities even jammed the BBC signal to prevent black communities from listening to foreign broadcasts. As Julie Frederikse notes,

> The first battle in the radio war was not waged directly against the guerrilla forces, but against the British Broadcasting Corporation—less out of fear that the BBC would foment revolution than out of a desire to prevent blacks from receiving any views other than those of the RBC. The target was the relay transmitter the BBC erected in Francistown, Botswana shortly after UDI. Demonstrating desperate overkill, RBC engineers clandestinely erected a 400,000-watt American made transmitter—one of the most powerful in Africa to jam the BBC signal. [45]

They went even further to ban the sale and distribution of shortwave receivers. The Rhodesian government subsidized the electronics industry to churn out thousands of cheap FM-only radios that were then distributed free to the rural population, targeting especially chiefs and village headmen to encourage listening to regime propaganda. [46] This was not lost to the guerrilla movements, who advised their supporters through radio to be wary of state propaganda churned out through official outlets. Commenting on the Smith Regime's reliance on lies, the VOZ announced on February 21, 1977:

> Here is a special announcement: whenever you turn your radio set on and hear the following announcement: "This is the Rhodesia Broadcasting Corporation," be prepared for gross distortions, shameless misrepresentation of facts. The regime is making all efforts to seal off every opportunity for disclosing the truth about the general state of affairs and the tremendous progress of Zimbabwe's national liberation war—hence, introduction of radios with only FM band. These radios are directed mainly at the African population, because the settler regime knows that . . . Zimbabweans won't be able to receive the Voice of Zimbabwe and broadcasts from any other progressive countries. [47]

Liberation movements thus made counter-propaganda an essential component of their communication in order to sustain their support bases.

CONCLUSION

This chapter points to the centrality of radio and spirit mediums in the "propaganda war of the air" to influence hearts and minds during the struggle for Zimbabwe's independence. It highlights that the ability of the two liberation movements to appropriate this technology as a tool for the advancement of their cause at a time when radio was considerably a new information and communications technology has a lot to do with an already existing communicative culture based on the use of mediums to convey messages. As technologies of the sign system, in the Foucauldian sense, the spirit mediums laid the foundation both for the adoption of radio as a medium and the messaging for the resistance. To extend John Durham Peters's metaphor of the act of radio broadcasting as "speaking into the air," [48] it can be argued that the communion of African communities in Zimbabwe with ancestral spirits and *Mhondoros* had long equipped them with the capacity to deal with absence and presence in their everyday communicative acts, making their relationship with radio almost a natural one. In a sense, radio became the amplifier of messages that had previously been produced and disseminated through traditional media—or through the ancient technology of spirit mediums. Song and oral traditions also played a part, as the chapter highlights.

While the study is not about effects, it points to the fact that where power is exercised without legitimacy, the power that often comes with ownership and control of powerful means of communication does not amount to much. It argues that despite limitations of being "stateless" and having to operate from exile, the two movements used sophisticated communication strategies that combined oral tradition, spirituality, song, modern technology in the form of underground radio, and face-to-face communication with villagers through evening gatherings to mobilize support for the struggle. Apart from using crude propaganda to sell a new Zimbabwe (the biblical land of Canaan), they played on the grievances that people already had around land dispossession, racial discrimination, disenfranchisement, and so on.

Overall, the importance of this study is to highlight the need for further studies that go into the archives and analyze the broadcasts from the two liberation movements from different perspectives, in order to build a fuller historical account of the centrality of radio in this historic moment. In addition, it points to the need for studies that look into listening cultures during the struggle, and how audiences used the messages they received, in light of the very complex listening processes occasioned by the restrictions created by the settler regime.

NOTES

1. Chimurenga is a Shona word: to fight or struggle for liberation. It is also widely used to mean revolutionary struggle. The First Chimurenga refers to the first uprising by Africans in the 1890s against colonial occupation.

2. See for instance, David Lan, *Guns and Rain: Guerrillas and Spirit Mediums in Zimbabwe* (London: James Currey, 1985). Spirit mediums (*masvikiro*, as they are known in Shona) are normal human beings who get possessed by the spirit of a "departed" clan or family member and give advice or warnings on issues affecting the family or community. They have powers to foretell the future, and have both cultural and political significance.

3. The shared belief in ancestral spirits has been an enduring feature in Zimbabwe's history. In more recent years, when the government of Robert Mugabe was facing serious economic challenges, it often turned for support from ancestral spirits. This explains how it was possible for Mugabe to be tricked by a woman pretending to be the medium of Nehanda into sending a delegation of ministers to witness how Nehanda was going to provide the country with diesel (flowing from a rock) at a time when the commodity was in short supply. Rotina Mavhinga insisted on the government availing a specified head of cattle and amount of money before "Nehanda" could roll out the diesel. It turned out all this was a sham.

4. Ngwabi Bhebhe, *The ZAPU and ZANU Guerrilla Warfare and the Evangelical Lutheran Church in Zimbabwe* (Gweru: Mambo Press, 2006); Terence Ranger, "Guerilla War in Zim-

babwe," *African Affairs* 324 (1982): 349–69; Michael Gelfand, "The African in Transition," *Central African Journal of Medicine* 5, no. 9 (1959): 486–88.

5. Foucault conceptualized four types of technologies: technologies of production; technologies of sign systems; technologies of power; and technologies of the self. Michel Foucault, "'Technologies of the Self': Lectures at the University of Vermont in October 1982," in *Technologies of the Self*, 16–49 (Boston: University of Massachusetts Press, 1988).

6. John D. Peters, *Speaking into the Air: A History of the Idea of Communication* (Chicago: University of Chicago Press, 2012).

7. Lan, *Guns and Rain*.

8. Interview with Jimmy Tambaoga, by Cris Chinaka, Harare, September 18, 2019.

9. Nicholus Cull argues in the historical encyclopedia on propaganda and mass persuasion that "Propaganda about Africa began in ancient times with legends about the savage lands beyond civilization." Zimbabwe's new colonial masters pursued a public relations program of painting their seizure of the country as part of a Christian/Western civilization mission, right from the start. Using books, diaries, newspapers, letters and communiques, public meetings, and sermons, they communicated a sense of conviction in a preordained, God-given task to advance development and to conquer paganism. In addition, as Cull argues, "For the European powers of the later nineteenth century, the conquest of colonies in Africa was a form of propaganda by deed, displaying the virility and prowess of the nation concerned. These colonial prophets included Cecil Rhodes." When it suited them, the settlers pushed the line that spirit mediums Mbuya Nehanda and Sekuru Kaguvi, who were driving the resistance war, were "witches" bent on keeping Zimbabwe in the Stone Age. See David Welch, "Introduction: Propaganda in Historical Perspective," in *Propaganda and Mass Persuasion: A Historical Encyclopaedia, 1500 to the Present*, ed. Culbert D. Cull and D. Welch, xix (Santa Barbara, Denver, and Oxford: ABC CLIO, 2003).

10. The Rhodesian whites had a generally low estimate of the African psyche, as evidenced for instance by depictions in a book that was given to all white immigrants upon arrival in the country. Titled *The Man and His Ways*, this book provided an oversimplified patriarchal view of the African as easily contented with basics such as tobacco, beer, and women.

11. Harold D. Lasswell, *Propaganda Technique in World War I* (Cambridge, MA: MIT Press, 1971).

12. Welch, "Introduction," xviii.

13. Julie Frederikse, *None But Ourselves: Masses vs. Media in the Making of Zimbabwe* (New York: Penguin, 1982), 116–47.

14. Jephias A. Dzimbanhete, "Reverberations of Rhodesian Propaganda in Narratives of Zimbabwe's Liberation War," *Africology: The Journal of Pan African Studies* 10, no. 1 (March 2017).

15. Ibid., 298.

16. See, for instance, Herb Friedman, *Rhodesia Psyop 1965–1980*, at http://www.psywarrior.com/RhodesiaPSYOP.html .

17. Alec J. C. Pongweni, *Songs that Won the Liberation War* (Harare: College Press, 1982); C. Pfukwa, "Black September et al.: Chimurenga Songs as Historical Narrative in the Zimbabwean Liberation War," *Muziki* 5, no. 1 (2008): 30–61; Mhoze Chikowero, *African Music, Power, and Being in Colonial Zimbabwe* (Bloomington: Indiana University Press, 2015).

18. Agrippa Mutambara, *The Rebel in Me: A Zanla Guerrila Commander in the Rhodesian Bush War, 1974–1980* (Solihul: Helion, 2014), 85.

19. Eliakim M. Sibanda, *The Zimbabwe African People's Union, 1961–1987: A Political History of Insurgency in Southern Rhodesia* (Trenton, NJ: Africa World Press, 2005), 222–23.

20. Interview with Rino Zhuwarara, by Cris Chinaka, Mutare, September 26, 2019.

21. Interview with Tambaoga.

22. Interview with Tambaoga.

23. Interview with Thomas Mandigora, by Cris Chinaka, Harare, September 15, 2019.

24. Interview with Andrew Moyo, by Cris Chinaka, Harare, September 12, 2019.

25. Interview with Gwaku Ndlovu, by Cris Chinaka, September 18, 2019.

26. See, for instance, Yvonne Vera, *Nehanda* (Harare: Baobab Books, 1993); Lene Bull-Christiansen, *Tales of the Nation: Feminist Nationalism and Patriotic History? Defining National History and Identity in Zimbabwe* (Uppsala: Nordik Africa Institute, 2004).

27. Ron R. Daly and Peter Stiff, *Selous Scouts, Top Secret War* (Johannesburg: Galago, 1982).

28. Interview with Kumurai Jeke, by Sifelani Tsiko, Harare, September 12, 2019.

29. Interview with Tambaoga.

30. Interview with Parker Chipoyera, by Cris Chinaka, Harare, September 14, 2019.

31. File: MS536/7/3 Letters to the Voice of Zimbabwe, Maputo, 1977. National Archives, Zimbabwe.

32. The Witwatersrand Native Labour Association (WNLA), popularly known as Wenela, was a program set up to recruit migrant labor to work in South African mines in the 1940s and 1950s. It recruited laborers from neighboring countries, including Botswana, Lesotho, Swaziland, Zimbabwe, Zambia, Malawi, and Angola.

33. Everette Ndlovu, "Radio as a Recruiting Medium in Zimbabwe's Liberation Struggle," *Westminster Papers in Communication and Culture* 12, no. 2 (2017), 53.

34. Bhebhe, *ZAPU and ZANU Guerrilla Warfare*, 104.

35. Eddison Zvobgo, cited in Frederikse, *None But Ourselves*, 101.

36. Lebona Mosia, Charles Riddle, and Jim Zaffiro, "From Revolutionary to Regime Radio: Three Decades of Nationalist Broadcasting in Southern Africa," *Africa Media Review* 8, no. 1 (1994): 13.

37. Ibid.

38. Zvobgo, cited in Frederikse, *None But Ourselves*, 101.

39. Mosia, Riddle, and Zaffiro, "From Revolutionary to Regime Radio."

40. Mutambara, *The Rebel in Me*, 81.

41. Ibid.

42. See Moyo 2009; Hayes M. Mbweazara, "'Pirate' Radio, Convergence and Reception in Zimbabwe," *Telematics and Informatics* 30, no. 3 (2013); Everette Ndlovu, "The Positioning of Citizen-Influenced Radio in the Battle for the Control of Minds," in *Participatory Politics and Citizen Journalism in a Networked Africa*, ed. Bruce Mutsvairo (New York: Palgrave Macmillan, 2016), 56–76.

43. See Matthew Preston, "Stalemate and the Termination of Civil War: Rhodesia Reassessed," *Journal of Peace Research* 41, no. 1 (2004): 65–83.

44. Friedman, n.d.

45. Frederikse, *None But Ourselves*, 96.

46. Ibid., 97.

47. "Voice of Zimbabwe Comment on Smith Regime's 'Reliance on Lies,'" February 21, 1977, Broadcast 1800 gmt.

48. Peters, *Speaking into the Air*.

Chapter Six

Zapu's "Voice of the Revolution" and the Radicalization of the Nationalist Struggle

Munyaradzi Mushonga, Lloyd Hazvineyi, and
Munyaradzi Nyakudya

Liberation movements in southern Africa—ANC, SWAPO, ZANU, and ZAPU, for example—did not confine their struggle for independence to armed combat only, but also resorted to the use of radio broadcasts in native languages and English to subvert white minority power. This chapter focuses on ZAPU's Voice of the Revolution (VOR) radio as an instrument of war against the Smith regime. Through political radio programs and news broadcasts in Shona, Ndebele, and English languages, ZAPU launched a new wave of war radio nationalism not only to agitate for militancy and insurgency against the Rhodesian government, but also to represent the state as a fetish, thus subverting its power into nothingness. Radical and jingoistic media representation complemented armed insurgency and struggle.

The purpose of this chapter is to examine ZAPU's radio broadcasts in terms of genesis, objectives, purpose of the broadcasts, and impact thereof on the masses and on the Rhodesian state. Using evidence gleaned from VOR transcripts, archival and newspaper reports housed at the National Archives of Zimbabwe (NAZ), and backed by secondary sources, we contend that ZAPU's VOR played a key role not only in radicalizing the nationalist struggle, but also in subverting the power of the Rhodesian state.

Historiographically, the first concerted attempt to influence political opinion in southern Africa by means of radio is traceable to the 1930s when the Nazi station, Radio Zeesen, used Afrikaans[1] to target sympathetic elements in both Namibia and South Africa before the Second World War.[2] After the end of the war, the African continent, like the rest of the world, was caught up in a wave (the Cold War), in which major world powers competed for influence. In southern Africa, the British colonial office helped to prepare the use of "saucepan radios" for political purposes. Also known as the "poor man's radio," the saucepan radio was a battery-powered four-valve tropicalized shortwave receiver that went on sale in the British colonies of Northern Rhodesia (Zambia), Southern Rhodesia (Zimbabwe) and Nyasaland (Malawi) in 1949. It took its name from its cabinet—an aluminum case 22.86 cm in diameter that looked like a saucepan without a handle.[3] This marked the genesis of war radio broadcasting in Rhodesia.

The Rhodesian government perceived the trendy saucepan radio as the new weapon to govern Africans, ostensibly through the spread of propaganda. The Native Affairs Department (NAD) saw its role as that of taming the native mind through the medium of radio, seeing it (radio) as the "new weapon" in the broader scheme to educate the natives in the "wisest sense."[4] Unlike in South Africa, where the introduction of radio to Africans generated debate on high possibilities of subversion, the Rhodesians perceived radio as just another tool that could be used to further entrench white domination.[5] They got it all wrong, because within the next decade, the saucepan radios were used by the nationalists to subvert white minority rule. However, it has to be said that on the African continent, it was Ethiopia and Egypt, having shaken off the colonial mantle, that were the first African states to use the radio for propaganda purposes by broadcasting anti-colonial messages beginning in the 1940s and 1950s. Ghana and Tanzania joined the fray in the 1950s and 1960s. The broadcasting facilities in these nations were later extended to nationalist movements—ANC, SWAPO, ZANU, and ZAPU, with Radio Tanzania playing a leading role.

Smith's Unilateral Declaration of Independence (UDI) from Britain on November 11, 1965 changed the course of the liberation struggle in Zimbabwe in a number of ways. First, the UDI led to the declaration of a state of emergency. Second, it led to the imprisonment of key leaders of the nationalist movements in the country. Third, it led to a massive exodus of nationalist leaders who sought refuge in neighboring African countries such as Zambia, Botswana, and Tanzania due to growing security concerns in Rhodesia. In Lusaka, Zambia, Zapu nationalists quickly embraced the need to embark not only on armed combat but also in massive political conscientization, propaganda, and radicalization of the liberation struggle through the medium of the radio, VOR. A war broadcasting instrument was seen as an important necessity to win the "hearts and minds" of the "masses" in Rhodesia.

When the African nationalists began to use Radio Zambia to transmit radical broadcasts into Rhodesia, the authorities panicked. They perceived the broadcasts as a ploy by the British and Zambian governments to cause a breakdown of law and order and render Rhodesia ungovernable so as to justify a military intervention in the wake of the UDI. Indeed, the Rhodesians were adamant that the purpose of the broadcasts was to create violence in Rhodesia so that the UDI could be vindicated from having "led to bloodshed and chaos."[6] They saw the infiltration of saboteurs and fighters into Rhodesia and the transmission of radio broadcasts/propaganda as complementary elements of the same plan—Rhodesian authorities charged that the main purpose of the broadcasts was to call on Africans "to give active support to terrorists operating in this country from Zambia."[7]

In this chapter we contend that the VOR, together with the Zimbabwe African National Union (ZANU)'s Voice of Zimbabwe (VOZ) war radio, which broadcast from Maputo, Mozambique, helped to mobilize, conscientize, and radicalize the masses in Zimbabwe for the liberation struggle, hastening the collapse of the Smith regime. The significance of our pioneering study lies at four different levels. First, it adds to the relatively underdeveloped historiography of guerrilla war radios in southern Africa, thus filling a historiographical gap. Second, it enables readers to appreciate how postcolonial state-owned radio stations were shaped by the guerrilla traditions of the 1960s and 1970s.[8] Third, it makes the contention that there is a direct relationship between war radio broadcasts and the intensification of the guerrilla war, thus showing the agency of guerrilla war radio broadcasts in radicalizing the struggle. Fourth, while both ZAPU and ZANU played key roles in liberating Zimbabwe, the process of state making and nation building in independent Zimbabwe became a ZANU-PF project that was exclusionary and subordinating in nature. By drawing on a diverse archive, and focusing on ZAPU's VOR, this study raises the visibility of ZAPU's contribution to the struggle, hitherto understated in popular narratives.

THE PURPOSE OF
THE VOICE OF THE REVOLUTION BROADCASTS

In this section of the chapter we demonstrate how, on one hand, the broadcasts sought to legitimize the struggle against the Rhodesian government, at the same time countering Rhodesian propaganda, and how, on the other hand, they sought to educate and appeal for the support of the masses and the African working class, including educating them on aspects of insurgency such as property vandalism, sabotage, and even carrying out cold-blooded murder against white Rhodesians.

Legitimation of the Liberation Struggle and Appeal for Support

One of the major purposes of the war broadcasts by both VOR and VOZ was to justify and legitimize the liberation struggle by appealing to the people's memory and history of the first Chimurenga of the 1890s. For example, in one of the many broadcasts, Rusike, one of the VOZ broadcasters, had this to say in response to the question "why fight another war after the First Chimurenga of the 1890s?"

> The answer is because there is no other way to get democracy, justice and majority rule. We have tried negotiation but this has failed. Once again today Britain and Smith are holding talks for the independence of Rhodesia. We are not represented at these talks, so we can never have taken part in these negotiations. We have only one way left—which is to fight bravely like the guerrillas who fought in the battle near Sinoia in order to get what we want.

Nationalists drew connections between their current suffering and the people's history in order to portray armed insurgency as not only reasonable, but also legitimate. In one of the many broadcasts, Jason Ziyapapa Moyo, one of the senior ZAPU cadres in exile, once remarked on VOR, "Today I want to stress and remind you that these days in our country are not happy days. We are at war in our country, war to fight for freedom." George Silundika, another ZAPU leader, implored the masses on VOR: "The nation of Zimbabwe will be rescued by you yourselves, the people of Zimbabwe. Therefore, even if you hear that the soldiers of the British will come and rescue you, we say to you that you just realise that the English stand on the side of their people." George Nyandoro reiterated Silundika's message by stressing that it was "up to us to take it [the country] back because the country was taken by force by the ogres."

Legitimation of the struggle was a key component of the broadcasts, as was appeal for support and unity. "In order that our work to free Zimbabwe goes according to plan, it is necessary that there is cooperation among the children of Zimbabwe," once bellowed Edward Ndhlovu of ZAPU in a broadcast. Soon after the UDI, on November 28, 1965, James Chikerema, then ZAPU vice president, made the following appeal to the people of Zimbabwe: "take your bows and break the government of Ian Smith and all his robbers, because it is true they are robbers, thieves. Take your bows, your axes, your spears and smash that government. If blood spills, even if blood is shed, that government must be broken." The same message was repeated by George Nyandoro in a direct and forthright manner on March 17, 1966: "Children of the soil, rise up. Rise up, the black man. Take your country."

Diverse groups of people were appealed to for support. For example, Africans working for the Rhodesian government, particularly teachers, nurses, and policemen, were encouraged to revolt. On December 16, 1965, for instance, Ronald Isaac Sibanda's broadcast targeted teachers and nurses: "It is known that in war, when you are at war, there are teachers, there are nurses, there are doctors, there are drivers, there are riflemen, but you are all soldiers, you are all at war fighting. . . . Therefore, teachers and nurses, in everything which you do, use your sense to do that work to free the nation." In the same broadcast, Stephen Parirenyatwa pleaded with teachers: "We ask you to discard everything which deceives you. In your teaching, in your talking with your parents, in all your actions, try everywhere to instil in their thoughts that they must fight for the freedom of the country."

A separate broadcast by Sibanda appealed to chiefs, noting that chiefs were "not something of today, [but] something which [was] part of tradition. The chiefs are part of the customs and therefore the customs must be pre-served." In essence, VOR was determined to legitimize the role of traditional leaders as the vanguards of rural nationalism, although the institution of chieftainship had been compromised by its incorporation by the state as a cog of colonial administration. Joseph Mtisi, Munyaradzi Nyakudya, and Teresa Barnes aver that chiefs were generally viewed with suspicion, seen as ap-pendages of the colonial regime, bent on advancing the interests of the Rho-desia Front government.[9] In a broadcast of December 22, 1965, Sibanda lamented: "The Europeans [were] riding on [chiefs] like horses so that . . . they can rule." VOR therefore sought to win the "hearts and minds" of chiefs by portraying the regime as bent on abusing them, thus legitimizing their role in the nationalist struggle. VOR and ZAPU were careful not to attack or question the legitimacy of chiefs despite the popular view that they were serving the interests of the colonial government.

African entrepreneurs (shop owners, farmers, bus owners) were appealed to equally for support. For example, Sibanda's broadcast of March 20, 1965 addressed entrepreneurs as follows: "Firstly, I want [you] to realise . . . that we are not telling you to stop your businesses. What are we trying to show you is that at this time when there is work to be done you must do it." Mosia, Riddle, and Zaffiro similarly note that VOR broadcasts were used to recruit fighters and supporters, as one broadcast revealed: "We wanted to get people to rally behind the war [and] form a link with the fighters, so that whatever they did was played back in a two-way flow of information: those inside Zimbabwe could get news of the outside and those outside got news of the movement."[10]

The broadcasts were also meant to give the people the opportunity to know about guerrilla activities and exploits on which the Rhodesian media was not reporting. One VOZ broadcast hailed the heroic successes of the freedom fighters at the Sinoia (Chinhoyi) Battle; this was intended to con-vince the people that the guerrillas were fighting a successful war. VOR broadcasts, just like VOZ broadcasts, sought to provide reliable information on the military aspects of the struggle, to "combat the misinformation of the Smith regime" and to "project the role of ZAPU as the leading and first party in the struggle, via its leadership in the fighting." One trait stands out among VOR broadcasters. Unlike other guerrilla broadcasters in southern Africa, most VOR guerrilla personalities used their real names. The former VOR broadcasters Jane Ngwenya, Jason Ziyapapa Moyo, James Chikerema, George Nyandoro, George Silundika, and Stephen Parirenyatwa did not use noms de guerre to disguise their real identity because, according to Ngwenya, they had committed themselves to the struggle and their role in it was public knowledge.[11]

In order to reach and appeal to the wider Rhodesian society, including the white community, VOR broadcast in the three major languages, isiNdebele, Shona, and English. Many VOR broadcasters were conversant in these three languages. VOR broadcasters claim that they did not even know who their listeners were; neither did they know the identities of people who gave them feedback in the form of letters, because, according to Jane Ngwenya (see chapter 7 of this volume), everything took a guerrilla approach because they were fighting a guerrilla war.[12] This suggests that, unlike the ANCs Radio Freedom, which freely shared via the *Sechaba* and *Mayibuye* journals, VOR did not share frequencies with listeners because listening to war radios was illegal.

VOR broadcasts were also used to appeal to the international community, thus internationalizing the struggle and drawing attention to the plight of Zimbabweans on one hand, and to the intransigency of the Rhodesia Front regime on the other. Following the proclamation of the UDI, the radio became important in not only educating the African masses, but also in internationalizing the Rhodesian crisis. This objective was clearly articulated by J. Z. Moyo in a broadcast on December 10, 1965: "English troops will come if there is terrible disorder in our country. That is when they can come. That is when all nations can come. This is when our country can be freed." The need to internationalize the Rhodesian crisis was expected to trigger a military intervention by British forces.

Not to be outdone, the Rhodesian regime, through its parliament, appealed to the British government and some sections of the international community to take punitive action against Radio Zambia, which was piggybacking on the VOR. It also dismissed any claims of insurgency, choosing to portray the internal political climate as peaceful.[13] In fact, the Rhodesian regime appealed to the British. There are two major reasons that the nationalists on one hand and the Rhodesians on the other were scrambling for British sympathy and support. First, the British government, through the BBC, was aiding Radio Zambia and had invested equipment to facilitate shortwave broadcasting; hence the British government's decision would determine the future of guerrilla broadcasting in Zambia. Second, the British government had earlier threatened Rhodesia with military intervention following the proclamation of the UDI. Such an intervention would have hastened the independence of Rhodesia through the removal of the white supremacist regime.

Educating the Masses about the Struggle and Various Tactics of Insurgency

Educating the masses about the struggle, its objectives, and its execution, including the expectations the war placed on the masses of Zimbabwe and how to subvert the regime, were important aspects of the liberation struggle. In the aftermath of the UDI, VOR broadcasts were used to explain why it was now necessary to resort to armed resistance. Chikerema once told listeners: "As there is no longer legal rule in Zimbabwe you must do whatever you want to do, so that the government of the enemy, Ian Smith, is destroyed." [14] The ZAPU president, Joshua Nkomo, always argued that the objective was "not to seek to avenge, dispossess, oppress, dismantle or subjugate any groups of people, but rather . . . to establish a just society with opportunities for all, irrespective of colour or creed, based on the freedom of the individual." [15]

Most of the broadcasts were packaged in combative language meant to send the Rhodesian regime into a state of nervousness. Some broadcasts contained detailed methods of how to carry out sabotage. Others gave expert advice on knifing and stabbing, how to stab and where to stab, even when the only available weapon was a kitchen knife. Yet other broadcasts gave specialist knowledge on how to coordinate underground guerrilla bands, maiming cattle and slashing down crops in the white-owned commercial farms, including how to desert and how to burn down telephone and power cables. There were also broadcasts that focused on how to make explosives such as petrol bombs using locally available resources. Other broadcasters even encouraged arson against the African middle and upper classes, most of whom were civil servants and parliamentarians seen by guerrillas as sellouts. Following her visit to Rhodesia, the Canadian journalist J. L. Howson described VOR broadcasts as "giving star billing to a specially chosen corps of black extremists, all of whom are trained and enthusiastic specialists in the deadly arts of mayhem." [16]

The broadcasts also put stress on key strategies and modalities of advancing the war. The main message was obviously the need to take up arms. To this end, various tactics of sabotage were spelled out. The broadcasts show that sabotaging the tobacco plantations and crippling the manufacturing industry through industrial strikes remained one of the main strategies. Tobacco was the backbone of the Rhodesian economy. In a broadcast on November 28, 1965, Chikerema urged the people of Zimbabwe:

> Form groups at night and go to the European farms and cut the tobacco which has been planted. Form parties at night, small separate groups, and go and cut down the Dutchman's tobacco which he covets. Kill many cattle. Go to the farms and take many cattle. If you are not able to take them, hamstring them. Children of the soil, do everything, go forward, cause chaos in Rhodesia. [17]

George Nyandoro repeated the same message and tone of economic sabotage on the farms a few days later when he called on the people to "drive away or remove the louse which is biting you," urging them to take over the farms.[18] He repeated the same message the following day: "Those farms where tobacco is being grown must be burnt. The factories must be burnt. . . . Do what I told you about the electricity cables. They are not difficult to burn. You are able to build fires beneath the cables. Then all Salisbury will be in darkness."[19]

As can be seen, many of the VOR broadcasts were targeted. The main aim was to incite rebellion against the Smith regime in order to hasten its collapse, and the main message was economic sabotage.

IMPACT OF THE VOICE OF THE REVOLUTION BROADCASTS ON THE MASSES AND THE RHODESIAN STATE

In this section, we examine the impact of the VOR broadcasts at two main levels: first, the impact of the broadcasts on the masses and, second, on the Rhodesian state, including counter-reaction measures by the minority regime. Consequently, we contend that VOR broadcasts helped to intensify and radicalize the struggle for liberation.

Impact of the Voice of the Revolution on the Masses

The call by ZAPU's VOR and ZANU's VOZ to "take up arms" was heeded; there is evidence of increased subversion and sabotage. This pointed to the fact that most of the masses were inducted into the realms of radical nationalism through the airwaves (VOR could not of course have successfully done this without Radio Zambia's support). Evidence of the impact of the broadcasts comes in different forms. We therefore contend that it could not have been a coincidence that the violence widely reported in many parts of the country came at a time when VOR broadcasts were agitating for violence. Although our study did not manage to capture the voices of specific listeners who joined the war because of VOR radio messages, a study by Everette Ndlovu shows how a number of listeners were influenced by the broadcasts. One listener, a certain Max Dube, is quoted as stating:

> The voice on (VOR) punctuated by songs from the Zipra forces would make you stand up and walk all the way to cross the Plumtree border into Botswana to join the struggle. The indignity we were subjected to in the land of our forefathers by this settler regime as narrated on the radio would make you feel an urge to restore your dignity by confronting the regime. The hope the VOR gave us was inspirational. Most of us were inspired by the likes of Joseph

Masuku and some voices of the people we knew who had crossed before us to also cross into Botswana on route to Zambia for training.[20]

In our study, we contend that listeners were inspired to take on the Rhodesian state in various ways. There seems to be a direct correlation between ZAPU's calls for violence and violent scenes that began to be witnessed in Rhodesia during this period. For example, on November 16, 1965, the *Rhodesia Herald* reported occurrences of violence linked to ZAPU in Highfield and Mufakose, Harare's oldest high-density suburbs (or townships). Highfield was one of ZAPU's strongholds. Sixty Africans reportedly attacked a school in the location and 500 students fled. Violent scenes linked to ZAPU were also reported in Bulawayo, Zimbabwe's second-largest city. "A series of strikes closed at Bulawayo this afternoon. About 1 500 Africans walked out of the factory at the lunch break and refused to return to work. Six factories were affected by this development."[21]

On November 20, 1965, the *Rhodesia Herald* also reported that there was evidence of ZAPU nationalist activities in Bulawayo. Zapu was also believed to be behind the violence in Bulawayo that led to the arrest of two thousand Africans, in sync with the messages broadcast by VOR. According to the *Rhodesia Herald*, one African was shot dead by the police in the bus-stoning incident. The violence led to the closure of shops. The violence was not only confined to Bulawayo and Salisbury. The *Rhodesia Herald* went on to report that on November 27, 1965, twenty-six Africans were arrested in Sipolilo (present-day Guruve) in Mashonaland Central province after they went on a rampage, damaging crops and property in the area. Similarly, on December 15, 1965, a news bulletin on VOR reported that in the Kwenda area in Charter District (Chivhu) in Mashonaland East Province, "all the tobacco there has been destroyed, poultry houses have been burnt and cattle killed and goats and pigs destroyed in their kraals. All the dips have been destroyed and others have been burnt by the freedom fighters this week." The previous day, the VOR bulletin had reported the destruction of eight fields of tobacco in the Rafingora area, in Mashonaland West Province. As the violence intensified, seven Africans were sentenced in the Bulawayo Regional Court on June 16, 1966, "accused of attempted murder, burning of property, power line and telephone lines, car stoning and other acts of sabotage."

According to the magistrate who presided over the trial for these acts of sabotage, Mr. D. Close, the acts of violence "were occasioned by inflammatory broadcast from Zambia." This statement by the magistrate only serves to confirm the effectiveness of VOR broadcasts and in particular of inciting insurgency against the colonists. We therefore posit that small-scale yet countrywide acts of insurgency, arson, banditry, sabotage, industrial strikes, and destruction of property could be directly or indirectly linked to VOR broadcasts. Further testimony of the impact of VOR is that the war radio was able to draw listeners from different social classes and different ethnic groups in Rhodesia. The majority of the broadcasts were in Shona and Ndebele, and only a few in English. Thus, VOR drew its listenership from the Shona, Ndebele, and European communities.

Impact of the Voice of the Revolution on the Rhodesian State

The Rhodesian authorities approached the threat of liberation war radio in a systematic manner. The impact of VOR broadcasts on the Rhodesian state is discernible at several levels. First, the government sought to appeal to the conscience of the British government to stop rendering support to VOR. Second, they resorted to periodic jamming. Third, they stepped up the use of propaganda and counter-propaganda measures through the Rhodesia Broadcasting Corporation (RBC). Fourth, they chose to deny that there was a crisis in Rhodesia and tried to depict the country as peaceful. Institutions of the Rhodesian state became important conduits of assessing the impact of VOR broadcasts.

As early as February 1966, the regime had already initiated a diplomatic offensive to try to quell the broadcasts. A comprehensive pamphlet spelling out the broadcasts and their "inflammatory" content was generated from the prime minister's office and sent to all members of the British House of Commons and the House of Lords. The pamphlet, titled "Britain's Part in the Incitement of Murder, Arson, Sabotage and Destruction in Rhodesia," was meant to appeal to the conscience of British parliamentarians by making them feel complicit in the violence being perpetrated by the Africans in Rhodesia. The Rhodesian regime argued that the British were not just complicit, but also condoned the "vile crimes" and "campaign of incitement to murder and violence" being carried out in Rhodesia through the aid that they were advancing to the broadcasting and television services of Zambia. In particular, the British Government was accused of supplying transmitters that were then used to transmit the broadcasts into Rhodesia. The pamphlet lamented the British failure to withhold aid to Zambia, to induce them to stop the broadcasts:

> In view of the massive aid Zambia receives from British taxpayer, the steps the British could have taken are obvious. A blunt warning that there would be no more aid if the incitement continued would have been quite enough; it might perhaps have saved innocent lives. Instead of taking such action, the British Government has given every indication of condoning Zambia's sick broadcasts. [22]

Indeed, there is evidence linking British money to the growth of the broadcasting institutions in Zambia between 1964 and 1965. In 1964, the Zambia Broadcasting Corporation received new transmitters for Ndola and Livingstone. In addition, Kitwe had seen the erection of new studios that were completed at the end of 1964. A new medium-wave transmitter was also set up in the same year at Broken Hill, in addition to a twenty-kilowatt short-wave transmitter from the United States that was set to bring a versatile look to the face of Zambia's broadcasting.[23] A sum of £35,000 was also spent in the installation of new machinery at Twin Palms Radio Station. Later, in 1965, the British government, through the BBC, offered human resources to Zambia following the establishment of a broadcasting training school that same year. Under this mutual relationship, broadcasters such as Susan Booth were deployed to Zambia to spearhead and oversee the sharpening of the Zambian broadcasting sector. During this period, a British medium-wave transmitter was set up in the Livingstone area, strategically located near the Rhodesian border.[24] Britain was clearly opposed to Smith's UDI.

Besides Zambia, Bechuanaland (Botswana) also played its part in aiding the VOR. Radio Francistown also offered the VOR airtime in the period following the UDI. Although VOR broadcasts from Bechuanaland were evidently restrained, Francistown conducted excessive repetitions of broadcasts that had the effect of inciting and unsettling both the Rhodesian working class and the state. In a bid to blackmail and unmask VOR's operations in Francistown, in 1966 a combined team from the RBC and Rhodesia Television tried to visit the establishments in Francistown. However, the crew was denied access to Bechuanaland. The Rhodesians then figured that one way of dealing with the VOR threat was to invest in jamming infrastructure. Consequently, a radio signal transmitter known as the Big Bertha Transmitter was erected near the Rhodesia-Botswana border. Later, in 1975, the transmitter was used by the Rhodesian government in setting up a Ndebele channel known as Radio Mthwakazi.[25] Furthermore, in 1976, the Rhodesian state embarked on a massive crusade to counter VOR broadcasts by installing FM transmitters throughout the country. Besides the jamming of nationalist shortwave frequencies, other measures taken by the Rhodesian authorities included "prohibition of all but FM receivers in rural areas, regulation of battery sales, and prohibition of listening to any station but RBC in rural settlement hamlets, or 'keeps,' where an estimated 750 000 Africans had been moved."[26] Yet, by its own admission, the Rhodesian government was aware of VOR broadcasts from as early as 1965. It is therefore evident that the installation of FM transmitters as a coping strategy by the Rhodesians was introduced when many Africans had already been radicalized by nationalist broadcasts. By the time this chapter was being finalized, the extent of investment in jamming infrastructure, in monetary terms, was not known to the researchers.

Yet it would seem that the installation of FM transmitters around Rhodesia, which started in earnest in 1976, was a little too late in the scramble for "hearts and minds." This is because as early as 1958, the VOR had already started beaming nationalist broadcasts into Rhodesia from Egypt as part of a working relationship established between Zapu and President Nasser's administration. Broadcasts also began to reach Rhodesia from Moscow in 1969.[27] By 1976, most Africans had already developed diverse networks with the guerrillas themselves and had cultivated a fairly realistic grasp of the war.[28] By this date, a number of Africans had had physical contacts with the guerrillas during underground political meetings (*pungwes*) and other forms of sensitization campaigns. This tardy reaction resulted in the RBC preaching to a people who had already been used to nationalist conscientization for a long time.

The setting up of Radio Mthwakazi in 1975 was a direct reaction to VOR broadcasts. This Ndebele radio station made use of FM frequency through the Big Bertha Transmitter.[29] Its broadcasts were deliberately packaged in the Ndebele dialect. Through Radio Mthwakazi, the regime hoped to foment ethnic discord between the Ndebele and the Shona. Radio Mthwakazi also sought to magnify, along ethnic lines, the differences between ZAPU and ZANU. Broadcasts that emphasized ideological and historical differences between diverse ethnic groups were therefore given primacy in order to counter mass sensitization by VOR. It was Radio Mthwakazi's objective to manufacture divisive tribal and ethnic broadcasts that would promote ethnic instability within the ZAPU and ZANU party structures and among the rank and file of the Zimbabwe People's Revolutionary Army (ZIPRA) and the Zimbabwe African National Liberation Army (ZANLA) and their diverse followers.[30] It was being emphasized that ZAPU was a party of the Ndebele-speaking people and ZANU of the Shona-speaking people; ZAPU and ZANU were depicted as perpetually vulnerable to tribal animosity and were on the verge of an ethnic implosion.[31] However, it is important to note that the leadership of both ZAPU and ZANU was made up of people from diverse ethnic groups Ndebele, Karanga, Manyika, and Zezuru, among others.

A retrospective assessment of the divisive strategies of the RBC shows that it was successful, to some extent, in fomenting ethnic divisions. Radio Mthwakazi systematically emphasized these conflicts, which have received sufficient treatment in Sithole's seminal works.[32] To deny ethnic tensions would be denying fundamental internal schisms within the revolutionary parties.

It is plausible to argue that the Rhodesian government, confronted with radical nationalist broadcasts by the VOR, embarked on a campaign to systematically produce a counter-narrative through the RBC. The counter-narrative sought to defuse nationalist broadcasts that depicted the Rhodesian political milieu as guerrilla-engulfed. Yet the very process was complex. The counter-narrative was multi-layered. First, in the late 1960s, it involved direct rebuff of the entire nationalist narrative as "misinformation."[33] This process involved several attempts to depict the situation as calm, and Rhodesia as omnipotent. Several reports by the Rhodesians during this period portrayed the country as peaceful.[34] The second level involved subject creation, the creation of new radio content to divert the attention of both the settler citizens and the African subjects from following the political struggle. Focus shifted to music, entertainment, drama, culture, folk tales, and community programs. Rhodesia sought to counter nationalist broadcasts by not reporting about the war at all. The third stratum involved the use of all manner of propaganda, through Radio Mthwakazi and the RBC, including portraying ZAPU as a disjointed and disarticulated party plagued by ethnic conflict.

Yet another observable impact of VOR broadcasts is the way RBC strategies against VOR produced an unintended outcome that proved detrimental to the entire colonial broadcasting scheme. The Rhodesian settler government failed to comprehend that it was broadcasting to a people, Africans and Europeans alike, who were experiencing war every day. On one hand, Africans in the rural areas were experiencing the devastating effects of the war, with about a quarter of a million of them staying in concentration camps known as "protected" villages (*makipi*)[35] under what was known as Operation Overload.[36] The majority of these villages were concentrated in the northern and eastern parts of the country. On the other hand, the settlers were experiencing the persistent guerrilla menace that escalated as the regime upped its counter-measures and repressive tactics. In spite of this, the Rhodesian government kept denying this reality to the listeners. Writing in 1976, the journalist Henry Maasdorp vividly captured this scenario. He reported that the "RBC encourages listeners to feel the cozy sense of community and a tendency natural to a small group facing outward for security, not to want to be informed about matters close to the bone."[37]

This apparent bias on the part of the RBC resulted in public trust and listener confidence being swept away.[38] There was a marginal shift in listening trends by both the white settlers and Africans. Statistics of listenership in 1973 indicate that daily listenership had dropped by 50 percent compared to the previous decade.[39] This drastic decline was a sign that the listening communities were beginning to look elsewhere for alternative news. Against this background the VOR became an alternative voice, yet this does not suggest in any way that the RBC was now preaching only to the converted. Rather, various actors across the political divide listened to RBC broadcasts to familiarize themselves with Rhodesian propaganda in order to counter it effectively. ZAPU guerrillas and nationalists, within and outside the geographical frontiers of Rhodesia, listened to the RBC for reasons ranging from knowing the "tools" of the enemy to familiarizing with the strategies of the enemy. ZANU guerrillas and nationalists did the same.

Jane Ngwenya, a veteran ZAPU Radio broadcaster, explains that VOR, in particular, responded to the RBC broadcasts, including Radio Mthwakazi's propaganda, by producing broadcasts whose content directly lampooned their propaganda. The Rhodesian broadcasts chose to highlight, as already indicated, divisions in the liberation movement along ethnic lines. However, VOR rebutted this by placing emphasis on unity and oneness among the nationalists. In this regard, use was made of songs that were composed specifically to chide the Rhodesians, particularly their cruelty against civilians and their ineffectual war efforts.[40] In their radio broadcasts and counter-propaganda, VOR and VOZ broadcasters exhibited a pragmatic grasp of the RBC broadcasting techniques and propaganda. For example, one VOZ broadcast aired in 1977 showed in-depth knowledge of the nature of RBC radio broadcasts:

> Here is a special announcement: whenever you turn your radio set on and hear the following announcement: "This is the Rhodesia Broadcasting Corporation," be prepared for gross distortions, shameless misrepresentation of facts. The regime is making all efforts to seal off every opportunity for disclosing the truth about the general state of affairs and the tremendous progress of Zimbabwe's national liberation war.

People began to listen to nationalists' broadcasts in search of political realities,[41] making VOR and VOZ credible sources of alternative news. Indeed, the excessive propaganda by the RBC had a boomerang effect on the entire "hearts and minds" scheme of the colonial period.

The Rhodesian propaganda that attempted to depict the internal political climate as stable contributed to the perception and use of VOR as a source of alternative news. According to Zaffiro, the white settler community made up a considerable percentage of listeners accessing guerrilla broadcasts through Radio Zambia.[42] Nyasha Donald Musiiwa explains that what attracted white listeners to broadcasts from the guerrilla movements was their disappointment with the propaganda they were fed by the RBC—propaganda that either exposed the Rhodesian government's sense of denial or its intention to dupe the whites into a false sense of security.[43] Many found the broadcasts both palatable and reassuring as Zapu was clear in espousing a nonracial society with opportunities for all, irrespective of color or creed. Moreover, the white settler community in Rhodesia was at odds with several fundamental political aspects of Rhodesia.[44] This resonates with Selby's findings that because of their vulnerability to guerrilla attacks in the outlying areas and the need to protect their investments, the majority of the white farmers indicated as early as 1975 that they accepted the idea of majority rule.[45] As a result, ZAPU had a considerable network of sympathetic European supporters with varying degrees of loyalty to the VOR. Conscious of this, ZAPU sought to exploit this sympathy with VOR broadcasts that were specifically targeted at sympathetic settler communities.[46]

There are two key issues that this brief chapter has been unable to explore: details of white listenership to VOR broadcasts and their reactions, and songs that are considered to have shaped and won the struggle. Both require further investigation.

CONCLUSION

This chapter has argued that the introduction of radio in the British colonies of Northern Rhodesia, Southern Rhodesia, and Nyasaland was accompanied by the state's miscalculation and overestimation of the impact of radio on the entire colonial project. Unlike in apartheid South Africa, where the white supremacists were aware of the political consequences of radio for Africans, the Rhodesian state lacked this political foresight. The introduction and popularization of the saucepan radio sets that had been introduced as the "new weapons" in governing Africans backfired a decade later, when the VOR began broadcasting radical nationalist propaganda from Zambia through the same radio sets.

The chapter has brought to the fore the very purpose of VOR, the impact of VOR on the masses, and the impact on the Rhodesian state, including its reaction. We therefore contend that the insurgency and the violence that began to be experienced following the UDI were not a coincidence but, rather, a consequence of the broadcasts by the war radios, in this case, VOR. The VOR broadcasts were successful not only in radicalizing the masses, but also in triggering perceptible panic and nervousness on the part of the state, thus subverting the state's power. It has also been shown that in a bid to demonize VOR broadcasts, the Rhodesian state ended up inadvertently reducing the listenership of RBC while increasing that of VOR.

NOTES

1. In 1937, the British Broadcasting Corporation (BBC) also began broadcasting in Afrikaans to counter the Nazi threat and propaganda.

2. L. Mosia, C. Riddle, and J. Zaffiro, "From Revolutionary to Regime Radio: Three Decades of Nationalist Broadcast in Southern Africa," *Africa Media Review* 8, no. 1 (1994): 4.

3. R. Smyth, "A Note on the 'Saucepan Special': The People's Radio of Central Africa," *Historical Journal of Film Radio and Television* 4, no. 2 (1984): 195.

4. NAZ/ *Radio Post Magazine* 1, no. 5 (October 1956), *The Magazine for the Southern Rhodesian African Broadcasting*, 12.

5. Mosia, Riddle, and Zaffiro, "From Revolutionary to Regime Radio," 4.

6. NAZ/RG-P/INF 43, *Murder by Radio*, Report to the British Parliament on Subversive Radio Broadcasts from Zambia.

7. Ibid.

8. Mosia, Riddle, and Zaffiro, "From Revolutionary to Regime Radio." See also J. Frederikse, *None But Ourselves: Masses vs. Media in the Making of Zimbabwe* (Oxford: James Currey, 1988).

9. J. Mtisi, M. Nyakudya, and T. Barnes, "War in Rhodesia," in *Becoming Zimbabwe: A History from the Pre-colonial Period to 2008*, ed. B. Raftopoulos and A. S. Mlambo, 157 (Harare: Weaver Press, 2008).

10. Mosia, Riddle, and Zaffiro, "From Revolutionary to Regime Radio," 13.

11. Jane Ngwenya interviewed by Lloyd Hazvineyi on June 21, 2017 in Bulawayo, Zimbabwe.

12. Ibid.

13. Ibid.

14. NAZ/S3279/62/16: Zambia Broadcasts, East Africa and Rhodesia.

15. *Rhodesia Herald*, November 1, 1965.

16. Ibid., quoting the *Toronto Daily Star*.

17. NAZ/RG-P/INF 43, *Murder by Radio*.

18. Ibid.

19. Ibid.

20. Everette Ndlovu, "Radio as a Recruiting Medium in Zimbabwe's Liberation Struggle," *Westminster Papers in Communication and Culture* 12, no. 2 (2017): 52–58.

21. *Rhodesia Herald*, November 16, 1965.

22. Ibid.

23. Ibid.

24. Ibid.

25. J. J. Zaffiro, "Broadcasting and Political Change in Zimbabwe, 1931–1984" (PhD diss., University of Wisconsin–Madison, 1984) , 3–25.

26. Mosia, Riddle, and Zaffiro, "From Revolutionary to Regime Radio," 16.

27. Ibid.

28. Joshua Nkomo, *The Story of My Life* (Harare: SAPES Books, 1991).

29. Ibid.

30. Zipra and Zanla were the fighting wings of Zapu and Zanu respectively.

31. Ibid.

32. See M. Sithole, "Class and Factionalism in the Zimbabwe Nationalist Movement," *African Studies Review* 27, no. 1 (1984); M. Sithole, *Zimbabwe: Struggles Within the Struggle* (Harare: Rujeko Publishers, 1999).

33. NAZ/RG-P/INF 43, *Murder by Radio*.

34. Ibid.

35. For a detailed discussion on this, see M. Mushonga, "The Formation, Organisation and Activities of the Catholic Commission for Justice and Peace in Rhodesia with Particular Reference to the Rhodesian War, 1972–1980" (BA Honors diss., History Department, University of Zimbabwe, 1990).

36. Ibid.

37. H. Maasdorp, "New Rhodesian Censorship Rule Remains Untested," *IPI Report* 25, no. 8 (August 1976): 3.

38. Zaffiro, "Broadcasting and Political Change in Zimbabwe," quoting the *Standard Encyclopedia of Southern Africa* .

39. Ibid.

40. Interview with Ngwenya.

41. Maasdorp, "New Rhodesian Censorship Rule," 3.

42. Zaffiro, "Broadcasting and Political Change in Zimbabwe," 5–14.

43. Nyasha Musiiwa, interview with Munyaradzi Nyakudya and Lloyd Hazvineyi, Harare, July 12, 2017.

44. D. Caute, *Under the Skin: The Death of White Rhodesia* (Evanston, IL: Northwestern University Press, 1983), 1.

45. A. Selby, "Commercial Farmers and the State: Interest Group Politics and Land Reform in Zimbabwe" (DPhil diss., Oxford University, 2006), 78.

46. NAZ/S3279/62/16: Zambia Broadcasts, East Africa and Rhodesia.

Chapter Seven

Reminiscences of Zimbabwe's War Radio Broadcasters

Munyaradzi Nyakudya, Lloyd Hazvineyi, and Munyaradzi Mushonga

This chapter is a collection of the lived experiences of two Zimbabwean nationalists and liberation war radio broadcasters. It sketches their experience of colonialism and as war radio broadcasters-cum-nationalists. The two are Jane Lungile Ngwenya (see figure 4) and Nyasha Donald Musiiwa. Jane broadcast for the Zimbabwe African People's Union (Zapu) war radio, the Voice of the Revolution (VOR), based in Lusaka, Zambia, while Nyasha broadcast for the Zimbabwe African National Union (Zanu) war radio, the Voice of Zimbabwe (VOZ), based in Maputo, Mozambique. The reminiscences of Jane and Nyasha captured here bring to the fore the oppressive nature of minority regimes in southern Africa, and their individual and collective efforts toward the liberation struggle. These reminiscences are not only worthwhile but a timely contribution to the historiography of the liberation struggle in southern Africa. The dominance of state-centered narratives, deliberately silent on certain aspects of the liberation struggle, has triggered the need to appreciate the contributions of unsung heroes such as these.

RATIONALE AND CONTEXTUALIZATION OF THE STUDY

During the liberation struggles in southern Africa, nationalist hotspots such as Tanzania, Zambia, and Mozambique hosted African political exiles.[1] With the assistance of the host governments, the African political exiles went on to establish guerrilla radios in the host nations in order to counter white settler propaganda broadcasts. Although there is a growing scholarship on guerrilla radios in southern Africa,[2] there is none that focuses on the persons behind the broadcasts. Lebona Mosia, Charles Riddle, and James Zaffiro focus primarily on the nexus between nationalist radio and postcolonial broadcasting cultures in southern Africa with an emphasis on Zimbabwe, Namibia, and South Africa[3] while Dina Ligaga, Dumi Moyo, and Liz Gunner grapple with radio broadcasting landscapes in parts of independent Africa.[4] Earlier works by Frederikse,[5] Smyth[6] and Zaffiro[7] can be said to represent pioneering work in the historiography of media and broadcasting in Zimbabwe. Mhoze Chikowero discusses the history of broadcasting in post–Cold War central and southern Africa and shows how Africans subverted colonial radio in the formative years of the broadcasting scheme.[8] His study grapples with how the entire war effort was influenced by radio technology and music.[9] However, none of these writers has attempted to capture the voices and experiences of individual broadcasters; hence this study's efforts to bridge this knowledge gap.

The lived experiences of these war radio broadcasters are an important story of the liberation struggle. The specific focus on the lives of broadcasters enables us to have an appreciation of the relationship between personal encounter and the broader struggle for independence. The reminiscences of Jane Lungile Ngwenya offer a worthwhile trajectory in understanding the intersection between gender and war radio broadcasting. It goes a long way toward dispelling the myth of female apathy during the liberation struggle in Zimbabwe.[10] Nyasha Donald Musiiwa represents the nationalist intelligentsia that engineered revolutionary propaganda through underground guerrilla radio stations.[11]

RESEARCH METHODOLOGY

This is a qualitative study largely informed by the oral historical approach, which was found to be the best method to get in-depth information and personal views regarding war radio broadcasting during the liberation struggle for Zimbabwe. David E. Russell argues that because of their focus on the subjective, oral histories can provide insights not normally found in more traditional sources such as correspondence files, diaries, and personal notes.[12] It is a fact that when it became clear that majority rule was inevitable, colonial governments systematically destroyed files and records just before the transition.[13] Patrick O'Meara, reviewing Frederikse's *None But Ourselves*, posits that "when it became clear that Robert Mugabe would be the first prime minister of an independent Zimbabwe, white Rhodesian authorities began to burn and shred many of the records of the liberation war."[14] In the absence of written primary and secondary sources, oral history proved to be the key design through which the narratives of war radio broadcasters could be captured. The two broadcasters forming the basis of this chapter were purposively sampled on the basis of their availability and easy access to the researchers, and their presumed knowledge of the subject of study as the best-placed informants to provide information, what some methodology gurus call "expert interviews."[15] Because there are several layers of meaning in every story of life, we have tried to keep as close as possible to the original words spoken in order to allow our readers to relive the experiences of these war radio broadcasters. Again, because we wanted this to be a story told by the broadcasters themselves, we did not see it worthwhile to find informants who could either validate or counter their voices. We were mainly interested in, as Alessandro Portelli puts it, the "acts . . . the remembering and the telling."[16] This is because our primary aim was not to interpret but to record factual evidence and to create a record from which other historians and researchers can reconstruct the past. Such narratives are therefore useful in the absence of, or beyond, the written records.[17]

The reminiscences recorded in the pages that follow are therefore largely built around oral interviews of the researchers with the war radio broadcasters[18] and interviews carried by two state-run newspapers, the *Sunday News* and the *Chronicle*, in the case of Jane Ngwenya. Since the interviewees shared their experiences in the English language, the researchers were spared the laborious and challenging tasks of translation. All the interviews were transcribed verbatim because verbatim transcription is thought to be central to the validity, reliability, and veracity of qualitative data collection.[19] However, there were a few limitations. First, there was a tendency by the interviewees, due to lapses in memory, to chronologically distort their narratives by lumping together events that do not belong to the same period. Second, there was a discernible tendency toward selecting what to report and what not to report, or a tendency to omit or overemphasize certain aspects of the liberation struggle. Third, the verbatim transcription was time consuming; we needed no less than seven hours to transcribe one hour of interview time.

THE REMINISCENCES OF JANE LUNGILE NGWENYA

Early Life and Education

Jane was born on June 15, 1935, in Buhera District, Manicaland, Southern Rhodesia, to a Mosotho father who migrated to Southern Rhodesia as a Methodist Church missionary and to a Shona mother from Chikwaka in Mashonaland East Province.[20] She lost her father at the age of three and grew up under the care of her grandparents. In 1944, Jane did Standard 1 at Gwebu Primary School in Buhera; she claims that she was the only pupil at Gwebu to attain a pass.[21] She then proceeded to do Standard 2 at Madende Primary School, again in Buhera, in 1945. Then in 1946 she did her Standard 3 in Kwekwe under the care of her uncle, who worked for the British South

Africa Police (BSAP). In the same year, Jane's uncle was posted to Hwange in Matabeleland. As a result, in 1947, she relocated to the mining town of Shurugwi, where she stayed with her stepfather. She finally completed Standard 6 in 1949 at Charles Wraith African School.[22] At fourteen, Jane was unable to enroll for a teaching course because she was below the recommended age of nineteen. As a result, she was only able to work as an untrained teacher at Globe and Phoenix School, a mine-owned school in Kwekwe.[23]

Jane Ngwenya Enters Politics

At the age of twelve, Jane witnessed and experienced intimidation by police, arrest, destocking, and forced removals.[24] On three separate occasions between the 1940s and 1950s, she witnessed the arrest of her grandfather for refusing to relocate into the Gwebu villages that had been set aside for African settlement.[25] Colonial brutality was decisive in influencing her to enter politics. Narrating how she joined the liberation struggle, Jane drew connections between her childhood experiences and the broader social and political developments of the time:

> I can liken colonialism to a greedy husband who wants to have the bigger share at the expense of the wife and children; an oppressive husband . . . who always wants to have the bigger share. . . . It will definitely become apparent that this is outright oppression. So, I can really say I joined the liberation struggle because of my resentment against this system . . . since childhood.[26]

Jane is emphasizing here that the oppression of Africans that she witnessed in Buhera between the 1940s and early 1950s made her conscious of the need to change the status quo through the liberation struggle.

At the age of eighteen, in 1953, Jane was married. She became a young African mother, a social status that hindered most African women from taking frontline roles in society and politics.[27] But for Jane, motherhood did not take away her consciousness of the need to confront colonial oppression head-on. She says that it was while she was on her way back from Saint Patrick's Cathedral in Bulawayo, with her firstborn son on her back, that she found herself entering politics in the late 1950s. She came across some men who were engaged in heated conversations. According to Jane, the political dialogue of these men was characterized by political grievances.

> Mineworkers lamenting retrenchment, textile industry workers airing grievances about low wages, peasants grieving evictions to tsetse-infested areas such as Binga and farmers from Tsholotsho criticizing destocking policies. Stunned by [my] "gate-crashing" of [a male-dominated meeting], Benjamin

Burombo,[28] who was addressing the crowd, paused for a moment and asked, "How may we help you?"[29]

Following this historic encounter with Benjamin Burombo and other trade unionists in Bulawayo, Jane became part of the underground political networks that met often, organizing campaigns and demonstrations.[30] The banning of all political gatherings by the colonial regime made political activism a risky endeavor. What made Jane different from other African women of her time was that she was prepared to part ways with her husband and take up the role of a nationalist fighter. The campaigns gathered momentum and hype; they had been torched by the countrywide strikes that had swept across Southern Rhodesia earlier in 1948.[31] Jane participated in the 1960 *Zhii* riots that took place in Bulawayo,[32] which sets her apart from the majority of women, challenging Francis Nehwati's and Terence Ranger's assertions that "except for women, everybody came out to fight" while the women either locked themselves "in their houses, venturing out only to loot, . . . and if necessary . . . move off into the countryside."[33]

Following the intervention of the BSAP, these riots were contained and several leading members of the National Democratic Party (NDP) led by Joshua Nkomo, including Jane, were arrested and detained for two weeks.[34] The NDP, formed in 1960, was banned in 1961. According to Jane, these arrests radicalized her even more.[35] Subsequently, Jane's marriage broke up; her husband eventually became impatient with her involvement in politics.[36]

> My husband was not happy with my involvement in politics because on several occasions the Rhodesian police came to our home looking for me. He always complained about that; *ethi ngumfazi onjani otshona edingwa ngamapholisa?* (what kind of wife is always wanted by the police?).[37]

Even after the banning of the NDP and the subsequent formation of Zapu in the same year, Jane still found herself in the top leadership structures of the leading nationalist movement. Her ascendancy can be attributed to the roles she played in the *Zhii* riots and to several underground political meetings. Together with the likes of Joshua Nkomo, Josiah Chinamano, Ruth Chinamano, and Joseph Msika, Jane was arrested in 1964 and sent to Wha Wha Detention Camp in Gweru, Grey Street Prison in Bulawayo, and subsequently Gonakudzingwa Restriction Camp.[38] She spent seven years in prison, from 1964 to 1971.[39] She escaped from prison and left for Zambia, where she joined other exiled Zapu nationalists. It was in this nationalist hotspot where she began a new life in war radio broadcasting. While the arrests were expected to slow down the liberation struggle, they actually drove more and more people toward the war effort.

Jane Lungile Ngwenya and Voice of the Revolution, Lusaka, Zambia

Following her escape from Gonakudzingwa Restriction Camp, Jane left for Zambia via Botswana in 1971.[40] In Botswana, she was warmly welcomed by Sir Seretse Khama, then president. It is important to note that before she went to Zambia, Amnesty International had organized a scholarship for Jane to study law in Canada, but she "sacrificed" that chance and opted to "work for the party (Zapu) [that] needed people to reorganize it and so I felt I could not leave for Canada."[41] Once in Lusaka, Jane was deployed as an administrator to Zapu's Voice of the Revolution Radio hosted by Radio Zambia.[42] The appointment was originally meant to be momentary—however, due to a leadership void that had been left by the departure of George Nyandoro and James Chikerema from Zapu, Jane saw herself, from 1971, doubling broadcasting responsibilities and other administrative roles.[43] We contend that VOR was established in order to counter Rhodesian propaganda and legitimize the struggle against the regime; to educate and appeal for support from the masses and groups of African professionals and nonprofessionals; and to educate the masses on various aspects of insurgency such as property vandalism, sabotage, and even carrying out cold-blooded murders against white Rhodesians.[44]

Asked by the *Sunday News* about the strategy they used to mobilize people to join the armed struggle, Jane replied, "On the radio I would say '*Buya mntanami uhlaleleni, owakho umbhobho nanku, ufanele wena*'" (come and get your gun).[45] Jane says that people came to Zambia in droves and were shocked to find that as soon as they arrived they had to "undergo a rigorous military training exercise before taking the gun and returning home to fight the Rhodesians."[46] On the nature of her broadcasts, Jane intimated that the message was clear and straightforward:

> Our message to the people was straightforward; we spoke openly, "Come and take your gun and fight the colonists. Why are you still there? You are living under oppression, you do not have a job, the children are not going to school . . . " because schools had been shut and leaders imprisoned. "Come, we are fighting for our country, let us liberate ourselves."[47]

It can be deduced from this excerpt that the messages were packaged in a manner that reflected the people's everyday colonial experiences. Jane's personal encounter with colonial oppression since her youthful days in Buhera clearly shaped the content of her messages. With her personal experiences of colonial oppression and marginalization, Jane used the VOR to good effect to churn out nationalist propaganda. She says that at times she had to use intimidation to appeal to African men to join the liberation struggle.

Why are you African men silent when things are like this? You do not have access to schools, you do not have houses, you do not have land, you do not have jobs, your cattle are being taken, you are not being paid . . . what are you doing about all this? If a man raised his hand saying that he was really a man, I could tell them that he was no man, but a wife/woman of the colonists. [48]

It could be thought that the unique and complex tone in Jane's broadcasts was shaped by personal tragedies such as witnessing the persecution of family members at a tender age; getting married at an early age; the subsequent collapse of her marriage; and her encounter with systematic segregation in the Southern Rhodesian colony. [49] Jane used the airwaves to challenge gender barriers and to invoke a reconceptualization of the notion of "men" in the broader need to incite insurgency. This awareness, interwoven with her personal experience, ultimately became the focal point of content creation for VOR Radio. Although Jane insists that she used the radio to awaken people to their colonial plight, there is evidence that her message went beyond the political and economic problems of land alienation, taxation, disenfranchisement, destocking, and racial exclusion.

Jane had considerable control over content. As a member of the Zapu National Executive Committee (NEC), her radio programs were not subjected to editorial sifting or censorship. This flexibility gave her the leeway to be creative and to be as detailed as she wished. During her tenure at VOR Radio, Jane intimated that she did not follow the conventional methods of broadcasting such as scriptwriting. Although she had received informal training in Tanzania, she says the environment she operated under and the audience they targeted required a great deal of dynamism. [50] For her, broadcasting to Africans in Rhodesia was a task that demanded more than scriptwriting; the issues to be covered were not only diverse but also complex. She says that the broadcasts constantly reminded Africans of their colonial plight.

We spoke about our problems. The problems we were facing determined what we spoke about on radio. We encouraged people to come and join the war and fight for our common cause. We told them to come and fight for their children in order to guarantee them access to education. One could not merely go and broadcast. We told the people about their real grievances. The programs were coherent with the situation that was prevailing on the ground; we told them that we were fighting against hate and oppression. [51]

It is important that although the use of pseudonyms was not restricted to the guerrillas on the front line, Jane and other leading nationalists in Zapu did not use any nom de guerre because they believed that they represented the face of the struggle. They sought to maintain their real names because they had become the face and the vanguard of the revolution. After all, Jane had been actively involved in mass mobilization from as early as the 1950s; consequently her role in the nationalist struggle in Rhodesia was no longer covert but, rather, public. Using her real name also helped to portray the revolution as a nongendered endeavor. But an interesting aspect in VOR broadcasting circles was the continued use of the name "Jane Ngwenya" by a young female guerrilla by the name of Chipo Mabuwa, even after Jane had left VOR Radio.[52]

There were two important reasons for choosing to perpetuate the name "Jane Ngwenya." First, the VOR wanted to maintain the loyalty of the listener base and the buoyancy that Jane had cultivated over the years.[53] Jane's broadcasts contributed immensely to the guerrilla recruitment effort. One former freedom fighter, Sithabile Sibanda, who joined the Zimbabwe People's Revolutionary Army (Zipra) in the 1970s, told the reporter of one state-run newspaper that "the spirit of what I heard on radio began to move my interests towards Zapu."[54] Secondly, as part of the guerrilla strategy, the use of the alias "Jane Ngwenya" by Chipo Mabuwa was meant to protect the young guerrilla broadcaster and her family back home, as well as to deflect any counter-insurgency strategies by the Rhodesian state.

Jane says that it is difficult to judge the effectiveness of the VOR broadcasts, but the fact that even some of those who were working for the Rhodesian state could heed their broadcasts and subvert the authorities is a measure of success. In her view, these forms of feedback were critical because her work was subversive. "When you make up your mind to become a witch, no one else will know the exact nature of your witchcraft . . . if it is poisoning water sources to kill people, or sorcery at night; only the doer knows better. Everything worked in its unique way."[55] To underline this, Jane went on to emphasize that because "the kind of warfare we fought was guerrilla war," even broadcasting assumed the same dimension, as did listenership.[56] Jane was a key player in this "game" where it was not only illegal to listen to VOR or VOZ, but also illegal to give any form of feedback to war radio stations.

In concluding remarks to our interview, Jane revealed that she was seriously considering writing a book along the lines of Joshua Nkomo's *The Story of My Life*, or Nelson Mandela's *Long Walk to Freedom*.

THE REMINISCENCES OF NYASHA DONALD MUSIIWA

Early Life and Education

Nyasha was born at Mpilo Hospital in Bulawayo, Zimbabwe, on October 7, 1959 and grew up in Kadoma, Mashonaland West Province, where his parents had bought a house. He did his primary education at Kuredza Primary School in the same town. His home area was Mhondoro. Growing up in Kadoma, Nyasha experienced institutionalized racial discrimination; there were whites-only suburbs. The park in the city was for whites only, and he was not allowed to play there. There was discrimination even in toilets: those for whites were labeled "No Africans." Accommodation was discriminatory. Whites were clearly affluent while blacks were clearly poor.[57]

Nyasha claims that the levels of discrimination against blacks forced his father to resign his job as a policeman. Nyasha developed an early political consciousness because of the experiences around him. He often listened to local radio broadcast from the BBC African Service and to two channels for whites, the European Service and Radio Jacaranda. Listening to these, Nyasha says he was able to discern the underlying racial undertones in the broadcasts. His favorite broadcaster, who inspired him, was Webster Shamu. "He had the voice," Nyasha remarks.[58] Little did he know that one day they would work together on the VOZ as part of the struggle for independence.

For his secondary education, Nyasha went to Goromonzi Secondary School, where he did Forms 1 to 4 before going to Hartzell High School for advanced levels. Hartzell was a Methodist Church–run school and political activism there was quite high. Nyasha thinks this was so because Bishop Abel Muzorewa, leader of the African National Council (ANC), the umbrella party under which all nationalist parties tried to forge unity in the 1970s,[59] was a bishop of the Methodist Church. The knowledge that some students from Hartzell had already crossed into Mozambique further encouraged Nyasha to join the liberation struggle.

In 1978, Nyasha enrolled at the University of Rhodesia to read for a bachelor's degree in business studies, but he could not continue because the Rhodesian government directed that blacks be compulsorily conscripted. Students were now required to serve in the army before they could proceed to university or vocational training (call-up for military service had initially been reserved for whites). Black university students demonstrated against call-up and vowed never to fight on the side of the regime. Consequently, Nyasha and some students decided to cross into Mozambique to join the liberation struggle. He left with two fellow students, Thomas Tagwira, a second-year student, and Donald Chimbodza, who was studying politics and administration.

Crossing into Mozambique: Joining the War and Military Training

Nyasha and his two colleagues took a bus to Hartzell in Umtali (now Mutare), where they met a Mr. Sithole, an activist in the area whom Nyasha knew about from his days at Hartzell High School. Mr. Sithole took them to Mr. Muringapi, a teacher, who housed them for a week before Mr. Sithole took them to meet with the guerrillas. They met the guerrillas at Nyabadza Business Centre along the Nyanga Road, on the Rhodesian side of the border, and walked until they reached the Mozambique camp of Chimoio. At Chimoio, Nyasha received his nom de guerre, Magwaza Chimurenga, after the first commander who received them. The commander decided to name Nyasha so after Nyasha had successfully repaired the commander's malfunctioning radio. The act of repairing the radio was quite symbolic in that, unbeknown to all, Nyasha would end up working for the VOZ war radio in Maputo.

From Chimoio, they left for Tembwe by the Chingaira Bus Service, a bus they hijacked along the way.[60] The first high-level commander Nyasha met was Cde Rex Nhongo, whose real name was Solomon Mujuru.[61] On the way to Tembwe, he also had the opportunity to meet Cdes Josiah Tongogara, Zanla's chief of defense, and Joshua Dube, the director of training, and this inspired Nyasha. At Tembwe, Nyasha received basic training for three months and instructor's training for another three months before he became an instructor. Thereafter, he did artillery training and antiaircraft training before becoming an antiaircraft squad commander. When the war had reached a stage at which there was need for antiaircraft guns at the front, Nyasha was deployed there.

Deployment to the Voice of Zimbabwe

In 1979, Nyasha was deployed to Maputo, to the Zanu Publicity Department's VOZ where he joined the printing and publishing unit. The director was Charles Ndlovu, aka Webster Shamu. Other members included Sobusa Gula-Ndebele, Grey Tichatonga, Shingirai Tungwarara, Nyasha Maphosa, Tichatonga Muchazosiya, Anna Mugwara, and Darlington Munyoro.[62] Nyasha was engaged in the printing of the *Zimbabwe News*. In this capacity, he also wrote news for broadcasts. His main role was compiling war communiqués; he received reports from all sectorial commanders through Cde Josiah Tongogara, and consolidated them, as Tongogara passed them on in their raw state. The reports carried narratives of what was happening at the front where "every incident, every battle, was reported on"[63] and were therefore an accurate reflection of what was happening at the front. However, in order not to compromise and jeopardize the security of the guerrillas and their families, the writers of the communiqués had to decide on what and what not to report, as well as how to report it.

When Nyasha was deployed to VOZ, he had no prior training in publishing and printing. He relied solely on his personal abilities and writing skills from his university days and the on-the-job induction he received on deployment to the publicity department. Later, he was sent to Yugoslavia, where he received training in journalism in 1979. At VOZ, the sources of news were the reports from the front and Agência de Informação de Moçambique (AIM), as well as from international news agencies such as the BBC and Agence France Presse (AFP). They also interviewed people who had come to join the war from Rhodesia and the diaspora, and Nyasha recalls interviewing the late Dr Felix Muchemwa, who was later to become a brigadier in the Zimbabwe National Army. War captives were also another source of news for the war communiqués.

The main thrust of war communiqués was primarily two-fold—reporting on what was happening at the front and spreading the war ideology. Reporting the happenings at the front was important to counter the propaganda being churned out by the Rhodesia Broadcasting Services.[64] Much of the Rhodesian propaganda sought to assure the white community by reaffirming their beliefs that the liberation movements were communist-inspired and led by terrorists, and to win the "hearts and minds" of black people. Nyasha observes that he had grown up listening to these propaganda broadcasts and when he began working in broadcasting, he knew for sure that the Rhodesian broadcasts were mere fabrications of the truth. It was important, therefore, that the broadcasts from the VOZ countered the Rhodesian state propaganda, to dispel the myth of invincibility that the Rhodesians tried to portray.[65] Rhodesian propaganda broadcasts also sought to convince whites that the war was being waged effectively and successfully.[66]

However, there were several challenges that the VOZ encountered. The greatest challenge was the shortage of resources, both financial and technical. Scarcity of funds precluded the broadcasters from going to the front to personally collect news; hence the overreliance on the war reports brought in by the guerrillas. Nyasha says that although they trusted the reports they received from the guerrillas, the new recruits and the captives, the ideal was for a professional journalist to gather firsthand information.[67] The other challenge was that they had to rely on the goodwill of Radio Mozambique/Radio Maputo, which gave them thirty minutes a day to air their broadcasts.

Nyasha believes that the VOZ made a huge impact by making people know what was happening; many people tuned in to the station across the country. He says that his uncle was one of the very few Africans who owned a radio set, and people often gathered at his house in Harare in National Township, Salisbury (now Harare) to listen together to the broadcasts every evening at eight. This brought about a sense of solidarity. The broadcasts were also useful both in motivating people to go to war and in inspiring them to fully support the guerrillas in every possible way. According to Nyasha, the use of music as a mode of communication made this possible because several songs were by guerrillas and refugees. All these educative and informative war songs were constantly played in the broadcasts.

CONCLUSION

The reminiscences captured in this chapter present exciting accounts of the important role of war radio broadcasts in the liberation of Zimbabwe. Their stories reveal the power of war radio broadcasts in inspiring the masses to join the war effort. Jane's story is particularly fascinating because it reverses the frequent undermining of women's role in the liberation struggle. She was not only a member of Zapu's supreme governing body, the NEC, but also a dedicated broadcaster. Fluent in four languages (Nyanja, Ndebele, Shona, and English), she is the only surviving member of the Zapu NEC of the 1970s and 1980s, and "a household name in the story of the country's liberation struggle."[68] On the other hand, not only is Nyasha's story intriguing for its invaluable contribution to war radio broadcasting, but it also shows the resolve and agency among students in Rhodesia to liberate their country by voluntarily stepping forward to join the war. Nyasha's reminiscences are especially important for two reasons: they show the importance of the people behind the scenes in the broadcasting industry (particularly those charged with writing war communiqués); and they offer insights into broadcasting in independent Zimbabwe. Jane and Nyasha decry the apparent failure of independence to transform the lives of the majority of Zimbabweans. They are also disappointed that radio broadcasting in the new Zimbabwe continues to be used as a propaganda tool to prop up the interests of the ruling elite.

NOTES

1. See Lebona Mosia, Charles Riddle, and James Zaffiro, "From Revolutionary to Regime Radio: Three Decades of Nationalist Broadcasting in Southern Africa," *Africa Media Review* 8, no. 1 (1994): 3–10.

2. See Marissa Moorman, "Guerrilla Broadcasters and the Unnerved Colonial State in Angola, 1961–1974" (paper presented at a Workshop on Liberation Radios in Southern Africa, Universidade Pedágogica, Maputo, Mozambique, 2017); R. Heinze, "'It Recharged Our Batteries': Writing the History of the Voice of Namibia," *Journal of Namibian Studies* 15 (2014); S. P. Lekgoathi, "You Are Listening to Radio Lebowa: Bantustan Identity, Censorship and Subversion: The African National Congress's Radio Freedom and its Audiences in Apartheid South Africa, 1963–1991," *Journal of African Media Studies* 2, no. 2 (2010), 139–53.

3. Mosia, Riddle, and Zaffiro, "From Revolutionary to Regime Radio," 3–10.

4. Dina Ligaga, Dumi Moyo, and Liz Gunner, eds., *Radio in Africa* (Johannesburg: Witwatersrand University Press, 2011).

5. See Julie Frederikse, *None but Ourselves: Masses vs. Media in the Making of Zimbabwe* (Johannesburg: Ravan Press, 1982).

6. R. Smyth, "A Note on the 'Saucepan Special': The People's Radio of Central Africa," *Historical Journal of Film, Radio and Television* 4, no. 2 (1984).

7. James J. Zaffiro, "Broadcasting and Political Change in Zimbabwe, 1931–1984," (PhD diss., University of Wisconsin–Madison, 1984).

8. Mhoze Chikowero, "Is Propaganda Modernity? Press and Radio 'for Africans' in Zambia, Zimbabwe and Malawi during World War II and its Aftermath," in *Modernization as Spectacle in Africa*, ed. P. J. Bloom, S. Miescher and T. Manuh (Bloomington: Indiana University Press, 2014).

9. See Mhoze Chikowero, *African Music, Power and Being in Colonial Zimbabwe* (Bloomington: Indiana University Press, 2015).

10. Examples include Francis Nehwati, who argues that women remained in the peripheries of early nationalist activism by running away to the rural areas in colonial Zimbabwe. See

Nehwati, "The Social and Communal Background to '*Zhii*': The African Riots in Bulawayo, Southern Rhodesia in 1960," in *African Affairs* 69, no. 276 (1970).

11. The educated Africans who led and directed the liberation struggle in Zimbabwe are generally referred to as the intelligentsia. For a rendition of this argument, see Terence Ranger, *Are We Not Also Men?: The Samkange Family and African Politics in Zimbabwe, 1920–1964* (Harare: Baobab Books, 1995).

12. D. E. Russell, "Oral History Methodology, The Art of Interviewing," Oral History Program, University of California–Santa Barbara, n.d., 1–2.

13. See Moorman, "Guerrilla Broadcasters."

14. P. O'Meara, review of *None But Ourselves: Masses vs. Media in the Making of Zimbabwe* by Julie Frederikse, 571.

15. A. Bogner, B. Littig, and W. Menz, "Introduction: Expert Interviews—An Introduction to a New Methodological Debate," in *Interviewing Experts,* ed. A. Bogner, B. Littig, and W. Menz, 1–13 (New York: Palgrave), 2009; R. Kumar, *Research Methodology: A Step-By-Step Guide for Beginners* (London: Sage, 2005).

16. Alessandro Portelli, *The Order Has Been Carried Out: History, Memory, and Meaning of a Nazi Massacre in Rome* (New York: Palgrave, 2003), 14.

17. Jan Vansina, *Oral Tradition as History* (Madison: University of Wisconsin Press, 1985); D. Henige, *Oral Historiography* (London: Longman, 1982).

18. Jane Ngwenya, interview with Lloyd Hazvineyi, Bulawayo, Zimbabwe, June 21, 2017; Nyasha Musiiwa, interview with Munyaradzi Nyakudya and Lloyd Hazvineyi, Harare, Zimbabwe, July 12, 2017.

19. E. J. Halcomb and P. M. Davidson, "Is Verbatim Transcription of Interview Data Always Necessary?" *Applied Nursing Research* 19 (2006), 38–42.

20. Interview with Jane Ngwenya, Bulawayo, Zimbabwe, June 21, 2017.

21. Ibid.

22. Charles Wraith African School was a community school. It was founded by a social worker and philanthropist, Charles Wraith, who had worked in Shurugwi in the 1940s.

23. Interview with Jane Ngwenya.

24. This followed the enactment of the Land Apportionment Act of 1930, which divided land along racial lines. Between 1930 and the 1940s there was massive land dispossession of Africans as white settlers appropriated land.

25. Forced removals or evictions were common during this period. Francis Musoni has documented the settlement of Ndebele speakers in Buhera who had been forcibly removed from various parts of Matabeleland and Midlands provinces between the 1920s and 1950s. See F. Musoni, "Forced Resettlement, Ethnicity, and the (Un)Making of the Ndebele Identity in Buhera District, Zimbabwe," *African Studies Review* 57 (2014).

26. Interview with Jane Ngwenya.

27. Josephine Nhongo-Simbanegavi, *For Better or Worse: Women and ZANLA in Zimbabwe's Liberation Struggle* (Harare: Weaver Press, 2000), 23.

28. Benjamin Burombo was one of Zimbabwe's pioneer political activists; see N. M. Bhebe, *Benjamin Burombo: African Politics in Zimbabwe: 1947–1958* (Harare: College Press, 1989).

29. Interview with Jane Ngwenya.

30. For a detailed discussion of the nature of underground political networks of this time, see A. S. Mlambo, "From Second World War to UDI, 1940–1965," in *Becoming Zimbabwe: A History from the Pre-colonial Period to 2008,* ed. B. Raftopoulos and A. S. Mlambo, 104–8 (Harare: Weaver Press, 2009).

31. Ibid.

32. Interview with Jane Ngwenya; *Zhii* referred to riots by Africans in the city of Bulawayo in July 1960. According to F. Nehwati, the closest equivalent of *Zhii* in English is "devastating action," "destroy completely "or "reduce to rubble." This is what happened in July 1960 following the banning of an NDP rally without any warning or explanation. Jane claims that she was the only woman in the sixty-five-member NEC of the NDP. See F. Nehwati, "The Social and Communal Background to '*Zhii*': The African Riots in Bulawayo, Southern Rhodesia in 1960," *African Affairs* 69, no. 276 (1970).

33. Nehwati, "Social and Communal Background to '*Zhii*,'" 233–34.

34. Interview with Jane Ngwenya.

35. Ibid.

36. Interview with Jane Ngwenya; the *Sunday News*, June 11, 2017. She is the only survivor of the PF-ZAPU National Executive that was there at Independence in 1980.

37. The *Chronicle*, "Jane Ngwenya: A Woman Married to Politics," November 2, 2013.

38. Ibid.

39. National Archives of Zimbabwe (NAZ), interview with Jane Lungile Ngwenya as part of the National Archives of Zimbabwe Project on "Capturing Fading National Memory," October 26, 2013, Gonakudzingwa Detention Camp, Zimbabwe.

40. Working with some Africans in the Rhodesian security forces, some ZAPU members facilitated her escape from prison after they learned that her name was on the death list that had been compiled by Rhodesian security forces.

41. Jane Ngwenya in an interview with the *Sunday News*, June18, 2017.

42. The *Sunday Mail*, "Zim's Freedom Cost Jane Ngwenya Marriage," June 11, 2017.

43. Chikerema and Nyandoro left Zapu due to a leadership crisis in 1971. They proceeded to form the Front for the Liberation of Zimbabwe (FROLIZI). See, for instance, J. Mtisi, M. Nyakudya, and T. Barnes, "War in Rhodesia, 1965–1980," in *Becoming Zimbabwe: A History from the Pre-colonial Period to 2008*, ed. B. Raftopoulos and A. S Mlambo, 144 (Harare: Weaver Press, 2009); D. Dabengwa, "ZIPRA in the Zimbabwe War of National Liberation," in *Soldiers in Zimbabwe's Liberation War*, ed. N. Bhebe and T. Ranger, 30 (Harare: University of Zimbabwe Publications, 1995).

44. L. Hazvineyi, M. Mushonga, and M. Nyakudya, "ZAPU's Voice of the Revolution War Radio and the Radicalisation of the Nationalist Struggle in Post-UDI-Rhodesia, 1965–1980" (paper presented at a workshop on Liberation War Radios in Southern Africa, 1960–1990s, Universidade Pedágogica, Maputo, Mozambique, 2017. See this paper for details on its target audience and the extent of VOR's influence.

45. The *Sunday News*, June 18, 2017.

46. Ibid.; See also National Archives of Zimbabwe (NAZ) (uncataloged), interviews with Walter Ntando Khumalo and Colonel Magwizi under the National Archives of Zimbabwe Project on "Capturing Fading National Memory," Bulawayo, Zimbabwe, July 14, 2014 and July 19, 2014 respectively.

47. Interview with Jane Ngwenya.

48. Ibid.

49. In *For Better or Worse*, Nhongo-Simbanegavi discusses how the majority of female combatants during the liberation war had been affected by different personal tragedies such as divorce and early marriages. Some chose to join the liberation struggle in order to escape these problems.

50. Interview with Jane Ngwenya; Nhongo-Simbanegavi, *For Better or Worse*.

51. Interview with Jane Ngwenya.

52. Ibid.

53. The popularity of the VOR is testified by a number of former Zipra guerrillas who were first conscientized by the broadcasts before crossing to Zambia for military training. See the *Sunday Mail*, "Untold Story of ZIPRA Women's Brigade," November 16, 2016.

54. *Sunday Mail*, "Untold Story."

55. Interview with Jane Ngwenya.

56. Ibid.

57. Interview with Nyasha Donald Musiiwa, Mt. Pleasant, Harare, July 2017.

58. Ibid.

59. See, for instance, Abel T. Muzorewa, *Rise and Walk: An Autobiography* (London: Evans, 1979) for the history of the ANC.

60. During the war, guerrillas occasionally commandeered buses that plied rural routes to ferry them and their arms to certain destinations within Rhodesia. It is interesting to note that in this case, the bus was taken across the border.

61. Solomon Mujuru was a former guerrilla and former commander of the Zimbabwe National Army. He died in 2011 in mysterious circumstances at his farm, 60 km southwest of Harare. He was generally regarded as one of the most feared men in Zimbabwe.

62. We invite those interested in the personal stories of the liberation struggle to track some of these liberation heroes and document their stories.

63. Interview with Nyasha.

64. For details on Rhodesian propaganda, see Hazvineyi, Mushonga, and Nyakudya, "ZAPU's Voice of the Revolution War Radio."

65. Ibid.

66. O'Meara, review, 571.

67. Interview with Nyasha.

68. *Sunday News*, June 11, 2017. Among liberation war heroes in southern Africa, and Zimbabwe in particular, it is a tradition to prefix their names and of those who participated in the liberation struggle with "Cde," short for "comrade," to mean a fellow combatant or fellow fighter.

Chapter Eight

SWAPO's Voice of Namibia as an Instrument of Diplomacy

Robert Heinze

Analyses of media usually concentrate on the circle of production, content, and reception in a given medium—that is, the specific communication between producers and readers, listeners or viewers. This is particularly inviting when looking at international propaganda broadcasting, as it seems to be the most direct way to gauge their impact in target societies. The impact of such stations often seems to have been comparatively small—in some cases, jamming facilities blocked communication completely. This chapter argues that judging impact from a more or less direct, if circulatory, communication misses other important functions of international radio, especially in the case of guerrilla radios that had to reach extremely diverse audiences with limited means.[1] There are other ways that guerrilla radio made an impact on anticolonial and anti-apartheid struggles. Most importantly, radio had a role to play in the diplomatic efforts of national liberation movements to establish the fight against colonialism and apartheid as a legitimate one, covered by international and human rights law, and morally justified. But also, these radios produced and reproduced specific media ethics and a culture around journalism that would influence media in independent countries in the years to come.

The Voice of Namibia (VoN) lends itself particularly to such an analysis, because its very existence and setup was embedded in UN efforts to educate journalists for an independent Namibia, and to provide the South West African People's Organization's (SWAPO's) radio station with educational, financial, and infrastructural support during the years of struggle. Thus, more than a contemporary instrument of propaganda, the Voice of Namibia was an instrument of diplomacy, and it looked to the future: to train journalists who would be able to take over and balance out the media in an independent Namibia.

The role of the Voice of Namibia in SWAPO's international diplomacy was twofold. One, the station itself was the result of the UN's growing involvement in the Namibian liberation struggle. From petitioning by individual anti-colonial leaders to pushing for more and more concrete involvement in UN processes, SWAPO had successfully established itself as the main partner for the UN General Assembly. It was granted observer status in 1976 and given institutionalized political and material aid. The latter came in the form of a Commissioner for Namibia, the Council for Namibia, and the United Nations Institute for Namibia. Furthermore, programs were designed to educate and train Namibians in exile to take over important roles in political administration and in core societal institutions such as the army and media after the country's independence. Part of these programs was material and educational aid for the Voice of Namibia, which was given studio equipment and transmitters, and organized broadcasting courses and on-the-spot training. The UN support for the Voice of Namibia was in accordance with its Resolution 435, which in 1978 demanded that the South African occupational forces prepare the transition to an independent, democratic Namibia by holding elections that included SWAPO on the ballot. Receiving such clear ideological and material support from the United Nations distinguished the Voice of Namibia from other guerrilla radios and gave it a basis in international law through the UN mandate for Namibia, which the organization had retracted from South Africa in 1966. It is thus useful to look at the role that the United Nations played in the setup and operation of the station, and how the Voice of Namibia used this as a diplomatic instrument.

The second role of the VoN in SWAPO's "diplomatic front" was as an instrument of diplomacy. The radio addressed two different audiences at once. First was Namibians "at home." In order to break through the South African media curfew, which tried to keep the war in the north as much out of the news as possible,[2] the VoN targeted Namibian listeners with information about the progress of the war, commentaries by SWAPO leaders on the goings-on in Namibia, but also music and news from the People's Liberation Army of Namibia (PLAN) camps. It provided a communication line to exile, a daily reminder that SWAPO was still there, just outside the borders, and still fighting. For Namibian listeners, tuning in to the VoN was a first act of resistance, which many who later joined SWAPO in exile integrate in their narratives of politicization. But secondly, and more relevant to the question of the VoN's role on the "diplomatic front," it addressed international audiences. It intervened in international public discourse in order to counter South African propaganda broadcast through Radio RSA and to bring international public opinion on Swapo's side thus increasing pressure from the international anti-apartheid movement on the South African government. To do so, UN support and other diplomatic successes, together with increasing pressure on the apartheid government in South Africa, provided the basis for intervening in a wider media circulation on which the VoN, lacking transmitter power, relied to bring its point across.

THE UNITED NATIONS AND NAMIBIA

In the Treaty of Versailles, South Africa had been granted a League of Nations mandate to rule the former German colony of "South West Africa." After the supersession of the League by the United Nations in 1946, South Africa refused to give in to demands to place Namibia under UN trusteeship (which would have enabled closer international monitoring), and went even further in arguing that the mandate had lapsed; from then on, it effectively administered Namibia as a fifth province of South Africa. Since 1946, this situation had prompted the international community and Namibian politicians and activists, including anti-colonial leaders such as Hosea Kutako, Hendrik Witbooi, and Andimba Toivo ya Toivo, to petition the United Nations to enforce the placement of Namibia under UN trusteeship.[3]

Namibian anti-apartheid leaders, including Sam Nujoma, had ample experience with leveraging UN support and close ties with its institutions. Not just the body itself, but particularly the African countries joining it (through, for example, the Africa Group, lobbying, advice, and diplomatic assistance) supported the petitioners. One of the results of these petitions and lobbying was that in 1966 the United Nations revoked the mandate, arguing that the League of Nations mandate had been continuously violated.

The process remained slow, however, and the support for the apartheid regime and derailing of SWAPO's diplomatic efforts among South Africa's Western trading partners in the Security Council and General Assembly meant that the UN's intervention possibilities were limited. This was one of the reasons for SWAPO's decision to take up armed military struggle in the summer of 1966 (before the mandate was revoked). While most of the UN General Assembly remained sympathetic to Namibian nationalists, SWAPO and other Namibian nationalist organizations also remained in close contact, using diplomacy and military struggle as "two complementary fronts."[4] These diplomatic efforts played a major role in establishing SWAPO as the single most important national liberation movement in Namibia.[5] SWAPO's media—posters, print magazines, books, and radio—would become an essential part of this two-pronged strategy, uniting content geared at mobilizing Namibians to join the struggle with international (counter-)propaganda designed to report on and support the movement's diplomatic efforts at the Organization of African Unity (OAU) and the United Nations.[6]

During the 1970s, this strategy paid off in that the UN General Assembly repeatedly called upon South Africa to end its "illegal occupation," legitimized the armed struggle and recognized SWAPO as the "sole and authentic representative of the Namibian people." The Security Council also became increasingly involved and sympathetic. The involvement culminated in 1978 in the famous Resolution 435, which called for South Africa to implement a democratic transition process leading up to independence, starting with free elections including SWAPO. The movement's diplomatic successes translated into concrete, material support. The UN Council for Namibia, established in 1967 as the legal administering authority for Namibia, and the UN Commissioner acted as symbolic government-in-waiting. Through the United Nations Fund for Namibia, they also mobilized UN resources to establish institutions geared at supporting SWAPO and preparing Namibians for independence. Commissioner Sean McBride proposed in 1974 to fund a research and training institute for Namibians in order to provide tertiary education to produce qualified staff for vital institutions in a future independent Namibia. The United Nations Institute for Namibia (UNIN) was established the same year with the explicit aim "to enable Namibians to acquire the necessary skills to man the public service of an independent Namibia."[7] A second program, the Nationhood Program for Namibia, was implemented two years later. This was operated by the Office of the UN Commissioner in consultation with Swapo. Under the Nationhood Program, a Communications Training and Equipment project was set up "to develop broadcasting and communication systems to meet the needs of the Namibian people and their national objectives."[8] Although some of the projects in the Nationhood Program were organized by UNIN, the broadcasting project was supervised directly by the Office of the Commissioner for Namibia.[9] It thus provided training in programming and production for SWAPO's media, including print media, broadcasting, and the operation of a news agency. It also provided studio facilities to enhance the quality of broadcasts, including mobile transmission equipment.[10] The establishment of a mobile studio van operating throughout southern Angola probably goes back to this program. Although the program was in planning from 1979, it was not completely implemented until 1983. From then on, every broadcaster for the Voice of Namibia (both new recruits and people who had worked in the station for years) underwent the training courses provided by Robin Makayi, a veteran Zambian journalist. Broadcasters also received stipends through the program.[11]

The United Nations provided two important avenues of support for the nationalist cause of SWAPO in general and its media in particular: one, through material and financial support, and two, through the ideological and diplomatic support of its continuous resolutions. SWAPO media could refer to UN resolutions emphasizing the legitimacy of SWAPO as a representative of Namibians and the illegality of South African occupation, an ideological and diplomatic advantage that was used in abundance. More than that, Voice of Namibia broadcasters were trained specifically with Namibia's independence in mind, in order to have qualified staff operating radio in an independent Namibia.

ORGANIZING A DECENTRALIZED RADIO

The Voice of Namibia was established as a coordinated broadcasting effort at SWAPO's 1976 Enlarged Central Committee Meeting in Nampundwe in Zambia. It grew out of the hour-long program "Namibian Hour," which had been broadcast on the external services of the Tanzania Broadcasting Corporation (TBC) mostly run by Mvula Ya Nangolo (with occasional support from another cadre) since 1966. The "Namibian Hour" had been a relatively improvised undertaking, for example relying largely on Namibian students in Dar es Salaam for translations instead of dedicated staff. The Voice of Namibia, however, became an extensive and coordinated institution controlled by Swapo's Politburo and its Department of Information and Publicity, at its largest operating seven different studios all over the African continent, including a mobile van in the war zone in southern Angola.

Starting from Radio Cairo, more and more national broadcasters in Africa had in the previous decades established so-called external services, specific departments hosting radio programs developed by nationalist movements from southern Africa, the last colonial holdout on the continent. Radio Cairo had supported and broadcast anti-colonial movements (including SWAPO, although not represented with its own program) since the 1950s. In the early 1960s, the TBC and the Ghanaian Broadcasting Corporation followed suit and hosted regional anti-colonial movements on their external services. But in the following decade the increasing pan-African support for southern African nationalist movements and guerrillas saw the exponential rise of such services, giving these movements the opportunity to develop bigger radio stations broadcasting regularly scheduled and diverse daily programming.

The different studios were established at different times: while the TBC, which had started giving airtime to nationalist movements in Zambia and Malawi in the early 1960s, hosted a SWAPO program from 1966, the Zambia Broadcasting Services followed in its footsteps only in the 1970s. Originally, the radio operation moved with SWAPO's headquarters—from 1962 Dar es Salaam, from 1974 Lusaka, and finally, from 1979 Luanda—but with the establishment of the Voice of Namibia, the radio branched out across the continent. To enable listeners to manage the differences in broadcast times and shortwave frequencies, SWAPO magazines carried big full-page "advertisements" listing both.

The region's governments became important supporters of anti-colonial and anti-apartheid movements, providing infrastructure, education, and financial and military support. For SWAPO, this support was invaluable, materially and as a propaganda tool, both in Namibia and on the global stage. Not only could the movement rely on material and financial backing, but it could also argue that the broad support coming through many avenues, including but by far not limited to one of the two major blocs in the Cold War, demonstrated the legitimacy of its struggle. As other regional governments and liberation movements, it deftly navigated the regional and global conflicts to its diplomatic advantage. Marissa Moorman has argued that the support networks both the new governments and movements established in this context can be seen as a continuation of the political and diplomatic practices of the non-aligned movement. Radios such as the Voice of Namibia, and the external services supporting them, can be described in her words as an instrument of "enter[ing] and manag[ing] the geopolitical world through decolonization."[12] Not only did SWAPO use the support as a means to manage diplomatic relations and to propagate the legitimacy of its struggle, but the governments providing the external services also emphasized their contribution to solidarity against the continuity of colonialism and apartheid.

The Voice of Namibia was part of a larger media operation. SWAPO's Department of Information and Publicity, first under Peter Katjavivi and then Hidipo Hamutenya, organized and coordinated not only the radio operation, but also the publication of newsletters, magazines such as *Namibia Today* or the *Combatant*, leaflets, posters, and books. It also produced music and mounted concerts, in coordination with the radio. With information offices established in London and other cities in Europe and the United States, it deliberately targeted an international public. Media content was circulated among the different publications—an interview with an important representative or chief of state conducted by the broadcaster in Addis Ababa during one of the OAU sessions would be printed in the *Combatant* after broadcast; music recorded by the Voice of Namibia in the guerrilla camps in southern Angola would be rerecorded in the studio and/or performed at solidarity events by the *Ndilimani Cultural Troupe*.

By the time the Voice of Namibia was established, it could draw from a large number of Namibian exiles coming into Zambia and Angola, mostly via Botswana, in several waves between 1974 and 1979. Many of them were young students—thus, furthering education became one of the central tasks of the movement in exile, with a view toward independence. This provided a useful avenue for UN support, since military support was out of the question.

VoN staff were recruited from the PLAN camps in Zambia and Angola, where Namibian refugees had been placed and received basic military training. Potential broadcasters were selected according to proficiency in Namibian languages and English, commitment to SWAPO's cause, and whether they had shown talent when operating recording equipment in the camps (for example, during music contests that were held by the VoN).[13] Although in theory they were supposed to first receive training in Lusaka (and, later, Luanda) before being sent to the individual studios, this was not always possible, and many were trained on the spot. The lack of broadcasting skills became a problem in the late 1970s, and the station's first director, Vinnia Ndadi, complained to the Swapo Information Department that the recruits sent to him were "not trained, or with very low education; such comrades found it very difficult to perform their duties at the broadcasting [*sic*] satisfactorily. You will find them not even able to translate a script from [the] English version into vernacular languages."[14] There was an urgent need for trained broadcasters able to operate independently in the difficult situation in exile.

While in theory the hierarchy of the VoN was very centralized, the actual setup was not. In fact, the hierarchical structure might have been an answer to the tendency toward decentralization that came with having seven studios scattered over a vast continent. The station's central department with its director (first Vinnia Ndadi, later Sackey Namugongo), was placed at the headquarters in Lusaka (later Luanda). The stations in the different cities consisted of three to five broadcasters under the direction of a supervisor. Because the stations were situated far away from each other, control was not easy to achieve. Much of the time, the stations operated separately, and they were often seriously understaffed, to the point of one person having to perform all three tasks. The supposed team hierarchy with one supervisor was not always adhered to, probably because the ideal number of four broadcasters in each station—one producer, announcer, and translator under one supervisor—was seldom reached. Thus, the broadcasters found themselves fulfilling all of these roles consecutively, or even all at once.

Broadcasters experienced a strong disconnect between SWAPO (and VoN) headquarters in Luanda and their respective station. Although Luanda produced much of the content (for example, interviews with SWAPO cadres or PLAN songs), the commentary and news items were selected and presented locally—so although the structure looks very hierarchical, in practice most broadcasters had significant agency in how to design broadcasts.

> Vinnia Ndadi used to visit us once a year, but there was not really that control. I think maybe there was that trust. . . . Maybe the only comment we would receive would be when, say, Robin Makayi comes over, then obviously he would stay for a week, and he would be with you as you are producing, then he would advise that here maybe this is better or bring this.[15]

This points to the importance of Robin Makayi's role as the project coordinator of the UN's media program for SWAPO/Namibia. Makayi trained Voice of Namibia broadcasters, he regularly toured the stations, and he was placed in the SWAPO headquarters in Lusaka (from 1979, Luanda). More than training broadcasters, he also assisted in editing SWAPO print publications and contributed to speeches and SWAPO's election manifesto. Makayi would, in 1987, also set up SWAPO's news agency, the Namibian Press Association (renamed the Namibian Press Agency, or Nampa). During this, he remained employed by the Office of the UN Commissioner for Namibia. [16]

Makayi was a Zambian journalist with a long career under his belt when he came to SWAPO. He had been an editor for one of Zambia's two biggest newspapers, the government-owned *Times of Zambia*, and worked as a correspondent for the BBC. In this role, he had covered the southern African liberation movements stationed in Zambia for some time. He lost his position when he reported on the trafficking of South African arms for the National Union for the Total Independence of Angola (Unita) through Zambia "with the full knowledge of the Zambian government."[17] After Kaunda's "watershed speech," in which the president took an anti-communist turn, Makayi was marked as "Marxist" and an MPLA (People's Movement for the Liberation of Angola) supporter and detained for six months. A friend from SWAPO had recommended him for the consultant position; although his role was as a UN project coordinator, SWAPO was actively involved in the selection process.

Although the project was intended to train broadcasters for an independent Namibia, Makayi spent only half the year in Luanda with courses, and toured the stations for the remaining six months to supervise operations and provide on-the-spot training. Additionally, the project description envisaged expenses for VHF transmitters, studio and office equipment, and the stipends (called "in-service training subsistence allowances") for the broadcasters. [18] Thus, although the ultimate aim of this UN project was stated as preparing qualified broadcasters to operate a station in independent Namibia, it enabled and supported the operation of the Voice of Namibia to a significant extent. Makayi was aware of the tension between the more urgent need to operate a propaganda radio and the long-term goal of training professional broadcasters for an independent, democratic society; in his mind, the fact that so many Voice of Namibia broadcasters went on to work for the public broadcaster after Namibia's independence speaks to his success in balancing those needs. [19]

This is visible in the operation of Makayi's courses. He provided courses in Lusaka and Luanda, where the Office of the Commissioner for Namibia and the VoN's main studio (including its director) were situated. These courses were held in the offices of the Commissioner for Namibia (underlining his direct responsibility for the training program, rather than the

UNIN's). Aspiring broadcasters would be trained and then sent to the different stations, but there was also a rotation, especially at the beginning, when broadcasters who had operated for years in places like Addis Ababa or Brazzaville were sent back to Lusaka or Luanda for training.[20] For half of the year, Makayi toured the studios to organize on-the-spot training courses, supervise the operations, and negotiate with host countries for more infrastructure and airtime. Experiences could be ambivalent: "There was a lot of cooperation because of the support they had for the Namibian liberation struggle, but you could also encounter bureaucratic problems, because somebody wanted you to feel his weight."[21] People who knew him from his earlier role could be suspicious, taking him for an unaccredited journalist.

Makayi had to develop his own modules for the course, comprising basic radio journalism, especially scriptwriting, theory of mass communication, and the history of Namibia—the latter probably taught by using SWAPO material such as Peter Katjavivi's *History of Resistance in Namibia* (published with UNESCO support) or SWAPO's *To Be Born a Nation*. But more than simply training, he was actively involved in the setup and running of the different studios. He held close contact through his networks in other media organizations, liberation movements, and UN institutions, negotiated with host countries for better equipment and more airtime, and from broadcasters' statements, seems to have been more involved in day-to-day operations than Vinnia Ndadi or Sackey Namugongo, the two successive directors of the Voice of Namibia, who could not tour the studios as regularly.[22]

SWAPO's campaigning at the UN, over time, had resulted in important material support for the liberation movement's diplomatic and civilian operations. From 1976, UN institutions provided much-needed infrastructure, particularly for SWAPO media, in terms of educational opportunities and technical assistance. The training in the context of the nationhood program project was also enhanced by broadcasters being sent to other institutions, including Sofia and Moscow University, the Werner Lamberz Solidarity School in Potsdam, the Thompson foundation, and the Harare Polytechnic.[23] But because of the exigencies of the liberation struggle, and the limited possibilities and staff shortages at the studios, the day-to-day propaganda work took precedence over the proclaimed reason for the establishment of the project, training for future independent media: "our priorities were on the liberation struggle itself."[24] This is corroborated by broadcasters themselves: most report being sent into the field without much training, and only later being given opportunities to educate themselves further.[25] Kaomo Tjombe was put on the air in 1981—fresh out of the camps—after "some short crash course," and was expected to establish the new studio in Harare (which did not work out for different reasons; the studio was established in 1983, when Tjombe had been sent to Addis). He would only be sent for further education to the Werner Lamberz Solidarity School in 1989.[26] Johanna Mwatara was the only broadcaster interviewed who had previous experience—she had worked for Radio Ovambo, an apartheid "Radio Bantu" station in Namibia, before going into exile after her husband had been arrested for "aiding terrorists"—both were SWAPO members. [27]

It is difficult to gauge the importance of the UN support for the Voice of Namibia. Certainly, there were alternative structures, and the offers to use external services from other African countries existed independently from it. But the UN project provided an important support structure, both financially and infrastructurally, to SWAPO's radio (and media in general). Although SWAPO's relationship with the United Nations was far from conflict-free, the individual institutions were an integral part of the infrastructure of the movement in exile. More than this material support, though, the backing from the United Nations provided SWAPO with an invaluable ideological advantage. Being supported by the United Nations allowed SWAPO to transcend Cold War divisions, argue against South African efforts to brand it as "'communist," and infuse its anti-imperialism with a strong evocation of international law and human rights. It used this to address a broader international audience and influence international media discourse in Swapo's favor.

BROADCASTING ON THE DIPLOMATIC FRONT

The Voice of Namibia targeted two specific, distinct audiences: Namibians at home—to provide an alternative to South African media, engage them in a shared culture of resistance, and mobilize them to join the liberation struggle—and an international audience to counter South African propaganda through Radio RSA and influence global public opinion in the liberation movements' favor. These two audiences were addressed differently, and with different effect. [28] Sarri Xoagus-Eises explains the complexities of talking to these audiences:

> The other thing was also important: that SWAPO's programs in exile to be known to the world. It was not only on the military front, but on the military front, the diplomatic front, and also locally to understand why SWAPO was there. It was also very good for the citizens of the countries in which we were operating to understand the role of the Voice of Namibia, and to understand what role we are playing. Otherwise they wouldn't have allowed us. But it was also to sensitize the leadership within those countries, the diplomatic community, and all those that were there to support the national liberation struggle. [29]

To work on the diplomatic front, the Voice of Namibia had one disadvantage: the South African external propaganda broadcaster, Radio RSA, had strong shortwave transmitters that could reach a global audience directly. In contrast, the smaller radios "piggybacking" on other countries' external services had much less coverage outside of the African continent. A workaround to nevertheless reach a global audience came in the form of two newsletters produced by the BBC and the CIA, respectively. The BBC produced the "Summary of World Broadcasts" (SWB), a daily and weekly (depending on subscription) newsletter sent out mostly to media and NGOs. A powerful receiver in Reading enabled the BBC monitoring team to listen in to even small and weak shortwave signals. They transcribed programs and produced a digest of the most important news, especially concerning specific events—military, political, or diplomatic—that gave differing versions from different sources. This was then sent out to subscribers. The CIA's "Foreign Information Broadcasting Service" provided a similar newsletter, although the intended audience was slightly different. While the CIA's newsletter was mostly distributed to other intelligence services, academia, political advisers, and think tanks, the SWB was mostly subscribed to by international media. Both cooperated and shared material.[30]

The importance of the SWB for SWAPO is visible in information secretary Peter Katjavivi's papers: he subscribed to the SWB, read them studiously and noted specific VoN broadcasts. Since it quoted verbatim and extensively from important broadcasts, SWAPO could use the SWB as a multiplicator to reach an international audience via established media. This is also borne out by VoN broadcasters, who obsessively and continuously listened to international radio stations, checked international print media for items on Namibia, used telex services where possible, and included them in their broadcasts.[31]

> You had to work really fast. Most of the times, even at lunchtime, we had to re-post what we heard lunchtime in the afternoon program, because the program goes out in the evening. So whatever we hear from morning up to our five o'clock, we have to re-post it. Over our little transistor radio, we listened to Voice of America, BBC, Radio Moscow, Holland, we listened to all the stations. In some of the stations, many of the SWAPO leaders are even interviewed. That's where you pick up and you use your ear. If you have a pen, you are lucky. You have to just jot down quickly what they said. And that is your news stuff. You had to write a news story.[32]

Another reason for this reliance on international news was more practical. Broadcasters could simply not go and work on stories in Namibia:

> And because of the circumstances we were in, we didn't have the luxury of them going out to develop stories, to interview people and whatnot. Sometimes, we could interview the president or the secretary for whatever, or the people in the refugee camps. But the ordinary type of story was not there; we could not have our sources in society.[33]

Kaomo Tjombe, who spent most of his career in the VoN in Addis Ababa, recounts a typical workday:

> We would come in around eight o'clock, then we would look at the wires, what has come in. We'd see if Nujoma or any other leader maybe was in London, and had been recorded. Then we'd use that for our bulletins, we could also use it as the basis for our commentary. And while preparing this, we'd also get telexes from Luanda on the latest military reports from PLAN, we'd also get the latest publications—the *Combatant, Namibia Today*—and would also make use of those. But basically we would compile a news bulletin, looking more on the Namibian angle, stories related to Namibia and southern Africa, or of course to the sister liberation movements which were there. And then we'd write a commentary on a particular issue. After that we would translate that and then you go and record. So that was the daily routine. And then, especially in Addis Ababa where the OAU is, around February, there used to be the ministerial meetings, and in June/July also ministerial and then the summits. So that time used to be really very hectic. If you are alone, you have to see how to divide your time, run there, get an interview, run back, record, and then to Luanda, they are waiting for you also. [34]

The Addis Ababa studio was, after headquarters in Lusaka/Luanda, the most important studio in the VoN network because it could record and distribute material from OAU sessions and, during these sessions, could conduct interviews with prominent politicians and heads of state from throughout the continent. It was headed by Charles Mubita, who went on to take over the main studio in Luanda. [35] Kaomo Tjombe, stationed in Addis, produced such interviews and circulated them among other Voice of Namibia stations and the wider SWAPO media network. The support from the OAU itself, the Africa Liberation Committee, and individual leaders of state such as Julius Nyerere and Kenneth Kaunda was a major point to emphasize in SWAPO media, as a reminder for the backing of SWAPO as the "sole and authentic" representative of Namibians, and a diplomatic tool publicizing the negotiations with which Swapo tried to put more pressure on the United Nations and Western powers.

The UN support for SWAPO became a major advantage in its propaganda, lending legitimacy to the movement through an international, non-bloc institution. Being recognized not just by the OAU but also the United Nations as the "sole and authentic representative of the Namibian people" effectively invalidated South African propaganda, which tried to brand SWAPO as part of the communist "total onslaught" that necessitated a similarly total defense and military mobilization of South African society. Voice of Namibia news and commentaries used UN reports as a source, [36] commented on ongoing negotiations between UN bodies and the South African government, [37] broadcast UN representatives' statements on Namibia (particularly if they were critical of South Africa or the Western Contact Group) [38] and regularly used UN language to emphasize the support. Although the movement took some ideological turns—sometimes emphasizing its socialist aspects more strongly—it remained consistent in its anti-imperialism. It combined this with human rights discourses, which proved useful to speak to a broad audience of Christian, socialist, social democratic, and liberal supporters. The VoN translated this into scandalizing the South African administration's human rights abuses—especially when the army targeted civilians in SWAPO camps in Zambia and Angola—strongly resisting the latter's varying efforts at "internal solutions," and reporting on the broad support for SWAPO as a democratic alternative in Namibia.

In coordination with other SWAPO media, the VoN constantly denounced the various South African efforts to implement "democratic" governments without actually relinquishing control over Namibia. This "internal solution" (superficially adhering to the demands of UN Resolution 435 while excluding SWAPO) was accepted by no negotiation partner outside of Namibia, and even the Namibian parties that took part in the succession of governments constituted during the 1980s protested to being constantly shackled by the South African administration, and let these governments fail. But in the run-up to the first elections in 1978, SWAPO intensified pressure on the diplomatic community via the Voice of Namibia:

> The South African fascist regime is using very sophisticated intrigues to get the UN to support the so-called free elections in Namibia and so pave the way for continued illegal occupation of the country by South Africa. The SWAPO president, Ndugu Sam Nujoma, is in Dar es Salaam to brief Mwalimu Nyerere on the new development in Namibia after the formation of the so-called Constituent Assembly. He said today that the recent election was an ongoing process of the Balkanization of Namibia. The elections, Ndugu Nujoma said, were forced on Namibians in order to try and camouflage the implementation of the 1976 Turnhalle [proposals] which (?adopted) the creation of homelands and bantustans for ethnic groups in Namibia. He hoped that the so-called elections will be rescinded if the UN (?and) all its member-states put in force the economic sanctions as passed by the UN Security Council [words indistinct]. He said short of that, Swapo will intensify the struggle, including the mobilization of the masses inside Namibia to isolate the puppets [words indistinct] the imposition of homelands and bantustans in their country.[39]

The station continued to emphasize the sham nature of the successive governments instituted by the South African administration and didn't let South African propaganda get away with presenting the "internal solution" as a contribution to the 435 transition process. For example, in 1985, after the failure of yet another "interim government," the Voice of Namibia commented:

> What the Botha regime is up to in 1985 is nothing new. It is its old game of
> delaying tactics. The idea of yet another interim government aimed still more
> at preventing Namibia from achieving its independence, is one more ample
> testimony that racist South Africa is determined to turn Namibia into its client
> state and sphere of economic plunder.[40]

The SWB contrasted conflicting reports from Radio RSA and the VoN, a
newsletter structure true to the BBC's "neutral" stance, and that broadcasters
might have been aware of. In any case, their technique of listening in to
Radio RSA, answering and correcting reports from that radio lent themselves
to the format of the SWB. While the tactic of petitioning the United Nations
subsided after its successes in the formation of the Commissioner for Namibia and the passing of Resolution 435, SWAPO media enabled the movement
to address an international public in order to support its position in negotiations, denounce the Western powers that, against UN resolutions, cooperated
with South Africa, and mobilize anti-apartheid movements in Europe and the
United States.

It is important to note that in doing so, the Voice of Namibia rarely could
directly address an international listenership; however, it could influence
international public discourse. I have argued elsewhere[41] that rather than
analyzing this aspect of the radio as a question of reaching direct listeners
who would tune in to the Voice of Namibia, we need to look at this relationship as one between broadcasters and an international audience constructed
through intervention in public discourse. Broadcasters in places like Addis
Ababa and Luanda, when addressing this international audience, entered into
a dialogue with other media, which they obsessively consumed and checked
for reporting on Namibia, in order to use it or refute it. Together with the
material connections to the United Nations via the UNIN and Nationhood
Program, the Voice of Namibia can be seen as being deeply embedded in
Swapo's wider diplomatic network.

CONCLUSION

Looking at guerrilla radios as instruments of diplomacy provides us with a
unique location to gauge their role in liberation struggles in southern Africa.
Mobilizing international support was an integral part of liberation movements' strategy, and using their own media to do so became more and more
important as South Africa became more and more isolated in the international community.

The Voice of Namibia is a peculiar example in that it not only engaged in
swaying international public opinion, but it was itself a result of SWAPO's
diplomatic successes with the United Nations. The concrete help through
several UN institutions showed the UN's commitment to SWAPO's struggle,

and the movement made ample use of this. Although the communications project under the Nationhood Program for Namibia stated its aim as providing education for Namibians to take over media in an independent country, it also enabled the professional operation of a radio station broadcasting from eight different locations. Robin Makayi, as a UN representative, was deeply involved with the operation of the VoN and effectively helped it to install and operate its studios. SWAPO continued to leverage the movement's influence with the United Nations and employed the UN support in its media. Although the movement itself changed ideological allegiances several times,[42] sometimes using more clearly socialist language in manifestos and communication, anti-imperialism remained a constant, and SWAPO referred to human rights and international law discourses in supporting this anti-imperialism.

Looking at the Voice of Namibia from the diplomatic angle also shows that the material groundings, the infrastructure, the financial connections, and wider support networks of guerrilla radios cannot be separated from the content broadcast, and vice versa. The station constantly interacted with UN institutions, used the language of UN resolutions to get its point across, and pressured an international community facing South African efforts at deflection to stay on course.

Understanding the Voice of Namibia as an integral part of SWAPO's diplomacy also helps to bring into focus the disconnect between the radio's addressing an international public and its limited resources to actually build a direct international listenership. Why, if listening to the Voice of Namibia was technically difficult outside of southern Africa—and interest would have probably been relatively low anyway—would a guerrilla radio put so much effort in speaking to an international audience? The reason lies in their targeting of international media and multiplicators such as the SWB, but the VoN also tried to speak to a global diplomatic community. Through these carefully constructed and addressed audiences, SWAPO could influence international public and diplomatic discourse, put pressure on the United Nations to uphold its promises and not accept any sham "solutions," and get its version of events into the spotlight, particularly when it came to human rights abuses. Thus, even if the station didn't reach many direct listeners, its effectiveness should be gauged through how successfully it conceptualized and targeted specific *audiences*. Although international listenership might not have gone far beyond radio enthusiasts collecting station IDs (who did send reception reports to SWAPO), through institutions like the SWB the station could influence wider circulating media discourses in SWAPO's favor. Referring to UN support and UN language concerning Namibia was a valuable asset in order to speak to this international public and legitimize SWAPO's anti-imperial project.

152 Robert Heinze

NOTES

1. Robert Heinze, "Dialogue between Absentees? Liberation Radio Engages Its Audiences, Namibia, 1978–1989," *Participations* 16, no. 2 (2019): 489–510.
2. Interview with Robin Tyson, Windhoek, November 6, 2007.
3. Dennis U. Zaire, "Namibia and the United Nations until 1990," in *Namibia's Foreign Relations: Historic Contexts, Current Dimensions, and Perspectives for the 21st Century*, ed. Anton Bösl, André Du Pisani, and Dennis U. Zaire, 37–50, 40 (Windhoek: Macmillan Education Namibia, 2014).
4. Ibid., 44. See also Richard Dale, *The Namibian War of Independence, 1966–1989: Diplomatic, Economic and Military Campaigns* (Jefferson, NC: McFarland & Company, 2014).
5. Chris Saunders, "Namibian Diplomacy before Independence," *Namibia's Foreign Relations*, ed. Anton Bösl, André du Pisani and Dennis U Zaire, 27–36, 29 (Windhoek: Macmillan Education Namibia, 2014).
6. William Heuva, "Voices in the Liberation Struggle: Discourse and Ideology in the SWAPO Exile Media," in *Re-Examining Liberation in Namibia: Political Culture since Independence*, ed. Henning Melber, 25–34 (Uppsala: Nordiska Afrikainstitutet, 2003).
7. United Nations Institute for Namibia, *Namibia: A Direct United Nations Responsibility* (Lusaka: United Nations Institute for Namibia, 1987), 164.
8. United Nations Council for Namibia, Nationhood Programme for Namibia: Project Document, 1978, 3. UNAM Achives Special Collections, Katjavivi Documents Series E, 2.
9. Interview with Robin Makayi, Lusaka, December 29, 2007.
10. Ibid.; UN Council for Namibia 1978, 2–5.
11. Interview with Kaomo Tjombe, Windhoek, November 11, 2007; UN Council for Namibia 1978, 4f.
12. Marissa J. Moorman, *Powerful Frequencies: Radio, State Power, and the Cold War in Angola, 1931–2002* (Athens: Ohio University Press, 2019), 131.
13. Interview with Sackey Namugongo, Windhoek, August 11, 2006.
14. V. Helao la Ndadi: The Department of Information and Publicity (Radio Section) Supplementary Report or Recommendation, undated, UNAM Archives Special Collections, SWAPO Documents of Dr. Peter Katjavivi, 14/1.
15. Interview with Kaomo Tjombe, November 27, 2007.
16. Interview with Robin Makayi, Lusaka, December 29, 2007.
17. Ibid.; Patrick Wele, *Zambia's most Famous Dissidents: From Mushala to Luchembe* (Solwezi: PMW, 1995), 79–89).
18. UN Council for Namibia, Nationhood Programme for Namibia: Project Document, Communications Training and Equipment, UNAM Archives: Katjavivi Collection Series E; Dep. Sec. for Information and Publicity to UNIN Commissioner for Namibia, 9.5.1980, SPARC 02001355; see also interview with Charles Mubita, Windhoek, August 18, 2006.
19. Interview with Robin Makayi, Lusaka, December 29, 2007. The transition, however, was not without conflicts. One broadcaster ran into problems for appearing at Swapo party rallies; most had difficulties adapting to an institution that expected them to work with former pro-apartheid broadcasters; especially the NBC newsroom became a tense environment in the first years. See Robert Heinze, *Promoting National Unity: The Role of Radio Broadcasting in the Process of Decolonisation in Namibia and Zambia* (Konstanz: University of Konstanz, 2012).
20. Interviews with Robin Makayi, Lusaka, December 29, 2007, Kaomo Tjombe, Windhoek, November 27, 2007, Charles Mubita, Windhoek, August 18, 2006; Theofilus Ekandjo, Oshakati, November 10, 2007.
21. Interview with Robin Makayi, Lusaka, December 29, 2007.
22. Interviews with Sackey Namugongo, Windhoek, August 11, 2006; Kaomo Tjombe, Windhoek, November 27, 2007; Kauku Hengari, Windhoek, November 15, 2007.
23. Robert Heinze, "'It Recharged Our Batteries': Writing the History of the Voice of Namibia," *Journal of Namibian Studies* 15 (2014): 25–62.

24. Interviews with Robin Makayi, Lusaka, December 29, 2007; Charles Mubita, Windhoek, August 18, 2006; Sackey Namugongo, Windhoek, August 11, 2006.

25. Interviews with Kauku Hengari, Windhoek, November 15, 2007; Charles Mubita, Windhoek, August 18, 2006; Sarri Xoagus-Eises, Windhoek, November 21, 2007.

26. Interview with Kaomo Tjombe, Windhoek, November 27, 2007.

27. Interview with Johanna Mwatara, Windhoek, November 17, 2007. See William Heuva, *Media and Resistance Politics: The Alternative Press in Namibia, 1960–1990*, Basel Namibia Studies Series 6 (Basel: P. Schlettwein, 2001), 66.

28. Heinze, forthcoming.

29. Interview with Sarri Xoagus-Eises, Windhoek, November 21, 2007.

30. "Measures against Hostile Broadcasts: Monitoring and Jamming: Draft Briefing Note by CRO for Sir W. Oliver," CRO 968/698, no. 104, in *Central Africa, Part 2: Crisis and Dissolution*, ed. Philip Murphy, British Documents on the End of Empire, Series B, Vol. 9, 3 (London: TSO, 2005).

31. Interview with Kaomo Tjombe, Windhoek, November 27, 2007; interview with Johanna Mwatara, Windhoek, November 17, 2017.

32. Interview with Isaac !Karuxab, Windhoek, October 26, 2007.

33. Interview with Robin Makayi, Lusaka, December 29, 2007.

34. Interview with Kaomo Tjombe, Windhoek, November 27, 2007.

35. Interviews with Charles Mubita, Windhoek, August 18, 2006; Theofilus Ekandjo, Oshakati, November 10, 2007.

36. For example, US arms shipments to SA, BBC SWB ME/7797/B/8, VoN Addis Ababa, 7.11.1984.

37. ME/7079/B/8f., VoN Addis Ababa, 14.07.1982.

38. ME/7173/B/4, VoN Harare, 1.11.1982.

39. BBC SWB, ME/6004/B/5, bc. 28.12.78.

40. BBC SWB ME/7871/B/3ff. (here B/4), bc. 06.02.1985.

41. Heinze, forthcoming.

42. Lauren Dobell, *Swapo's Struggle for Namibia, 1960–1991: War by Other Means*, Basel Namibia Studies Series 3 (Basel: P. Schlettwein, 1998).

Figure 2. Rádio Nacional de Angola (formerly Emissora Oficial de Angola). The building was under construction from 1964 to 1967. Angolan architect Fernão Lopes Simões de Carvalho designed the building. Photo from collection of Fernão Lopes Simões de Carvalho and used with his permission.

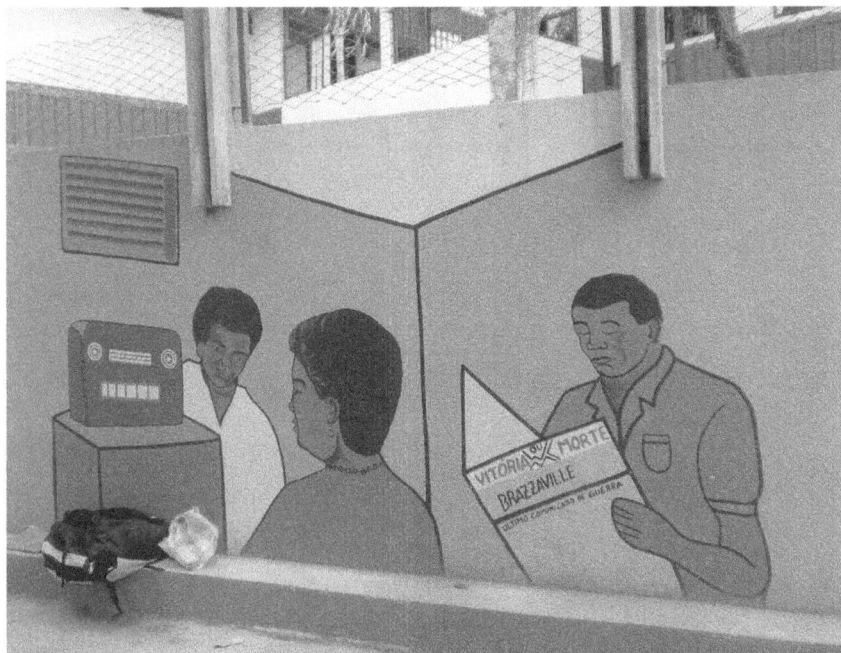

Figure 3. Mural on the wall of the Luanda military hospital. This panel of a larger mural shows the significance of media (newspaper and radio) in that fight. Initially painted by Teresa Gama and a number of art students shortly after independence, it is today one of the few works of public art from that period that remains and is re-painted. Photo by Margarida Paredes and used with her permission.

Figure 4. Photograph of Jane Lungile Ngwenya, one of the most prominent broadcasters of ZAPU's Voice of the Revolution. *Source*: *Sunday News*, Zimbabwe.

Figure 5. Thabo Mbeki, one of the major figures in the ANC's Department of Information and Publicity (DIP) where Radio Freedom belonged. *Source*: Photographer-agency/africamediaonline.com.

Figure 6. Pallo Jordan, another major figure in the ANC's Department of Informa-tion and Publicity who played a prominent role in *Radio Freedom*. *Source*: Photographer-agency/africamediaonline.com.

Figure 7. Winston Nkondo, also known as Victor Matlou—one of the broadcast-ers of Radio Freedom. He was the voice in the signature tune of Radio Freedom. *Source*: Photographer-agency/africamediaonline.com.

Figure 8. Thami Ntenteni, one of the broadcasters of Radio Freedom in Lusaka, Zambia. *Source*: Photographer-agency/africamediaonline.com.

Figure 9. Solly Mokoetle, Radio Freedom broadcaster in Lusaka, Zambia. *Source*: Photographer-agency/africamediaonline.com.

Figure 10. Golden Mphaphuli, also known as Golden Neswiswi, Radio Freedom broadcaster in Lusaka, Zambia. *Source*: Photographer-agency/africamediaon-line.com.

Figure 11. An anti-apartheid sticker bearing the logo of the ANC's Radio Free-
dom. This was developed by *Omroep Voor Radio Freedom*, a Dutch solidarity
group of media workers based in Amsterdam, which was affiliated to the Dutch
Anti-apartheid Movement (AABN). Translation: Support the underground South
African resistance transmitter Radio Freedom, bank account: 580900, account
name: AABN (Anti-Apartheid Movement Netherlands), payment reference: 'Radio
Freedom' Tune into the resistance! Anti-Apartheid Movement Netherlands.
Source: Photographer-agency/africamediaonline.com.

Figure 12. A drawing depicting listenership to Voice of PAC. *Source*: Flora More (artist).

Chapter Nine

The Struggle for the Airwaves in South Africa

Sifiso Mxolisi Ndlovu

The period when the African National Congress (ANC) was in exile was not only marked by the military struggle. It was also marked by a struggle for the hearts and minds of the people, inside and outside South Africa. This battle defined what I call the propaganda battle. The Department of Information run by Dr. Connie P. Mulder, the minister of information and the interior, engaged in a great deal of clandestine work for the apartheid regime. The Department of Information was established in 1960. Funds for the secret operations came from the Special Defense Services account that was protected from scrutiny by the Defense Special Account Act—money could be transferred without reference to the Treasury or Parliament. Further protection lay in the Defense Act, which prevented publication of information relating to defense matters without ministerial permission.[1] Later, protection was made stronger still by creating a special Secret Services account, with a specific Act of Parliament, to remove it from any public scrutiny. Les de Villiers, who was the deputy secretary of information in Mulder's department, wrote:

> Out of 20 trips a year to overseas countries only one or two resembled my travels before I became involved in secret work- attending embassy parties, meeting openly with people I liked, conducting interviews with the Press and television, and addressing audiences about South Africa. . . . We had started building a network of front organisations in South Africa and abroad; appointed tens of collaborators across the globe; bought publications and established some abroad; recruited spies in vital areas and bribed statesmen into our pay and debt; and even have men elected to a party we had created somewhere in Europe. We had, in short, a massive task on our hands.[2]

Endeavors by the Department of Information, whose budget had risen from R5,000 in 1948 to R13.8 million in 1976, were aided by publications such as *The Paper Curtain* by Dr. Eschel Rhoodie, a high-ranking official in Mulder's department.[3] The Commonwealth Summit held in New Delhi in 1983 decided that concrete steps should be taken in countering apartheid propaganda, including pro-apartheid propaganda emanating from countries in the world, particularly the United States and the United Kingdom. It was in the realization of this New Delhi mandate that the London-based Commonwealth Secretariat, jointly with the United Nations Committee Against Apartheid, organized a workshop on this theme on May 20–22, 1985. More than a hundred countries attended the workshop, at which Nathan Shamuyarira, minister of information of Zimbabwe, dealt with the distortion of African news that stemmed from what he referred to as the "fly-in-by-night correspondent," and said that he preferred a resident correspondent. He also reported about attempts of the Southern African Development Coordination Conference (SADCC) to free itself—even in the field of information—from dependence on Pretoria. He discussed destabilization maneuvers by the apartheid regime, using, for example, Radio Republic of South Africa (known as Radio RSA), Radio Truth, and Radio Venda:

> Beamed at a tribal section of the Zimbabwe population, and other clandestine radio stations, stationed and operated inside South Africa but beamed to various SADCC countries. The official Radio RSA has an extensive external broadcasting service that distorts and slants news about Africa, and especially the OAU and the Frontline States. In Zimbabwe, we have warned the South Africans that we are going to reply positively to their information aggression. We plan to establish an external service of the Zimbabwe Broadcasting Corporation in the next financial year. It will be beamed to the broad masses of South Africa and Namibia to provide a link between them and the progressive peoples and organisations who support them. We are willing to join hands with any member of the Commonwealth on this project. The broadcasts will be prepared by the liberation movements of South Africa.[4]

These and many other concrete suggestions were made during the workshop by the likes of General J. Garba, chairman of the United Nations Special Committee Against Apartheid, Archbishop Trevor Huddlestone, president of the British Anti-Apartheid Movement, and Abdul Minty of the World Campaign Against Nuclear and Military Collaboration with South Africa.[5]

THE ROLE OF RADIO REPUBLIC OF SOUTH AFRICA (RADIO RSA)

Robert Horwitz writes that in 1976, the South African Information Bureau, which came into being during the Second World War, communicated information about South Africa to the international community. The bureau was designed to keep the press and broadcasting services adequately supplied with information within the limits of wartime security. With the victory of the Nationalist Party in 1948, the bureau was expanded as a self-accounting section of the Department of External Affairs, under the title "State Information Office." The department's task was to promote the image of South Africa internationally and deflect criticism of apartheid policies; the bureau's tasks included the distribution of written, televisual, and cinematic informational materials in overseas countries. Such material typically defended apartheid policies and government action.[6]

The bureau worked hand in hand with the South African Broadcasting Corporation (SABC), created by an Act of Parliament in 1936 and amended by Act 73 of 1976 to accommodate television in South Africa. The 1936 Act enabled the SABC to assume the duties of the Bureau/State Information Office and establish an external service, on a very powerful set of transmitters designed to broadcast the apartheid regime's propaganda to the world. This shortwave external radio service, to be known as Radio RSA, "the voice of South Africa," was formally established on May 1, 1966 and broadcast from Johannesburg to many corners of the world. Radio RSA's rapid development led to its being able to broadcast in eleven languages (which included English, French, Portuguese, German, Dutch, Afrikaans, and Spanish) in order to scupper the influence of the international solidarity movement. In 1974, there were four SABC all-day services in African languages inside South Africa and Namibia. By 1977, there were eleven. In Namibia, the Damara-Nama Service and the Herero became all-day services; the areas they covered were increased, and a new Kavango service was set up. Within South Africa, in the northeast Transvaal, the XiTsonga and TshiVenda services were separated; Setswana services became separate; and each, with the North Sotho or Sepedi and Setswana services, became all-day services. With the isiZulu service, there was an expansion of programs in siSwati and isiNdebele. South African border areas and the southern African region emerged clearly as the target area. In addition to these African languages, Swahili, Chichewa, Lozi, and Tsonga were languages used for broadcasting purposes, the last four African language groups targeting a sizable number of listeners in both southern and east Africa. This was aimed at undermining the influence of the Organization of African Unity (OAU) member states that supported the liberation struggle in South Africa. Portuguese was used to target listeners in Angola and Mozambique; French in west Africa, North Africa, and Madagascar; Spanish in Latin America. Radio RSA also offered Afrikaans language lessons through the medium of English, French, Dutch, and German. By the 1980s, Radio RSA broadcast 208 hours a week and received well over a hundred thousand letters a year from listeners from North America, Europe, and the African continent.[7]

On May 20, 1965, during the Department of Posts, Telegraphs, Telephones and Radio Services parliamentary debate, a member of parliament representing the opposition party, MP Durrant, supported the government proposal to establish an external radio service to be operated by the SABC. Durrant acknowledged that four powerful new transmitters would be erected and would be beamed toward the African continent. He supported this because "we know that as far as the African continent is concerned, we are faced with considerable animosity as a result of unjustified propaganda about our country." Furthermore, he emphasized, "we on these benches have pleaded for many years for the institution of the service. We have recognised the need for it for many years." Although the minister of posts and telegraphs would be responsible for the policy that would apply to the messages to be broadcast, the opposition MP was concerned about the consequences; he elaborated that the "transmitters will in fact become part of our foreign policy; they will be the mirrors in which many people in the emergent countries in Africa will have their first glimpse of South African conditions and of the people of South Africa." His main reason for caution was not the implementation of the policy of setting up Radio RSA as an external wing of the SABC broadcasting services, but considered the minister of posts and telegraph unsuited to the promotion of a positive image of, and propaganda about, South Africa. This was because the minister had a reputation for being an unrepentant racist, and Durrant confessed to parliament that "what I am afraid of is that if the policy is in the hands of this minister we may find that material will be broadcast which is in fact going to bedevil South Africa's foreign relations further as far as the African continent is concerned."[8] Furthermore, Durrant elaborated, "it is of no use saying there will be no propaganda service. Talks will be presented on those [shortwave radio] services. There will not only be music but talks as well because without talks the service as a propaganda service to tell the truth about South Africa is worthless."[9] MP Greyling, a member of parliament representing the ruling Nationalist Party, was forthright in his reply to the opposition MP.

> The content of those [shortwave] broadcasts will be directed positively towards the outside world. It will not be positive propaganda because it is of no avail to try and refute propaganda with propaganda. The SABC will give a positive picture of South Africa as a civilised country. We shall make the outside world acquainted in a positive way with the fact that we are not, for example, a police state, that we are not living in the dark ages, that there is no slavery here and that one worships God here in South Africa. We shall give the world a positive picture of the fact that we in South Africa are civilised and highly developed nation. That will be our image.[10]

Radio RSA broadcasts' signature opening line informed listeners that "you are listening to Radio RSA, the voice of South Africa, broadcasting on shortwave to our listeners around the world." By the 1980s, the SABC could boast that Radio RSA powerful shortwave transmitters operated at 100, 250, and 500 kW and its target areas were Africa, North America, and Latin America. It also targeted the Middle East and Europe, particularly Germany, Austria, Switzerland, the Netherlands, Belgium, France, the United Kingdom, and Ireland. Radio RSA, like other shortwave broadcasts, targeted a global audience. When the new powerful transmitters were installed in 1966, Radio RSA changed from a regional broadcaster to a world radio station. The first step into the wider world involved establishing services for North America. The Middle East and North Africa were also incorporated. Not until 1967 were the broadcasts extended to Europe on a larger scale; the African continent still dominated in terms of total transmission time to each targeted geographical area. In one of its undated promotional magazines, *This Is the SABC*, the broadcaster boasted, "but response from listeners abroad shows that it [Radio RSA] is also heard loud and clear in countries well outside its target areas—even in Japan."[11]

Radio RSA promoted itself as an instrument of goodwill, its main purpose being to encourage and foster understanding of South Africa by other nations. Its objectives were listed as to broadcast comprehensive, reliable, accurate, and objective information, to present a positive and correct image of South Africa to listeners abroad, and, where necessary, to counter and refute false propaganda against South Africa. Radio RSA also committed itself to promoting South African trade abroad, to strengthening existing bonds of friendship, and to winning new friends for South Africa. Programs broadcast by the services of Radio RSA included music, magazines, actuality, sport, religion, and current affairs (discussions). Direct contact with listeners was maintained through a weekly program in which listeners' questions on subjects such as politics, tourism, and the "South African way of life" were discussed.[12] Hendrik Verwoerd, the prime minister of South Africa, noted the following when he launched Radio RSA in 1965:

> The primary aim of the external service would be to present to the world a faithful picture of the South African way of life, and the traditions, growth and ideals of the people of Africa. The Voice of South Africa, as the service is known, would not be used as a weapon against any country or people, but would be an instrument for promoting goodwill, understanding and cooperation between nation and nation, and a medium to disseminate factual and objective knowledge of the Republic of South Africa. . . . The Voice of South Africa (Radio RSA) will beam truth and goodwill to all parts of the globe. . . . It will counter that which is so harmful to the welfare of this continent and civilisation as a whole.[13]

John Laurence notes that on August 16, 1966 a draconian amendment to the South African Radio Act was published. It gave permission to South Africa's postmaster general to "name" any radio station in the world that he considered "guilty of injuring the morals, religion or morale of any section of the South African population." Anyone living in South Africa who in any way supported and endorsed the activities, broadcasts, or policies of any of the "named" stations was liable to a fine of a thousand pounds and six months in jail, or both, for every day on which the offence was committed.[14]

By 1971 nearly 45 percent of the Radio RSA program time was directed toward disseminating information and propaganda to North America, Europe, Australia, and New Zealand.[15] The 1970 Annual Report of the SABC noted that, as in the case of other services, the Portuguese services of Radio RSA oriented its program to highlight the relationship between South Africa and its targeted areas. One example was a series titled *Relacoes Bilaterais* (mutual relations), focusing on South Africa's and Portugal's interests on the African continent and on the cooperation between the two countries. As a result, until 1974 several programs were beamed to Portuguese soldiers fighting against "terrorists" in the Portuguese colonies Angola and Mozambique; the purpose was to offer psychological and ideological support to Portuguese soldiers. Such radio programs also included messages to Portuguese soldiers from friends and relatives in Portugal and South Africa, as well as messages from the soldiers to their families and friends. A series of Radio RSA programs was conceptualized around the theme "mutual relations"—leading to a series called "South Africa and her neighbours." Another series was termed "Southern Bastion"; the content was mainly propaganda that emphasized the "stability" of this strategic region, and South Africa's economic, political, and military value to the Western world was highlighted.[16]

According to Magnusson, the Africa-oriented services of Radio RSA focused on three main geographical areas. The first targeted area was referred to as "Africa General"; as the name implies programs were directed to the whole continent and the services were in English and Afrikaans. The second geographical area was southern and east Africa, which comprised Lesotho, Botswana, Swaziland, Rhodesia (Zimbabwe), Angola, Mozambique, Madagascar, Kenya, Tanzania, Zambia, Malawi, and Uganda. In 1971, content beamed to these twelve states filled 55 percent of the total time allocated to the African continent. North and west Africa formed the third targeted geographical area for Radio RSA—shortwave radio broadcasts were beamed to Ghana, Nigeria, and Francophone west Africa, which included countries such as the Ivory Coast. These broadcasts extended to North Africa, also dominated by French-speaking countries. More coordinated and regular broadcasts to French-speaking west Africa commenced in 1972. Shortwave radio broadcasts, as an ideological tool in the foreign policy arsenal of techniques, were thus implemented with one aim of pursuing dialogue and détente with countries on the African continent.[17]

In 1969, the Summit of the Heads of States and Governments in East and Central Africa adopted the Lusaka Manifesto, which stated the preference of African countries for nonviolent solutions to the problems of white minority rule and apartheid on the subcontinent. In conciliatory terms, the African states urged the South African regime to become more accommodating. The Manifesto reaffirmed its commitment to the principles of human equality and self-determination as the only basis for peace and justice in the world. This was seen by the African National Congress (ANC), however, as a retreat from the earlier uncompromising stance against the white regimes.[18] The most contentious clause of the Lusaka Manifesto was the pro-dialogue Clause 12, which read as follows:

> On the objective of liberation as thus defined, we can neither surrender nor compromise. We have always preferred and we still prefer to achieve it without physical violence. We could negotiate rather than destroy, to talk rather than kill. We do not advocate violence; we advocate an end to violence against human dignity which is now being perpetrated by the oppressors of Africa. If peaceful progress to emancipation were possible, we would urge our brothers in the resistance movements to use peaceful methods of struggle even at the cost of some compromise on the timing of change.[19]

The ANC voiced four main objections to the Lusaka Manifesto. First, it noted that the Lusaka Manifesto, ironically, emphasized peaceful change in southern Africa at the time when ANC forces were engaged in armed combat in Wankie and Sipolilo in Rhodesia. Second, and possibly more worrying to the ANC, the Lusaka Manifesto undermined one of the ANC's main diplomatic trump cards: the hitherto indisputable argument that the apartheid regime was illegal. Whereas the ANC regarded the apartheid regime as illegal, the document played up South Africa's independent, sovereign status as recognized by the United Nations. For that reason, and on a very legal basis, apartheid was considered an internal affair to be resolved exclusively by the people of South Africa. Third, implicit in the Lusaka Manifesto was the separation of the South African liberation struggle from those in Rhodesia and South West Africa. Finally, the major difference between the ANC and some signatories of the Lusaka Manifesto was about the official status of other oppressive white minority regimes such as in Mozambique and Rhodesia.[20]

One of the dominant news items produced by Radio RSA during the late 1960s and early 1970s was about worsening divisions within the OAU as a result of détente and dialogue between the apartheid regime and African states. Most French-speaking countries, except Algeria, supported the Lusaka Manifesto and most of the English and Portuguese-speaking African countries did not. The ANC in its message pointed out the danger to OAU unity if John Vorster's dialogue and détente foreign policy frameworks were adopted as OAU official policy. It used both Radio Freedom and *Sechaba* to point out the dangers posed by the apartheid regime's propaganda machinery. But the liberation movement faced an uphill struggle.[21] To pursue the apartheid regime's policy of trying to improve its relations with the international community and the African continent, Radio RSA was broadcasting forty-five news items a day by the 1980s.

THE RESPONSE BY THE AFRICAN NATIONAL CONGRESS

The ANC's Department of Information and Publicity (DIP) was charged with fostering an understanding of ANC policies and objectives among elements outside South Africa who normally supported apartheid South Africa, with the intention of eventually winning their support.[22] The ANC was striving to nullify apartheid's formidable propaganda machine. The plan was also to diminish the regime's credibility and counter its efforts to foster disunity and isolate the ANC so that its support from the international community dried up.

The DIP adopted multimedia communication strategies. It effectively utilized the arts, artists, musicians, actors, live cultural performances, plays, poetry, exhibitions, films, and freedom songs to good effect.[23] It also operated radio stations by collaborating with various broadcasters internationally to broadcast its content through Radio Freedom,[24] and it arranged for ANC officials to be interviewed on foreign television and radio stations and to present speeches at public meetings, seminars, international conferences, and other gatherings.[25] It also mounted annual commemorations and celebrations of important historical events. It organized mass demonstrations, pickets, protests, and boycotts in conjunction with solidarity groups such as the Anti-Apartheid Movement. The DIP produced press statements, memoranda, fact papers, posters, leaflets, published books, journals, pamphlets, and newsletters. Some of its publications included *Mayibuye*, *Sechaba*, *Spotlight in South Africa*, *Vukani-Awake*, and *Voice of Women*.[26]

ANC publications relied on disparate sources of information. The organization informed itself through ensuring a regular flow of source material from and about South Africa:[27] sources published in South Africa and abroad; information obtained directly from South Africa through uMkhonto we Sizwe (MK) cadres in the field; information obtained from experts and other reliable informants.[28] Information was also gleaned from the research findings of various universities, institutes,[29] and individuals[30] and also sourced from ANC missions and solidarity groups.[31]

During 1978 the ANC restructured its Department of Information and Publicity for the second time since 1971, to counter gains acquired by the apartheid regime's Department of Information. During a parliamentary debate on March 4, 1977, Mulder acknowledged that the propaganda "war of words" was a fight for control of the human spirit. Such a war of words was far more subtle and dangerous than a conventional war, for the enemy was not always identifiable. He further acknowledged the crucial role played by the apartheid government's information officers, "which South Africa has in the front lines overseas and who have to wage this struggle against people who are sometimes not only mercilessly but also diabolically engaged in launching attacks 'by distorting facts.'"[32] The restructured ANC's Department of Information and Publicity now consisted of three main branches—Internal Propaganda, External Propaganda, and Research. Pallo Jordan (see figure 6), Gill Marcus, Sizakele Sigxashe, Frene Ginwala, Thabo Mbeki (see figure 5), and Yusuf Dadoo played prominent roles within the restructured DIP. The ANC had realized that propaganda was a useful arsenal in the liberation struggle, and understood the ingredients that made it an effective strategy: What was the overall political objective and specific purpose of a propaganda output? Who was the targeted recipient? What was the correct propaganda vehicle to utilize on a specific occasion? How should the package be prepared and distributed? In August 1976, Pallo Jordan recalled having a "long discussion" with Tambo, who said things had changed inside South Africa as a result of the Soweto Uprisings. The ANC needed to jack up its propaganda effort and Jordan recalled:

> Typing this programme of propaganda was, and what I sought with it was first of all to move away from what I thought was a very conventional approach to propaganda which the ANC had up until then; which was to see propaganda as having to bear the stamp of the ANC which of course limited its utility . . . there was a certain degree of political space inside the country which we had not occupied in the main because of the dogmatic insistence that things must be identified as ANC . . . so the important thing was to occupy that space and fill it with your concepts, your ideas and the sense of political problems such as that you wanted to put before the people. So we proposed in that, that we had three levels in this propaganda effort. There must be open ANC propaganda which should assume two forms; overt and covert; then there must be general liberatory propaganda which could be overt. Then there was a more subtle type of propaganda which was that, if you like, subterranean . . . by suggesting certain ideas which are intrinsically subversive but not overtly seen as subversive and would nonetheless in the long term achieve or dovetail with one's objectives (like adapting subversive African labourers work songs to the struggle for national liberation).[33]

The overall objectives of the ANC's propaganda output were to project the organization inside South Africa and internationally as the alternative government. The ANC was also portrayed as the main vehicle for democratic change and had developed a program that embodied the aspirations of the majority of the people in South Africa. The ANC's propaganda and communication policy served to mobilize the masses and to channel their grievances and anger into a politically oriented and effective strategy. Its main objective was to prepare the oppressed masses to support the armed struggle, and to raise the level of their consciousness so that they regarded MK cadres as their only hope for liberation. This, it was hoped, would lead the masses to support, protect, and actively assist MK units that had infiltrated into the country. The presence of MK guerrillas would build and consolidate the morale of the ANC's supporters, give them confidence, and inculcate a belief in the certainty of the movement's victory and the defeat of the apartheid regime.

Another task of the propaganda and communication unit was to develop an understanding of ANC policies and objectives among elements inside and outside South Africa who normally supported apartheid South Africa, with the sole intention of eventually winning their hearts, minds, and support.[34] The ANC's strategy strove to nullify the enemy's formidable and vicious propaganda machine, spearheaded by the government's Department of Information whose budget was the meagre figure of R5,000 in 1948 and R13.8 million in 1976.[35] The plan was to diminish the opponent's credibility and counter the enemy's efforts to foster disunity and isolate the ANC so that it could no longer receive support from the international community. This necessitated a propaganda plan that created disunity and despair in the enemy camp and would also inspire a conviction of the inevitability of their defeat. After the Muldergate scandal of the late 1970s, the functions of the department of information were split. The Department of Foreign Affairs took over control of Radio RSA.

RADIO RSA AS AN ALTERNATIVE
SOURCE OF INFORMATION FOR THE ANC

The ANC's Internal Propaganda Section included the Publication Section and the maintenance of six radio broadcasting facilities for Radio Freedom offered to the ANC by Angola, Zambia, Tanzania, Madagascar, Ethiopia, and the USSR.[36] External Publicity constituted of *Sechaba*, the official organ of the ANC, the relaunched *Mayibuye*,[37] books, posters, publications, films, and so on. The Research Section carried out operational research on the political, economic, and military positions of the South African government. Research was also intended to address strategic questions of interest about the struggle for liberation. The Research Section was responsible for organizing the systematic collection of information for the ANC, from published and other sources, including from information officers based in various offices and from ANC members.[38] It was also responsible for organizing and maintaining ANC libraries, ensuring that information required by various ANC departments was readily available.[39] The South African government reacted with venom, banning all ANC publications and waging unsuccessful wars of the airwaves by trying to jam Radio Freedom signals. According to the DIP, the gloves were off between Radio Freedom and Radio RSA:

> One of the best weapons in this enemy confrontation has been and continues to be the political weapon through our mass media especially our radio— "RADIO FREEDOM, THE VOICE OF THE PEOPLE OF SOUTH AFRICA." Through our radios we are able to address our people and give timely political leadership to all our underground internal units. We therefore see our radios as directly responsible for the mass political mobilisation and direction of our revolution now and tomorrow. As a result of the power of our work, the enemy has resorted to all sorts of methods to frustrate our work and win over the minds and hearts of our people. One of the latest methods is by jamming our radios, counter-radio broadcasts through Radio RSA in over eleven different international languages beamed by their FM radios. . . . We intend to monitor the enemy FM radios through our own radios to confront it and intensify our political work among the masses for the eventual and inevitable overthrow and seizure of power by the people sooner than later.[40]

Radio Freedom provided alternative news and was influential to the youth in African townships. Soweto's school-going youth and activists included those who belonged to students' organizations such as the South African Student Movement (SASM) and subscribed to the Black Consciousness philosophy. Murphy Morobe remembers:

> Now in all of these years (as a high school student), when I was an affiliate or I was a committed black consciousness activist, it was you know, there was something you really wanted to know, that were either not spoken about or you got a hint off. That related to the banned organisations. And it was really in 1973–74 that I became slowly to be exposed to the ideas of the African National Congress, mainly through Radio Freedom when some of us used to have short wave radios and we would invite each other to listen to Radio Freedom. My friend, Supa Moloi, had an uncle who was a SACTU stalwart, comrade Elliott Shabangu who slowly Supa got to introduce us to him . . . you listen to Radio Freedom and then once in a while you will luckily run across a copy of *Sechaba* or *u Msebenzi*. If you are luckier you will stumble across upon a copy of the *African Communist.* Now, the point this was . . . it was us that in 1974 we began a process to resuscitate SASM. Then at the time it was the generation of myself, Amos Masondo who is now the mayor of Gauteng, Billy Masethla, Supa Moloi, Roller Masinga, Mosala and in those days it was very difficult but then when the situation in the Portuguese colonies turned in the early 1970s . . . 1973–74, culminating in the independence [of Mozambique] and of the Pro-Frelimo rallies that were held [inside South Africa] in 1974, those events actually raised the level of consciousness and awareness to a very new dimension.[41]

In 1979, the ANC obtained a slot on Rádio Nacional de Angola's international channel. The program, Radio Freedom, was aired for fifteen minutes twice a week until 1984. The program was aimed at propaganda, mobilizing guerrillas on all fronts, and supporting refugees.[42] In 1986 the BBC summarized a hundred broadcasts made in English on the ANC's Radio Freedom. Seventy-four of the broadcasts were made from Addis Ababa and the remainder from Dakar, Dar es Salaam, Lusaka, and Maputo. Prominent members of the ANC hierarchy conducted these broadcasts, which took the form of articulating ANC policy and strategy, comments on events inside South Africa, and interviews and discussions.[43]

But in terms of counter-broadcast, it was also important to listen to the enemy's radio at the ANC military camps in Angola. Radio RSA powerful airwaves penetrated the entire continent, including some parts of Europe, for it had to spread propaganda through European languages. The ANC had to monitor Radio RSA broadcasts in order to have a sense of what was happening inside South Africa. This radio had a strong signal that reached Angola and other countries in southern Africa. Andrew Masondo, while still based in the camps in Angola during the late 1970s, remembers when Radio RSA news confirmed to them, as camp commanders, that the ANC camps in Angola were infiltrated by enemy spies:

> You know, comrade Mzwai Piliso and I, as commissars, together with other MK people had inculcated the habit of listening to news broadcast through radio, right through, and once we listen to news, we analyse the radio news. . . . Not only did we listen to BBC Africa, we listened to all news, particularly Radio South Africa while we were in the camps in Angola, we listened to it, every day if we could get the signal. One day Radio South Africa broadcast propaganda news claiming that the MK soldiers were dissatisfied about the fact that the leadership of the ANC no longer want to return to South Africa and fight for freedom, they are having it nice in exile—enjoying luxurious life and doing nothing to advance the struggle for national liberation. Then suddenly we began to face problems at the various camps in Angola, there was a rebel group standing up against the ANC there in the camps in Angola, repeating some of the allegations broadcast by Radio RSA . . . the influence of the rebel group spread right through from Angola to Tanzania and Lusaka. This point was emphasised in Radio South Africa during that Radio South Africa news broadcast. Also, the ANC security and intelligence section monitored Radio South Africa broadcasts and proclaimed: "No, this is a concerted action influenced by the enemy," and that is when the ANC conducted a thorough security sweep within itself. Many people were arrested, and in Lusaka some people were beaten up very seriously, you know, in the course of this interrogation and arrests. They were sent to Angola, where they were jailed.[44]

In 1979 Radio RSA came to their rescue again as it provided the Angola-based ANC commissars with valuable information about pending military attacks by the South African Air Force's fighter jets. As a result, the ANC was able to avoid a massacre. Andrew Masondo accentuates:

> You know, in 1979 . . . the South African regime attacked us in Nova Ca-tengue ANC camp in Angola. . . . Now, before the actual attack, comrade Mzwai Piliso and I had a long discussion with Cuban comrades. This is after we had been listening to Radio South Africa, we heard John Vorster say they are going to attack a Swapo camp in Catengue. But we said: "Catengue is us, not Swapo." We discussed the Radio South Africa news broadcast with the Cubans, and we said to the Cubans, we must do something about saving our people if those South African Defense Force fighter jets attack. We had differ-ence and quarreled, the Cubans were saying: "No, it's not possible for the South African fighter jets to come here, it's too far for the bombs." We told them: "No! they are capable." We then went to inform their commander about the implications . . . that we disagree with his chaps, and we want to devise a strategy to defend MK cadres, and we got our chaps, MK cadres, to build dugouts, they built them. Yes, the South African air force attacked us.[45]

Masondo elaborates that in terms of implementation of a defensive strategy against the attack,

> comrade Mzwai and I changed the anti-aircraft positions, the South African Air Force [SAAF] attacked where the anti-aircraft positions were. They at-tacked the headquarters, they attacked the women's quarters with bombs, and they threw a lot of bombs at the Catengue MK camp. When that place was bombed, it was bombed when I was at the ANC headquarters in Luanda. I had to return the next day to the camp because I was one of the commissars. I got a report on my arrival from Luanda . . . in fact, at one point as we were analysing the damage, a South African fighter jet flew over, and we had to take cover, I took cover on a live bomb, which had not yet been defused . . . what happened, the SAAF came at a time, when MK cadres were just out of the breakfast hall, which was late. At that exact time, we wouldn't been at breakfast, we would have been on the parade, they would have been exposed in the open and they were going to hit them, but fortunately the chaps were underground, we had only 11 people above the ground . . . we only lost one South African, comrade whom we used to call, Chief, and one Cuban comrade, but if we hadn't taken those precautions with comrade Mzwai, we would have had a massacre of MK cadres.[46]

Now because the SAAF jet fired bombs at the same time when MK cadres were supposed to be involved in military drills, Masondo continues:

> We investigated the incident as we did with other security related incidents in the camps. We discovered that the chap, who poisoned our people earlier, just panicked, this planned attack should have happened when he had poisoned the

cadres at the camp. You can imagine if people were sick with running tum-
mies, as they did earlier in September, we would have had the whole camp
destroyed and all MK cadres dead. We would have had a massacre. Now, I
think he was worried about the consequences; we were beginning to suspect
him after the poison incident. . . . I think he also was scared. . . . I mean, the
signs were there that people were investigating, although we didn't say that to
people in the camp but . . . [47]

Radio RSA footprints extended into southern Africa and its programs were
extensive. I will use a case study underpinned by its broadcast of the following three historical events: the first meeting between President Kenneth
Kaunda and Prime Minister John Vorster on August 25–26, 1975; the Nkomati Accord signed between the republic of South Africa and Mozambique
on March 16, 1984; and the South African Defense Force cross-border raid
into Botswana that took place on June 14, 1985. [48]

In the Radio RSA broadcast on the Victoria Bridge conference in August
1975 it is noticeable that Vorster and Kaunda met Prime Minister Ian Smith
of Rhodesia, who was leading a five-man delegation; the opposing side included a twelve-member delegation representing a group called the African
National Council that was led by Abel Muzorewa. This twelve-member delegation incorporated delegates from the Zimbabwe African National Union,
Zimbabwe African People's Union, and the Front for the Liberation of Zimbabwe. Both Vorster and Kaunda were given the status of mediators who
promoted peace between black and white Rhodesians. Chris Morgan was the
newsreader for the BBC who mentioned that Vorster's stature was now being
transformed from a bogeyman to one of the most influential political leaders
in southern Africa. Other accolades referred to Vorster as the "leading states-
man in Africa." In his address Vorster mentioned that he was following the
proposals of the Lusaka Manifesto and therefore his commitment to dialogue
and peace in southern Africa because "wholly new vistas have been opened
with the prospect of détente in Southern Africa and the promise to end race
discrimination in South Africa." Friendly placards, which welcomed Vorster
at the luxurious hotel Musi-o-Tunya where president Kaunda was waiting,
read, "Vorster you are brave" and "Mr Vorster today you have become a
great man in Africa." On his return to South Africa, Vorster said, in an
address covered by Radio RSA, "it was certainly worthwhile that the minister of foreign affairs and I went to the Falls, not only with the view of talks
between the delegation of the Rhodesian prime minister, Mr. Smith, but also
especially for the opportunity which gave us to have a long and penetrating
discussion with Kenneth Kaunda of Zambia and his government. With regard
to Kaunda I was impressed with his sincere desire, just like South Africa's to
try and bring peace to Southern Africa."

Through the recordings by Radio RSA, we have recordings of the events
that were also covered by the BBC TV and the BBC Radio's famous ten

o'clock news with the unmistakable signature sound of Big Ben. The BBC referred to the talks as constitutional talks on Rhodesia and noted that the UK government was stymied by the new turn of events. It reported that "White-hall has been silent on the future of southern Africa which will be decided by southern Africans who are engaged in talks." The BBC radio news report also linked the talks to détente, Vorster's new strategy for South Africa's foreign policy.[49]

In September 1974, with the help of the French government, Vorster paid a secret visit to Houphouet-Boigny in Ivory Coast. In February 1975, he visited Liberia and held talks with President Tolbert. In short, during the 1970s South Africa was not isolated from the rest of the continent, as some would argue. But also, in 1974 the apartheid regime's efforts at pursuing its "outward looking policy" with African states collapsed as a result of the Portuguese coup of April 1974. Vorster was quick to grasp the implications of these profound political changes for the continued survival of apartheid South Africa. The imminent independence of Mozambique and Angola necessitated a change in terms of strategy from "outward looking policy" (or "dialogue") to "détente." Six months after the coup, Vorster launched his détente initiative—a variant of the earlier strategy. Détente was underpinned by a diplomatic strategy to try to delay more African countries, including South Africa, attaining independence. South Africa needed to formulate a strategy that would enable it to safeguard the position of the white minority during these changing times. Hilgard Muller confirmed this during a parliamentary debate in September 1974; in his response to a question from the floor, he admitted:

> Now I come to the events in Portugal since 25 April and their repercussions for Southern Africa and especially for our two neighbouring states Angola and Mozambique. The government has been keeping a very close check on and studying the situation all the time . . . and will not allow us to be caught off guard or on the wrong foot.[50]

One of the leading South African newspapers, the *Rand Daily Mail*, put forward the view that the Victoria Bridge talks were the highlight of détente in southern Africa.[51] Presenting a report about the talks to a South African audience during a luncheon at the Durban Club on October 31, 1975 (an event also covered by leading newspapers and by Radio RSA), Vorster informed his audience that:

> Now if you fail as far as Rhodesia is concerned, does that mean that your whole mission has failed? Then I want to say to you all in all earnestness that Rhodesia is but one aspect, but one facet of the whole problem. It does not mean of necessity that if you fail as far as Rhodesia is concerned, that the whole exercise has gone down the drain. Because what are the positive re-

sults? . . . we have achieved certain things. First, we no longer shout at each other from a distance, we talk to each other around a table . . . there is progress in every sense of the word. But secondly, we have built bridges, not only as far as the Rhodesia issue is concerned. We have built bridges between South Africa and many countries in Africa, and I stress the question of Africa, because it is clear to me that as far as the outside world is concerned we will never be able to sell ourselves to them unless we succeed in selling ourselves to Africa . . . we have opened certain avenues and lines of communication and I am not giving away secrets unnecessarily. [52]

Vorster was elaborating on what was not outside the diplomatic circles, links between the apartheid regime and the African continent. Various South African government departments were collaborating with their counterparts in the continent. These networks included parastatal institutions such as the Council for Scientific and Industrial Research, Bureau of Standards, Industrial Development Corporation, South African Broadcasting Corporation, Institute for Medical Research, and numerous other bodies that focused on hotels, mining, and agriculture. The private sector also extended its tentacles into the African continent; examples were health services that were being arranged by the Development and Management Foundation, which included management workshops and training courses for government representatives and businessmen from African states. [53]

Responding to the turn of events, an enlarged session of the ANC's National Executive Committee of March 17–20, 1975 met in Morogoro to debate the apartheid regime's strategic intentions. The deliberations focused on the inroads made by Vorster's government on the African continent. The ANC noted that for the first time in its twelve-year history, the OAU was convening a special session on South Africa. The ANC resolved not to take these important developments for granted but to use the opportunity they offered to stop Vorster's détente and dialogue policies. The ANC's strategy was now to consolidate its status as the "undisputed leader of the people's revolutionary onslaught against apartheid oppression" and to seek to convince as many African states as possible. [54] Representatives of the ANC's external missions were encouraged to use media—including Radio Freedom and *Sechaba*—to canvass mass public support. This meant projecting the ANC as the only viable alternative to the apartheid regime. The democratic international movements and other mass movements—such as the Anti-Apartheid Movements, the World Peace Council, Afro-Asian Peoples' Solidarity Organization (APPSO), Women's International Democratic Federation (WIDF), the Pan African Youth Movement (PAYM), and the World Federation of Democratic Youth (WFDY)—were to be encouraged to attend the forthcoming OAU special session on South Africa to strengthen the voice calling for economic sanctions and the international isolation of South Africa. The ANC's overall intention was to win friends and influence people. [55]

The Ninth Extraordinary Session of OAU Council of Ministers on South Africa duly met in Dar es Salaam from April 7 to 10, 1975. The ministers discussed their response to Vorster's cunning political maneuvers through détente. In his address, Tambo told the OAU session that the apartheid regime had responded to the 1974 Portuguese coup and the impending independence of Mozambique and Angola by launching its détente initiative, which was supported by the United States, France, Germany, and the United Kingdom as part of the Cold War. This was demonstrated in October 1974, when the United States sent its former assistant secretary of state for Africa, Donald Eassum, to lobby several African states in support of South Africa. The British foreign secretary also paid a visit to several African states and South Africa and in 1975 the French president visited the Central African Republic, where he met several leaders from Francophone Africa in a mini-summit. A high-level delegation from the Central African Republic had paid a "goodwill" visit to South Africa prior to the French president's visit.[56] They not only met Vorster but also had an opportunity of touring the soon-to-be independent Transkei on a "fact finding mission." Tambo further told the foreign ministers:

> The problem that Africa has to face in South Africa is essentially a colonial problem, and like colonialism elsewhere it has to be removed root and branch. . . . This is why the legitimacy of our armed struggle has been endorsed at successive meetings of the OAU and by the international community as a whole. It was reaffirmed by the East and Central African Heads of States in the Mogadishu Declaration. Earlier, as part of the struggle to transfer power to the majority in South Africa, independent Africa had adopted the demand of the African people for the complete international isolation of South Africa in all spheres—diplomatic, political, military, economic and cultural. The implementation of this policy was spearheaded and enforced by the OAU.

Tambo rejected détente as proposed by Vorster, which specifically excluded dialogue about the ways in which apartheid might be eliminated. He reassured the foreign ministers that the ANC would emerge victorious, regardless of Western support for apartheid.

> Our organisation is aware of the forces of evil and oppression that are arraigned against it. Events have fully borne out the fact that international imperialism is committed to defend and buttress the regime of terror in our country. We are also aware of the fact that with trickery and duplicity, our enemy is frantically attempting to seduce the so-called uncommitted forces all over the world. Time and irreversible course of events are, however, working in our favour. The revolutionary mood of the oppressed masses of our country is surging forward. The whole of the democratic world is on our side. We shall win.[57]

Even though Tambo predicted that the ANC would finally win the battle of the minds, it was really a tough struggle. The final session of the foreign ministers unanimously adopted the Dar es Salaam Declaration on South Africa. It confirmed that the OAU, like the UN, opposed the apartheid regime, not because it was white but because the regime rejected and fought against the principles of human equality and national self-determination. Despite Vorster's claims at the end of 1974 that given six months the world would be surprised by the changes that would be initiated from within apartheid South Africa, in April 1975 the situation in South Africa had taken a turn for the worse as evidenced by the mass trial of the students, the consolidation and strengthening of the bantustans, and the vast increase in South Africa's military budget. Clearly, Vorster's government was not about to ditch apartheid. If anything, Vorster's measures had been designed to strengthen the security of the system within South Africa. Confronted with this intransigent determination of the apartheid regime to maintain racial discrimination, "Africa should continue to maintain the economic, political and cultural boycott of South Africa. The OAU and the UN should work in concert for the total isolation of the apartheid regime."[58]

The Dar es Salaam Declaration observed further that there was nothing to be gained by the leaders of free Africa talking to the leaders of apartheid South Africa. If the current or future leaders of the apartheid regime "should desire to begin to move away from the policy of racism in South Africa and to seek cooperation of Africans to that end, they could initiate the necessary contacts and negotiations from within." The Dar es Salaam Declaration also underscored the importance of all African states to "remain firmly united in the policy of isolating South Africa and ostracising the apartheid regime." It reiterated support to the national liberation movements of South Africa and called for the intensification of international efforts to eradicate apartheid.[59]

But when Vorster was ousted in 1978, the apartheid regime continued with its efforts to try to foster relations with African countries. It continued to use Radio RSA as a communication channel to broadcast its policies. If we analyze the radio programs dedicated to the signing of the Nkomati Accord, we note that the SABC had a multi-faceted strategy in terms of addressing different audiences within and outside the borders of South Africa; it broadcast in southern Sotho through Radio Sesotho based in Bloemfontein and the footprint of this FM station extended to Lesotho; it also used Afrikaans, English, and Portuguese; all these languages covered southern Africa. The broadcast in Portuguese focused on Samora Machel's speech, including the opinions of Portuguese-speaking current affairs analysts; its footprint included Angola, Mozambique, and South Africa, and probably Portugal and Guinea Bissau if the shortwave broadcasting could reach those shores. What is interesting in the Portuguese broadcasting schedule is the entry reading "restrict none," meaning that there was to be no censorship. The SABC had to be extra careful since Machel's speech was also broadcast in apartheid South Africa and there were possibilities that the president of Mozambique might articulate propagandist views that supported the liberation struggle in Africa. But because this was a different historical event the powers that might have been at the SABC were conscious that the chances of this taking place were not high. Machel's speech was businesslike and also contextualized the importance of the Lusaka Manifesto in terms of promoting peace, conflict-resolution mechanisms, and the commendable role of President Kaunda in promoting peace in southern Africa—including the geopolitics and geo-economic development of the SADCC region. Although listening to voices and broadcasts by leaders of the banned ANC and leaders of the frontline states who were their supporters could land one in jail, Machel's speech made history. It was the first time that the apartheid regime did not censure a speech from a leader who supported what it perceived as a terrorist organization. Machel's voice bellowed from radio stations in apartheid South Africa.[60] For example, Radio RSA's archival record of the Nkomati Accord collection is as follows:

SERVICE: AFRIKAANSE DIENS

CLASS: DOKUMENTER

PROGRAM MONITOR: BRANDPUNT

TITLE: NKOMATI-VERDRAG

CONCEPT: 'N PROGRAM OOR DIE AGTERGROND EN BETEKE-NIS VAN DIE VERDRAG VAN NKOMATI TUSSEN SUID-AFRIKA EN MOSAMBIEK SAAMGESTEL DEUR ANDRIES CORNELIUS

CATNO: T 84/192

RECORDBC: 19840316

DURATION: 18:25

PRODUCER: CORNELIUS ANDRIES

PARTPERF: CORNELIUS ANDRIES, AD OMROEPER SAUK

REFER: SOUTH-AFRICA MOZAMBIQUE KOMATIEPOORT

RECTECHN

SERVICE: RADIO SESOTHO

CLASS: ACTUALITY

TITLE: NKOMATI ACCORD RSA AND MOZAMBIQUE

CONCEPT: A SPECIAL PROGRAMME IN WHICH WE TAKE A LOOK AT THE DESCRIPTION OF THE PROCESSION LEADING TOWARDS THE WHITE TRAIN COACH WHERE THE ACCORD WAS TO BE SIGNED BY HIS EXCELLENCY SAMORA MACHEL AND THE HONOURABLE PRIME MINISTER PW BOTHA

CATNO: BT(SS/84)4

RECORDBC: 19840316

DURATION 30: OO

CONTENTS: A DESCRIPTION OF THE PROCESSION OF SIGNA-TORIES OF BOTH COUNTRIES SA AND MOZAMBIQUE LEADING TOWARDS THE WHITE TRAIN COACH WHERE THE ACCORD WAS TO BE SIGNED

PARTPERF LEKHELEBANE SEBOTA:

SERVICE: RADIO RSA: PORTUGUESE SERVICE

CLASS: SPEECH

PROGRAM: PRESIDENT SAMORA MOISES MACHEL

TITLE: PRESIDENT SAMORA MOISES MACHEL

CONCEPT: A SPEECH BY PRESIDENT SAMORA MOISES MACH-EL OF MOZAMBIQUE DURING THE SIGNING OF THE NKOMATI ACCORD

CATNO: T 86/303

RECORDBC: 19840316

DURATION: 19:15

RESTRICT: NONE

PARTPERF MACHEL SAMORA MOISES, PRES, MOZAMBIQUE

REFER: NKOMATI-ACCORD

RECTECHN

VIEWNAME ARCACTIV

The Radio Sesotho program was different. It was based on translating P. W. Botha's English version of his speech at Nkomati. In the opening parts of this speech Botha trumpeted an interpretation of Afrikaner nationalist history as he claimed that South Africa was the first country to confront colonialism but emphasized white Afrikaner resistance against the British colonizers, including the Anglo-Boer War. He also mentioned the "scramble for Africa" as one of the reasons that exacerbated differences among Africans, including the fact that existing borders were arbitrarily drawn and decided by the colonizers, including Portugal. He therefore contextualized the Nkomati Accord as an exercise in conflict resolution in southern Africa, which was enmeshed in anti-colonial struggles for centuries.

Other guests included Prince Bhekimpi Dlamini, prime minister of Swaziland, and other official guests from Malawi. Swaziland and South Africa had already signed a secret peace agreement in 1982. It is worth pointing out that only two indigenous South African languages are spoken in Mozambique, Tsonga, and isiZulu, and one would have expected that the broadcast was going to be in these two languages. The broadcast was in Sesotho, perhaps in order to persuade the Lesotho government to follow suit; and later the government of Botswana might be persuaded to sign a treaty. But, as we will discuss later, both these countries were attacked by the SADF during cross-border raids broadcast on Radio RSA.

This program, officially dubbed "Tlhakisetso," was produced by Lekhelebane Sebota, but the announcer was Mosolodi Mohapi, who was responsible for the voice-over and interpretation and translation of Machel's speech in Portuguese and P. W. Botha's English speech into Sesotho. Botha's speech focused on peace and conflict resolution. He also used the occasion to address issues of poverty, disease, ignorance, and other socioeconomic ills in southern Africa. Botha argued that South Africa and Mozambique should work for promoting stability and peace in order to uplift the standard of living in both countries. What was interesting in this broadcast was the use of Miriam Makeba's signature *mbaqanga* tune, a freedom song celebrating the struggle for national liberation in Mozambique; the lyrics glorify the people of Mozambique and Makeba refers to herself as one of them, hence the lyrics, "my people, my people," "my brothers and sisters." She also invokes the stature of a heroic Samora Machel, as a great African leader in the forefront of the liberation struggle, by repeatedly calling out Machel's name and the famous slogan "a luta continua." This impressive and catchy song was used throughout the program as an opening and closing tune. It is important to remember that freedom songs were banned by the SABC—including the music of Makeba, who was a prominent cultural activist and a member of the ANC. She was also banned by the SABC and was not part of the official playlist so she would not be interviewed by SABC disc jockeys.

The Afrikaans broadcast was very different. Botha's speech was fiery—the tone and intonation were forceful enough to be termed belligerent, which was understandable; his main audiences were white Afrikaner nationalists and committed white supporters of the apartheid regime. This broadcast included current affairs broadcast by Radio RSA, anchored by Andries Cornelius. In Afrikaans, he interviewed senior white historians and political scientists from the University of the Free State, University of South Africa, University of Port Elizabeth, and University of Pretoria. These academics offered different interpretations of the Nkomati Accord with the professor from the University of Port Elizabeth, noting that such a historic agreement had a precedent in terms of both the geo-economics and geo-strategic facts because the old South African Republic under the rule of prime minister Paul Kruger wanted access to the sea via Delagoa Bay in Lourenço Marques, then controlled by the Portuguese colonizers. Their analysis was predicated on what they construed as Botha's foreign policy on Africa as a continent, particularly the policy on the Constellation of African States (Consas); they argued that the Nkomati Accord was part of this strategy.[61]

But there was a noticeable difference in the way John Vorster and P. W. Botha dealt with the "Africa question" during radio broadcasts. P. W. Botha, a former minister of defense in Vorster's government, preferred military confrontation to resolve challenges facing the apartheid regime as far as relations with other African countries were concerned. In the end, however, resistance from the majority of OAU members and certain dynamics within the apartheid regime undermined Vorster's diplomatic efforts at détente. When Vorster was ousted and P. W. Botha assumed power in 1978, he adopted an official policy that he called "total strategy." This led to the restructuring of South Africa's regional policy in important ways. Botha emphasized the idea of a "constellation of states" and this became his regional objective. Neighboring states were to be lured into "a regional alliance" in which South Africa would play a pivotal role.

To the uneducated eye, these dramatic diplomatic maneuvers seem to suggest that they would bring peace to the region. But the opposite was true. The whole exercise was accompanied by the regime's propaganda campaign, referring to the "open-minded" and "considerate" South African government that cared for its "needy" neighbors. Unsurprisingly, many of the ANC's allies were confused by this turn of events, but others could see what the apartheid regime was trying to do—bolster white minority rule, which was becoming increasingly shaky. The ANC was under no misapprehension. Despite the Nkomati Accord, which the regime had pressured Mozambique to sign, the ANC never wavered from seeing Mozambique, its government, and the Front for Liberation of Mozambique (Frelimo) as its allies and friends. It had no intention of denouncing Samora Machel; its attack was directed against the apartheid regime.

But Botha adopted a carrot-and-stick approach defined by the cross-border raids into southern African countries, and thus the 1985 attacks in Botswana. The most gruesome attack on members of the liberation movements and some Batswana citizens was the raid in June 1985. Prior to this there had been several bombings by South African agents targeting so-called terrorists. On February 13, 1983, a bomb destroyed the home of South African refugees in a suburb called Jinja.[62] Earlier, a refugee, Nat Serache, had become suspicious when he noticed several cars in the area with South African number plates. He remained alert and watchful in his home and when the attackers arrived, he escaped through the back door; a bomb reduced his home to rubble.[63]

Another bomb killed Nathan Moagi Mooketse on May 14, 1985 when he tried to start his car. The bomb was so powerful that his "body was blown to pieces, while shrapnel from the ill-fated sedan was sent flying in all directions."[64] Another bomb killed four people and two were injured in the village of Mochudi.[65] The dead included Ramontsho Ralefala (age thirty-two); Charity Mokoko (twenty-one); Mmilo Molotsi (six); and Tumelo Molotsi (one). These bombings and others were the prelude to the June 14 raid—they were in fact a warning that more would come, because the Pretoria regime believed that there were ten ANC hideouts in Gaborone from which the ANC was planning to launch subversive activities.[66]

The June 14, 1985 raid took place in the early hours of the morning. The Botswana-based *Guardian* newspaper described the incident as follows:

> a convoy of 12 white Datsun E20 kombis and six Ford Cortina vans had rumbled across the border, somewhere in the region of Tlokweng gate. Behind them, it is rumoured, waited a back-up force of tanks and armoured vehicles in case the operation should run into trouble. At the Tlokweng round-about, the vehicles split up, each with its own target of the so-called terrorist bases. The road to the Tlokweng border gate was littered . . . with thousands of pyramid shaped twists of wire designed to shred tyres. Then the killers got to business.[67]

The Batswana citizens killed included Eugena Kakale Kobole (a student at the Catholic Cathedral commercial school in Gaborone) and Gladys Kelape Kesupile (a housemaid). The rest of the victims were South African refugees. At Tuli Court in Gaborone, Dick Nkukwana Mtsweni (refugee) was killed while Ellen Mtsweni and Busisiwe were injured; at Tsholofelo, Cecil George Phahle (refugee) and Lindiwe Maude Phahle (refugee) were killed; and at Tshweneng, Joseph Malaza (a visiting South African student) and Amos Zondi (refugee and businessman) were killed. Also, in Gaborone near Maruapula, Themba Duke Machobane (refugee and teacher) and Peter Kamohelo Mafoka (refugee) were killed. In Gaborone's Extension 10, Michael Frank Hamlyn (a second-year science student at the University of Botswana and treasurer of the Medu Ensemble) and Ahmed Gheer (a Dutch citizen of Somali origin with association to the liberation struggle) were killed. [68]

After these raids, General Constand Viljoen the chief of the SADF conducted a media briefing that was broadcast by Radio RSA. He pleaded innocent of the murder of the citizens of Botswana and insisted that the casualties were well-known ANC "terrorists." He inferred that attacks were conducted because they had received reliable intelligence that the ANC was planning to intensify raids into South Africa in June 1985 and therefore the SADF's strike was meant as a deterrent. Their strategy was based on a lightning attack that would allow the SADF to enter Gaborone, hit their target, and leave rapidly to avoid engaging the Botswana Defense Force. Viljoen claimed that only one Botswana citizen had been killed; he had listened to Botswana's English radio broadcast, which announced that two children were wounded during the attack and probably one of them had died afterward. The operation was a great success as far as he was concerned and he informed journalists that white tourists from other parts of the world were safe, offering them assurance by claiming that "Botswana is safe, we take a lot of time planning carefully and caring, [white] tourists will not be affected." [69] The majority of white South Africans believed this propaganda spewed by their leader, and believed that damage during the cross-border raid was negligible and casualties did not include citizens of sovereign countries attacked by the SADF.

CONCLUSION

The apartheid regime considered propaganda a vital weapon in its efforts to secure internal and external support for its racist policies. The perspective was set out by the then minister of posts and telegraphs, Hertzog, when in 1964 the SABC established Radio Bantu as a broadcasting network for Africans. The minister opined:

> The radio is the only way to get through to the Bantu and to reach his soul. It has an important role to play in the creation of good relations and goodwill between white and black. . . . The establishment of Radio Bantu is an even greater security measure for the country than the police force, and for that reason the whole population must help put it on sound footing. [70]

The same view can be extended to the formation of Radio RSA. The Radio Bantu message was specific and placed emphasis on language and separate identity such as the Sesotho language and Basotho; it focused on bantustans and the advantages of ethnicity and separate development. This can be contrasted with the messages beamed by Radio RSA outside the borders of South Africa that focused on what it defined as the "tribal conflicts" and "oppression by majorities" in independent African countries; the dangers posed by "communism" in countries such as Angola and Mozambique, and the dangers of the presence of "the Cubans in Angola." The use of Radio RSA to promote the sudden conversion of the apartheid regime to "dialogue" and "détente" in the 1970s was a tactic designed to cope with collapsing Portuguese colonialism. Similarly, the so-called reforms of the 1980s were a response to continuing resistance, the escalating armed struggle, and the mounting international pressure. As a result, the apartheid regime used Radio RSA to undermine the SADCC, preventing the consolidation of independence of countries in the region, weakening them by military, political, and economic actions and various forms of destabilization thereby trying to ensure these regional countries were unable to support the liberation movements or withstand incorporation into South Africa's sphere of influence. This is what the Nkomati Accord stood for.[71]

NOTES

1. S. M. Ndlovu, "The ANC's Diplomacy and International Relations," in *Road to Democracy in South Africa, Volume 2 [1970–1980]*, ed. South African Democracy Education Trust (hereafter SADET), chapter 12 (Pretoria: Unisa Press, 2006); S. M. Ndlovu, "The Geopolitics of Apartheid South Africa in the African Continent: 1948–1994," in *Road to Democracy in South Africa: Volume 5, African Solidarity, Part 1*, ed. SADET, chapter 1 (Pretoria: Unisa Press, 2014). See also J. Laurence, *The Seeds of Disaster: A Guide to the Realities, Race Politics and Worldwide Propaganda Campaign of the Republic of South Africa* (London: Gollancz, 1968), 78; A. Magnusson, *The Voice of South Africa* (Uppsala: Nordic Afrika Institute, 1975), Research Report No 35, 15–17; South African Department of Information Annual Report (Pretoria: Government Printers, 1972).

2. L. de Villiers, *Secret Information* (Cape Town: Tafelberg, 1980), 98; E. Rhoodie, *The Real Information Scandal* (Pretoria and Atlanta: Orbis, 1983), chapters 4 and 5.

3. University of the Western Cape (UWC), Mayibuye Archives, ANC-London Papers, MCH02-9, Box 9; see letter from the ANC addressed to Mr. Idris, UNESCO officer in Dar es Salaam, October 16, 1979.

4. "Countering Apartheid Propaganda," *Sechaba*, July 1985, 8–9.

5. Ibid.

6. R. B. Horwitz, *Communication and Democratic Reform in South Africa* (Cambridge: Cambridge University Press, 2001), 73; A. Hepple, *Censorship and Press Control in South Africa* (Johannesburg: self-published, 1960).

7. SABC magazine, *This Is the SABC* (Johannesburg: SABC, n.d.), 6; "Countering Apartheid Propaganda," *Sechaba*, July 1985, 10.

8. South African Parliamentary House of Assembly Debates (Hansard), May 21, 1965, columns 6476–6477.

9. Ibid.

10. South African Parliamentary House of Assembly Debates (Hansard), May 21, 1965, column 6478.

11. *SABC Magazine*, "This Is the SABC," 6.

12. *SABC Magazine*, "This Is the SABC," 8–9.

13. Laurence, *Seeds of Disaster*, 78.

14. Ibid., 155.

15. Magnusson, *Voice of South Africa*, 25.

16. Ibid. See also SABC Annual Reports, 1969, 1970, 1971, and 1972.

17. Magnusson, *Voice of South Africa*, 27. On South Africa's foreign policy, see S. M. Ndlovu, "The ANC and the World," in *Road to Democracy in South Africa*, ed. SADET, chapter 13 (Cape Town: Struik, 2004); Ndlovu, "Geopolitics of Apartheid South Africa"; R. Pfister, "Apartheid South Africa's Foreign Relations with African States, 1961–1994" (PhD diss., Rhodes University, 2003); S. Nolutshungu, *South Africa in Africa: A Study of Ideology and Foreign Policy* (Manchester, UK: Manchester University Press, 1975).

18. Ndlovu, "ANC's Diplomacy and International Relations"; Ndlovu, "ANC and the World."

19. *Africa Contemporary Record, 1969–1970*, "Lusaka Manifesto on Southern Africa: Joint Statement by Thirteen Governments, Lusaka" (April 1969), C 41. See also Ndlovu, "ANC's Diplomacy and International Relations."

20. University of Fort Hare (hereafter UFH), ANC Archives, Oliver Reginald Tambo (hereafter ORT) Papers, "The Report of the (Morogoro) Secretariat covering the last two years, 1971"; UFH, ANC Archives, "The Aggressive and Expansionist Foreign Policy of the White Minority Regime of South Africa"; T. Mbeki, "Domestic and Foreign Policies of New South Africa," *Perspective and Policy Options*, Carleton University, Ottawa, February 1978, 19–22; Ndlovu, "ANC's Diplomacy and International Relations"; S. Thomas, *The Diplomacy of Liberation: The Foreign Relations of the African National Congress since 1960* (London: I. B. Tauris, 1996); C. Legum, "Dialogue: Africa's Great Debate," *Africa Contemporary Record Special Issues Series* (London: Rex Collings, 1972).

21. UFH, ANC Archives, ORT Papers, Box 17, Statement by O. R. Tambo, Acting President General of the African National Congress of South Africa to the Ninth Extraordinary Session of the Council of Foreign Ministers of the Organisation of African Unity held in Dar es Salaam from April 1975. See also the editorial by R. Uwechue, "Real-Politik," *Africa* 45, May 1975, 11.

22. UFH, ANC Archives, ORT Papers, Box 35, "ANC and Information Policy."

23. The ANC has deposited important archival materials that includes films, videos, music cassettes, and records as part of the ANC Archives at UFH. See also "The Fantastic 'Amandla,'" *Sechaba*, July 1981; Ndlovu, "ANC's Diplomacy and International Relations."

24. UFH, ANC Archives, ORT Papers, Box 34, Statement of the NEC broadcast by Radio Freedom on the sixty-seventh anniversary of the foundation of the ANC, January 8, 1979; UFH, ANC Archives, ORT Papers, Box 17, transcribed copy of an interview with Comrade Oliver Tambo, president of the African National Congress of South Africa, Radio Freedom, Madagascar, May 31, 1980.

25. UFH, ANC Archives, London Papers, Box 18, ANC Submission, "The Liberation of South Africa: Perspectives," International Conference of Experts for the Support of Victims of Colonialism and Apartheid in Southern Africa, Oslo, April 9, 1973.

26. J. Ngani, "Voice of Freedom: Clandestine ANC Propaganda Inside South Africa," *Sechaba*, Fourth Quarter, 1976; UFH, ANC Archives, ORT Papers, Box 31, Statement of the African National Congress of South Africa to the Conference of Foreign Ministers of the Coordinating Bureau of Non-Aligned Countries, New Delhi, 1977; statement made by African National Congress of South Africa Delegation to the sixth Pan African Congress held in Dar es Salaam, June 19–27, 1974; UFH, ANC Archives, Lusaka Papers, Box 4, "The Racist South Africa Regime is Not A Sovereign and Independent State"; UFH, ANC Archives, Lusaka Papers, Box 5, "Memorandum Submitted by the African National Congress to the UN Committee of Twenty-Four on Decolonisation," Dar es Salaam, May 30, 1970; UFH, ANC Archives, ORT Papers, Box 29, "Memorandum of the African National Congress to the UN Special Committee on Colonialism." On the ideological role of pamphlets see I. Greig, *Subversion,*

Propaganda, Agitation and the Spread of People's War (London: Tom Stacey, 1973), chapter 1; See also V. I. Lenin, *What Is To Be Done?* (London: Panther Books, 1970) on the question of establishing or using an underground newspaper or journal as one of the most effective weapons for propaganda purposes.

27. UWC, Mayibuye Archives, ANC London Papers, "The Battle for South Africa: Armed Resistance in South Africa." See also in the same collection Anti-Apartheid Movement National Action Conference on "Southern Africa after Zimbabwe," May 31, 1980.

28. "Colonial Border Industries," *Sechaba*, January 1970; "The Case against Winnie Mandela," *Sechaba*, March 1979; "Inside South Africa: Apartheid in Crisis," *Sechaba*, April 1981; UFH, ANC Archives, ANC Morogoro Papers, Box 4, "Brief on Exposes [*sic*] of British Business in South Africa," Morogoro, March 28, 1973; UFH, ANC Archives, ORT Papers, Box 29, Report on the South African Defense Force.

29. UFH, ANC Archives, Lusaka Papers, Box 5, Report: Re African-American Institute Conference, January 24, 1972; UFH, ANC Archives, Lusaka Papers, Box 77, Re: Invitation to attend the fourth African Association of Political Science Conference in Maputo, April 9–12, 1979.

30. UFH, ANC Archives, ORT Papers, Box 35, W. Geisler, "The Military Cooperation between the Federal Republic of Germany and South Africa in the Nuclear and Conventional Field," FRG AAM, West Berlin, May 1978; see in the same collection, B. Rivers, "The Role of South African Oil and of Western Oil Companies and Possibilities of Oil Embargo against South Africa," testimony before the United Nations Special Committee Against Apartheid, December 1, 1977.

31. UFH, ANC Archives, Lusaka Papers, Box 8, November 1975, ANC Toronto Committee, "Multinational Corporations and the Perpetuation of Apartheid in South Africa," paper prepared for the World Conference on Multinational Corporations, Toronto; UFH, ANC Archives, London Mission papers, Box 20, "New Zealand AAM, Apartheid: A Conference to Examine New Zealand's Relationship with Racism and Colonialism in Southern Africa."

32. South African Parliamentary House of Assembly Debates, March 4, 1977, col. 2781.

33. Interview with Pallo Jordan conducted by Luli Callinicos, April 12, 1993.

34. UFH, ANC Archives, ORT Papers, Box 35, "ANC and Information Policy."

35. UWC, ANC-London Papers, MCH02-9, Box 9, Mayibuye Archives, letter addressed to Mr. Idris, UNESCO officer in Dar es Salaam, from the ANC, October 16, 1979.

36. See UFH, ANC Archives, Lusaka Papers, Box 36, Zambia Broadcasting Services, "External Service," April, May, and June 1980. Radio Freedom broadcast in the 31 meter band short wave, unless otherwise stated. The transmission times were Central and South African. Radio Freedom Madagascar broadcast in the 49- and 60-meter bands; Rebecca Matlou was in charge. See also the available Radio Freedom transcripts and memoranda and reports about the ANC's propaganda division.

37. UFH, ANC Archives, Lusaka Papers, Box 36, ANC Archives, "Minutes of Mayibuye Staff Meeting," August 22, 1980; memorandum on Mayibuye to the Department of Information and Publicity and Office of the President, March 25, 1980.

38. UFH, ORT Papers, Box 35, ANC Archives, Marius and Jeanette Schoon, "A Report on the South African Situation"; V. Matlou, "South Africa: Social Production, Social Deprivation and Social Emancipation" (paper presented at the CODESRIA Conference on "Another Development for Southern Africa," University of Zambia, Lusaka, September 3–7, 1979. See also UWC, Mayibuye Archives, ANC-London Papers, MCH02-9, Box 9, on manuscripts about a film/play on Mandela and a plan of a cartoon magazine project concerning the struggle for liberation.

39. UFH, ANC Archives, Lusaka Papers, Box 36, DIP-Research (Lusaka) Progress Report, ANC. See also acquisitions lists for the ANC Library in the same collection.

40. UFH, ORT Papers, Box 35, ANC's Department of Information and Publicity, "Re: RADIO FREEDOM (SA) MINIMAL AND URGENT REQUISITION," October 25, 1978. See also UWC, Mayibuye Archives, ANC-London Papers, MCH02-9, Box 9, Radio Freedom broadcast, "n NUWE WOONBUURTE VIR CROSSROADS," October 4, 1978; "WAAROM HAAT HULLE DIE KOMMUNISTE." See also the interview with Pallo Jordan conducted by Luli Callinicos.

41. Interview with Murphy Morobe conducted by Ben Magubane and Greg Houston, March 3, 2004, SADET Oral History Project.

42. On Radio Freedom, see S. P. Lekgoathi, "The ANC's Radio Freedom , Its Audiences and the Struggle against Apartheid, 1963–1991," in *The Road to Democracy in South Africa, Volume 6, 1990–1996*, ed. SADET, chapter 13 (Pretoria: Unisa Press, 2013).

43. South African Institute of Race Relations (SAIRR), *Race Relations Survey, 1986, Part 1* (Johannesburg: SAIRR, 1987), 132.

44. Interview with Andrew Masondo conducted by Sifiso Mxolisi Ndlovu, SADET Oral History Project, May 15. 2001. About the rebellion in various MK camps and commission of inquiry in Angola see www:/anc.org.za/historical docs.

45. Interview with Andrew Masondo conducted by Sifiso Mxolisi Ndlovu.

46. Ibid.

47. Ibid.

48. For elaborate discussion of these historical events, see SADET, The Road to Democracy in South Africa, multi-volume series.

49. Radio RSA broadcasts in possession of the author.

50. South African Parliamentary House of Assembly debates, September 10, 1974, columns 2588 and 2589.

51. *Rand Daily Mail*, August 20, 1975.

52. O. Geyser, ed. *B. J. Vorster: Select Speeches* (Bloemfontein: INCH, University of the Free State, 1977), 282.

53. South African Parliamentary House of Assembly debates, March 7, 1975, column 2186.

54. UFH, ANC Archives, Lusaka Papers, Box 74, O. R. Tambo, Presidential Address submitted to the extended meeting of the National Executive of the ANC held in Morogoro, March 1975.

55. Ibid.; UFH, ANC Archives, Morogoro Papers, Declaration of the African National Congress Executive Committee-Morogoro March 17–20, 1975.

56. UFH, ANC Archives, ORT Papers, Box 17, Statement by O. R. Tambo, Acting President General of the African National Congress of South Africa to the Ninth Extraordinary Session of the Council of Foreign Ministers of the Organisation of African Unity, held in Dar es Salaam from April 1975. See also "Africa at Dar es Salaam," *Africa* 45 (May 1975), 15–17; R. Uwuche, "Real-Politic," *Africa* 45 (May 1975), 11; "African Strategy in Southern Africa" (paper presented by Tanzania to the Ninth Extraordinary Session of the OAU Council of Ministers, April 1975), 11.

57. Statement by O. R. Tambo, Acting President General of the African National Congress of South Africa to the Ninth Extraordinary Session of the Council of Foreign Ministers of the Organisation of African Unity; also cited as O. R. Tambo, "Increase Our Strike Power," Statement to the Ninth Extraordinary Session of the Council of Foreign Ministers of the OAU, Dar es Salaam, April 1975, in A. Tambo, *Preparing for Power: Oliver Tambo Speaks* (London: Heinemann, 1987), 95.

58. *Africa* 45 (May 1975), "The Dar es Salaam Declaration," 18–19.

59. Ibid.

60. South African Broadcasting Corporation (SABC) Archives, Radio RSA broadcasts about Nkomati Accord and Botswana.

61. South African Broadcasting Corporation (SABC) Archives, Radio RSA broadcasts about Nkomati Accord and Botswana.

62. P. T. Mgadla and B. Mokopakgosi, "Botswana and the Liberation Struggle of South Africa: An Evolving Story of Sacrifice," in *Road to Democracy in South Africa: Volume 5, African Solidarity, Part 1*, ed. SADET, chapter 10 (Pretoria: Unisa Press, 2013); L. Nyelele and E. Drake, *The Raid on Gaborone: June 14, 1985: A Memorial* (Gaborone: self-published, 1987), 5. Jinja is a suburb in the northern part of Gaborone.

63. Mgadla and Mokopakgosi, "Botswana and the Liberation Struggle of South Africa"; Nyelele and Drake, *Raid on Gaborone*.

64. Ibid.

65. Nyelele and Drake, *Raid on Gaborone*, 4.

66. Ibid., 6.

67. BNARS, (Botswana) *Guardian*, June 19, 1985; and article by G. Ansell, *Guardian*, June 19, 1985.

68. See Mgadla and Mokopakgosi, "Botswana and the Liberation Struggle of South Africa."

69. Radio RSA broadcasts in possession of the author.

70. *Die Transvaler*, March 4, 1964.

71. Ndlovu, "Geopolitics of Apartheid South Africa"; C. Legum, *Southern Africa: The Secret Diplomacy of Détente* (London: Rex Collings, 1975).

Chapter Ten

Radio Freedom, Black Consciousness, and the Struggle for Liberation in South Africa

Tshepo Moloi

In 1953, five years after ascending to power, the National Party (NP) won a landslide victory in the whites-only general elections in South Africa. This convinced the party that it had the support of the majority of the white population and it became fixated on upholding white supremacy. The Congress Alliance, led by the African National Congress (ANC), and the Pan Africanist Congress (PAC), which had split from the ANC in 1958, opposed the NP regime. However, on April 8, 1960, a few weeks after the gruesome shooting of anti-pass protesters in Sharpeville, the regime responded by proscribing the ANC and PAC. For the next thirty years the two movements executed the struggle for liberation from exile.[1]

Although the ANC and PAC were banned from operating legally, the regime could not totally suppress their political ideologies. To inspire and reassure their members that they still existed inside the country, the two movements established military wings. The ANC launched uMkhonto we Sizwe (MK, the Spear of the Nation) and the PAC, Poqo (later renamed the Azanian People's Liberation Army, or APLA). MK embarked on a sabotage campaign by blowing up the regime's properties throughout the major cities in the country between 1961 and 1963.[2] Poqo, on the other hand, planned to attack and kill whites and Africans perceived to be collaborating with the regime.[3]

In 1961, the leadership of the Congress Alliance established Radio Freedom (then known as "Freedom Radio" or "ANC Radio") secretly. In his chapter in this volume and elsewhere, Sekibakiba Lekgoathi elaborates on this radio's first and only broadcast from inside the country.[4]

In 1963 the regime managed to quell the campaigns by the ANC and PAC when it arrested en masse the leadership and members of the two movements. Many were imprisoned for long spells on Robben Island. Those who escaped the regime's net fled into exile and a few operated underground.

In exile, the ANC and PAC devised ways of communicating with their members and potential supporters in South Africa, which included underground units scattered across the country, through print media, and guerrilla radio. This chapter will focus on the latter, especially the ANC's Radio Freedom, which was revived in exile in the mid-1960s. For its part, the PAC established "The Voice of the Pan Africanist Congress of Azania," which broadcast from African countries where it was based (see Ali Khangela Hlongwane's chapter in this book).[5] Radio Freedom's functioning from exile happened during the time when the Black Consciousness Movement (BCM) was active and vibrant. This chapter will argue that through programs broadcast on Radio Freedom the ANC's politics were revived inside the country (Radio Freedom's transmissions also assured the supporters of the ANC in South Africa that the movement existed in exile). More importantly, the chapter will contend that Radio Freedom exposed many of the supporters of the BCM to the ANC and its politics, and also inspired some to flee the country to join the ANC's military wing in exile. To achieve the above, the chapter will, inter alia, discuss how members of the BCM within South Africa were exposed to Radio Freedom, how they listened to it, and how they interpreted the message or messages they received from it.

Substantial work on radio in South Africa and elsewhere in Africa has been produced,[6] but little scholarly attention has been paid to the role of guerrilla radio or liberation radio in the struggle for liberation. Notable exceptions are Marissa Moorman, who has written on two of Angola's guerrilla radios, Angola Combatente aligned to the People's Movement for the Liberation of Angola, and the National Liberation Front of Angola's Voz de Angola Livre; Mhoze Chikowero on guerrilla radio in Zimbabwe; and Lebona Mosia et al., Sekibakiba Lekgoathi, and Stephen Davis on South Africa's Radio Freedom.[7] For the purpose of this chapter, the publications by the three last-named are most important because their focus is on Radio Freedom, starting from the reason Radio Freedom was established and how it broadcast from South Africa (albeit briefly) in the early 1960s and then shifting focus to Radio Freedom's operating from exile. In certain respects their work is distinct though. Mosia, Riddle, and Zaffiro, for example, provide an overview of Radio Freedom's operations in exile and how the radio expanded from broadcasting from Tanzania, then being provided with broadcasting time on Radio Zambia External Services in 1972, then Radio Luanda External Services in Angola in 1977, and two years later on Radio Madagascar.[8] Lekgoathi, on the other hand, goes further and discusses how Radio Freedom was structured under the ANC's Department of Information and Publicity (DIP).

He also writes about the programs and content broadcast on Radio Freedom in the 1970s through to the 1980s. More notably, Lekgoathi elaborates on aspects of listenership in South Africa during the 1970s, which is particularly important for my own work.[9] Using oral interviews, I also demonstrate how the proponents of the Black Consciousness Movement (BCM) listened to Radio Freedom.

Davis, in his work, centers Radio Freedom within the tension that was brewing between the ANC and the South African Communist Party (SACP) in exile. He contends that the ANC, through its National Intelligence and Security unit, commonly known as Mbokodo (Grinding Stone), exerted pressure on the staff of the DIP responsible for Radio Freedom, to not "stray away from the external image of the movement from the SACP's policies and objectives."[10] The main issue for Davis was that the members of Mbokodo were concerned that the DIP staff, many of whom were Western-educated and were able to source funding from the Western nations, might, if given free rein, use Radio Freedom to tarnish the image of the communist-led countries, particularly the USSR. This was the era of the Cold War, and the USSR was the major supporter of the ANC, monetarily and militarily.

As to its methodology, this chapter is based primarily on oral history interviews with former supporters of the BCM, some of whom later joined the ANC. Because it was illegal to listen to Radio Freedom in South Africa, the interviews help to shed some light about the risk involved. They also help us to understand the methods people used to listen to Radio Freedom. Additionally, secondary sources, as alluded to above, have been used; and audio materials, which include Radio Freedom broadcasts and revolutionary songs from the Robben Island Mayibuye Archives at the University of the Western Cape. Other sources include documentary films that feature some of the former high school and university students in the 1970s.

To fully comprehend the role of Radio Freedom in the 1970s, it is valuable first to understand the political environment in South Africa during the period under review, with a particular focus on the influence of the BCM.

SOUTH AFRICA AFTER THE BANNING OF THE ANC

South Africa of the 1960s was characterized by fear. The regime's police were vigilant and everywhere, assisted by an army of informers. Furthermore, the regime passed a battery of suppressive laws to intimidate political activists or anyone contemplating causing political disorder. Between 1961 and 1963, for example, it passed a variety of General Law Amendment Acts that prohibited certain gatherings and authorized the detention of anyone suspected of political crime for a period of ninety days without access to a lawyer. After a number of acts of sabotage by members of MK,[11] the regime passed the "Sabotage Act" by which contravention was punishable by sentence to death.

The NP regime's determination was evident when, in 1969, its security police cracked the ANC's underground cell that operated between Soweto and Alexandra, a township north of Johannesburg. The cell included Snuki Zikalala, Wally Serote, Joyce Sikhakhane, and Winnie Mandela. Its task was to source ANC banned literature from Botswana to distribute inside the country.[12] Members of this cell were arrested and tortured.[13] For her involvement, Winnie Mandela, wife of Nelson Mandela, former member of MK's High Command incarcerated on Robben Island for life, was detained and locked up for eighteen months in solitary confinement. Reading such reports instilled fear in many and discouraged them not only from participating in extra-parliamentary opposition politics but also from even discussing the ANC.

The fear that had engulfed the parents was evident in the way they tried to protect their children from politics. Duma Ndlovu, who was part of the Medupi Cultural Group and later a journalist at the *World* newspaper (and now director of a series of local television dramas) remarked in a documentary film that in the mid-1960s when he was learning to read, he was traveling with his father, who was illiterate, to the train station. On the wall at the station he saw graffiti: "Release Mandela or bombs."[14] He read the message aloud. His father turned around and slapped him, because he had shouted the name Mandela in public.[15] Joseph Litabe, who, in 1976, was a student at Bodibeng High School in Kroonstad in the northern Free State, recalled a time in the early 1970s when his parents rebuked him for uttering the name Mandela: "Be careful, these walls have ears. Never mention the name of that person in this house."[16] Because parents avoided discussing politics many young people grew up not having heard about the ANC. Joel Netshitenzhe, who was born in 1956 in the rural village of Sibasa, in Venda (and now an influential figure in the ANC) admitted that his understanding of the ANC came much later at the University of Natal in 1975.[17] Khosi Xaba, born in 1957 and raised in Ndaleni Township in KwaZulu, confessed that by 1970 she had not heard of the ANC.[18]

Fear of reprisal by the regime paralyzed even the literate. Enos Ngutshane, who in 1976 was the branch secretary of the South African Student Movement (SASM) at Naledi High School in Soweto, recalls reading graffiti on the wall of his school, Busisisiwe Primary, "Release Nelson Mandela." As young and inquisitive learners they wanted to know who this person was. When the teachers overheard them debating this issue, they said that Nelson Mandela was the former principal of the school.[19] Ngutshane's teachers may have deliberately misled the learners to protect them, but maybe also to shield themselves from suspicion of teaching opposition politics (teachers suspected of contravening the Bantu Education Act of 1953 could be forced out).[20] Not too long after this incident, however, Ngutshane came to know the truth about Mandela. This was after he started listening to Radio Freedom.

The systematic efforts of the regime to erase the ANC from people's memories was further compounded by the South African Broadcasting Corporation (SABC). The SABC was established in 1924 and by the 1940s it had introduced African language radio on a small scale.[21] In 1960 it launched Radio Bantu as a fully fledged radio station. According to Lekgoathi, "the expansion phase of the SABC's African language radio service in the early 1960s . . . was a response to the upsurge of political activism in African communities in town and the countryside in the previous decade."[22] The NP's technocrats were aware that radio, as a mass medium of communication, could reach larger audiences in both the towns and rural areas, and by using African languages it would be able to counter the ANC's activities. But, most importantly, the NP was aware that it could use Radio Bantu, which broadcast in different African languages for each ethnic group to promote the policies of separate development.[23]

Khosi Xaba, who fled the country in the mid-1980s to join MK and ended up working for Radio Freedom as a broadcaster in Zambia, recalls being an avid listener to radio from the 1960s through the 1970s. South Africa did not have television until 1976, so radio, newspapers, and magazines were the sources of entertainment and knowledge. In Xaba's household they listened to three radio stations: Radio Zulu, Lourenço Marques (based in Maputo), and Springbok, a commercial station broadcasting in English and Afrikaans. Xaba recalls that Radio Zulu in the 1960s started broadcasting for fifteen minutes; in time its slot was extended to thirty minutes, and by the time Xaba started school it had been given more time. On Radio Zulu she listened to plays, *imidlalo yo moya* (plays of the air). "I remember some plays that we used to listen to and some of them were censored by my parents."[24]

Radio Bantu, which Radio Zulu fell under, was established to depoliticize Africans. It broadcast programs (and news) that would not ignite their political conscientization and it became the regime's propaganda machinery to tarnish the liberation movements. Some of the plays aired on Radio Zulu were produced to instill fear or abhorrence of freedom fighters. One of these was Bhekifa ("Watch your inheritance"), aired in the 1970s. One of the terms that featured frequently in Bhekifa was *amaphekulazikhuni* (What blows over the burning faggots).[25] *Amaphekulazikhuni* were associated with the Bolshevists or militant communists; in the play, these were terrorists from outside of whom the locals had to be wary because they were there to destroy. In one episode of the drama these "outsiders" were depicted as being from Zambia and called *amaphekulazikhuni zamakhomanisi* (terrorist lackeys of the communists).[26] The ANC's freedom fighters, some of whom were

based in Zambia, were pejoratively referred to in the South African media as
amaphekulazikhuni.

In line with the SABC's mandate of psychological engineering, Xaba
does not recall hearing Radio Zulu broadcasting about the Soweto student
uprising—at least, not in detail:

> I wasn't aware there was censoring. But I was very aware that on Radio
> Springbok I got different kinds of stories. You know, like the reporting of the
> '76 uprising. I got it from Radio Springbok. I didn't listen to isiZulu radio for
> that. Radio Springbok was talking about '76 like hour to hour reporting in
> terms of what was actually happening on the ground. They were not just
> reporting . . . but there was analysis. [27]

Although the news about the Soweto student uprising may have been broadcast from the white South African perspective on Radio Springbok, it nevertheless left an indelible mark on Xaba's memory and also demonstrates the
strong influence of radio. "I wanted to be in Soweto. I wanted to be where it
was happening."

The NP regime, in its endeavor to consolidate apartheid, passed the Bantu
Authorities Act, which introduced the self-governing territories, known as
homelands or bantustans, divided into different African ethnic groups. The
regime envisaged that Africans were to establish themselves in their own
territories and not in the white urban areas where they were only allowed as
long as they met the needs of the white population. From the 1960s, the
regime stopped developing the townships and channeled funds to the homelands. It was also in the homelands that Africans were encouraged to engage
in their politics. To popularize the homelands, the regime introduced a newsletter. Ngutshane recalls:

> My father actually used to read the apartheid propaganda magazines printed in
> all the languages called *Intuthuko*. In Setswana it was called *Tswelopelo*. It
> was written by the regime and distributed free of charge. And when you
> opened that magazine it spoke about nothing but bantustans. It promoted the
> regime's idea of separate development; the benefits of that for black people.
> The regime used such magazines to tame our people, because it said "we want
> you to develop on your own." [28]

Against this background, thousands who listened to Radio Bantu (and read
government-produced magazines) in the 1970s came to associate the ANC
(and PAC) with terrorism, bent on attacking the NP regime that was doing
everything it could to better the lives of Africans in their homelands. This
view was pumped into people's minds by the NP through its mouthpiece, the
SABC's Radio Bantu. Mostert van Schoor, the SABC's political editor, is
remembered for his staunch support of apartheid policy, which was reflected

in the broadcaster's news. In addition to vilifying the ANC's freedom fighters as "terrorists" and communist-inspired, he is notorious for seeking "to conscientise the people listening to radio that the Bantustans were their real homes."[29]

RADIO FREEDOM BROADCASTING FROM EXILE

Radio Freedom was forced to disband after the leadership of the ANC and SACP was arrested in 1963. It was reestablished in exile as part of the ANC's External Mission in 1967 and placed under the Department of Information and Publicity (DIP). It first broadcast from Tanzania (then Tanganyika), on Radio Tanganyika's External Services. This was not coincidental. Tanzania saw the promotion of nationalist movements in southern Africa as one of its foreign policy objectives and was in the forefront of attempts to organize forces directed against South Africa and its administration in Namibia. Radio Freedom was allocated fifteen minutes to broadcast and as the years progressed the time was extended. In 1972, Radio Freedom was granted time to broadcast on Radio Zambia. Because of differences between the ANC and Zambia's president Kenneth Kaunda, this station was closed in 1975. After a year, when the two had ironed out their differences, Radio Freedom again broadcast from Radio Zambia's External Services. Following the independence of Angola in 1975, Radio Freedom was given a time slot on Radio Luanda in 1977; two years later it broadcast from Radio Madagascar.[30]

Lekgoathi notes that "by the early 1970s, the news was certainly a central feature of Radio Freedom broadcast in Lusaka, Zambia,"[31] aired six times a week, except on Sunday, in English and one African language, Sesotho, SeTswana, isiZulu, or isiXhosa, used alternatively with English. Each news bulletin took thirty minutes. In addition to the news, other programs included Africa reconstruct; Writers and the People; Heroes of the Struggle; Speaking my Mind; and Pictures of History. On Saturday and Sunday the programs were Music and Freedom, and Religion, respectively.[32]

Programs on Radio Freedom were broadcast at different times. On Radio Tanzania External Services, for example, Radio Freedom went out on Monday, Wednesday, and Friday at 20:15; then Tuesday, Thursday, and Saturday at 18:15; and finally on Sunday at 20:45 (all South African time).[33] On Radio Luanda it was on the same days as Radio Tanzania, but at 19:30. On Radio Zambia it was from 18:10.[34] Ardent Radio Freedom listeners would tune in at these times. This information was easily accessed in the ANC's print media such as *Sechaba*, and by word of mouth.

In 1971, broadcasting from Tanzania's External Services, Radio Freedom beamed messages about the ANC's response to the NP's "outward looking policy" through which the prime minister, B. J. Vorster, attempted to lure

African leaders into accepting South Africa as a "good neighbor." Notwithstanding the OAU's position on isolating South Africa as long as it upheld
apartheid, leaders such as Hastings Banda of Malawi bought into Vorster's
idea and visited South Africa to address white South Africans defending the
NP regime's position.[35] Ndlovu notes that the ANC used Radio Freedom to
"keep the international community fully informed about crimes perpetrated
against the African masses by the apartheid government."[36]

In the same year, Radio Freedom's broadcasts also focused on black
workers inside the country. Leaders of the South African Congress of Trade
Unions (SACTU), an ANC ally, used this platform to conscientize the workers and encourage them to mobilize because they strongly believed that "the
workers in various factories, shops and farms within the country . . . would
make genuine trade union work effective[ly]."[37] This segment was broadcast
by Mark Shope, the secretary general of SACTU, who said the time had
come "when every single factory and workshop in South Africa must be
organized into a trade union branch; every worker must become a member of
a trade union."[38] Although there is no hard evidence to connect this broadcast to the development of worker militancy in the early 1970s, judging by
the strikes and work stoppages from 1973 (beginning in Durban and later
spreading to the Rand, particularly the East Rand, now Ekurhuleni) we can
infer that Radio Freedom made a strong impact on black workers inside the
country,[39] forcing the regime to allow black workers to form their independent trade unions.

It was from 1973 that Radio Freedom began to operate optimally. The
historian Hugh Macmillan contends that this was because in that year high-
powered Chinese radio transmitters were installed in Zambia, enabling Radio
Freedom to beam more effectively into South Africa.[40]

RADIO FREEDOM AND THE BLACK
CONSCIOUSNESS MOVEMENT (BCM)

"To keep the organisation intact"[41] inside the country in the 1970s, the ANC
used its members who had recently been released from prison, its underground operatives, and print media to inform and influence the oppressed
masses about its heroes, heroines, and activities. However, I contend in this
section that it was through Radio Freedom that the ANC managed to reach
members of the BCM. Here I will demonstrate how members of the BCM
were exposed to Radio Freedom, how they listened to it, and how they
interpreted its messages.

> I think contact with the ANC was growing. More people from outside were
> coming into the country, books were coming from outside. There was a dearth
> of material at that time: published material of the ANC was particularly valu-

able and one treasured it as if it was gold. We even had a "mobile library"—books which moved from hand to hand amongst selected people. You see, we knew the ANC was underground, but the problem was finding the underground members of the ANC. At that time more and more of them were coming out of prison and coming to see us, SASO, to see who we were. We used to listen to Radio Freedom every day when there was a broadcast.[42]

From this we can construe that members of the BCM listened to Radio Freedom although the ANC was nonracial and the BCM was exclusively black.

In 1968 some disgruntled African students who were members of the National Union of South African Students (NUSAS), terminated their membership and formed the South African Student Organization (SASO). They argued that NUSAS, which was predominantly white, paid lip service to the total destruction of the apartheid government while its white members were content with the status quo because they benefited from it. A year later they launched SASO at the University College of the North (now the University of Limpopo) and elected Stephen Bantu Biko as the organization's first president. SASO adopted black consciousness as its guiding philosophy. It disputed the term "nonwhite," as the oppressed masses were described. Its members considered the term inappropriate and chose "black" to identify themselves.[43] For SASO, "black" encompassed all the groups oppressed by the regime: Africans, Indians, and coloreds. For the adherents of the black consciousness philosophy, black pride was closely linked to self-reliance. The dual effects of state repression and poverty had paralyzed many black people and reduced them to a state of perpetual dependence. Mamphela Ramphele, citing Biko, wrote that "some even began to believe that they deserved the oppression they suffered because of innate inferiority."[44] To reverse this, self-reliance was the only solution. For them, this would lead to black liberation from white domination. They refused to be in an alliance with whites or white organizations in the fight for liberation.

As noted above, listening to Radio Freedom was illegal in South Africa. "It carried a maximum sentence of eight years in prison."[45] This undoubtedly caused people to be very cautious about who they shared information with about Radio Freedom. People heard about Radio Freedom in different ways and from different sources. Bafana Sithole, who was recruited to work for the ANC underground in the early 1970s, was introduced to Radio Freedom by a friend.

Remember this was the period of the Black Consciousness. We then met a certain young man from the Makhaya family in Alexandra. This young man was a member of the BCM. His older brother knew about Radio Freedom and he had informed him about it. So Muzi Makhaya introduced us to Radio Freedom. We were a group of about 12 young people from Alexandra. It was

Hlongwane (Ntsizwa), Jappie Vilankulu, Toto Skhosana, Muzi Makhaya, Gama Magagula, Absolomon "Steshi" Mazibuko and others. We'd meet at Gama's house. They had a spare room detached from the main house. We'd congregate there and listen to Radio Freedom. After listening we'd ask "Where can we find this ANC?" But no one would provide us with answers.[46]

From Sithole's reminiscence we can infer that the message they received from Radio Freedom inspired them to find the ANC—even though they supported the BCM.

Oupa Maluleke, who fled the country in 1976 and after receiving military and journalism training in Moscow, joined Radio Freedom as a broadcaster.

I had a friend Khehla Nkutha, also known as "Bra K." He was ambushed in exile and died there. He was older than me but very instrumental in me going into exile. He was friends also with Wally Serote. I got to know about Radio Freedom through him.[47]

Both Sithole and Maluleke came to know about Radio Freedom from people who had been exposed to it and who trusted them sufficiently to alert them to it.

Similarly, Jabu Moleketi, who joined SASM, a BC-oriented high school student organization, was introduced to Radio Freedom by people who trusted him. Moleketi, who was born in 1957 in Pimville, Soweto, was expelled from school in Intshanga, Natal, for involvement in a solidarity strike with fellow students who had been expelled for smuggling girls into the dormitories. He returned home and joined the branch of SASM at his new school, Musi High, where he met Elias "Roller" Masinga, Billy Masetlha, Murphy Morobe, and Zweli Sizane, all members of SASM and BCM. Moleketi recalled that the group used to meet at 8:00 or 9:00 at night at Musi High by candlelight to speak about politics and leaders and listen to Radio Freedom.[48]

Conversely, other young people knew about Radio Freedom through "trial and error": tuning from one station to the other on their radio until they landed on Radio Freedom. Writing about how he was exposed to Radio Freedom, Wonga Welile Bottoman, who left the country to join MK at the beginning of the 1980s, summed it up as follows:

One quiet night as I twiddled a transistor radio, searching for a disco music station, I heard the statement, "The terrorist regime of Ian Douglas Smith," delivered in thick African tones. The broadcast went out of tune and I twiddled the dialling knob; the crackling thick voice came back and my body tensed with every turn of the knob I'd had to make, to keep the broadcast in focus. After the deliverance, a familiar song from the political rallies started. At the end, I heard that the broadcast was Radio Freedom.[49]

Others, like Stanley Manong, who also later left the country in the mid-1970s to join MK in exile, were introduced to Radio Freedom by politically conscientized friends. Manong was introduced to Radio Freedom in 1974 by his classmate at Mmadikoti Technical College in Polokwane, northern Transvaal (today, Limpopo Province), Ronald "Rocks" Mokete Mashinini, who was from Soweto, and while he was a student at Morris Isaacson High School he was taught and conscientized by Onkgopotse Tiro.[50] Manong writes that he came to know through the Radio Freedom program "Heroes of the Struggle" about the assassination of Tiro and Boy Adelphus Mvemve, also known as John Dube in MK, who was killed by a parcel bomb in Lusaka in 1974.[51]

Some listeners, who were operating underground, recruiting members for the ANC, used Radio Freedom as an educating tool about the ANC and the struggle for liberation. Describing political mobilization in Natal in the mid-1970s and the role of Radio Freedom, Sithole avers.

> ANC structures were organised into cells of two or three people. The responsibility of each cell was to explore ways of reviving the ANC, to conduct political education, to identify young men and women who could be recruited for military training. . . . Radio Freedom was identified as a particularly important medium for educating recruits about the ANC and making potential recruits aware of the ANC.[52]

The year 1973, the time the ANC's Radio Freedom broadcast optimally inside the country, coincided with the harassment of the BCM activists. Some within the BCM were beginning to question the movement's anticonfrontational stance, complaining that the movement believed in talking and conscientization and not in fighting.[53] Young people who had begun to tune into Radio Freedom were inspired by the messages to take up arms and fight. Writing about this moment, James Ngculu, who left the country to join the ANC in exile, recorded the following in his political memoir:

> We . . . listened to the ANC's Radio Freedom, broadcast from Lusaka, and the sound of the opening tune, "Hamba Kahle Mkhonto" followed by a burst of gunfire, excited us. We would imagine ourselves pulling that trigger.[54]

In similar vein, Maluleke, after listening to Radio Freedom, wanted to take up arms and fight.

> Listening to RF made me more militant, because I was getting frustrated. As young people we were militant. We wanted to fight these guys. Take them head on. We felt that talking won't help us. So when we listened to RF we felt that the time for talking was over. We needed to take up arms. We were all itching to get our hands on the guns.[55]

For this generation, the message they were receiving from Radio Freedom was clear. The time for talking was over. It was now time to face the regime head on. And to do this, they first had to leave the country to receive military training in exile and return to fight.

Maluleke's inspiration was also drawn from the Voice of Zimbabwe, which was the guerrilla radio for the Zimbabwe African National Union (Zanu) during the liberation struggle in Southern Rhodesia against Ian Smith's regime. He explains:

> We didn't listen to Radio Freedom only. We also listened to the Voice of Zimbabwe, [Robert] Mugabe's guys. They used to say *Phambiri ne Chimurenga* (Forward with the Struggle). Basically, what they were telling us was that we should take up arms and fight the white minority regime. They were trying to convince us that the white minority regime was not invincible. It could be defeated. So, we young people must stand up and take up arms and fight. [56]

Such militant broadcasts helped to strengthen Maluleke's resolve to flee the country and join the ANC's military wing, MK. This happened in 1976.

Finally, Nkululeko Sineke, one of the few women who attended the BCM meetings in Alexandra Township in the early 1970s, describes how Radio Freedom inspired her to leave the country to join MK:

> Because Bafana [Sithole] would allow women to talk during their meetings, I liked attending the meetings and became involved. We would then listen to Radio Freedom. So, after imbibing all this information I asked myself how to change this situation. I had to go to exile and train and come back to fight to liberate Alexandra (not South Africa). My thinking was still narrow. [57]

Because it was illegal to listen to Radio Freedom in South Africa, people who listened to it had to be extra careful. Bheki Nkosi, a student at Siyamu-kela High School in Madadeni, Newcastle, describes how they listened to Radio Freedom in the early 1970s:

> We heard about Radio Freedom from our friend's father. His name was Snicks Levuno. Although he was a pastor but he also associated with gangsters in the township. He was wealthy. He had a good portable radio which we used to listen to Radio Freedom. We were six friends from school. We would put it down in the middle of the room and lie down on our bellies to listen to Radio Freedom. We tuned in at 6:00 in the evening. [58]

Judging by the time they tuned in they probably received the broadcast from either Zambia or Tanzania, where Radio Freedom broadcast from 18:15 during the week from the external services of the national radios of those two countries. People listening to Radio Freedom took measures to ensure that it was safe. Maluleke recalls:

I remember the first time I listened to it, it was at 19th Avenue in Alexandra. It was scary because we knew that it was banned. And we'd warn each other, whispering, saying "Hey, don't play it too loud. People might be spying on us." There was that excitement and fear. We were scared that we might be arrested for listening to this radio. So, we used to play it very, very low. We never played it out loud. The volume was always low. [59]

Gregory Malebo, on the other hand, remembers that they employed children playing in the streets to alert them if they observed suspicious cars approaching. "If we were listening to it from someone else's house, there would be kids outside who had to inform us if there were police approaching. They would give us a sign if they suspected any car that stopped next to where we were." [60]

Radio Freedom produced several programs, including poetry, plays, news, and music. Maluleka was inspired by revolutionary music played on Saturday. "There was one song that they used to play a lot: 'M'hlasibuyayo Kuyokhala umbambayi' (When we return there'll be a sound of gunfire). That song used to excite us a lot. Then we'd discuss amongst ourselves that these guys are serious. They say when they return all hell will break loose." [61] Maluleke confessed that he was inspired by the song to join MK to fight the regime. [62] Other revolutionary songs played on Radio Freedom included "Freedom is Our Guiding Light" and "Ikhaya Lam' lise South Africa" (My home is in South Africa) by Amandla Cultural Ensemble, the ANC's cultural group. [63] Some of the revolutionary songs were chanting songs, interspersed with whistling, clapping of hands, and stamping of feet, a dance known as *toyi-toyi*. Another song is "Amaqhawe" (Heroes and heroines) in which the singers, possibly Amandla, pay tribute to the heroes and heroines of the ANC, calling out their names (including O. R. Tambo's and Lilian Ngoyi's (the first president of the ANC Women's League who led the women's march to the Union Buildings in 1956), and saluting them for their unrelenting involvement in the struggle for liberation. In the middle of the song, the singers change and ask the government why it hates them so much.

Some of the young BCM supporters who listened to Radio Freedom began to shift allegiances and identified with the ANC. For example, Lekgoathi writes "in the early 1970s, Nompumelelo Setsubi, a student at Fort Hare University, was influenced by Radio Freedom to join the ANC." [64] Murphy Morobe, a leading figure within SASM, also shifted to the ANC, as early as 1974. "We began slowly to be exposed to the ideas of the ANC." [65]

Not all the young BCM supporters who listened to Radio Freedom decided immediately to shift allegiance to the ANC. Malebo explains in his own words:

When we listened to Radio Freedom in the 1970s . . . we were not really ready. You see, we were listening to Radio Freedom but we did not consider ourselves as members of the ANC. But we were getting messages from outside saying here are some of the things which were supposed to be done. It was strange, because we listened to Radio Freedom but we were saying something different about the ANC. 18:00 was the time to listen to Radio Freedom. We had a small transistor radio. But I must say that it did not turn us into becoming members of the ANC. It did however update us about what was happening. It was more on telling us about what was happening even inside the country. It would brief us about what happened and who had been arrested. [66]

Observing the escalating politicization of young people and the increasing numbers fleeing into exile, the regime did not stand by. It jammed Radio Freedom's broadcasting into South Africa, which made it very difficult to hear. "The South African government reacted with venom . . . waging unsuccessful wars of the airwaves by trying to jam Radio Freedom signals."[67] Maluleke, who experienced the jamming first as a listener and later as a broadcaster, had this to say: "We used to listen to RF at Magagula's place. It was not quite audible but we could still hear it."[68] And "The regime would jam our signal a lot. We knew that it was doing that because we were reaching many people inside the country. . . . They jammed Radio Freedom especially in Zambia and Angola. But it cost the regime a lot of money. I think per minute it paid about R400 000."

CONCLUSION

After it was banned in 1960 the ANC had to operate from exile. The distance between it and its supporters in South Africa forced it to devise methods of keeping the lines of communication open. There were grave risks in using print media, underground operatives, and members who had been released from prison. The ex-political prisoners were under constant police surveillance and the chances of making contact with many people were thin. Underground operatives were overly cautious, only having contact with people they trusted. Through Radio Freedom the ANC was able to reach large numbers across the country. Notwithstanding the prison sentence for anyone caught listening to Radio Freedom, people took the risk, but surreptitiously. Those who listened to Radio Freedom learned about the ANC, its leaders, and its activities, and revolutionary songs that they copied and sang in the townships and villages when mobilizing people. More importantly, Radio Freedom inspired a significant number of BCM members, and supporters of black consciousness philosophy, to escape into exile, join MK, and receive military training—and return to fight. The ANC, through Radio Freedom, managed to achieve two objectives—to counter the SABC's propaganda and to attract large numbers to its ranks in exile, particularly after 1976.

NOTES

1. Luli Callinicos, *Óliver Tambo: Beyond the Engeli Mountains* (Claremont: David Philip, 2004), 254–57.

2. Nelson Mandela, *Long Walk to Freedom: The Autobiography of Nelson Mandel a* (Randburg: Macdonald Purnell, 1994); Thula Simpson, *Umkhonto we Sizwe: The ANC's Armed Struggle* (Cape Town: Penguin, 2016).

3. Brown Maaba, "The PAC's War against the State, 1960–1963," in *The Road to Democracy in South Africa, Volume 1 , 1960–1970*, ed. South African Democracy Education Trust (hereafter SADET), 273–85 (Cape Town: Zebra Press, 2004).

4. Sekibakiba Lekgoathi, "The African National Congress's Radio Freedom and Its Audience in Apartheid South Africa, 1963–1991," *Journal of African Media Studies* 2, no. 2 (2010): 141.

5. Waters "Bishop" Toboti, former broadcaster, discusses his role and that of the PAC's guerrilla radio in the fight for liberation in South Africa. *The Other Side of Freedom: Stories of Hope and Loss in the South African Liberation Struggle 1950–1994*, ed. Gregory Houston et al., 127–32 (Cape Town: HSRC Press, 2017).

6. See, for example, Liz Gunner, Dina Ligaga, and Dumisani Moyo, eds., *Radio in Africa: Publics, Cultures, Communities* (Johannesburg: Wits University Press, 2011).

7. Marissa J. Moorman, "Airing the Politics of Nation: Radio in Angola," in *Radio in Africa: Publics, Cultures, Communities*, ed. Liz Gunner, Dina Ligaga, and Dumisani Moyo (Johannesburg: Wits University Press, 2011); Mhoze Chikowero, "Is Propaganda Modernity? Press and Radio Broadcasting to Africans in Colonial Zambia, Zimbabwe and Malawi, 1939–1950s," in *Modernization as Spectacle in Africa*, ed. Stephan Miescher, Peter Bloom, and Takywa Manuh (Bloomington: Indiana University Press, 2014); Lekgoathi, "ANC's Radio Freedom"; Stephen R. Davis, "Voices from Without: The African National Congress, Its Radio, Its Allies and Exile, 1960–84," in *Radio in Africa: Publics, Cultures, Communities*, ed. Liz Gunner, Dina Ligaga, and Dumisani Moyo (Johannesburg: Wits University Press, 2011); Lebona Mosia, Charles Riddle, and Jim Zaffiro, "From Revolutionary to Regime Radio: Three Decades of Nationalist Broadcasting in Southern Africa," in *Africa Media Review* 8, no. 1 (1994).

8. Mosia, Riddle, and Zaffiro, "From Revolutionary to Regime Radio," 8.

9. Lekgoathi, "ANC's Radio Freedom."

10. Davis, "Voices from Without," 233.

11. Davis estimates that these were more than 200. Stephen Davis, "The African National Congress, Its Radio, Its Allies and Exile," *Journal of Southern African Studies* 35, no. 2 (2009): 350.

12. Interview with Mongane Wally Serote by Gregory Houston. Pretoria, April 11, 2002; also see Gregory Houston, "The Post-Rivonia ANC/SACP Underground," in *The Road to Democracy in South Africa, Volume 1, 1960–1970*, ed. SADET (Cape Town: Zebra Press, 2004).

13. Interview with Serote.

14. Graffiti on the walls of buildings was inscribed by members of the Congress Alliance. See Houston, "Post-Rivonia ANC/SACP Underground," 605.

15. Duma Ndlovu was interviewed for the documentary film *Amandla: A Revolution in Four-Part Harmony*, directed by Lee Hirsch, 2002.

16. Interview with Joseph Litabe by the author, Kroonstad, January 27, 2007.

17. Sifiso M. Ndlovu and Miranda Strydom, *The Thabo Mbeki I Know* (Johannesburg: Picador Africa, 2016), 239.

18. Interview with Khosi Xaba by Sekibakiba Lekgoathi and Tshepo Moloi, Wits University, December 15, 2016.

19. Interview with Enos Ngutshane by the author, Braamfontein, Johannesburg, n.d.

20. Abram Onkgopotse Tiro, a leading figure in SASO and teacher at Morris Isaacson High School, was forced out of his teaching position because the regime claimed that he was feeding the learners with "wrong" information—BC ideas. See, for example, Anne Heffernan, "Black

Consciousness's Lost Leader: Abram Tiro, the University of the North, and the Seeds of South Africa's Student Movement in the 1970s," *Journal of South African Studies* (2015).

21. Sekibakiba Lekgoathi, "Bantustan Identity, Censorship and Subversion on Northern Sotho Radio under Apartheid, 1960s–80s," in *Radio in Africa: Publics, Cultures, Communities,* ed. Liz Gunner, Dina Ligaga and Dumisani Moyo, 119 (Johannesburg: Wits University Press, 2011).

22. Ibid., 122.

23. Ibid., 117.

24. Interview with Xaba. Some of the dramas aired on Radio Zulu in the 1970s included "Ubongilinda Mzikayifani" (You must wait for me, Mzikayifani) and "Abangani Ababi" (Bad Friends).

25. Liz Gunner, "IsiZulu Radio Drama and the Modern Subject: Restless Identities in South Africa in the 1970s, in *Radio in Africa: Publics, Cultures, Communities,* ed. Liz Gunner, Dina Ligaga, and Dumisani Moyo, 175 (Johannesburg: Wits University Press, 2011).

26. Ibid., 176–77.

27. Interview with Xaba.

28. Interview with Ngutshane.

29. Lekgoathi, "Bantustan Identity," 130.

30. Sekibakiba Lekgoathi, "Radio Freedom, Songs of Freedom and the Liberation Struggle in South Africa, 1963–1991," in *The Soundtrack of Conflict: The Role of Music in Radio Broadcasting in Wartime and in Conflict Situations,* ed. M. J. Grant and F. J. Stone-Davis (Zurich and New York: Georg Olms Verlag, 2013).

31. Lekgoathi, "The ANC's Radio Freedom," 568.

32. Ibid., 570–71.

33. *Sechaba: Official Organ of the African National Congress South Africa,* March 1979.

34. Ibid.

35. Sifiso M. Ndlovu, "The ANC's Diplomacy and International Relations, " in *The Road to Democracy in South Africa, Volume 2, 1970–1980,* ed. SADET, 622 (Pretoria: Unisa Press, 2006).

36. Ibid.

37. Jabulani Sithole and Sifiso Ndlovu, "The Revival of the Labour Movement, 1970–1980," in *The Road to Democracy in South Africa,* ed. SADET, 214 (Pretoria: Unisa Press, 2006).

38. Ibid.

39. Ibid., 225–30.

40. Hugh Macmillan, *The Lusaka Years: The ANC in Exile in Zambia, 1963 to 1994* (Auckland Park: Jacana Media, 2013), 118.

41. Houston, "Post-Rivonia ANC/SACP Underground," 604.

42. Papi Mokoena, SASO activist expelled from Fort Hare University in 1973 for leading a student strike.

43. See, for example, Tshepo Moloi, *Place of Thorns: Black Political Protest in Kroonstad Since 1976* (Johannesburg: Wits University Press, 2015), 50.

44. Mamphela Ramphele, "Empowerment and Symbols of Hope: Black Consciousness and Community Development," in *Bounds of Possibility: The Legacy of Steve Biko and Black Consciousness,* ed. Barney Pityana et al. , 156 (Cape Town: David Philip, 1991).

45. Lekgoathi, "The ANC's Radio Freedom," 579.

46. Interview with Bafana Sithole by the author, Parktown, Johannesburg, August 15, 2017.

47. Interview with Oupa Maluleke by the author, Ennerdale, Johannesburg, February 15, 2017.

48. Houston, "Post-Rivonia ANC/SACP Underground," 384.

49. Welile Bottoman, *The Making of an MK Cadre* (Pretoria: LiNc Publishers, 2010), 18.

50. Stanley Manong, *If We Must Die: An Autobiography of a Former Commander of uMkhonto we Sizwe.* (Johannesburg: Nkululeko Publishers, 2015), 18; Tiro was a leading figure in the BCM. He fled the country in 1973 and settled in Gaborone, Botswana. In February 1974 he was assassinated by a parcel bomb. For a detailed account of Tiro, see Heffernan, "Black Consciousness's Lost Leader."

51. Ibid., 38.

52. Jabulani Sithole, "The ANC Underground in Natal," in *The Road to Democracy in South Africa, Volume 2, 1970–1980*, ed. SADET, 548–49 (Pretoria: Unisa Press, 2006).

53. Lindy Wilson, "Bantu Stephen Biko: A Life," in *Bounds of Possibility: The Legacy of Steve Biko and Black Consciousness*, ed. Barney Pityana et al, 32. (Cape Town: David Philip, 1991).

54. James Ngculu, *The Honour to Serve: Recollections of an Umkhonto Soldier* (Claremont: New Africa Books, 2010), 22.

55. Interview with Maluleke.

56. Ibid.

57. Interview with Nkululeko Sineke by the author, Pretoria, n.d.

58. Interview with Bheki Nkosi by the author, Madadeni, Newcastle, November 8, 2017.

59. Interview with Maluleke.

60. Interview with Gregory Malebo by the author, Hospital View, Thembisa, January 19, 2017.

61. Interview with Maluleke.

62. Interview with Malebo.

63. Tom Seeta Collection. RF555 Sunday Music, 1976. Robben Island Museum Mayibuye Archives.

64. Lekgoathi, "The ANC's Radio Freedom," 579–80.

65. Ibid., 580.

66. Interview with Malebo.

67. Ndlovu, "ANC's Diplomacy," 639.

68. Interview with Maluleke.

Chapter Eleven

International Solidarity and Support for the ANC's Radio Freedom

Sekibakiba Peter Lekgoathi

On February 19, 1993, Oliver Reginald Tambo, the president of the African National Congress (ANC) for nearly three decades in exile, gave the opening address at the International Solidarity conference held in Johannesburg, on the theme "From Apartheid to Peace, Democracy and Development." In his speech, Tambo paid tribute to the international community, governments, trade unions, and civil society organizations for their contribution to ending the system of apartheid in South Africa. He spoke eloquently about the "small and lonely voices of protest" in the early days of the international movement in the 1940s, the beginning of the boycott of Cape grapes and wines and Outspan oranges and the picketing at supermarkets. He also commented on how, over the years, this effort had grown into a massive movement with the capacity to bring the apartheid regime to its knees and to effect far-reaching changes in the country. In his own words,

> When we needed to fight with arms in hand, there were few countries even in Africa which had the possibility to extend assistance to us. . . . And yet, because apartheid is truly evil and because there are men and women of conscience such as you who are gathered here, who would not connive at the perpetration of a crime by refusing to act against it, the anti-apartheid movement grew into perhaps the strongest international solidarity movement of this century, bringing together citizens of all countries, governments and international organisations. [1]

Although scholars have begun to pay some attention to the role of international solidarity organizations and governments in isolating the apartheid regime and supporting the South African liberation movements in their strug-

gle against apartheid, not enough attention has been paid to the role of communication technology. This chapter fills the gap by focusing more sharply
on the support advanced to the ANC's Radio Freedom by some governments
and civil society organizations on the African continent and in Europe.
Against the backdrop of the Cold War, the chapter also probes the motives
behind the different forms of support that countries provided for the broadcasting venture. It also probes the extent to which this guerrilla radio shaped
the nature of the struggle against apartheid inside the country.

Based on a combination of archival evidence (audio and documentary
sources), interviews, and secondary literature,[2] the chapter makes an argument that revolves around the pivotal role that international solidarity played
in supporting the guerrilla radios of the liberation movements, thus deepening the struggle against white settler regimes in the region. Driven by political agendas or motivations such as the expansion of ideological influence,
pan-Africanism, and democratic values of media pluralism, international solidarity groups and some governments in eastern and western Europe and
Africa provided certain resources and facilities that enabled the ANC's Radio
Freedom to execute a protracted offensive of propaganda and counter-
propaganda against white minority rule. Through Radio Freedom, the ANC
and its allies were able to reach the people at home and to create alliances
with support groups and sponsors on the African continent and overseas in
the struggle against white domination in southern Africa.

THE INSEPARABLE COMPANION OF REVOLUTION

The idea of using broadcasting technology as one of the strategies within the
liberation movement came shortly after the adoption of the armed struggle in
1961.[3] By that time, the National Party government had effectively turned
the public broadcaster, the South African Broadcasting Corporation (SABC),
into its own mouthpiece. From the beginning of the 1960s, the apartheid
government had begun expanding its means of communicating its messages
over radio by incorporating the use of African languages in the country (as
well as in South West Africa, Namibia today) in what it called "Radio Bantu." In fact, "Radio Bantu" had already been launched as a fully fledged
station on frequency modulation (FM), with a mandate to strengthen ethnic
separatism (euphemistically referred to as "national consciousness") among
the different language groups. Considering these developments, the ANC and
its allies the South African Communist Party, Congress of Democrats, and
South African Indian Congress took a decision to contest the state's monopoly over the airwaves. This they did by establishing a pirate radio with the
intent of presenting the liberation movement's perspective on key issues such
as news and current affairs and challenging government propaganda, as well

as influencing public opinion and mobilizing support against apartheid. The development of ideas about revolutionary radio in South Africa did not happen in a vacuum—they were informed by a broad diversity of revolutionary movements on the African continent and globally.

Before the launch of its pirate radio inside South Africa in June 1963, the ANC already had some access to radio broadcasting in Ethiopia and Egypt from as early as the 1950s. The first to shake off the colonial cloak in Africa, the two countries were also the first on the continent to join the "propaganda war of the air" and to broadcast anti-colonial messages. Possessing a powerful broadcasting service from the beginning of the 1940s, Egypt extended its broadcasting facilities to the ANC and SWAPO (South West African People's Organization, in Namibia) on Radio Cairo in the following decade, a development that made the South African government very nervous.[4] Soon after Ghana's independence, Kwame Nkrumah announced plans in 1958 to purchase three 100-kilowatt transmitters to establish a radio service that would ensure "the liberation and unity of the entire African continent."[5] In good time, the white settler regimes down south were picking up these hostile broadcasts that sought to influence the people in their territories.[6]

In the meantime, the ANC surreptitiously launched its own radio within South Africa in June 1963, to reach and mobilize its supporters. Known initially as "Freedom Radio," or simply as "ANC Radio" (and "Radio Liberation" according to Rusty Bernstein, former activist and member of the Communist Party of South Africa), Radio Freedom was hosted at Liliesleaf farm, a twenty-eight-acre smallholding located in what was then a quiet and isolated rural part of Rivonia just north of the city of Johannesburg.[7] The property was purchased by the movement and then turned into a secret headquarters and hideout of the high command of the ANC's military wing, Umkhonto we Sizwe (MK), or "Spear of the Nation."[8]

The main impetus for the initial foray into radio was the failure of the spectacular MK bombings between 1961 and 1963 to activate the great majority of South Africans to revolution.[9] Although there were differences of opinions within the ANC, there was a strong feeling that the movement disregarded the crucial task of establishing the political means with which to capitalize on the armed struggle—political propaganda. The pirate radio venture was therefore a key component of the broader mass communication strategy (the other being print media) employed by the ANC and its allies to influence public opinion and mobilize support for its course, particularly after the adoption of the armed struggle. In a country where the majority of the people could not read or write, the ANC, just like the National Party government, had come to appreciate the importance of harnessing the power of the spoken word, using the modern technology of communication—radio.

Denis Goldberg, a member of the MK since 1961 and a civil engineer by training, was among the underground revolutionaries tasked with establishing the movement's pirate radio. He purchased the materials to set up the antenna for the first broadcast by Walter Sisulu scheduled for June 26, 1963.[10] Lionel Gay, a physics lecturer at the University of the Witwatersrand, had built the movement's mobile radio transmitter, which was small enough to be transported by car from place to place. The underground collective agreed that Sisulu would make the ANC's broadcast from somewhere in the country.[11] The speech was initially forty-five minutes long, but was eventually reduced to a maximum of fifteen minutes because of security concerns that a longer speech "would give the police too long a time to find the transmitter, and [its operator]."[12]

The speech was prerecorded and on the night of June 26, 1963 Denis Goldberg and his two old soldier comrades, Ivan Schermbrucker and Cyril Jones, drove from Rivonia to the home of Fuzzy and Archie Levitan in the suburb of Parktown.[13] There they assembled a custom-built aluminum antenna, with poles spray-painted black so that it should not be spotted by police searchlights "when pulled upright for the duration of the broadcast."[14] Jones parked a rented car nearby for Goldberg, and Schermbrucker stood watch, using torchlight and a pair of walkie-talkies to signal to Goldberg. Goldberg connected the jury-rigged transmitter to a tape recorder, then pressed the play button, and the inaugural broadcast of "Freedom Radio" went on air to an unknown number of listeners. "Sons and daughters of Africa, I speak to you from somewhere in South Africa. I have not left the country. I do not plan to leave," began the broadcast of Sisulu's address on Radio Freedom. Defiant and brave, Sisulu went on to apprise the listeners on the state of political repression in the country, which had forced many of the ANC leaders to go underground. He then urged them to "intensify the attack on the pass laws," to "fight against the removal of Africans from the Western Cape" and "to reject once and for all times, the Bantustan fraud."[15] He called upon his audiences to be united and to stand firmly behind the ANC, and to support the new method of struggle, the armed struggle. Sisulu concluded his broadcast as follows:

> Throughout the ages men have sacrificed—they have given their lives for their ideals. And we are also determined to surrender our lives for our freedom. In the face of violence, men struggling for freedom have had to meet violence with violence. How can it be otherwise in South Africa? Changes must come. Changes for the better, but not without sacrifice. Your sacrifice, my sacrifice. We face tremendous odds. We know that. But our unity, our determination, our sacrifice, our organisation are our weapons. We must succeed! We will succeed! Amandla!

The extract provides strong evidence that Radio Freedom was intended as a mobilizing instrument, to inspire the masses not to give up in the face of political repression but to continue supporting the ANC in its turn to armed struggle. By that time, the ANC was a banned organization but it continued operating underground. Therefore, such guerrilla radio broadcasts were intended to let the people know that the ANC was still inside the country and actively fighting against apartheid. It would be impossible to estimate the transmission range, or the number of listeners who actually managed to tune in to the first broadcast of Radio Freedom. No audience surveys were conducted, given the clandestine nature of its operation. It is likely that only those who had prior knowledge of the planned broadcast would have tuned in, which would probably narrow the number to the inner core and well-informed activists of the liberation movement. However, Goldberg notes that the ANC broadcast "created a stir throughout the country and was widely reported" in the media.[16]

Within two weeks of the first broadcast, however, police raided Liliesleaf farm and arrested seven leaders including Sisulu, Ahmed Kathrada, and Goldberg. In the famous Rivonia trial, the state prosecution, led by the infamous chief state prosecutor Percy Yutar, presented most flagrantly as evidence of treason and sedition the recordings of Freedom Radio, only now submitted under the provocative title of the "Eye for an eye" broadcasts. At the trial's conclusion in June 1964, the presiding judge, Quartus de Wet, sentenced the seven Rivonia defendants (including Nelson Mandela) to life in prison. The liberation movement was now in utter disarray and the remaining members faced arrest and intimidation. Many fled into exile, where they regrouped and continued the struggle against apartheid. While Raymond Suttner suggests that Radio Freedom broadcast intermittently within the country for a few more years thereafter, Bernstein states that the inaugural broadcast that featured Sisulu was intended to be only the first in a regular series—but it turned out to be the last.[17] Nevertheless, the ability of the liberation movement to broadcast from within the country's borders had been dealt a deadly blow and it was only in the late 1960s that Radio Freedom was able to come back on air, this time from outside the borders of South Africa.

AFRICAN SOLIDARITY AND
SUPPORT FOR RADIO FREEDOM

Following the political clampdown inside the country in the early 1960s, a significant number of political activists (from the ANC, PAC, SACP, and other anti-apartheid organizations) skipped the country and sought refuge, mainly in independent African countries where they immediately started rebuilding their nationalist movements. The idea of tapping into radio broadcasting as a medium of countering the propaganda messages of the apartheid state was not surrendered but kept alive by those in exile who joined the

ANC's newly established External Mission that was hurriedly set up by Oliver Tambo, Moses Kotane, and Tennyson Makiwane.[18]

It was to Tanzania (which attained independence from Britain in 1961) that the ANC and other nationalist movements in southern Africa turned for support in the use of radio as a means of counter-propaganda and connecting with their supporters back home. Under the leadership of Mwalimu Julius Nyerere, who was an ardent pan-Africanist, Tanzania became a political mecca of exiles from the entire southern African region and made the most sacrifice in the process. Taking a cue from independent Ghana and Algeria, Tanzania declared from the beginning that independence would only be complete and meaningful once the entire continent was free from colonial domination.[19] One of Tanzania's foreign policy objectives was the promotion of nationalist movements in southern Africa. As a result, this country played a pivotal role in the efforts of the Organization of African Unity (OAU) to organize forces directed against South Africa and its administration of Namibia. From March 1964, Tanzania began broadcasting daily news bulletins to South Africa that gave a strong voice to South African exiles and opposition leaders.[20]

The establishment of Radio Tanzania's External Service in 1968 gave a major boost to the nationalist movements. Its mandate included "the task of supporting the liberation of Africa, African unity, harmonising good neighbourliness and portraying Tanzania's image outside its boundaries."[21] The ANC was one of the eight nationalist movements whose radio broadcasts received this support. According to Thami Ntenteni, a former director of Radio Freedom in Lusaka, Radio Freedom came back on air courtesy of Tanzania nearly six years after its forced shutdown in Rivonia in 1963.[22] Along with other guerrilla radios in southern Africa, it was allocated fifteen minutes three times a week on the program called "Voice of Freedom," which was sponsored by the OAU's Liberation Committee. This program was broadcast to the entire region. A Voz da Frelimo for the Mozambican liberation movement, Voice of the Revolution (ZAPU's radio), Voice of Zimbabwe (ZANU's radio), Voice of Namibia (SWAPO's radio), and the guerrilla radio of the National Liberation Movement of the Comoro Islands were some of the other guerrilla radios broadcasting from Dar es Salaam at that time.[23]

Radio Freedom broadcasting from Tanzania was a legal radio service and the location of the transmission was legal and readily evident to listeners tuning in to Radio Tanzania anywhere on the continent, except in southern Africa where white minority regimes were still in charge. Individuals on the radio identified themselves publicly as representatives of their respective organizations. In this way, the appearance of the ANC on "Voice of Freedom," even if it was for as little as fifteen minutes three times a week, was a crucial acknowledgement that the external mission had survived in exile.

This provided the liberation movement with the opportunity to counter the apartheid government's propaganda messages, as well as to inform and educate—not only the people back home but also the international community—about the effects of the apartheid system and the importance of supporting campaigns to eradicate it.

The archival record gives some fragments of evidence of the kinds of messages that Radio Freedom was able to broadcast from Tanzania. Among the transcripts contained in the records on the Tanzania Mission in the Liberation Archive at the University of Fort Hare is Commentary No. 26, "Solidarity for Our Liberation Heroes" dated April 1, 1968. Presented by Dlangamandla Dingindawo (the presenter's nom de guerre), the commentary gives a systematic rebuttal of the South African government's propaganda dished out through a commentary program on the SABC's Radio Republic of South Africa a week earlier. A propaganda station of the apartheid government, Radio RSA had presented what amounted to the ruling National Party government's pro-Western view of the liberation movements, equating the struggle with communist-inspired terrorism. Radio RSA's commentator said, "Terrorism has become an accepted fact," and that "terrorists armed with communist weapons are causing havoc to public and private property and killing innocent people in Vietnam, Israel, Venezuela and Rhodesia." Quite palpable in this commentary is the language of the Cold War and the apartheid government's perspective of the regional and global political developments.

The Radio Freedom commentator retorts with a counter-analysis that emphasizes the importance of solidarity and explains the escalation of guerrilla warfare in four continents involving millions of people as a justified response against Western imperialism. He gives a detailed account of the links between struggles in southern Africa, the Frelimo-led resistance; the MPLA in Angola; and joint operations between the ANC and Zimbabwe African Peoples Union (ZAPU) guerrillas in colonial Zimbabwe in 1967 and 1968. He connects these resistance movements with other anti-imperialist confrontations such as the war in Vietnam against American imperialism, and with other conflicts elsewhere. Reflecting the 1960s optimism in the capacity of the armed struggle to bring about the revolution, Dlangamandla urges the listeners to rise up and show their support for underground military operations of the freedom fighters in the whole region. This commentary is worth quoting at length:

> Fellow South Africans. Oppressed, exploited and humiliated sons of the soil, we call upon you to take inspiration from the sacrifices of our guerrilla heroes. Their blood must not be allowed to flow in vain. We call upon you to develop the struggle for freedom and national independence like wildfire. The time for action is now. Stretch your courage to the needs of the day; invoke the only

> law of resistance to tyranny and Fascism, the law of violent retaliation . . . the struggle for freedom is an accumulation of the actions of a people at war. This is why we call upon you to show your solidarity with the guerrilla heroes of Southern Africa. Steady your determination, gather your courage and lash out with all the will you have. Hit the enemy in whatever way you can, for every action is a contribution to the weakening of the enemy, and to lowering his morale. [24]

The commentary clearly demonstrates the didactic role that Radio Freedom played in terms of highlighting the importance of solidarity in the transnational struggle against Western imperialism. It informed the listeners about revolutionary struggles in other parts of the world and suggested ways of unleashing guerrilla warfare in South Africa. The ANC used this modern technology of communication to urge its audience to join the freedom fighters in the struggle to liberate the country from racial oppression and exploitation. It is remarkable that the broadcast script was produced during the middle of the joint ANC/ZAPU military campaigns in the western and eastern fronts of Southern Rhodesia (the Wankie campaign from July to September 1967, and the Sipolilo campaign from December 1967 to July 1968). [25]

It is not very clear when Radio Freedom was established for the first time in Lusaka, Zambia, but Raymond Suttner suggests that this happened in 1967 under the aegis of the ANC's Department of Information and Publicity. [26] However, the authors Lebona Mosia, Charles Riddle, and Jim Zaffiro suggest 1972 as the year in which it went on air on Radio Zambia. [27] Hugh Macmillan provides May 1973 as the date when Radio Freedom broadcasts commenced for an hour a day on Zambia Broadcasting Services' (ZBS's) new shortwave radio transmitters supplied by China. These broadcasts were shut down in 1975 due to pressure from South Africa and President Kaunda's talks with B. J. Vorster (the prime minister of South Africa) during the period of détente (1974 to 1976). [28] But Thabo Mbeki insisted that the suspension of Radio Freedom broadcasts was related to the situation in Angola whereby "Zambia wanted us [Radio Freedom] to write scripts in favour of Unita [The National Union for the Total Independence of Angola], or at least not critical of it. We refused to take instructions on what we should say and as a result Radio Freedom was closed down." [29] It was only after the 1976 Soweto student uprising and as a result of the request made by Duma Nokwe (who was then involved in the sphere of ANC diplomacy and propaganda) to the Zambian government and the ruling party (UNIP) in December of the same year that the Radio Freedom broadcasts were later resumed on the ZBS. Nokwe's motivation for the resumption of the broadcasts was based on reports from people who had recently left South Africa that testified to the effectiveness of the broadcasts, which had even reached the prisoners on Robben Island. He concluded that their resumption would immensely enhance the morale of the oppressed masses of South Africa. [30] In April 1978,

Oliver Tambo and Thomas Nkobi, ANC treasurer, could inform the Swedish embassy in Lusaka that Radio Freedom was now transmitting regularly not only from Dar es Salaam but Luanda and Lusaka as well.[31] The Swedish government was one of the major financial sponsors of the ANC in exile, especially in the period after the Soweto students' uprising of 1976, so the organization had an obligation to give a full account of how the donated funds were disbursed. The Democratic Republic of Madagascar followed suit when the Radio Freedom unit was installed in Antananarivo in 1979, and later the revolutionary government of Ethiopia approved the launch of this station in Addis Ababa.[32]

In Angola, Radio Freedom was established on the external services of Radio Luanda in 1977, followed by Radio Madagascar in 1979, and Radio Ethiopia and Radio Zimbabwe in 1981.[33] The defeat of the Portuguese colonialists in Africa, and the independence of Angola and Mozambique in 1975, allowed the ANC to establish bases very close to home. The ANC drew on alliances with fraternal liberation movements and persuaded the governments in the two newly independent countries to allow for the establishment of military training camps, to permit the transit of guerrillas and arms through these territories[34] and to make provision for the use of state broadcasting facilities. Radio Luanda in Angola extended its services to Radio Freedom, giving it one hour daily.[35] Not only did Radio Freedom receive free airtime, but production facilities and access to the news wire services were made available free by host countries. For more than two decades Radio Freedom was broadcast from outside the borders of South Africa, and at its highest point in the 1980s it was put on air daily at spread-out times and frequencies from five African countries—Angola, Ethiopia, Madagascar, Tanzania, and Zambia.[36] While most of the broadcasters were selected from the ANC camps, especially those of the MK, some of these recruits actually received training in broadcasting and radio journalism in Eastern Europe, but following the independence of Zimbabwe in 1980, most were sent to the Harare Polytech.[37]

The outbreak of the Soweto student uprising on June 16, 1976 had huge implications for exile communities and the way that the liberation struggle unfolded. Thousands of politicized youth facing brutal state repression throughout South Africa skipped the country and joined the liberation movements in exile, many of them joining the ANC and undergoing military training as MK cadres.[38] Steven Ellis and Tsepho Sechaba state that "as many as 4 000 men and women had left South Africa by early 1977, most of them determined to find arms and to return to the country as soon as possible to carry on the fight."[39] Although the PAC might have been the natural home of many of these young insurgents, given their leanings to black consciousness philosophy, the PAC was wracked by internal conflict and the arrest of Zephania Mothopeng and the nucleus of its underground, and therefore ill-prepared to welcome large numbers of students into its fold. Being the more organized and relatively well-resourced of the two liberation movements in exile, the ANC took advantage of the situation and skillfully directed these youngsters into its headquarters in exile in Lesotho, Botswana, and Swaziland.[40] During this period many of the recruits from Soweto were able to access Radio Freedom within the country; this was a major source of information and inspiration for them to join the ANC.

The Radio Freedom broadcasts appealed to youthful political activists who wanted to establish some connection with the ANC in exile. This happened notwithstanding the risks involved and the knowledge that if arrested and convicted they could spend many years in prison. Thabo Chiloane, a former teacher and political activist who was part of the ANC underground in the Bushbuckridge area in the 1970s and 1980s, remembers the inspiration he and others derived from listening to Radio Freedom while studying toward a teacher's diploma at Setotolwane Teachers Training College in Polokwane in the mid-1970s:

> During the night of the 16th [of June 1976] we were chased by the soldiers at the college and we understood that everywhere in South Africa things were bad. We believed it was the work of the Black Consciousness Movement and the ANC guys who had come to mobilise everybody. And during our stay in the college we would listen to Radio Freedom. I had a small radio and I would tune in to Radio Lusaka, and then some guys. . . . I understand it was Thabo Mbeki who would broadcast from Lusaka. So their language, those guys, was persuasive some of the phrases they would say to you, they would say that "people of South Africa your courage, your sacrifices and your great determination are breaking the chains," they used to promise us when we were listening to Radio Freedom. So who are you, that you won't be influenced by that? . . . Some of the guys I remember, they decided that enough was enough, they will cross and go . . . undergo training.[41]

Another young activist who started listening to Radio Freedom broadcasts in the 1970s is Stanley Manong. Originally from the Eastern Cape, Manong was studying civil engineering at Mmadikoti Technical College (in the Polokwane area in present-day Limpopo) in the early 1970s when he was conscientized through listening to Radio Freedom and eventually decided to skip the country and train as an MK guerrilla. He recalls:

> One of my classmates at Mmadikoti was Ronald "Rocks" Mokete Mashinini. Rocks was the elder brother of Tsietsi Mashinini. Tsietsi was the most prominent student leader of the students uprising of June 16, 1976. A week after the schools opened, on 1 February 1974, news came of the assassination of Abram Onkgopotse Tiro, who was a teacher at St Joseph's College in Kgale, near Gaborone in Botswana. . . . Tiro was killed by a parcel bomb. In the same month of Tiro's death, Boy Adelphus Mvemve (MK John Dube) was killed on

February 12, 1974, also by a parcel bomb at the offices of the ANC in Lusaka, Zambia. At the time of his death, Boy Mvemve was the Deputy Chief Representative of the ANC in Zambia since 1971. It was during this time that Rocks introduced me to Radio Freedom. . . . As expected, the main feature of Radio Freedom during that month and beyond was the assassination of the two activists. That was what first attracted Rocks to listen to Radio Freedom, being able to listen to a live broadcast of the life and times of his hero, from the studios of Radio Zambia. For Rocks and I, that was the beginning of a lifelong addiction to listening to Radio Freedom. [42]

In the aftermath of the 1976 Soweto student uprising, the ANC was convinced that through Radio Freedom it could disseminate its ideas and effectively mobilize the oppressed masses. As a result, access to more broadcasting facilities became imperative. On September 3, 1979, Tambo wrote a very detailed five-page letter to the president of Ethiopia (which was then under a military government), Lieutenant-Colonel Mengistu Haile Mariam, requesting support for the liberation struggle, specifically in the form of radio facilities for the ANC in Addis Ababa. After a very detailed appraisal of South Africa's enormous industrial capacity and resources, as well as its huge and repressive army and police force "all of which threatened the stability and peace of neighbouring independent African states," Tambo drills down to the issue of the apartheid government's formidable propaganda machinery. [43] Thereafter he gives an account of the ANC's own capacity and challenges in this sphere before making a request for Radio Freedom to be accommodated on the Ethiopian state radio in Addis Ababa, as well as for support with other logistical materials. Tambo elaborates:

> Information on the life of our people and propaganda to mobilise support for the national liberation has been of a protest type when this was necessary. It successfully achieved its goal. But with the change in our forms of struggle to combat fascist violence and police terror by sabotage and armed resistance, it follows that our propaganda must reflect this revolutionary strategy. In short, propaganda to be effective (in peace and wartime) must be related to mass action or preparation for such action. In our propaganda work both at home and abroad we are shifting emphasis from mere appeals and protests to militant involvement of the people on the side of their vanguard movement, the A.N.C. This requires revolutionary and agitational material and fast methods of communication with the people. [44]

Tambo concludes his letter by providing a detailed list of things requested from the Ethiopian government, which would strengthen his movement's capacity to accomplish its mission. These included radio broadcasting facilities on Ethiopia's Voice of the Revolution for at least thirty to sixty minutes every day, which would be manned by two ANC broadcasters in Addis; technical equipment in the form of two Sony CF 950S tape recorders with

headphones; 200 cassettes; 50 tape reels, size 18cm; two portable tape recorders with accessories and tapes; one photocopier; one portable electric
typewriter and two heavy office ones; a camera with a variety of lenses,
filters, tripod, light meter, and film); one vehicle for transport; and passports
for at least six of the top functionaries in the Department of Information and
Publicity.[45] By the early 1980s, Radio Freedom was broadcasting from the
External Services of Socialist Ethiopia's Voice of the Revolution. This suggests that the ANC president's appeal in 1979 for support for radio broadcasting services did not fall on deaf ears in Ethiopia, and throughout the
1980s international solidarity with the liberation movement was at an all-
time high.

THE EASTERN BLOC AND
SUPPORT FOR RADIO FREEDOM

The type of support that the Eastern Bloc provided to the ANC's media
initiatives, particularly radio, is huge but very difficult to prove because of
inaccessibility of the archives in Moscow. In his book *ANC: A View from
Moscow*, Vladimir Shubin discusses the nature of support given by the USSR
to the ANC and its military wing, Umkhonto we Sizwe (MK). Shubin informs us that a real breakthrough in relations between the Soviet Union and
the South African liberation movement happened in 1963. Although this
process was initiated by the South African Communist Party (SACP), the
visit by Oliver Tambo to Moscow in April of that year and further talks in the
same city again, on his way back from Beijing, China, gave this process
major impetus. At his meetings with the officials of the Communist Party of
the Soviet Union (CPSU) on October 9 and 10, 1963, Tambo confirmed the
need to send new and larger groups of Umkhonto fighters (up to 300 at a
time) for training in the USSR. He explained that it was not possible either to
organize appropriate training in African countries, or to import Soviet military specialists to train ANC members in Africa.[46]

Besides military training and support with arms, the ANC received direct
financial assistance from the Soviet Union from 1963, and this would continue for many more years. The first allocation to the ANC was US$300,000
(compared to the SACP's US$56,000), which was an enormous sum of mon-
ey in those days. In fact, the ANC and the Indian Communist Party were
placed ninth and tenth among eighty-five recipients of financial support from
the USSR. The MPLA of Angola and Zapu of Zimbabwe received
US$50,000 each. In 1963 the newly established Communist Party of Lesotho
received US$52,000.[47] Some limited financial support had, in fact, been
given to the ANC even earlier.[48] The Soviet Union was the greatest pillar of
(financial and military) support for the liberation movement in South Africa,

particularly after the turn to the armed struggle; this is confirmed by fragmentary evidence from interviews with former MK fighters. In addition to receiving military training, some freedom fighters were offered training in print and radio journalism in the Soviet Union and East Germany. Since radio broadcasting was a core feature of the armed struggle, it can be deduced that part of the material support for the ANC's armed struggle from the Soviet Union trickled down to radio broadcasting—for example the purchase of broadcasting equipment and audiocassettes.

Oupa Maluleke is a former broadcaster of Radio Freedom in Angola and Tanzania, and director of this radio in Madagascar. After skipping the country in 1976 and undergoing six months of training in journalism and propaganda in the Soviet Union, Maluleke was deployed on Radio Freedom as a broadcaster for more than fifteen years of his political activism. He was a broadcaster in Angola for three years, from 1976 to 1979; Tanzania from 1979 to 1981; and Madagascar from 1981 to 1991. In Madagascar he served as the head of both Radio Freedom and the Department of Information and Publicity.[49] About the training he received in the Soviet Union, Maluleke had this to say:

> It was basically Journalism, because when we left we were not trained as journalists in terms of writing skills and how to counter misinformation or disinformation campaigns. Because we were always taught that the truth was very very [sic] vital when we were fighting the liberation struggle. You counter the enemy by speaking the truth because the enemy relied on lying. Like Hitler during the Second World War; you know, the Nazis they manipulated the minds of the German people through lies. We were taught that the truth will always prevail. It is not like . . . you know people have got this misconception that propaganda is lies. No, the Russians taught us that propaganda was telling the truth, depending on which side you are.[50]

Makhosazana Xaba is another former ANC activist to receive both military training and training as a journalist in the Soviet Union and the German Democratic Republic (GDR, or East Germany). Born in KwaZulu-Natal in 1957, Khosi, as she is popularly known, grew up at Ndaleni, where she attended school at Pholela and completed matriculation in 1975 at Inanda Seminary, a very progressive school that encouraged students to think critically and independently. Her political conscientization deepened in 1976 through listening to Radio Zulu and Springbok radio, which covered the news on the June 16, 1976 Soweto students' uprising. Between 1982 and 1984, she studied for a nursing administration degree at the University of Zululand, Ngoye, where she became active in the student movements and the Students Representative Council (SRC). She was one of the seven students who were expelled from the university in 1984, never allowed to return.[51]

At that time (mid-1980s) Khosi became connected to the MK operatives and in the same year she learned about Radio Freedom although she was never able to tune in to it—she never got the frequency right. Then in 1986 she skipped the country and went to Maputo in Mozambique, then to Zambia and on to Pango in Angola (1987) where she underwent military training. After a few months she was flown to Moscow for further training before she was brought back to Zambia, where she was assigned to the office of the ANC Women's League. She worked with Mavivi Myakayaka (later Manzini) who oversaw the ANC women's magazine *Voice of Women*. Then she was sent to the GDR for further training (a six-month crash course) as a journalist at the Werner Lamberz School of Journalism, focusing on both radio and paper journalism. Thereafter she returned to Zambia in 1988, where she was deployed to Radio Freedom. She was responsible for a daily news program in the morning, "The ANC International," and a weekend cultural program dealing with music and book reviews. Many other cadres received their military and journalistic training in the Eastern bloc.[52] For its part, the Soviet Union's support for the liberation movements in southern Africa was motivated not only by its abhorrence of colonialism but also by the desire to expand its sphere of influence within the context of the Cold War.

SWEDISH SUPPORT FOR ANC RADIO BROADCASTING

International support for the liberation movements in South Africa was not only limited to the Eastern bloc; there were also Western countries that played a major role in this regard. The Nordic countries in general (Norway, Sweden, Denmark, and Finland) played an important role, but Sweden topped the list. Whereas in many Western countries it was the civic society groups that vigorously supported the liberation movements in Africa, in Sweden it was the government itself that directly advanced financial assistance to the liberation movements, especially the ANC. Sweden, through the Swedish International Development Authority (SIDA), started giving direct financial assistance to the ANC in 1973. This is comparatively late when set against other liberation movements (such as Zanu, Frelimo, MPLA and even Unita) in the region. In the beginning, support for the ANC was seen as a stopgap measure, so only modest allocations were granted.

Sweden gave the support to the ANC despite the dissenting voices in favor of other organizations. This support "was made permanent and soon assumed a more pro-active political character than the assistance extended to the other Southern African liberation movements."[53] Swedish support for the ANC, which was based on long-term dealings between the two, increased significantly in the second half of the 1970s. The focus was on capacity building and on strengthening the internal base of the liberation movement on top of immediate humanitarian needs. By the late 1970s, this relationship had evolved into a form of institutional cooperation "outside the military field paving the way for support to central functions of the future South African ruling party."[54]

The Swedish government made a decisive intervention in support of the ANC after the independence of Angola and Mozambique, and in response to the need of the liberation movement after the Soweto student uprising when thousands of youth sought refuge in these countries. The social democratic government under Olof Palme took the initiative and bore the financial costs of the establishment of the ANC presence in Luanda, financing the onward transportation of recruits to Angola as well as the delivery of food and other daily necessities to the camps in that country. This support was then consolidated by Thorbjörn Fälldin's non-socialist coalition. Swedish involvement contributed significantly to the reemergence and visibility of the ANC as a major player in South African politics post-1976, which found expression through armed operations. The Swedish government extended this support on humanitarian grounds, which the ANC acknowledged at the time as "of decisive importance." "In an unsettled Southern African political environment and a divided Cold war context, a flexible interpretation of humanitarian assistance paved the way for special relations."[55]

Sweden accepted the ANC's calls around 1975 for assistance in the Department of Information and Publicity in order to break out of its isolation. It should be remembered that the host countries in Africa where the ANC had bases had very limited resources to keep them afloat, so financial support from Sweden was quite opportune.[56] The ANC included funds for "information, publicity and propaganda" as a line item in the 1975–1976 budget in its application for financial assistance from Sweden in February 1975. This financial support was needed to keep up the regular production of the fortnightly journal *Mayibuye*.[57] By mid-1975 the Swedish funding policy for the ANC was no longer only about commodity aid (money for daily necessities for the members in Tanzania and Zambia), but included a budget for information and publicity. Out of a total amount of one million Swedish krona (SEK) budgeted for 1975–1976, the amount of 419,000 SEK was specifically allocated to "miscellaneous" items and this money was used, inter alia, for "support towards ANC's information efforts." In subsequent years the ANC would use Swedish funds to issue not only *Mayibuye* but also *Voice of Women* (the journal of the ANC Women's Secretariat) and other publications inside the country.[58]

Noting that in the past the ANC had not given enough attention to information and publicity, Oliver Tambo drafted a section on information, publicity, and propaganda that was submitted in May 1976 with the funding request for 1976–1977. During his meeting in the same year with Anders Bjurner,

Tambo described information and publicity as "absolutely the most important [component]," and explained that the leadership of the ANC was busy
preparing the launch of an "information offensive" against the apartheid
state, and that the request to the Swedish government formed part of that
initiative.[59] By the early 1970s, only Zambia and Tanzania supported Radio
Freedom broadcasting on the external services of their state broadcasters.
However, by late 1975 Zambia had discontinued Radio Freedom broadcasts
to South Africa as part of the ill-fated "détente exercise," which meant that at
the time of submitting the 1976–1977 funding request to Sweden, Radio
Freedom had access to broadcasting services only in Tanzania. However, the
Angolan government had already made an offer to Radio Freedom and things
looked promising from that side, as well as from other friendly countries.
Against this background, the ANC submitted a request to Sweden for both
printing and radio equipment.[60]

The submission by the ANC finally bore positive results when, out of the
initial ANC allocation of three million SEK for 1976–1977, 281,000 SEK
was earmarked for "information component." From then onward, Swedish
support for the ANC's Department of Information and Publicity, within
which Radio Freedom was situated, would feature regularly in the program
of cooperation between Sweden and the ANC. In 1977–1978 the allocation
for this component was raised to 430,000 SEK, and in 1978–1979 to 600,000
SEK. By 1984–1985, this department was allocated over 1.9 million krona
and so work on the "information offensive" to which Tambo had referred
could get under way.[61]

In a meeting with Carin Norberg from SIDA in October 1976, Thabo
Mbeki, in his capacity as Tambo's assistant and head of information and
publicity, discussed the modalities of how the 1976–1977 grant for information would be used. Mbeki proposed that in addition to supplying telex
equipment, Sweden should supply the ANC with four shortwave radio units
for purposes of internal communications. These radio units would be installed in Dar es Salaam, Luanda, Lusaka, and Maputo. In addition, he included the training of two radio operators in the plan, which was formalized
through a written request. In the end, SIDA secured the services of Swedtel,
the official consultancy company, to implement this radio service. The same
consultancy had actually assisted the African Party for the Independence of
Guinea and Cape Verde (PAIGC) of Guinea-Bissau with the setting up of a
mobile radio station in that country in 1972, and the ANC project was only
implemented in 1977.[62] By that year, only Radio Tanzania in Dar es Salaam
provided some airtime to Radio Freedom,[63] which probably meant that reception of its broadcasts in South Africa was very limited. Several host
countries were still reluctant to launch Radio Freedom broadcasts, chief
among which was Zambia. However, the situation took a turn as a result of
the failure of détente and the aftermath of the 1976 Soweto students uprising.

Apart from assistance with the purchase and installation of equipment in the stations of Radio Freedom, Swedish support came in the form of daily necessities and cash allowances for Radio Freedom staff in their exile locations.[64] Funds allocated under the "home front component" were also used for clandestine distribution of the Radio Freedom broadcasts in South Africa, as had been done with the ANC's official publications. Shortwave radio receivers, cassette recorders and duplicating equipment were procured for purposes of disseminating ANC propaganda. The ANC was able to report triumphantly in January 1986, that "we have . . . formed radio clubs inside the country, where our units are able to monitor 'Radio Freedom,' dub our programmes, reproduce the dubbed material and distribute it as propaganda."[65] All this was made possible by the Swedish government's generous financial support for the ANC and its radio broadcasting initiatives.

DUTCH SUPPORT AND OMROEP VOOR RADIO FREEDOM

Unlike the situation in Sweden, where the government played a key role in providing financial support to the liberation movements in southern Africa, in the Netherlands the civil society groups were at the forefront of support. Part of this assistance coalesced around radio, primarily because the supporting agencies remained limited by the political sensitivities of the Cold War period within their respective nations. Rather than providing direct military aid, the Swedish and Dutch development agencies, and later the Dutch anti-apartheid movement's support group, Omroep voor Radio Freedom (literally "Broadcasting for Radio Freedom"), all devised creative strategies of supporting what they saw as a just struggle that conservative right-wing critics unfairly depicted as a communist cabal.[66]

Omroep voor Radio Freedom (OvRF) was officially launched in Amsterdam in November 1982, on the occasion of the seventieth anniversary of the ANC. It was but one among several campaigns mooted by the activists of the Anti-Apartheidsbeweging Nederland (AABN, or the Dutch anti-apartheid movement). A group of media workers—broadcasters, journalists, editors, and technicians—played a significant role in the formation of OvRF, or simply Omroep (as it was called within ANC circles), which was established at the behest of Thami Ntenteni, the director of Radio Freedom in Lusaka (see figure 8). Prior to the formation of Omroep, the Dutch public had very limited knowledge of the ANC and its radio station, so it is thanks to this support group that Radio Freedom became "a household word in Holland."[67] Omroep played a key role in raising awareness of the injustices of the apartheid system, state monopoly of the media, and the need to support campaigns for media pluralism in South Africa.

A group of AABN activists began their campaigning for Radio Freedom a few months before the formal launch in November. This campaigning culminated in a "Week of Action," during which anti-apartheid groups traveled around the country in an old Volkswagen minibus "modelled to represent a mobile studio of Radio Freedom."[68] Money was collected and flyers containing information about the apartheid system in South Africa and Radio Freedom were handed out. A small awareness-raising concert was held where a famous Dutch band gave a performance and all the takings were given to Radio Freedom.[69]

The first "Week of Action" laid the foundation for the second week, the beginning of a larger and more sustained campaign that involved radio and television broadcasters. Whereas the first week of action was spearheaded solely by the anti-apartheid activists under the banner of the AABN and without involving the media workers to any significant degree, in the second "Week of Action" the AABN activists placed the broadcasters at the center because this particular campaign concerned radio.[70]

In its formative stages Omroep had five people drawn from various radio stations with differing political orientations. These media professionals embarked on a recruitment drive within the media industry, managing to bring on board about sixty radio and television workers, predominantly journalists, from the thirteen broadcasting companies, three freelancers, and three other organizations (the Federatie Nederlandse Vakbeweging (FNV), AABN, and Radio Netherlands/Wereldomroep). Although the campaign was managed by the AABN, it was actually these sixty media workers who were the backbone of Omroep voor Radio Freedom and who made it possible for campaigners to have easy and unhindered access to the media.[71]

One of Omroep's founder members and activists was Dr. Karel Roskam, a radio journalist with the progressive broadcaster Vara, a socialist-aligned radio station.[72] Roskam was the first Dutch person to be banned from entering South Africa for a period of thirty years (1960–1990) on account of his views on apartheid articulated in his widely publicized book.[73] The book was based on his PhD dissertation that he had researched in the country in 1959, which was critical of the system of apartheid and its effects on interracial relationships. Upon arrival in South Africa in that year, Roskam attached himself for about seven months to the University of the Witwatersrand as a postgraduate student. During this visit he met and made friends with political activists such as Mendi Msimang, John Nkadimeng, Ruth First, Joe Slovo, Ben Turok, Bram Fischer, and Baruch Hirson. He even joined the Congress of Democrats and attended the Treason Trial where he met Nelson Mandela and other ANC leaders.[74]

Following the formation of Omroep in 1982, Roskam became a very important and central figure in the campaigns of this support group and as a journalist he made sure that the Dutch public was informed about the political developments inside South Africa, and also gave good coverage to the leaders of the ANC in exile in his radio broadcasts. According to Fulco van Aurich, a former member of Omroep, Roskam wrote a petition that included a statement proclaiming support for freedom of speech in South Africa and comparing the ANC's Radio Freedom to Radio Oranje, the Dutch underground radio that broadcast from exile in London into the Netherlands during the German occupation of 1940 to 1945.[75] This comparison was frequently drawn in promoting Radio Freedom to the Dutch public and in the end about 1100 media workers signed the petition.[76] These broadcasters gave enormous support to their colleagues at Radio Freedom, who worked hard to bring alternative views to the South African public, and in this way Omroep became a rather exceptional "collective effort of the broadcast workers themselves."[77]

From its beginning in 1982, Omroep's fund-raising campaigns were a success and the Dutch people proved receptive to the cause and gave it overwhelming support. The Dutch broadcasters donated free spots on radio and television that were quite short and simple. Usually, radio spots included the opening signature tune of Radio Freedom, which featured the heavy sound of machine guns, singing, and the opening address. The voice of Thami Ntenteni would come next as he provided the Dutch listeners with a short overview of the role of Radio Freedom in English, along with details of the bank where supporters could deposit their donations to the station. The recordings of these spots were then shared among the group of sixty members, who would circulate further to their respective broadcasting corporations where they were played on air. These recordings received daily airplay across stations, free of charge.[78]

The same principle was applied to the production of television spots. For example, a television spot was recorded at Galgenwaard soccer stadium in Utrecht, featuring the renowned Dutch comedian Freek de Jonge and the Surinam-born internationally renowned soccer player, Ruud Gullit, who would take a penalty, shooting the ball through the head of a figure constructed to resemble P. W. Botha, then president of apartheid South Africa. Botha's now decapitated head was substituted with that of de Jonge, begging audiences to sponsor Radio Freedom. Neither de Jonge nor Gullit expected to be paid for their services as this was their contribution to the cause. In addition, a benefit concert was held in a large venue simply known as "013," situated in the small town of Tilburg. This is the venue where Doe Maar, a very popular Dutch band among young teenage girls, gave a performance and all takings from the concert went to Radio Freedom.[79]

Omroep also devised many other methods in which the Dutch public could donate funds in support of Radio Freedom (see figure 11). On May 1–5, 1985, a Radio Freedom Festival was held in Tilburg, followed closely by another one in Amsterdam on May 12. This festival was made up of a series of cultural (all musical) events with a benefit character. The performers participating in the festival readily gave up their radio and television rights in order to increase the income for Radio Freedom. The event, which was broadcast for five hours on radio and one hour on television, was completely oversubscribed and about 1,600 people attended the festival. It succeeded in raising about €50,000, sufficient to finance a fully fitted mobile studio.[80]

Every autumn following the formation of Omroep in 1982, the supportive radio stations held a "Radio Freedom Day." This was a fundraising event in which listeners could give monetary donations, either to win the jacket of Ruud Gullit or to hear their favorite popular song. However, not everyone in Holland was necessarily keen on Omroep's activities for Radio Freedom; in fact, some were hostile. In 1983 (the first year of Radio Freedom Day), unknown attackers shot at the glass door of Vara studio four times.[81] In the following year (1984), Donald Gobane, then director of Radio Freedom in Lusaka, Zambia, came to visit Holland and, as was the usual practice with Omroep, stayed at the house of Huub Bammens, another Omroep activist. Many years later Bammens would discover that the Dutch government operatives in conjunction with the National Party government agents had tapped all the phones in the house, presumably to monitor the activities of the group.[82] Such activities, however, were not enough to deter the animated Dutch public from raising funds for a cause they considered noble—helping Radio Freedom to achieve its main objective of reaching listeners back home and challenging government propaganda.

Omroep assisted a great deal in collecting funds through publicity on radio and television, through advertisements, concerts, sponsoring, and so forth. The broadcasters were widely supported by artists in various fields: musicians, entertainers, writers, and painters. A successful benefit performance could be organized because all the artists appeared free of charge. An exhibition on censorship was composed of work by Dutch artists who, free of charge, drew impressive cartoons on the subject.[83]

Between 1982 and 1989, Omroep was able to collect well over US$750,000, money that was used to purchase broadcasting equipment (including audiotapes) for Radio Freedom studios in Lusaka, Addis Ababa, Luanda, Antananarivo, Dar es Salaam, and Mazimbu.[84] By 1985, Omroep had already contributed two studios to Radio Freedom—one in Antananarivo (1983), and the other one in Lusaka, (1984). Between 1985 and 1989, Omroep donated three more studios to Radio Freedom that were installed in Ethiopia, Angola, and Tanzania, respectively. The studios consisted of eight small channel mixers—an audio mixer with one turntable, three Otari tape recorders, tapes, and some microphones. A Dutch radio technician would typically travel with the studios to their locations. Upon arrival, the technician would install the equipment with the assistance of the Radio Freedom staff. Radio Freedom staff were trained "technically in using the equipment." In this way, if something would happen and nobody was around to help, they could also help themselves. The studios were purposefully made to be mobile since during the 1980s the Botha regime unleashed military attacks against neighboring countries that gave refuge to the ANC and there was constant fear that Radio Freedom would be targeted.[85]

Omroep also assisted in improving the system of Radio Freedom broadcasting by providing training in radio making to Radio Freedom workers. Omroep held its first training course at the ANC's Solomon Mahlangu College (SOMAFCO) in Mazimbu, Tanzania; this training was provided mainly by Huub Bammens and Karel Roskam.[86] Using a fraction of the funds collected by Omroep, about seven Radio Freedom workers (broadcasters and operators) were at the same time enrolled for international training courses in technique, maintenance, and journalism at the Radio Netherlands Training Centre (RNTC) in Hilversum.[87] By providing training and donating broadcasting equipment to the ANC radio, Omroep contributed immensely toward enhancing the quality of Radio Freedom programming and reception right at the time when there was growing demand among radio listeners for alternative voices inside South Africa.

In August 1988, the Dutch media workers, under the slogan, "Keep Radio Freedom on the Air!" launched a campaign to collect funds to buy a high-powered 250-kilowatt shortwave transmitter for Radio Freedom. Their intention was to have this transmitter installed in a secret location in a territory of an African country so that the people in South Africa would be able to receive the Radio Freedom broadcasts.[88] While Radio Freedom had access to the shortwave transmitters of host countries, these were not owned by the ANC, so when they broke down, Radio Freedom was incapacitated from broadcasting its programs into South Africa. Furthermore, the white minority regime had increased its technical capacity to obstruct the voice of the ANC through jamming. The shortwave transmitters in use by the ANC were too weak and always succumbed to the jamming signal, thus depriving certain parts of Africa from receiving Radio Freedom programs. It was thought that giving Radio Freedom its own transmitter would assist in overcoming reception problems.[89] The Omroep campaigners realized, however, that the Dutch people would not be able to launch such a shortwave transmitter on their own because it was too expensive—and thus started mobilizing internationally so that support groups in other countries could collaborate in the initiative.[90]

How, then, do we account for this overwhelming support for Radio Freedom in the Netherlands? Firstly, besides the relative strength of the Dutch anti-apartheid movement, the Dutch public provided specific support to Radio Freedom mainly because they still had vivid memories of how, during the Second World War, the Nazi occupation forces heavily censored the news in the Netherlands. Thus, the situation of the oppressed in apartheid

South Africa in the 1980s had some resonance. "In those years of misery, 1940–1945, the Dutch people listened clandestinely to Radio Oranje, a Dutch broadcasting station transmitting news in Dutch from London."[91] As was the case with Radio Freedom in apartheid South Africa, it was a crime to listen to Radio Oranje in the Netherlands during the Nazi occupation. Omroep capitalized on this history by drawing parallels between the two radios, knowing pretty well that the difficulties that Radio Freedom in exile had in its attempts to connect with audiences in South Africa would touch a raw nerve with the Dutch broadcasters and the audiences at large.

The second key reason that the Dutch supported the ANC's clandestine radio was the effectiveness of ANC propaganda and the global visibility of its campaign. By the 1980s, the stature of ANC figures such as Nelson Mandela and Walter Sisulu, who were serving life sentences on Robben Island, had gained international coverage. The use of their symbolism in the countrywide mobilization by the United Democratic Front (inside South Africa) served to attract followers for Omroep among the Dutch public and hence their support for Radio Freedom. In spite of the Cold War and the ANC's affiliation with Marxist-aligned countries and its adoption of the armed struggle, many in the Netherlands, particularly the progressive left constituting the bulk of supporters of Omroep voor Radio Freedom, and even moderates, strongly felt that Radio Freedom should have the right to broadcast without risking imprisonment.[92]

In 1990, while the "Keep Radio Freedom on the Air" campaign was in full swing, the ANC and other political organizations were unbanned, followed by the release of Nelson Mandela and other political prisoners. South Africans who had been in exile started finding their way back home, so the need for a powerful 250-kilowatt transmitter diminished. Omroep voor Radio Freedom was uncertain as to what to do with the funds it had collected at the same time that the ANC was forced to face the question of how to transform the broadcasting landscape, should the ANC become the new government. Against this background the "Jabulani! Freedom of the Airwaves Conference" was organized in Doorn in the Netherlands in August 1991, to discuss the new role that radio and television would have to play in a democratizing society. This conference was attended by about fifty delegates drawn from a broad range of South African organizations concerned with broadcasting. In the end, the funds collected by Omroep were diverted into an ill-fated Radio Freedom–related training initiative called the Johannesburg Radio Freedom Institute in Bertrams, and Omroep voor Radio Freedom finally closed shop in 1994.

At an event on the tenth anniversary of Omroep in December 1992, Nelson Mandela delivered a speech in which he acknowledged the pivotal role that Omroep played in galvanizing support for the liberation movement and ensuring that Radio Freedom was heard in the Netherlands. Mandela, in his own words, had this to say:

> I feel particularly honoured to be the one to express our heartfelt gratitude to the Dutch people in general, for the unrelenting support you have rendered to the ANC, and Radio Freedom in particular, during the most difficult period in the history of our struggle against apartheid....
>
> Today, Radio Freedom, like Radio Orange, its Dutch counterpart during the Second World War, has become a household name in Holland. Both radios came into existence under singularly difficult circumstances. It was a time when the forces of oppression had launched an all-out offensive against the forces of justice, peace and human dignity.
>
> The spirit of resistance of the Dutch people under the threat from Fascism was kept alive by Radio Orange. In South Africa, it became the task of Radio Freedom to mobilise and organise the people against the tyranny of apartheid. Both Radios were an expression of the resilience and indomitable nature of the human spirit when confronted with injustice and inhumanity.
>
> The honourable task of keeping our people informed in the face of disinformation and the conspiracy of silence then prevailing, was made easier by your unstinting support. Without your steadfast and principled support, it is difficult to imagine how we could have made these giant strides towards freedom and democracy in our country. [93]

CONCLUSION

Some independent African countries, particularly in eastern and southern Africa, that were pan-Africanist and anti-imperialist in political outlook and orientation, played a major role in giving various forms of support to the liberation movements in southern Africa, including their broadcasting ventures. The ANC's Radio Freedom was no exception. Support for the liberation movements' broadcasting was crucial for the prosecution of the struggle against white minority rule in southern Africa. The support received from the host countries in the form of broadcasting facilities, airtime, and so forth enabled Radio Freedom and other fraternal radio stations in the region to connect with their listeners back home, to mobilize the masses, to influence political developments, and to counter the white minority governments' propaganda messages disseminated through state radio stations. Equally, the support from solidarity groups in eastern and western Europe made it possible for Radio Freedom to accomplish its goals of broadcasting to audiences back home, influencing the struggle against apartheid, shaping public opinion, and countering apartheid propaganda both at home and abroad. All this happened despite the apartheid state's counter-strategy of signal jamming Radio Freedom's programs.

Despite its location outside South Africa's borders, and destabilization by the apartheid state, Radio Freedom was able to go beyond the purview of the state and to reach specific audiences inside South Africa. Through the financial and other forms of support received from the Nordic countries, particularly Sweden, as well as from support groups such as Omroep voor Radio Freedom, Radio Freedom was able to stay on air. Its broadcasters attained appropriate training, enabling the station to play a major role as an alternative popular voice to a captive audience inside the country during the heyday of apartheid. This radio offered a different perspective of the history of South Africa, and it gave political education to its listeners about what the ANC stood for. It provided information about the campaigns that the ANC supporters inside the country should engage in, and it became a major source of inspiration for political activists wanting to skip the country in order to join the liberation movement.

NOTES

1. See http://www.anc.org.za/show.php?id=4570 .

2. The secondary literature covers the following texts: Vladimir Shubin, *ANC: A View from Moscow* (Bellville: Mayibuye, 1999); Tor Sellström, ed., *Liberation in Southern Africa: Regional and Swedish Voices—Interviews from Angola, Mozambique, Namibia, South Africa, Zimbabwe, the Frontline and Sweden* (Uppsala: Nordiska Afrikainstitutet, 2002); Tor Sellström, *Sweden and the National Liberation in Southern Africa Volume II: Solidarity and Assistance 1970—1994* (Uppsala: Nordiska Afrikainstitutet, 2002); Christopher Munthe Morgenstierne, *Denmark and the National Liberation in Southern Africa: A Flexible Response* (Uppsala: Nordiska Afrikainstitutet), 2003; South African Democracy Education Trust (hereafter SADET), *The Road to Democracy in South Africa Volume 3: International Solidarity Part 1 & 2* (Pretoria: Unisa Press, 2008); as well as other volumes before and after.

3. For a more comprehensive analysis of the early years of Radio Freedom, see, for example, Sekibakiba P. Lekgoathi, "ANC's Radio Freedom and Its Audiences in Apartheid South Africa," *Journal of African Media Studies* 2, no. 2 (2010): 139–53; "ANC's Radio Freedom, Its Audiences and the Struggle against Apartheid in South Africa," in *The Road to Democracy in South Africa Volume 6, 1990–1996*, ed. SADET, 549–87 (Pretoria: Unisa Press, 2013).

4. Lebona Mosia, Charles Riddle, and Joseph Zaffiro, "From Revolutionary to Regime Radio: Three Decades of Nationalist Broadcasting in Southern Africa," *Africa Media Review* 8, no. 1 (1994): 5.

5. William A. Hachten, *Muffled Drums: The News Media in Africa* (Ames: Iowa State University Press, 1971), 117–18, cited in Mosia, Riddle, and Zaffiro, "From Revolutionary to Regime Radio," 6.

6. Mosia, Riddle, and Zaffiro, "From Revolutionary to Regime Radio," 6.

7. Rusty Bernstein, *Memory against Forgetting: Memoirs from a Life in South African Politics, 1938–1964* (London: Viking, 1999).

8. According to Nicholas Wolpe, the farm was bought by the SACP. In contrast, Nelson Mandela states that it was bought "by the movement" in August 1961 "for the purpose of having a safe house for those underground," including Mandela, who was himself an underground operative at the time. See Nelson Mandela, *Long Walk to Freedom: The Autobiography of Nelson Mandela* (Johannesburg: Macdonald Purnell, 1994), 268; Nicholas Wolpe, "Memory, Legacy, Heritage and Monuments Define Us as People and a Nation," *The Thinker* 52 (June 2013): 51.

9. Stephen R. Davis, "Voices from Without: The African National Congress, Its Radio, Its Allies and Exile," *Journal of Southern African Studies* 35, no. 2 (2009): 349–73.

10. At that time, Walter Sisulu was the general secretary of the ANC. He was banned following his conviction for furthering the aims of the illegal ANC, but was out on bail and

operating underground. See Denis Goldberg, *The Mission: A Life for Freedom in South Africa* (Johannesburg: STE Publisher, 2010), 99.

11. Ibid.

12. Ibid., 100.

13. Fuzzy and Archie Levitan were comrades who had long dropped out of open political activity but were, nonetheless, active underground. See Ibid.

14. Davis, "Voices from Without," 351; Goldberg, *Mission*, 100.

15. Walter M. Sisulu, "Document 72, Broadcast on ANC Radio, 26 June 1963," in *From Protest to Challenge: A Documentary History of African Politics in South Africa, 1882–1990 Volume 3*, ed. Thomas Karis and Gwendolen M. Carter, 759–760 (Stanford: Hoover Institution Press, 1977).

16. Goldberg, *Mission*, 100.

17. Bernstein, *Memory against Forgetting*, 229. However, Raymond Suttner suggests that clandestine broadcasting in the country continued for a short while after the conclusion of the Rivonia Trial and one of these broadcasts featured Wilton Mkwayi, another prominent ANC leader and head of the MK's High Command. Raymond Suttner, *The ANC Underground in South Africa, 1950–1976: A Social and Historical Study* (Auckland Park: Jacana Media, 2008), 68.

18. Luli Callinicos, *Oliver Tambo: Beyond the Engeli Mountains* (Cape Town: David Philip, 2004), 253–302.

19. Elias C. J. Tarimo and Neville Z. Reuben, "Tanzania's Solidarity with South Africa's Liberation," in *The Road to Democracy in South Africa Volume 5: African Solidarity Part 1*, ed. SADET, 202 (Pretoria: Unisa Press, 2013).

20. Mosia, Riddle, and Zaffiro, "From Revolutionary to Regime Radio," 6.

21. Ibid.

22. Cited in Mosia, Riddle, and Zaffiro, "From Revolutionary to Regime Radio," 7.

23. Mosia, Riddle, and Zaffiro, "From Revolutionary to Regime Radio," 7; James M. Kushner, "African Liberation Broadcasting," *Journal of Broadcasting* 18, no. 3 (June 1974): 299–309.

24. University of Fort Hare (hereafter UFH) Liberation Archives, Box 18, Folder 156: Radio Freedom Broadcasts, 1966–1968, The African National Congress of South Africa "Commentary No. 26: Solidarity for Our Liberation Heroes," April 1, 1968, ANC Morogoro.

25. For more details on the joint ANC/ZAPU military campaigns at Wankie and Sipolilo, see Rendani Ralinala et al., "The Wankie and Sipolilo Campaigns," in *The Road to Democracy in South Africa Volume 1: 1960–1970*, ed. SADET, 435–90 (Pretoria: Unisa Press, 2004).

26. Suttner, *The ANC Underground*, 68.

27. In Zambia, Radio Freedom programs were aired on the External Services of Radio Zambia in Lusaka on shortwave 31-megaband on 9505KHz. See *Sechaba*, June 1981.

28. Hugh Macmillan, *The Lusaka Years: The ANC in Exile in Zambia, 1963–1994* (Auckland Park: Jacana Media, 2013), 117–18.

29. Interview with President Thabo Mbeki, conducted by Hugh Macmillan, Johannesburg, October 11, 2011; cited in Macmillan, *Lusaka Years*, 118.

30. Ibid., 124.

31. Elisabeth Michanek, Memorandum "Meeting with Oliver Tambo on 11 April 1978," Swedish Embassy, Lusaka, 20 April 1978 (ANC), cited in Sellström, *Sweden and National Liberation in Southern Africa*, 603.

32. Sellström, *Sweden and National Liberation in Southern Africa*, 603.

33. Mosia, Riddle, and Zaffiro, "From Revolutionary to Regime Radio," 8.

34. Stephen Ellis and Tsepo Sechaba, *Comrades against Apartheid: The ANC and the South African Communist Party in Exile* (London: James Currey, Bloomington: Indiana University Press, 1992), 80–85; Baruch Hirson, *Revolutions in My Life* (Johannesburg: Witwatersrand University Press, 1995), 34.

35. Ellis and Sechaba, *Comrades against Apartheid*, 133.

36. Suttner, *ANC Underground*, 68.

37. Mosia, Riddle, and Zaffiro, "From Revolutionary to Regime Radio," 8.

38. Mayibuye Centre Archives (hereafter MCA), University of the Western Cape (UWC), 8, Papers of the Dutch Anti-Apartheid Organisations (1959–1994), Audiocassette 1204, interview with Christian Seleke and Ronnie Kasrils, conducted by Karel Roskam, Lusaka, August 1, 1986.

39. Ellis and Sechaba, *Comrades against Apartheid*, 84.

40. Ibid.

41. Interview with Thabo Chiloane, conducted by Tshepo Moloi, Bushbuckridge, Mpumalanga Province, November 19, 2013.

42. Stanley Manong, *" If We Must Die": An Autobiography of a Former Commander of Umkhonto we Sizwe* (Cape Town: Nkululeko Publishers, 2015), 38–39.

43. UFH Liberation Archives, Oliver Tambo Papers, Box 36: "Letter by Oliver Tambo to H.E. Lieutenant-Colonel Mengistu Haile Mariam," dated September 3, 1979.

44. Ibid.

45. Ibid.

46. Shubin, *ANC: A View from Moscow*, 62.

47. Ibid.

48. Shubin tells us that the Central Committee's decision on mass training of MK members was taken on the eve of Tambo's arrival. Special courses to train guerrilla commanders and various specialists were organized in Odessa, on the shores of the Black Sea. He also informs us that some of the ANC members who received military training in Odessa were Joe Modise (Thabo More), Moses Mabhida, Josiah Jele, Ronnie Kasrils, Chris Hani, etc. See Shubin, *ANC: A View from Moscow*, 63.

49. Interview with Oupa Maluleke, conducted by Tshepo Moloi, Ennerdale Extension 9, February 15, 2017.

50. Ibid.

51. Interview with Makhosazana "Khosi" Xaba, conducted by Sekibakiba Lekgoathi and Tshepo Moloi, December 15, 2016.

52. Thami Ntenteni (nom de guerre Don Hashe) is another broadcaster who underwent training in the Eastern bloc. He went on to join Radio Freedom and to be its director in Lusaka, Zambia in the 1980s.

53. Sellström, *Sweden and National Liberation in Southern Africa*, 580.

54. Ibid.

55. Ibid., 599–600.

56. Ibid., 600.

57. Ibid.

58. Ibid., 601.

59. Ibid.

60. Ibid., 601–2.

61. Letter from Thomas Nkobi to the Swedish Embassy, ANC, Lusaka, October 20, 1976 (SDA) cited in Sellström, *Sweden and National Liberation in Southern Africa*, 602.

62. Sellström, *Sweden and National Liberation in Southern Africa*, 603.

63. Memorandum submitted by African National Congress of South Africa to SIDA in support of a request for assistance for the year 1977–1978, ANC, Lusaka, [no date, but attached to the letter "Request for assistance from ANC from Anders Mollander, Swedish embassy, to the Ministry for Foreign Affairs," Lusaka, April 14, 1977] SDA, cited in Sellström, *Sweden and National Liberation in Southern Africa*, 603.

64. Swedish support to ANC in Madagascar and Ethiopia was introduced in 1982–1983 (Agreed minutes of discussion in Lusaka, May 1982, between the African National Congress of South Africa, ANC, and the Swedish International Development Authority, SIDA, concerning humanitarian assistance, Lusaka, May 24, 1982) (SDA), cited in Sellström, *Sweden and National Liberation*, 604.

65. Letter (Submission of budgets for 1986–1987 and consolidation of projects 1985–1986) from Thomas Nkobi, Treasurer General, to the Swedish Embassy, ANC, Lusaka, January 10, 1986 (SDA), cited in Sellström, *Sweden and National Liberation*, 604.

66. Sellström, *Sweden and National Liberation*, 23–39, 592–608.

67. This is according to Maartje van Weegen, chairperson of Omroep voor Radio Freedom, on the occasion of the opening of the "Jabulani! Freedom of the Airwaves" conference held in Doorn, Netherlands in August 1991. See *Jabulani! Freedom of the Airwaves: Towards Democratic Broadcasting in South Africa Conference Report*, Doorn, Netherlands, August 1991, Amsterdam: African-European Institute, 1991, 8, copy available in MCA, Dr. Karel Roskam Collection, MCA, Robben Island Museum-Mayibuye Archives, University of the Western Cape.

68. Kelsey Simon, "'Keep Radio Freedom on the Air!': The Dutch Support of ANC's Clandestine Radio Station, 1982–1996" (BA Hons Mini-diss., University of the Witwatersrand, Johannesburg, 2017), 63.

69. Ibid.

70. Ibid., 64.

71. Ibid., 65.

72. Hans Fortuin, a broadcaster at School Television, was another founder member. At the moment it is still unclear as to who the other three members were.

73. Karel Roskam, "Interracial Relationships in the Union of South Africa and the International Community" (PhD diss., Calvinist Free University, Amsterdam, July 1960).

74. MCA 8, Karel Roskam Collection, Papers of Dutch Anti-Apartheid Organisations (1959–1994); Karel Roskam, "Dutch Opposition to Apartheid: Facts and Fallacies" (paper presented to Mayibuye Center, University of the Western Cape, March 16, 1993); Karel Roskam—Biographical Sketch, Dr. Karel Roskam Collection, MCA 8, Robben Island Museum—Mayibuye Archives, University of the Western Cape.

75. Interview with Fulco van Aurich, conducted by Kelsey Simon, cited in Simon, "Keep Radio Freedom on the Air!'", 65.

76. Ibid.

77. Interview with Martin Jansen, conducted by Kelsey Simon, Johannesburg, July 3, 2017, cited in Simon, "'Keep Radio Freedom on the Air!'", 66.

78. Simon, "'Keep Radio Freedom on the Air!'", 69–70.

79. Interview with Fulco van Aurich, conducted by Kelsey Simon, September 28, 2017, cited in Simon, "'Keep Radio Freedom on the Air!'", 71.

80. Ibid., 72.

81. Ibid., 70.

82. Interview with Huub Bammens, conducted by Kelsey Simon, August 7, 2017, cited in Simon, "Keep Radio Freedom on the Air!'", 70.

83. Ibid., 72.

84. Ibid., 73.

85. Simon, "'Keep Radio Freedom on the Air!'", 74.

86. MCA 8: Karel Roskam Collection, "Documenting the Dutch AAM," *On Campus*, March 12, 1993.

87. *Sechaba*, September 1989, 5.

88. *Sechaba*, September 1989, 5; MCA, Dr. Karel Roskam Collection, *"Zuidafrikanen mogen niet alles weten (en buitenlanders ook niet)"* ("South Africans may not know everything [and that goes for foreigners too])," pamphlet by Karel Roskam, dated 1989, Robben Island Museum—Mayibuye Archives, University of the Western Cape.

89. MCA, Dr. Karel Roskam Collection, *"Zuidafrikanen mogen niet alles weten."*

90. *Sechaba*, September 1989, 5.

91. Ibid.

92. Skype interview with Fulco van Aurich, conducted by Kelsey Simon, September 28, 2017, cited in Simon, "Keep Radio Freedom on the Air!"

93. See www.mandela.gov.za/mandela_speeches/1992/9212_omroep.htm.

Chapter Twelve

In Search of PAC Footprints in Broadcasting

Ali Khangela Hlongwane

From the time of their emergence as a political formation within the African National Congress Youth League (ANCYL) in the 1950s, the Africanists who later established the Pan Africanist Congress of Azania (PAC)[1] took the propagating of ideas seriously. The platforms available to them at the time included the print media, which they generated through a cyclostyled publication, *The Africanist*, and distributed among the core members. Local and national newspapers were also utilized to spread the message of the PAC. A number of PAC activists across generations were journalists attached to various publications; their writings would be used as source materials by PAC broadcasters.

Radio broadcasting, the core subject of this chapter, was probably not even contemplated; it was a government-controlled machine in South Africa from its inception in 1924. The banning of the PAC in 1960 and new challenges to reach out to wider international audiences by the now exiled liberation movement made the option of engaging in radio broadcasts attractive. In 1961, offices were established in London, Accra, Cairo, Francistown, Dar es Salaam, and Leopoldville as operational bases of the PAC in exile.[2] Representatives based in these offices were the ones who had broadcast slots in the host countries and had begun to use radio as one tool for spreading the PAC message. Print was another mechanism used to propagate PAC ideas as evidenced by *Azania News*, which replaced *The Africanist* in 1966, and a variety of booklets, pamphlets, and *Azania Combat*. The *Combat* was a publication of the Azanian People's Liberation Army (APLA).

Literature on the use of radio by liberation movements exclude the PAC and its use of this medium. For instance, Lebona Mosia, Charles Riddle, and

Jim Zaffiro, writing as far back as 1994, document "the history of . . . four African nationalists stations: Radio Freedom of the ANC, the South West African People's Organisation of Namibia (SWAPO) station, the Voice of Namibia, and the two stations that broadcast to pre-independence Zimbabwe, the Zimbabwe African National Union (ZANU) station, Voice of Zimbabwe and the Zimbabwe African People's Union (ZAPU) station, Voice of the Revolution."[3] The latter stations, in Mosia, Riddle, and Zaffiro's view, "had the same central purpose—opposition to white minority regimes; they all have similar histories—relying on extensive help from, in the early stages, Nasser's Egypt and, later, Nyerere's Tanzania."[4] The authors further note that "for decades the stations attempted to reach supporters through a barrage of state jamming and censorship,"[5] challenges that also applied to the PAC's endeavors in this medium, and providing insight into the use of radio by interest groups in southern Africa to influence political opinion and direction from the time of the Second World War and, in the context of the Cold War, tracing the role of "the first African states to join the propaganda war . . . Ethiopia and Egypt" where the beginnings of the PAC relationship with radio begins. In another article, Mosia, Pinnock, and Riddle list eight liberation movements that were using Radio Tanzania from 1968, and include the PAC in the list.[6]

Sekibakiba Lekgoathi, in his study of the ANC's Radio Freedom (chapter 11 in this volume), notes that the literature on the use of radio by liberation movements is still scanty. His article on Radio Freedom and the struggle against apartheid, published in 2013,[7] builds on an earlier work by Stephen R. Davis, an article published in 2009 titled "The African National Congress, its Radio, its Allies and Exile." Both Davis and Lekgoathi are silent on the PAC. Nonetheless, their studies provide useful approaches to exploring "the social history of [radio], the motives behind [their] establishment, [their] modus operandi, program content, listenership and [their] impact in the struggle against apartheid."[8] Work by Rawia Tawfik is worth mentioning insofar as it provides background information on the role of Egypt in pan-African struggles of the 1950s and 1960s.[9] Egypt's contribution was in providing offices in Cairo to liberation movements as well as diplomatic, political, and military support to African liberation movements. Like Ghana, Egypt also had a Bureau of African Affairs.[10] However, when Tawfik goes through the names of leaders and organizations that were based in Cairo, the PAC is hardly mentioned. Proceeding along the same lines is Helmi Sharawy, who writes about his recollections of Cairo as host to African liberation movements in the 1950s. He notes that Egypt was not sectarian and did not go along the lines of "authentic" liberation movements. He also acknowledges that South Africa was not the only country with two or more liberation movements, but in his list of liberation movements that were based in Cairo the PAC is left out.[11]

The PAC, which has been in existence for sixty years at the time of writing of this chapter, has not had a single chronicler of its use of radio as a tool for the advancement of the liberation struggle. This chapter traces the PAC's footprint in radio from the 1960s in Ghana, 1963 in Cairo, also 1963 in the Congo, 1965 to 1967 in Algeria, and the radio operations in Dar es Salaam, Tanzania, which began in 1968.[12] It also outlines the profiles of the organization's media operatives—print and audio—the program and content of its broadcasts, and the ideological rationale that informed it.

A brief historical outline of the exile years of the PAC will suffice to situate the promising beginnings of PAC broadcasting in Ghana in the 1960s and the attempts to do the same in the Congo in the 1960s, gaps in the use of radio in the early 1970s, the sustained broadcasts in the 1980s from Dar es Salaam, and the commentary on a regular slot on Zimbabwean broadcasting in the 1980s. Three directorates played a critical role in the early phases: the Secretariat for Pan African Affairs under the leadership of Peter Hlaole Molotsi, the Secretariat for Foreign Affairs led by Selby T. Ngendane, and the Publicity and Information Secretariat under Z. B. Molete. In Molotsi's view, his secretariat was "supposed to engender studies of African political structures and develop groups that would have knowledge of what was happening in each African country."[13]

Right before its formation, the PAC had already established links with leaders of the emergent independent African states (as demonstrated by messages of support at its founding congress), as well as correspondence with A. K. Barden, who was the secretary of the Bureau of African Affairs.[14] The bureau was described by Ngila Muendane as "the nerve centre of African liberation movements."[15] This explains why the PAC was able to establish offices—and in some cases links—with broadcast centers in African countries.

Another critical secretariat, the Secretariat for Foreign Affairs, was meant to deal "primarily with people outside the African continent."[16] According to Molotsi, in the early days of the PAC they had held "the idea that we did not live in an empty world: that there were other people who lived outside the continent with whom we needed to have links."[17] Further, the Publicity and Information Secretariat led by Z. B. Molete from 1963 had propagated PAC ideas from Maseru, Lesotho. Molete would continue to hold this position as part of the Presidential Council but not much systematic propaganda work seems to have been implemented under his watch. For instance, the reissuing of the founding documents, PAC Basic Documents, with an introduction by Edwin Makoti, took place in Zambia.[18]

The PAC leadership conflicts intensified in the 1970s. This crisis dragged on until 1979, with the setting up of a Presidential Council consisting of Vusi Make, David Sibeko, and Elias Ntloedibe as secretary for publicity and information. The Presidential Council was short-lived; Vusumzi Make of the

Cairo days became the chairman of the Central Committee; and Elias Ntloe-dibe was replaced by Gora Ebrahim as director of publicity and information. Editions of *Azania News*, which replaced the *Africanist*, were published. Publications such as *The New Road of Revolution, The National Mandate in Azania,* and the *Field Marshall's Manual* were released. In 1981, Make handed over the political leadership of the PAC to John Nyati Pokela, who had just completed thirteen years on Robben Island after being kidnapped by agents of the colonial apartheid government from Lesotho during the days of the Presidential Council.

These developments are significant because they also mark the reorgan-ization of PAC propaganda work under the Department of Publicity and Information and the intersection of print, cultural activities, and broadcasting under one roof. The exception was the regular broadcasts in the 1980s by the late PAC activist Vusi Ndlovu, who had a regular slot on Zimbabwean radio.[19] PAC radio broadcasts in Zimbabwe are not covered in this chapter, largely because the archives of the Zimbabwe Broadcasting Corporation (ZBC) are not available electronically. Importantly, Raymond Fihla, former member of APLA High Command and a retired general, affirms that "Cde Vusi Ndlovu was employed by the ZBC but with the agreement of the PAC. He also had a PAC slot in his program and if I remember well it was a daily program. . . . I arrived in Zimbabwe in 1984 and Cde Vusi was already at ZBC."[20]

I have written elsewhere that with the return of Pokela to the leadership of the PAC there was renewed hope that finally the PAC had a leader who could pull the organization out of its factionalism and disorganization.[21] This hope was captured well by one foot soldier who cherished that hope and later rose to the position of commander of operations in the APLA High Command, Letlapa Mphahlele. He later wrote in his autobiography:

> Pokela's arrival and rise into leadership as chairman boosted the morale of PAC cadres in the camps. The new lease of life that he brought in the military was testified to by the arrival of about thirty recruits who came via Lesotho.[22]

These recruits were joined by groups trained in Lebanon, Sudan, Nigeria, and Guinea, as well as a group that had trained in Cambodia. In less than a month, Pokela had succeeded in bringing back to the PAC fold members who had earlier been "pushed out of the organization"[23] and who subsequently established the African People's Revolutionary Party (APRP). This group was led by Pokela's former comrade during the early days of Basutoland, Templeton Ntantala. In 1981, he led the process of restructuring APLA, creating a high command and appointing a youthful secretary for defense, Sabelo Phama.[24]

Internal [PAC] publications, such as Azania Today and Azania Combat, have gaps. They do not cover the entire period of the organisation. There were periods when these publications were not printed due to a shortage of funds. [In contrast] there is an abundance of these internal publications during the period starting from 1984 to 1990.[25]

FRAGMENTS AND GAPS: BROADCASTING THE SOUTH AFRICAN LIBERATION STRUGGLE

There is an archive of the scripts of the Voice of the PAC and the Azanian People's Liberation Army; it is part of the PAC archives at the University of Fort Hare. The archive covers the period from 1984 to 1994, including the leadership period of Nyati Pokela and Johnson Mlambo. But the earlier period has gaps that emerge in the archive as footprints laid by the Secretariat for Foreign Affairs in the early 1960s, the period in which Molotsi and Nana Mahomo left South Africa on the eve of the 1960 Anti-Pass Campaign that led to the shootings at Sharpeville and the setting-up of the first PAC office abroad. The historian Kwandiwe Kondlo is of the view that what are called PAC offices in Accra, London, and Cairo "were not fully-fledged offices with full infrastructure, as would be expected; they operated more as contact points for the PAC in these countries."[26] Molotsi nonetheless recalled that their "mission [in Ghana] was to publicise our name all over Africa and the world and to ask for assistance for our struggle."[27] Molotsi further recalls that the PAC

operated a radio station there [Ghana], so we could communicate with a wide variety of people in Africa and beyond. We had links with agencies that distributed news to the world; we were being heard all over the world. We even managed to send messages to South Africa. Some people used to hear the messages here on broadcasting station. But the regime here jammed up the broadcasts and when they did that we operated from Cairo as well.[28]

Molotsi's comment that the broadcasts from Ghana reached South African listeners is doubtful but cannot be completely dismissed. Certainly, radio in the 1960s was still underdeveloped in African countries. For instance, broadcasting relied largely on shortwave as the main means of transmission, but it could be interfered with easily and was subject to fading and distortion. In the early days of Nkrumah's Ghana, FM networks were not yet accessible. However, most of the radios had shortwave bands and ready access to international shortwave broadcasters such as the British Broadcasting Corporation (BBC).[29] This period relied on the technology of the 1940s, which saw the development of transistor radios that were portable and battery-operated and that became popular as African states were gaining independence in the 1960s.[30] Isaac Abeku Blankson notes that "in 1961, the government

launched the External Service of Radio Ghana to transmit information, propaganda, and solidarity messages to promote freedom and self-determination
among Africans on the continent and in the diaspora. The service also
reached North America, Europe, Japan, and Australia."[31] Paul Vianney Ansah further notes that "with four 100kw, and two 250kw transmissions, it
broadcast 110 hours a week and the signal was clearly received in several
parts of Africa and Europe."[32] This external service was only discontinued in
1979 by the military government of Jerry Rawlings.

The PAC's access to radio in Ghana did not represent broadcasting by the
organization; it was only part of free access to Ghanaian state radio. Kwesi
Kwaa Prah links the PAC's access to radio in Ghana to the establishment
soon after 1957 of the Bureau of African Affairs, involving George Padmore,
Ekou Barden (mentioned above, corresponding with the PAC leadership in
1959) and Ras Makonnen. Prah specifically recalls a program on Ghanaian
radio called *Down South* that broadcast on Saturday afternoon after lunch and
played South African music like the pennywhistle and mbaqanga.[33]

> That this interaction produced an interest in both the non-Ghanaian and Gha-
> naian public can be exemplified by the fact that one of the most popular
> programs was a programme that played predominantly South African music.
> The programme, called "Down South," went out on Saturday afternoon around
> lunchtime; Accra would virtually come to a standstill, with people rushing to
> their homes, from wherever they might have been, work, shopping and so on,
> to listen to this programme. People of Ghana identified themselves with South
> African music and could therefore understand when South Africans talked
> about their oppression and their struggles for liberation.[34]

The PAC office in Ghana was later joined by Elias Ntloedibe, who replaced
Molotsi when he relocated to Dar es Salaam. Ntloedibe would later play a
prominent role in the PAC's Department of Publicity and Information. The
PAC presence in Ghana was also boosted by the arrival of Peter Raboroko,
who was secretary for education at the founding of the PAC. Raboroko had
played a major role in the work of the Bureau of African Affairs and its
subsidiary the African Affairs Centre (AAC) as "the associate editor of a
monthly magazine called *Voice of Africa*."[35] Jeffrey S. Ahlman notes that
Raboroko "presented the magazine's local and continental readership with
accounts of the conflict in South Africa, but also with stories of the struggles
in neighbouring territories, such as those of the Portuguese colonies, Rwanda
and Burundi."[36] On leaving Lesotho, Potlako Leballo also joined the PAC
team in Ghana and equally contributed articles explaining the South African
situation from the perspective of the PAC. It is acknowledged that there was
a failed attempt by Nana Mahomo, acting in his individual capacity when he
was alienated from the PAC, who tried to raise funds to start a radio station
while based in the United States.[37] (I will return to Mahomo's other endeav-

ors in the Congo shortly.) The coup of 1966 closed the chapter on Ghana as the center for anti-colonial struggles.

EGYPT AND ALGERIA

Molotsi indicates that when the broadcasts from Ghana were jammed the PAC broadcast from Cairo. Mosia, Riddle, and Zaffiro write that "Egypt, by African standards, had a powerful broadcasting service dating back to the beginning of the 1940s."[38] The PAC veteran Hezekiel Mothopi recalls PAC broadcasts in Cairo beginning in 1963. The PAC was represented in that country by Vusumzi Make, who in turn was afforded a slot on Egyptian Radio.[39] When Make left Cairo, Sizake continued broadcasts; the radio slot was known as "force and rights."[40] Although there are no available documentary records of the PAC's broadcast scripts in Cairo (a major gap that the ongoing research of this project seeks to address), we nonetheless know from the available archival records that radio broadcasting continued in 1969 when the PAC office in Cairo was under Victor L. Mayekiso, who published *Africanist News and Views* monthly. Consequently, the PAC "appointed Comrade Jackie Mazibuko to assist him [Mayekiso] and also to be our broadcaster there."[41] Further, from oral histories of PAC activists we learn that as late as 1977 Ngila Muendane also had a slot on Egyptian Radio.[42] Muendane had joined the PAC after the launching of the Positive Action Campaign in 1960. In 1963 he was sentenced to seven years in prison under the Sabotage Act and spent this term on Robben Island. He joined the external mission in 1976 and served as chief representative to the Middle East, based in Cairo, up to 1978, when he was transferred to London.[43] Other PAC activities in Cairo were the training of the first group of PAC exiles at around the same time as another small group was being trained in Ethiopia and its involvement with the short-lived Southern Africa United Front.[44]

Mothupi recalls that Z. B. Molete also had a radio slot in Algeria from 1965 to 1967 before leaving for Zambia. There are no documentary or oral testimonies corroborating Molete's role in Algeria. However, there is no dispute that the PAC was first represented in Algeria by Manelisi Ndibongo, who was known as Nga Machema. He was later replaced by Patrick Duncan. The Algerian government gave the PAC a flat and an office with a telephone line. PAC activities, including military training for its cadres, the visit by Leballo and Raboroko in 1964, and fault lines are discussed in detail in C. J. Driver's book on the life history of Duncan.[45] There is also mention of a newsletter, *Pan African*, initiated by Duncan, but no mention of the use of radio.

PAC IN THE CONGO AND THE MUTED RADIO KATANGA

Apart from establishing the PAC office in London, Mahomo was also active-ly engaged in setting up a PAC office in Leopoldville in the Congo. Lazlo Passemiers cites the PAC veteran Hezekiel Mothopi, suggesting that the "PAC's Leopoldville office was very tiny with only a counter, a printing press and no telephone."[46] Other liberation movements housed together with the PAC in the same building were GRAE (Angola's Revolutionary Govern-ment in Exile), SWAPO (South West African People's Organization), ZANU (Zimbabwean African National Union), Udenamo (Uniao Democratica Na-cional de Mocambique) and the Movimiento Nacional de Liberacion de la Guinea Ecuatorial.[47] According to Passemiers:

> As part of establishing a permanent presence in Congo, Mahomo also tried to set up a project to transmit PAC radio broadcasts across the region. . . . Radio Katanga had good reception in South Africa, and in late August 1963 he [Mahomo] approached [Cyrille] Adoula[48] to allow the PAC to make use of it. The following year in May, Mahomo, aided by [John] Marcum whom Maho-mo had become close to, convinced the Congolese government to grant PAC permission to utilise Radio Katanga's facilities twice a week.[49]

The political developments in the Congo were fraught for the Congolese as well as for the PAC. The PAC veteran Ike Mafole, who was one of twenty-two PAC operatives who arrived there in 1963, described the Congo "as the beginning of disaster for the party."[50] Mafole writes in depth about their experiences in the Congo in his unpublished autobiography. For purposes of this chapter it will suffice to conclude that Mahomo's second radio initiative did not transpire. His contact Cyrille Adoula was replaced by Moise Tshombe as prime minister in July 1964. Passemiers notes that "in the end, in September 1964, the PAC's plans to use Radio Katanga were blocked be-cause of the disturbances in Congo and Tshombe's uncertain standing in Africa."[51]

DAR ES SALAAM: THE VOICE OF THE PAC

The PAC's sustained work on radio was part of the support the African Liberation Committee was giving to liberation movements. Available records and information suggest that the PAC began broadcasting in Dar es Salaam in 1979, when in fact there is a view that it had begun in 1960. The year 1960 in the context of Tanzania is questionable. Mosia, Riddle, and Zaffiro's study points to a later date. They write that in March 1964 Tanzania started broadcasts to South Africa and Namibia, and Radio Tanganyika (as it then was) began broadcasting daily news bulletins to South Africa, bulletins that emphasized statements by South African opposition leaders and exiles. Molotsi, who had a slot on radio in Ghana, initiated the broadcasts when he relocated to Dar es Salaam. Extensive archival records of radio broadcasts by the PAC are continuous under the leadership of John Nyati Pokela who assumed the leadership of the external mission in January 1981 until his untimely death in 1985. Oral testimonies by PAC activists who were engaged with radio trace their involvement in the 1970s.

These gaps are a legacy of internal contradictions in the organization. Pokela was succeeded by Johnson Mlambo in the middle of 1985 until the period of negotiations in the 1990s. The Department of Publicity and Information was led by Elias Ntloedibe and the as yet unappreciated thinkers from the ranks of the PAC, Edwin Makoti and Waters "Bishop" Toboti.

Who were these communication activists or journalists of the liberation movement? Ntloedibe, active from 1979 to 1981, was born at Hammanskraal in 1927. He spent his youth in the rural area where his parents lived, on the farm Goedgedacht near Vaalwater in the Waterberg District. He earned a BA degree from the University of South Africa (Unisa), but had started writing at a younger age, while at high school. He later contributed articles to several magazines and newspapers.[52] From 1963 to 1989, he represented the PAC in countries such as Ghana, Egypt, Algeria, Indonesia, Tanzania, Zambia, and Botswana.[53] During Ntloedibe's period, the Department of Publicity and Information operated the radio broadcasts of four programs a week handled by Vuyisile Dlova; the department's work with the Organization of African Unity (OAU) press; publishing *Azania News*; public talks at the University of Dar es Salaam; and interacting with embassies including those of Algeria, Egypt, Sudan, Syria, Yugoslavia, Czechoslovakia, a French anti-apartheid group, and the German Federal Republic.[54]

Another report from the Department of Publicity and Information, whose author is unknown but was dated June 1974, reports on *Azania News* from January 1972 to February 1974. The report says that at this time *Azania News* carried a feature, "Letter from America," "in solidarity with the Black liberation movement and to acquaint the political fighters in Africa with important trends in the struggle of our brothers and sisters across the Atlantic ocean and to show the internationalist link-up and the need for solidarity in the anti-imperialist struggle."[55] Regular features of the publication, according to this report, are "in depth on the review of the South African press under the titles 'Tit-Bits from racist South Africa' and 'Strategic thoughts and current events' . . . [it] serialised biographical writings on Mangaliso Sobukwe . . . and the review of books." After reporting on the circulation of the publication and financial challenges, the report ends with a note on broadcasting programs:

> *Azania News* plays an important role in the party's broadcasting programmes. All broadcasts' material are based in the main on articles in *Azania News*. Even dealing with current events *Azania News* is used as basic material. All party ideological broadcasts are a reproduction of material from *Azania News*. The party has regular ideological broadcasts every Sunday evening. Indeed the role the paper plays in our entire . . . cannot be overemphasised. [56]

Another communication activist, Edwin Makoti, was born in 1921 and received his primary education in Sterkspruit, in the former Transkei. He completed his secondary education in Johannesburg. He married while in Johannesburg and had three children. He left South Africa in 1961 for Lesotho and was part of the team that reissued *The Africanist*. After Lesotho, he stayed for short periods in Botswana and Zambia en route to Tanzania and was subsequently posted to Indonesia as a PAC representative. In 1968, he led an APLA unit for military training in China and on his return was appointed secretary for publicity and information. While fulfilling this role, he also served as secretary for defense.

Makoti, side by side with Pokela, is remembered for introducing a wide-ranging scheme to retrain PAC militants in the 1980s. He also introduced a variety of military and political education programs. He was considered articulate on PAC thought, and in turn contributed extensively to the writing of several PAC policy documents in the organization's exile period. Some of these documents are "Bogus Independence of Apartheid 'Republic,'" "The National Mandate in Azania" and "The South African Brand of Colonialism."[57] The former is described as setting out "the PAC position on the national question in Azania, with the land ownership issue having been placed at the heart of that question."[58] The three documents representing a few of his extensive writings are significant as their take on the nature of the liberation struggle underpinned most of the broadcasts.

In *Azania News*, Volume 20, No. 4 of April 1984, Makoti published an article titled "A Revolutionary Information Service" in which he summed up the revolutionary role of an information service aiding the struggle of the oppressed and exploited people in their quest for national liberation. He went further, to posit a view that asserts that an information service has an external and internal task, the external task being "to give our party, our movement of national liberation, our people and their struggle, a bold political character" and he cautioned against "an exaggerated view of ourselves, our attitudes and our activities," consequently asserting that "propaganda, to be believed, must be substantially true and restrained, so that it can also serve to enhance the integrity of our movement and the ingenuity of its leaders." Internally, the task of the information service was to "unify and revolutionise our party . . . unify the liberation movement . . . so that it speaks with one voice and act in unison on all matters of revolution." Broadly, the information service was to "report on the character of our struggle, explain the developments that are taking place among the people and counter the false, distorted or misleading and malicious propaganda of the enemy"—and to "expose those forces abroad which prop up the system and enable it to continue." Makoti also included seeking moral and material support for the struggle as an important task of an information service, and concluded by linking the work of this unit to the founding documents of the PAC, which pointed out that the organization wanted "an intelligent, informed and politically educated membership, a full-time information service."

Waters "Bishop" Toboti, active from 1981 to 1991, joined the Department of Publicity and Information shortly after escaping arrest and joining the external mission in the early 1980s. He was deployed first as a coordinator and then as director of publicity and information. His history with the PAC dates to his teenage years. He was imprisoned on Robben Island after the massive swoop of Poqo operatives by the police. On leaving the country and joining the external mission in the 1980s, Toboti recalls, "I became a broadcaster on the Voice of the Pan Africanist Congress, and my duty was to interview people like John Nyati Pokela, Johnson Mlambo and others. I interviewed all the political heavyweights of the PAC. And thereafter . . . I was taken to Zimbabwe for five years as the chief representative of the PAC."[59] Toboti notes that after he left the Department it "degenerated": "I was called back to the department in 1989. And then in 1991 the negotiations began in South Africa."[60] Indeed, the Voice of the Pan Africanist Congress broadcast during the period of negotiations articulated PAC perspectives of the process, including its walkout from the Convention for a Democratic South Africa (Codesa). The broadcasts continued to the eve of the 1994 first democratic elections. Makoti's view on the role of an information service is in line with that expanded in the guidelines the PAC developed in the 1980s on the work of the Department of Publicity and Information wherein the radio program was located. The document partly reads:

> The structural functions of this department embrace strategy and tactics in the interpretation and propagation of policy and programmes as clearly defined in the Basic Documents of our organisation, particularly as outlined in paragraph six to eighteen of our Disciplinary Code. In order to make the purpose of this re-organisation process clear beyond doubt we hereby summarise the tasks of publicity that our work demands as follows:
>
> • Maintain and enhance the organisational integrity of the PAC and the African Revolution of which our struggle for national independence, self-determination and social emancipation is an integral and indivisible part;
> • Project the dynamism of the National Mandate of the people of Azania;

- Highlight the essential value of the preparatory work necessary to assure that our revolution will take place and proceed, consciously and systematically, towards its dialectical conclusion;
- Refute and repudiate, without panic or rancour, the fallacious propaganda against our people, our party and our struggle at home and abroad; and
- Maintain and project the image of our organisation in the effort to unite and enable those who make revolution in Azania to acquire the revolutionary skills that are appropriate to the political situation in that country.[61]

At this point it will suffice to trace the profiles of the activists who had to embrace these tasks of publicity and played major roles behind the PAC broadcasts.

BROADCASTING PERSONNEL

The producers, initially Tanzanian nationals, were replaced over time by exiled PAC activists. The presenters, on the other hand, were at all times PAC exiles based in Tanzania who also had other responsibilities within the PAC and APLA. Some used their own names and are easily identifiable. Others used underground names and it is therefore not possible at the time of writing to confirm all the names as those of PAC militants in exile. Also, the names used in *Azania News* and those used in the publications of the APLA differ radically. Nonetheless, some of the personnel in APLA's information department also contributed to *Azania News* as well as the PAC radio broadcasts.

The presenters who were on other occasions referred to as "announcers" or "artists" included Peter Mana; Nicholus [*sic*] Molefe; Abel "Lumumba" Makhubela; Stanley Rasivhetshela, who was also the political commissar; Molefe Molapo;[62] Themba Hlaula; Brown Tasco; Waters "Bishop" Toboti (who joined the external mission in the 1980s and whose role is touched on above);[63] Sipho Majola;[64] Wandile Saji; Dudu Nosizwe; John Banyan Gwebityala; Gerald F. Malinga; Reggie Kumalo; Satch Gqajela; and Dan Mthimunye, a founding leader of the Azanian National Youth Unity (AZANYU), for which he held the position of secretary for publicity and information—he subsequently left the country following a police crackdown on the founding leadership. Mthimunye's writings appear in *Azania News* under his name.[65] Tswagare Kalf Namane,[66] whose poetry is published in *Azania News*, also developed playscripts for cultural programs in the camps. He had been a student at the University of the North (Turfloop), who joined the broadcast from 1979. Namane also recalls the names of Philemon Mohlahlane and Cecil Msomi. Maivha Mudhini, a former trade unionist and journalist who contributed articles to *Azania Combat* under the name "Muriel Dimpho"[67] remembers Msomi as a director in the Department of Publicity and Information during Gora Ebrahim's tenure, and a regular contributor to *Azania News* under the name "Izwe Lami."[68] On his return from exile Msomi worked as regional editor of television and radio in KwaZulu-Natal, served on the South African Broadcasting Corporation (SABC) board and at the time of writing was chief director of communications in the KwaZulu-Natal provincial office of the premier.

Othaniel Mackenzie was an actor who had worked internally with the poet Don Mattera and also performed in Namane's play. There were also Nkosana Mkhize and Edmund Ziba Jiyane who, on his return to the country, rejoined his earlier political home, now known as the Inkatha Freedom Party.[69] There was also Manqoba Qubeka, a former student at Orlando West High School and a PAC underground operative in the 1970s who was imprisoned in Botswana for APLA activities in 1986. He joined PAC Radio in 1986 when the Department of Publicity and Information was under the leadership of Gora Ebrahim, and was at the same time chairperson of the branch in Dar es Salaam. A musician in his own right who performed in the Mafube Band, Qubeka studied for a short period at the School of Journalism in Dar es Salaam but left before completing and later also studied at the National Social Training Institute known as Mwanza.[70] His broadcasts were largely on the national and colonial question.

While the directors of the Department of Publicity and Information played important roles, given that this was a department within a liberation movement, there are other players who may have been unintentionally silenced when they were part of the driving force of the propaganda machinery. These included Vusi Nomadolo, Vuyisile Dlova, and Charlie Maklemusi.[71] Only one woman activist's name, Dudu Nosizwe, appears in the archival records of the PAC radio. However, Mthimunye recalls the woman activist Casterlia Motshabi Moleke, formerly with the *Voice* newspaper in the early 1980s. The former journalist, writer, and publisher Mothobi Mutloatse, who was editor of the *Voice* at the time, recalls that Casterlia Motshabi Moleke "was from Diepkloof originally, a quiet but determined person who surprised all by going into exile 'to fight *maburu*.'"[72] Another known woman activist is the late Nombulelo Maphoyi.[73]

Most of these activists had abandoned formal education at home to take up arms against the South African regime. They would have had some form of high school education, one or two some higher education, like Namane, whose university education was disrupted by arrest and fleeing to exile. They were principally a product of the PAC's political education program in various camps and personal initiative in self-development. For instance, Namane recalls that he had unlimited access to Kwame Ture's (formerly Stokely Carmichael) private library while he was in Guinea. They also improved their hands-on experience through seminars organized by the PAC's Publicity and Information, where guest speakers included personnel from the Tanzania School of Journalism,[74] where a number of PAC cadres received formal training. The content of their training included broadcasting, editing and design, English, news writing, photojournalism, and practical work.

FORMAT AND CONTENT

From the extensive archive of the period 1981 to 1994 deposited in the PAC archives at the University of Fort Hare, we learn that the broadcasts were through the External Services of Radio Tanzania, Dar es Salaam. The Voice of the PAC was aired every Monday, Wednesday, and Saturday at 8:15 in the evenings. Further broadcasts were on Tuesday, Thursday, and Saturday, at the same time.[75] The transmission frequencies were consistently 50 kilohertz in the 60 meter band, 1035 kilohertz in the medium band, and 8.19 megahertz in FM.[76]

The broadcasts differed but a pattern defined them. There would be a theme and an interlude of freedom songs sung by selected APLA cadres who would be brought from the camps to record.[77] According to a radio program script compiled by John Marvin, "an army without culture is dull-witted army. In APLA, culture plays a very prominent role. It helps to build cadres of highest calibre, cadres who have the interest of the masses at heart and have love for their motherland."[78]

Each broadcast would have a theme drawn from diverse subjects reflective of the political thinking of the PAC. For instance, radio scripts of the period 1984 to 1994 ranged from those that dealt with South African history and the PAC's articulation on the national question; some aspects of South African History; the illegitimacy of South Africa; the role of imperialism in reforming apartheid; the national question; apartheid and the land question. Another major theme would be culture, cultural resistance, and cultural expression through music and poetry. Examples in the latter context were scripts with the themes of music and African musicians and their role in the liberation movement. These were broadcasts of an ideological nature. For example, freedom songs that were sung by APLA were those popularized inside the country from music cassettes accessed by members of AZANYU and related cultural groups such as the Bachaki Theater led by the late AZANYU member Thulani Sifeni; the Soyikwa Institute of African Theater (in which this author was a member as an actor and AZANYU activist); Busang Thakaneng, led by Gamakhulu Diniso, an AZANYU activist from Sharpeville who also contributed graphics in *Staffrider* magazine; and the Mafube Arts Commune.[79] Soyikwa members interacted with PAC representatives such as Lesoane Makhanda in New York and Pitika Ntuli and Bicca Maseko in Swaziland and later in the United Kingdom, and accessed PAC literature and music cassettes.[80] Mafube members were also connected with the PAC underground networks, which led to the conviction of one of its founder members, Jaki Seroke, to ten years on Robben Island;[81] the escape from trial to exile by Maropodi Mapalakanye, playwright, poet, and former secretary of the African Writers Association (AWA), and Mpikayipheli Figlan, also a member of Mafube writing for *Azania New*s under the name Pencil Sword[82] and contributor to *Staffrider* magazine. Seroke, also a former member of AWA and employee of Skotaville Publishers, recalls that

> the underground of the PAC distributed the cassettes and videos of the Party to popularise APLA and Pan Africanism. I smuggled from Botswana, Swaziland and Lesotho some of the APLA music production and recorded political education sessions. We distributed copies widely. The response was overwhelming. Especially among young people. . . . Besides APLA we also had the solidarity group Azania Kommittee's products on the PAC brought into the country.[83]

Indeed, AZANYU had the most developed underground network; sometimes it was not possible to tell who was not, in various ways, an underground operative. Tom Lodge has observed that "by 1985, AZANYU was functioning as an effective transmission belt for APLA recruits."[84] Lodge further writes, "By then a variety of other organisations were using the Africanist symbolic repertoire—a cluster of trade unions, the African Women's Organisation, and the Pan-Africanist Student Organisation."[85] Consequently, PAC literature, audio-visual cassettes of public addresses by PAC leaders such as Mlambo, and cassettes of PAC freedom songs were distributed through AZANYU networks and those of the National Council of Trade Unions (NACTU).

A program presented by Peter Mana under the theme "Revolutionary Songs" will illustrate the nature and character of a cultural program:

> Welcome dear listeners on our quarter hour revolutionary programme. In today's edition we will have a line-up of revolutionary songs by APLA combatants. We will open up our today's programme with the song *"Basebenzi nani balimi manyanani."*
>
> > *Basebenzi nani balimi manyanani*
> > *yekelani ubuhlanga*
> > *nani zinsizwa nezintombi manyanani*
> > *yekelani ubuhlanga*
> > *Bakithi manyanani yekelani ubuhlanga*
> > *ngoba bona*
> > *kobulala izwe*
> > *izwe lakithi izwe lawokhokho*
> > *sizwe sakithi soshonaphi na?*

Those were army cadres calling on our mothers and fathers who are the workers and peasants to unite in the march to the total liberation of Azania. Our
next song is titled "*We mama sizophekani*."

> *We mama sizophekani?*
> *izindleko zomkhosi wethu*
> *abalimi nabasebenzi*

"*We mama sizophekani*" is a song dedicated to the selfless and supreme sacrifices paid by the masses of our country in their revolutionary struggle. Our
next song is "*Manyanani*." Unite all the people of Azania under one banner of
African nationalism, that was the message from the song, "*manyanani*," "we
shall serve, we shall suffer, we shall sacrifice."

> We shall serve, we shall suffer, we shall sacrifice
> freedom fighter
> forward ever backward never
> freedom fighter
> forward to independence now!
> and tomorrow the United States of Africa

This song indicates once more militant determination of APLA cadres in guiding the revolutionary struggle to its logical conclusion. The next song is "*Sizo-
hamba no Sobukwe*."

> *Sizohamba hamba noSobukwe*
> *Sizohamba*
> *We Sobukwe sikhokhele*
> *Sizongena e Azania no Sobukwe*
> *Bazohamba o John Vorster*
> *Bazohamba*
> *Nge bazooka bazohamba*

The late Professor Mangaliso Sobukwe, the first and founder president of the
PAC. Azanians will always draw inspiration to [*sic*] his uncompromising and
militant revolutionary teachings. We will always be there in the battle front
where Sobukwe had always urged us to be.

Dear listeners we had [*sic*] now come to the end of our quarter-hour
revolutionary programme. On behalf of the Voice of PAC and APLA, our
producers Lucy Uriyo, our technician, Brown Tasco, our compiler, thank you
for listening. Tune in again. I am Peter Mona saying Long Live PAC, viva
APLA, viva Clarence Makwethu, viva Phillip Mlambo.[86]

Culture was not conceived as playing revolutionary songs. There were programs that engaged the theory of cultural struggle, drawing from the writing
of Sékou Touré, who is quoted from his address at the second Congress of
Black Writers and Artists in Rome in 1959, making the point that

> to take part in the African revolution it is not enough to write a revolutionary
> song: you must fashion the revolution with the people. And if you fashion it
> with the people, the songs will come by themselves, and of themselves. In

order to achieve real action, you must yourself be a living part of Africa and her thoughts; you must be an element popular energy which is entirely called forth for the freeing, the progress, and happiness of Africa. There is no place outside that fight for the artist or for the intellectual who is not himself concerned with and completely at one with the people in the great battle of Africa and suffering humanity.[87]

In this broadcast, Dan Mthimunye weaves the theory of cultural struggle to unpack the historical development of the arts as a tool of struggle across generations in South Africa. In particular he traces the historical emergence of cultural voices such as Miriam Makeba, Hugh Masekela, Spokes Mashiane; the emergence of Mahlathini Nkabinde and, in the 1970s, the voices of Malombo Jazz Makers led by Phillip Tabane; Victor Ndlazilwane; Dashiki, which included the poet and visual artist Lefifi Tladi; and the impact of the Black Consciousness Movement in shaping new notions and practices of cultural struggle. Mthimunye looks at cultural struggle in contestation with racist South Africa as an "imperialist base"[88] where South Africa "has become a second US culturally."[89]

There were commemorations of national days such as Sharpeville Day, June 16, 1976; the founding of the PAC on April 6; and tributes to fallen leaders and cadres of APLA.[90] Leaders of the PAC based in different parts of the world were interviewed and people from the home front were also featured in the program; there were profiles of PAC leaders such as Jafta "Jeff" Masemola[91] on his release after serving twenty-seven years of a life sentence. Toward the 1990s, internal leaders such as Zeph Mothopeng, Clarence Makwethu, and Dikgang Moseneke were interviewed during their visits to Dar es Salaam.[92] Current affairs in South Africa and the world were featured prominently. The sources were drawn largely from newspapers published inside the country. Manqoba Qubeka includes South African radio as a source of news as well as a propaganda machine.[93] In some instances, the broadcasters would read the newspaper reports from (inter alia) the *Rand Daily Mail*[94] and the *Sowetan*, analyze them, and give the PAC perspectives on the subjects covered.[95] Examples of how newspaper reports about current news were utilized can be gleaned from features in *Azania News* under the title "Tid-Bits from and About RSA."[96]

WHO WERE THE LISTENERS?

The only time the PAC made claims of reaching out to listeners in South Africa was the comment by Molotsi that the South African regime jammed their broadcasts from Ghana in the 1960s. When the broadcasts were introduced, it was to listeners in central, eastern, and southern Africa.[97] In conversations with Dlova, the dominant view was that the radio program was directed to listeners in the continent of Africa and any other part of the world that could access Radio Dar es Salaam; this was because the PAC placed emphasis on building solidarity with peoples of the countries in which its exile community was based. Indeed, it is affirmed in the policy document cited earlier by Edwin Makoti and in the minutes of meetings of the PAC Central Committee. The archive of the broadcasts is silent on public responses. These are, hopefully, areas for further research on the histories of the PAC.

According to former APLA operative Zongezile Sishuba,[98] PAC cadres in the two APLA camps in Bagamoyo and Ruvu listened to the radio broadcasts and used them as part of political education. Ruvu was a multipurpose center where new arrivals were stationed to give them an opportunity to decide whether they wanted to go for military training or pursue educational studies. In the camps, according to Zongezile, they had access to small radio sets brought to the camps by cadres who were trained in Guinea. Manqoba Qubeka recalls receiving feedback from listeners based in Botswana and internally in South Africa,[99] but qualifies the recollection by noting that these listeners were already part of the PAC underground machinery. Dan Mthimunye also concurs on the availability of portable radio sets in the camps: "at the camps we had small radios. [In addition to PAC Radio] we listened to most international radio stations like BBC, Radio Deutsche Welle, Radio France International and produced articles with our analysis of the story according to the ideological interpretation of the PAC."[100]

Cadres at the camps were not only consumers of news and ideological messages. They were equally generators of news and messages. Mthimunye recalls:

> there was also a Publicity team: Kalf [Namane], Letlapa [Mphahlele], Reuben Molefe, the late Mazambane[101] including our greatest graphic artist the late Velile [Velile Christopher Gcweni]. We added the [camp] newspaper [Bagamoyo Daily][102] with what we called local news to add humorous flavour of our situation at the camp, like, cultural events, football matches and interviews with the readers—the comrades at the camp. We would work the whole night compiling the newspaper/newsletter. By 5.00 am the newsletter would be ready when comrades came back from training and breakfast. It used to be so useful, with interesting headlines and graphics by Veg that left comrades in stitches. It ran on a daily basis and we rotated ourselves. We would sleep during the day and at 7:00 p.m. start again until the following morning. The "Voice of the PAC" was aired in the evening and the comrades listened— some other days it would be in the morning because we were alternating with Radio Freedom from Monday to Saturday.[103]

THE REACTION OF THE
APARTHEID SETTLER COLONIAL REGIME

PAC broadcasts seem to have mostly targeted citizens of countries where they were hosted as exile communities and where there were camps of PAC and APLA operatives, as well as the international community in general. However, as Manqoba Qubeka notes:

> We were really engaged in a propaganda war, where as a result of our revolutionary media and cultural activities, the racist regime was forced to establish a counter revolutionary medium called Radio RSA, created through funding from the Department of Foreign Affairs. They recruited broadcasting announcers from African states. They were to broadcast in Kiswahili, French, Portuguese, Silozi and Chichewa. [104]

Consequently, Qubeka further notes, "We also had to monitor and counter their reactionary propaganda." [105] An undated *Azania News* (Volume 21, No. 1) reported under the title "RSA supports subversive broadcasts to neighbours on counter broadcasts by the South African government." The report reads:

> In August, 1984, the British Broadcasting Corporation's Monitoring Service, which records radio transmissions from around the world, confirmed that clandestine broadcasts to Zimbabwe emanated from racist South Africa through Radio Truth. The General Post Office in South Africa is charged with policing the airwaves but its deputy postmaster-general declined to say whether or not the frequency was licensed. He did say, however, that the station was not their concern and nothing was being done about it since the report was made in August. A spokesman of the radio section of the post office admitted that the transmission was illegal. [106]

CONCLUSION

This chapter has utilized biographies of PAC activists, their oral testimonies, and the paper trail of PAC activities from the time of its formation in 1959 to its relocation on South African (Azanian) soil after the unbanning of liberation movements. The paper trail of PAC activities in Ghana, Cairo, Algeria, and the Congo is quite thin, with numerous gaps. Many activists who were based in Ghana, Egypt, and Algeria have since passed on. However, in recent years in-depth attention has been given to PAC activities in Ghana and the Congo, in particular by the scholars Matteo Grilli (on Ghana) and Lazlo Passemiers (on the Congo). Two PAC veterans who were based in these two countries in the 1960s, the late Lucas Rammonaseswa Molomo and Ike Mafole, have recorded their experiences in as-yet-unpublished memoirs along the lines of Philip Kgosana's autobiography, which touches on Ghana and the Congo. *Patrick Duncan: South African and Pan African* by C. J. Driver is an important secondary source on the PAC in Algeria, as is Ngila Muendane's biography of Vusumzi Make. This chapter builds on the scholarly work of Grilli and Passemiers as well as the unpublished memoirs of Molomo and Mafole and Driver's book on Duncan by exploring an area of PAC practice that has not been studied at all. Consequently, the chapter has traced the PAC's relationship with radio in Ghana, Cairo, Algeria, the Congo, and Dar es Salaam. Further research remains to be undertaken on PAC broadcasts under the auspices of the United Nations, as well as in Zimbabwe in the 1980s.

This chapter explores the broadcasts in the Dar es Salaam Radio External Service with better insight because they were aired consistently. The PAC activists who operated in Dar es Salaam left a trail of handwritten and typed scripts showing corrections by activists at work. A number of scripts have the name of the compiler and the date on which the scripts were broadcast; there are a few scripts with the name of a compiler and the broadcaster, but with no date. However, the content of those scripts and the identifiable compiler assist in the better understanding of PAC messages. Reports to the Central Committee by the Department of Publicity and Information provides insights into the strengths and weaknesses of the PAC radio, although there are no records suggesting its impact was ever evaluated, even though senior leaders—in particular Nyati Pokela—understood the critical value of propaganda and attended the workshops and seminars of the Publicity and Information secretariat. A number of PAC radio announcers have been willing to share their recollections of their activities in the broadcast studios and camps of PAC exiles.

This chapter has attempted to highlight the profiles of the heads of the PAC's Publicity and Information Department. It has also made an attempt, though sketchy, to profile the broadcasters, the foot soldiers of the Voice of the Pan Africanist Congress of Azania whose experiences are dwarfed by the biographies and autobiographies of leaders. In the archival records there is a name that reads like that of a woman, Dudu Nosizwe, and this study has found that there was also the late Casterlia Motshabi Moleke, formerly with the *Voice* newspaper in the early 1980s, and the late Nombulelo Maphoyi. The challenge to track and document the experiences of these foot soldiers (particularly women activists in the PAC) remains, and this chapter has hardly started that process.

But the chapter has also thrown light on PAC underground activities, an area that has also not yet been researched and written about. The role of cultural activists inside the country—the Bachaki Theater, the Soyikwa Institute of African Theater, the Mafube Arts Commune, Busang Thakaneng, individual members of the African Writers Association—who popularized the political messages, the freedom songs, and the literature of the PAC side by side with political formations such as AZANYU, Awo, and some affiliates of NACTU, to mention but three.

The PAC Radio was an important tool for the political education of PAC cadres in camps, but more research still needs to be undertaken to identify listeners in the host countries and to attempt a summation of its influence. Some PAC activists quoted here hint that the broadcasts were also meant to politicize people on the home front, but as yet there are no corroborating sources that the PAC Radio was listened to inside South Africa, except for the recorded material in the form of cassettes and, in the 1980s, videos of leaders addressing international constituencies.

Lastly, the ideological message on available scripts followed closely the political views of the PAC articulated in its publications, particularly *Azania News*. Its ideological views consistently built on the PAC's founding ideas published in the *Basic Documents*. Subsequent to the national democratic elections in 1994, a number of PAC Radio broadcasters and contributors to PAC publications were integrated into the South African Defense Force; a few took up positions in the SABC, while others are working as independent writers of books.

NOTES

1. The PAC adopted the name Azania in reference to South Africa in 1961. See the PAC Statement on Azania in David Dube, *The Rise of Azania, The Fall of South Africa* (Lusaka: Daystar Publications, 1983).

2. Lucas R. Molomo, untitled memoirs in the author's possession.

3. Lebona Mosia, Charles Riddle, and Jim Zaffiro, "From Revolutionary to Regime Radio: Three Decades of Nationalist Broadcasting in Southern Africa," *Africa Media Review* 8, no. 1 (1994).

4. Ibid., 3.

5. Ibid., 4.

6. Lebona Mosia, Don Pinnock, and Charles Riddle, "Warring in the Ether," *Review*, July 1992.

7. Sekibakiba P. Lekgoathi, "The ANC's Radio Freedom, Its Audiences and the Struggle Against Apartheid in South Africa, 1963–1991," in *The Road to Democracy in South Africa Volume 6, 1990–1996,* ed. South African Democracy Education Trust (hereafter SADET) (Pretoria: Unisa Press, 2013).

8. Lekgoathi, "The ANC's Radio Freedom," 550.

9. Rawia Tawfik, "Egypt and the Transformation of the Pan-African Movement: The Challenge of Adaptation," *African Studies* 75, no. 3 (2016): 297–315.

10. Ibid., 302.

11. Helmi Sharawy, Memories on African Liberation (1956–1975) https://www.pambazuka.org/pan-africanism/memories-african-liberation-1956-1975 .

12. Telephone conversation with Hezekiel Mothopi, September 2019.

13. Tom Lodge, "The Pan-Africanist Congress, 1959–1990," in *The Long March: The Story of the Struggle for Liberation in South Africa,* ed. Ian Liebenberg, Bobby Nel, Fiona Lortan, and Gert van der Westhuizen, 38 (Pretoria: HAUM, 1994).

14. See letter to Potlako Kitchener Leballo, October 28, 1959, the *Africanist* 4 (November 1959), Gerhart M. Gail, Papers A 2422 Box 3, University of the Witwatersrand Historical Papers.

15. Ngila M. Muendane, *The Leader South Africa Never Had: The Remarkable Pilgrimage of Vusumzi Make* (Johannesburg: Soultalk, 2007), 73.

16. "Peter Hlaole Molotsi," in *The Road to Democracy in South Africa: South Africans Telling Their Stories, Volume 1, 1950–1970*, ed. SADET, 38 (Johannesburg: Mutloatse Arts Heritage, 2008).

17. Ibid.

18. Edwin Makoti, "Foreword to the Second Edition," in *The Basic Documents of the Pan Africanist Congress of Azania (South Africa)* (Lusaka: Pan Africanist Congress of Azania, 1965).

19. Telephone conversation with Maivha Mudhini, September 7, 2019.

20. WhatsApp conversation with Raymond Fihla, September 27, 2019.

21. Khangela A. Hlongwane, *We Are Our Own Liberators: A Biography of John Nyati Pokela* (Johannesburg: RM Sobukwe Institute of Pan African Thought, n.d.).

22. Letlapa Mphahlele, *Child of This Soil: My Life as a Freedom Fighter* (Cape Town: Kwela Books, 2002).

23. I am indebted to Mfanasekhaya Gqobose for this expression.

24. During Nyati Pokela and Johnson Mlambo's tenure a number of young cadres, particularly from the class of 1976, were appointed to senior positions in the Azanian People's Liberation Army, including membership of the High Command.

25. Kwandiwe Kondlo, *In the Twilight of the Revolution: The Pan Africanist Congress of Azania (South Africa) 1959–1994* (Basel, Switzerland: Basler Afrika Bibliographien, 2009), 177.

26. Kondlo, *In the Twilight of the Revolution*, 101.

27. Muendane, *The Leader South Africa Never Had*.

28. Ibid., 44.

29. Graham Mytton, "A Brief History of Radio Broadcasting in Africa," http://www.transculturalwriting.com/radiophonics/contents/usr/downloads/radiophonices/.

30. Ibid.

31. Isaac Abeku Blankson, "Broadcasting in Ghana: Opportunities and Challenges of a Plural Media in an Evolving African Democracy," in *Transitional Media: Concepts and Cases*, ed. Suman Mishra, and Rebecca Kern-Stone (New York: John Wiley & Sons, Inc., 2019).

32. Paul Archibald Vianney Ansah, "Kwame Nkrumah and the Mass Media," in *The Life and Work of Kwame Nkrumah: Papers of a Symposium Organised by the Institute of African Studies, University of Ghana, Legon*, ed. Kwame Arhin (Trenton, NJ: Africa World Press, Inc., 1993).

33. Telephone conversation with Kwesi Kwaa Prah, July 2019.

34. Muendane, *The Leader South Africa Never Had*, 90.

35. Pan Africanist Congress, "Joint Programme of the Tombstone Unveiling: Peter 'Rocks' Nkutsweu Raboroko," May 15, 1915 to January 4, 2000. May 15, 2010. Copy in the author's possession.

36. Jeffrey S. Ahlman, "Road to Ghana: Nkrumah, Southern Africa and the Eclipse of a Decolonizing Africa," *Kronos* 37 (2011), 23–40.

37. I am indebted to Lazlo Passemiers, "Long Time Back Room Boy of the Pan Africanist Congress: An Appraisal of Nana Mahomo's Anti-Apartheid Struggle" (paper presented at Trails, Traditions and Trajectories: Southern African Historical Society, 27th Biennial Conference, Rhodes Makhanda University, June 24–26, 2019).

38. Mosia, Riddle, and Zaffiro, "From Revolutionary to Regime Radio," 5.

39. Telephone conversation with Hezekiel Mothopi, September 17, 2019.

40. Ibid.

41. Potlako K. Leballo, "P.A.C. Affairs Abroad: Resolution by Comrades," August 15, 1968. I am indebted to PAC veterans Philip A. Kgosan and Lucas R. Molomo for sharing this item, which is part of their papers in my possession.

42. WhatsApp conversation with Ngila Michael Muendane, September 17, 2019.

43. Ngila M. Muendane, *Confrontation with Apartheid Colonialism: The Role of the Pan Africanist Congress and the Influence of Sobukwe and Africanism in the Azanian Struggle* (London: Jacobin Books & Muendane Publishing), 1988.

44. "Gasson Ndlovu," in *The Road to Democracy in South Africa: South Africans Telling Their Stories, Volume 1, 1950–1970*, ed. SADET, 371–82 (Johannesburg: Mutloatse Arts Heritage, 2008).

45. C. J. Driver, *Patrick Duncan: South African and Pan-African* (Cape Town: David Philip, Oxford: James Currey, 1980).

46. Lazlo Passemiers, "The Pan Africanist Congress and the Congo Alliance, 1963–1964," *South African Historical Journal Special Issue: The Politics of Armed Struggle in Southern Africa* 70, no. 1 (March 2018): 95.

47. Ibid.

48. Cyrille Adoula succeeded Patrice Lumumba as Prime Minister of the Congo.

49. Passemiers, "Pan Africanist," 95.

50. Ike Mafole, *The Road to Exile: Wanted PAC-POQO Underground Activist: On the Run Inside and Itinerary Outside South Africa. History of a Generation of Resistance.* Unpublished autobiography; copy in the author's possession.

51. Passemiers, "Pan Africanist," 95–96.

52. See Elias M. Ntloedibe, "An Africanist View—Race and Nationhood," *The New African* (September 1962).

53. Elias M. Ntloedibe, *Here Is a Tree: Political Biography of Robert Mangaliso Sobukwe* (Mogoditshane: Century-Turn Publishers, 1995).

54. Vuyisile Dlova, "Report of the Publicity and Information to the Central Committee, 1981." I am indebted to PAC veterans Philip A. Kgosana and Lucas R. Molomo for sharing this item, which is part of their papers.

55. Anon. Azania News Brief Report. 1974. I am indebted to PAC veterans Philip A. Kgosana and Lucas R. Molomo for sharing this item, which is part of their papers in my possession.

56. Ibid.

57. Edwin Makoti, "The South African Brand of Colonialism," *Ikwezi: A Black Liberation Journal of South African and Southern African Political Analysis* 11 (March 1979); see P. Leballo, (made submission on behalf of the PAC), "Bogus Independence of Apartheid 'Republic,'" in *Time for Azania* (Toronto: Norman Bethune Institute, n.d.); "Pan Africanist Congress of Azania," in *The National Mandate in Azania* (Dar es Salaam: Pan Africanist Congress Publications, 1980).

58. Mazambane Willie [real name, Wilberforce Willie Mbuyiseni Zweni], "PAC Remembers Its Fallen Ex-Secretary for Defence," *Azania Combat: Official Organ of the Azanian People's Liberation Army* (APLA) 8 (1989): 6.

59. "Toboti 'Bishop' Waters," in *The Other Side of Freedom: Stories of Hope and Loss in the South African Liberation Struggle 1950–1994*, ed. Houston Gregory et al. (Cape Town: HSRC Press, 2017).

60. Ibid.

61. Pan Africanist Congress of Azania, Administrative Structures, Guidelines and Rules. n.d. I am indebted to PAC veterans Philip A. Kgosana and Lucas R. Molomo for sharing this item, which is part of their papers.

62. Molefe A. Molapo, "Profile of an Artist," *Azania News: The Official Organ of the Pan Africanist Congress of Azania* 26, no. 2 (n.d.).

63. See "Toboti 'Bishop' Waters," in *Other Side of Freedom*.

64. Sipho Majola, "Democracy and the Azanian Revolution," *Azania News: The Official Organ of the Pan Africanist Congress of Azania* 26, no. 6 (October–December 1990).

65. Dan Mthimunye, "Azanian National Youth Unity (AZANYU)," *Azania News* 19, no. 7 (July 1983); "The Role of the Youth in the Liberation Struggle," *Azania News* 21, no. 1 (n.d.); "PAC at Kumrovec [Yogoslavia]," *Azania News* 22, no. 6 (1986).

66. Tswagare K. Namane, "Bright Star of the Morning (Mangaliso Son of Sobukwe)." *Azania News: The Official Organ of the Pan Africanist Congress of Azania* 26, no. 2 (n.d.).

67. Muriel Dimpho [Maivha Mudhini], "Mugabe's Statesmanship Shines Once More as Unity Dawns in Zimbabwe," *Azania News* 26, no. 2 (n.d.).

68. Izwe Lami [Cecil Msomi], "Sobukwe on Internecine Violence," *Azania News* 26, no. 2 (n.d.); "Frankly Speaking," *Azania News* 26, no. 2 (n.d.); "From the Chairman's File," *Azania News* 26, no. 2 (n.d.).

69. Telephone conversation with Tswagare Kalf Namane, July 18, 2019.

70. Telephone conversation with Manqoba Qubeka, September 5, 2019.

71. Telephone interview with Nomadolo, former broadcaster and PAC representative in London, and Dan Mthimunye, founder member of AZANYU, broadcaster, and APLA operative, July 18, 2019.

72. WhatsApp conversation with Mothobi Mutloatse, September 10, 2019.

73. An email correspondence with Dan Mthimunye, September 3, 2019.

74. See Edwin Makoti, "A Revolutionary Information Service," *Azania News* 20, no. 4 (April 1984).

75. "Pan Africanist Congress of Azania—Radio Programme Scripts: Department of Publicity and Information," PAC Tanzania Box 80. University of Fort Hare, Liberation Archives.

76. Ibid.

77. Interview with Tswagare Namane (Kalf), August 14, 2019.

78. Ibid.

79. Khangela A. Hlongwane, "Reflections on a Cultural Day of Artists and Workers on 16 April 1989," in *Politics and Performance: Theatre, Poetry and Song in Southern Africa*, ed. Liz Gunner (Johannesburg: Witwatersrand University Press, 1994).

80. Khangela A. Hlongwane, "Journeys, Memories, Recollections, Diaries and Landmarks of Cultural Struggles: Reminiscences on the 1980s," unpublished autobiographical essay, 2019.

81. Interview with Mayaba Jabulani by Brown Maaba, Wits Oral History Interviews, historicalpapers.wits.ac.za/inventories/inv_pdfo/A3402-B48-00/jpeg/pdf.

82. Pencil Sword [Mpikayipheli Figlan], "South African Legal System Part of Pretoria's Arsenal to Murder Opponents," *Azania News* 26, no. 2 (n.d.).

83. WhatsApp conversation with Jackie Seroke, September 6, 2019.

84. Lodge, "Pan-Africanist Congress."

85. Ibid., 121.

86. Peter Mona, "Revolutionary Songs," "Pan Africanist Congress of Azania, Radio Programme, Poetry and Songs," University of Fort Hare Liberation Archives, Box 80. January 18, 1994.

87. Sekou Toure quoted by Dan Mthimunye, "African Musicians and Their Role Together with the LM [liberation movement]," (Monday) "Pan Africanist Congress of Azania, Radio Programme, Poetry and Songs." University of Fort Hare Liberation Archive, Box 80. February 23, 1987.

88. Ibid.

89. Ibid.

90. "Pan Africanist Congress of Azania, Radio Programme, Poetry and Songs," Liberation Archive, Box 80. University of Fort Hare Liberation Archive.

91. See Ike Molefe, *Uncompromising Till Death: Jafta Kgalabi Masemola, The "Tiger of Azania": Reclaiming the History of the Pan Africanist Congress of Azania (PAC)* (Johannesburg: Centre for the Study of Violence and Reconciliation, 2007).

92. "Pan Africanist Congress of Azania, Radio programme, Poetry and Songs," Liberation Archive, Box 80, University of Fort Hare.

93. Telephone conversation with Manqoba Qubeka, 5 September 2019.

94. Makoti, Edwin. "Apartheid in Practice, Radio Tanzania". n.d. I am indebted to PAC veterans Philip A. Kgosana and Lucas R. Molomo for sharing this item, which is part of their papers in my possession.

95. Telephone conversation with Vusi Nomadolo, Dan Mthimunye, July 2019.

96. "Azania News, Tid-Bits from and About RSA," *Azania News* 22, no.6 (1986); "Tid Bits from and about RSA: J. N. Pokela: Developments inside Occupied Azania," *Azania News* 21, no.1 (n.d.).

97. "Pan Africanist Congress of Azania, Radio Programme, Poetry and Songs," Liberation Archives, Box 80. University of Fort Hare.

98. WhatsApp conversation with Zongezile Sishuba, August 23, 2019.

99. Telephone conversation with Manqoba Qubeka, September 5, 2019.

100. WhatsApp conversation with Dan Mthimunye, August 30, 2019.

101. Mazambane (Wilberforce Willie Mbuyiseni Zweni) joined APLA in 1976 after the June 16 uprisings. He received military training in Tanzania, Kampuchea, and Sudan. He became a director of publicity and information in the APLA High Command. He obtained a national diploma in mass communication in Harare, Zimbabwe and a certificate in communications in Canada.

102. See Molapo, "Profile of an Artist."

103. WhatsApp conversation with Dan Mthimunye.

104. Email correspondence from Manqoba Qubeka, September 10, 2019.

105. Ibid.

106. "Azania News, "Tid Bits from and about RSA."

Selected Bibliography

Ainslie, Rosalynde. *The Press in Africa*. London: Victor Gollancz, 1966.

Anderson, Benedict. *Imagined Communities: Reflections on the Origin and Spread of Nationalism*. New York: Verso, 1990.

Baines, Gary. "The Battle for Cassinga: Conflicting Narratives and Contested Meanings." *BAB Working Paper 2*. Basel: BAB, 2007.

Barbosa, Ernesto. *A radiodifusão em Moçambique: O caso do Rádio Clube de Moçambique*. Maputo: Promédia, 2000.

Basson, Nico, and Ben Motinga. *Call Them Spies: A Documentary Account of the Namibian Spy Drama*. Windhoek/Johannesburg: African Communication Projects, 1989.

Bezdrob, M. Anne. *Winnie Mandela: A Life*. Cape Town: Zebra Press, 2003.

Bhebhe, Ngwabi. *Benjamin Burombo: African Politics in Zimbabwe: 1947–1958*. Harare: College Press, 1989.

———. *The ZAPU and ZANU Guerrilla Warfare and the Evangelical Lutheran Church in Zimbabwe*. Gweru: Mambo Press, 1999.

Bhebhe, Ngwabi, and Terence Ranger, eds. *Soldiers in Zimbabwe's Liberation War*. Vol. 1. London: James Currey, 1995.

Binda, Alexandre. *The Saints: The Rhodesian Light Infantry*. Johannesburg: 30° South Publishers, 2008.

Bogner, A., B. Littig, and W. Menz, "Introduction: Expert Interviews—An Introduction to a New Methodological Debate." In *Interviewing Experts*, edited by A. Bogner, B. Littig, and W. Menz. New York: Palgrave, 2009.

Bösl, Anton, André Du Pisani, and Dennis U. Zaire, eds. *Namibia's Foreign Relations: Historic Contexts, Current Dimensions and Perspectives for the 21st Century*. Windhoek: Macmillan Education Namibia, 2014.

Bottoman, W. Welile. *The Making of an MK Cadre*. Pretoria: LiNc Publishers, 2010.

Bower, R. T., and S. Ervin. "Translation Problems in International Surveys." *Public Opinion Quarterly* 16, no. 4 (1953).

Bragança, Aquino, and Immanuel Wallerstein. *Quem é o inimigo* (II). Lisboa: Iniciativas Editorials, 1978.

Brennan, James. "Radio Cairo and the Decolonization of East Africa, 1953–1964." In *Making a World after Empire: The Bandung Moment and its Political Afterlives*, edited by Christopher J. Lee, 173–95. Global and Comparative Studies Series 11. Athens: Ohio University Press, 2010.

Bull-Christiansen, L. *Tales of the Nation: Feminist Nationalism and Patriotic History? Defining National History and Identity in Zimbabwe*. Uppsala: Nordik Africa Institute. 2004. https://www.academia.edu/832397/Tales_of_the_Nation.

Callinicos, Luli. *Oliver Tambo: Beyond the Engeli Mountains*. Claremont: David Philip Publishers, 2004.

Caute, David. *Under the Skin: The Death of White Rhodesia*. Evanston: Northwestern University Press, 1983.

Chikowero, Mhoze. *African Music, Power and Being in Colonial Zimbabwe*. Bloomington: Indiana University Press, 2015.

———. "Guerrilla Radio: Liberation Broadcasting, Engineering the Post-Colonial African Nation State." Paper presented at workshop on Liberation War Radio, Johannesburg, February 2017.

———. "Is Propaganda Modernity? Press and Radio 'for Africans' in Zambia, Zimbabwe and Malawi during World War II and its Aftermath." in *Modernization as Spectacle in Africa*, edited by Peter J. Bloom, Stephan Miescher, and Takyiwaa Manuh. Bloomington: Indiana University Press, 2014.

Chitando, Ezra, Munyaradzi Nyakudya, and Government Phiri, eds. *Resilience Under Siege: The Zimbabwean Economy, Politics and Society*. Newcastle: Cambridge Scholars Publishing, 2016.

Chitando, E., and J. Tarusarira. "The Deployment of a 'Sacred Song' in Violence in Zimbabwe: The Case of the Song 'Zimbabwe Ndeye Ropa Ramadzibaba' (Zimbabwe was/is Born of the Blood of the Fathers/Ancestors) in Zimbabwean Politics." *Journal of the Study of Religion* 30, no. 1 (2017): 5–25.

Chung, Fay. *Re-Living the Second Chimurenga, Memories from Zimbabwe's Liberation Struggle*. Uppsala: Nordik Africa Institute & Weaver Press, 2006.

Coplan, David. "South African Radio in a Saucepan." In *Radio in Africa: Publics, Cultures, Communities*, edited by Liz Gunner et al. Johannesburg: Wits University Press, 2011.

Cruz e Silva, Teresa. *A Rede Clandestina da FRELIMO em Lourenço Marques (1960–1974)*. Licenciatura thesis. Maputo: UEM, 1986.

Cull, Nicholas. J. "Africa." In *Propaganda and Mass Persuasion: A Historical Encyclopedia, 1500 to the Present*, edited by Nicholas J. Cull, David Culbert, and David Welch. Santa Barbara, Denver, and Oxford: ABC CLIO, 2003.

Curry, Dawne Y. *Apartheid on a Black Isle: Removal, and Resistance in Alexandra, South Africa*. New York: Palgrave Macmillan, 2012.

Dabengwa, Dumiso. "ZIPRA in the Zimbabwe War of National Liberation." In *Soldiers in Zimbabwe's Liberation War*, edited by Bhebe Ngwabi and Terence Ranger. Harare: University of Zimbabwe Publications, 1995.

Dale, Richard. *The Namibian War of Independence, 1966–1989: Diplomatic, Economic and Military Campaigns*. Jefferson, NC: McFarland, 2014.

Daly, Ron R., and Peter Stiff. *Selous Scouts, Top Secret War*. Johannesburg: Galago Publishing, 1982.

Davis, Stephen R. "Voices from Without: The African National Congress, Its Radio, Its Allies, and Exile, 1960–84." *Journal of Southern African Studies* 35, no. 2 (2009): 139–53.

Diploma Legislativo Ministerial #28, de 19 Outubro de 1961. *Boletim Oficial de Moçambique*, 1ª série, #45(5º suplemento).

De Roche, Andrew. *Black White and Chrome: The United States and Zimbabwe, 1953 – 1998*. Trenton: Africa World Press, 2001.

De Villiers, Les. *Secret Information*. Cape Town: Tafelberg, 1980.

Dobell, Lauren. *Swapo's Struggle for Namibia, 1960–1991: War by Other Means*. Basel Namibia Studies Series 3. Basel: P. Schlettwein, 1998.

Dzimbanhete, Jesias A. "Reverberations of Rhodesian Propaganda in Narratives of Zimbabwe's Liberation War." *Africology: The Journal of Pan African Studies* 10, no. 1 (March 2017).

Evenson, John, and Dennis Herbstein. *The Devils Are Among Us: The War for Namibia*. London, New Jersey: Zed Books, 1989.

Fanon, Frantz. "This Is the Voice of Algeria." In *A Dying Colonialism*, 329–35. New York: Grove Press, 1965.

Foucault, Michel. "'Technologies of the Self': Lectures at University of Vermont in October 1982." https://foucault.info/documents/foucault.technologiesOfSelf.en/.

Franklin, Harry. *Report on the Development of Broadcasting to Africans in Central Africa.* Salisbury: Government Printer, 1949.

Frederikse, Julie. *None But Ourselves: Masses vs. Media in the Making of Zimbabwe.* New York: Penguin, 1982.

Fullard, Madeleine. "State Repression in the 1960s." In *The Road to Democracy in South Africa, Vol.1, 1960–1970,* edited by South African Democracy Education Trust (hereafter SADET). Cape Town: Zebra Press, 2004.

Geyser, O., ed. *B. J. Vorster: Select Speeches.* Bloemfontein: INCH, University of the Free State, 1977.

Good, Robert C. *UDI: The International Politics of the Rhodesian Rebellion.* London: Faber and Faber, 1973.

Greig, Ian. *Subversion, Propaganda, Agitation and the Spread of People's War.* London: Tom Stacey, 1973.

Gunner, Liz, Dina Ligaga, and Dumisani Moyo. *Radio in Africa.* Johannesburg: Witwatersrand University Press, 2013.

Halcomb, E. J., and P. M. Davidson. "Is Verbatim Transcription of Interview Data Always Necessary?" *Applied Nursing Research* 19 (2006).

Hale, Julian. *Radio Power: Propaganda and International Broadcasting.* Philadelphia: Temple University Press, 1975.

Hancock, Ian. *White Liberals, Moderates and Radicals in Rhodesia, 1953–1980.* New York: St. Martin's Press, 1984.

Hazvineyi, Lloyd, Munyaradzi Mushonga, and Munyaradzi Nyakudya. "ZAPU's Voice of the Revolution War Radio and the Radicalisation of the Nationalist Struggle in Post-UDI Rhodesia, 1965–1980." Paper prepared for the Comparative Workshop on Liberation War Radios in Southern Africa, 1960–1990s, November 2017.

Hedges, David, and Arlindo Chilundo. "A contestação da Situação Colonial, 1945–1961." In *História de Moçambique: Moçambique no auge do Colonialismo , 1930–1961,* coordinated by David Hedges. Maputo: Imprensa da UEM, 1993.

Heffernan, Anne. "Black Consciousness's Lost Leader: Abram Tiro, the University of the North, and the Seeds of South Africa's Student Movement in the 1970s." *Journal of South African Studies* (2015).

———. *Lipompo's Legacy: Student Politics and Democracy in South Africa.* Johannesburg: Wits University Press, 2019.

Heinze, Robert. "Dialogue between Absentees? Liberation Radio Engages Its Audiences, Namibia, 1978–1989." *Participations* 16, no. 2 (2019).

———. "'It Recharged Our Batteries': Writing the History of the Voice of Namibia." *Journal of Namibian Studies* 15 (2014): 25–62.

———. *Promoting National Unity: The Role of Radio Broadcasting in the Process of Decolonisation in Namibia and Zambia.* Konstanz: University of Konstanz, 2012.

Henige, David. *Oral Historiography.* London: Longman, 1982.

Hepple, Alex. *Censorship and Press Control in South Africa.* Johannesburg: Self-published, 1960.

Heuva, William. *Media and Resistance Politics: The Alternative Press in Namibia, 1960–1990.* Basel Namibia Studies Series 6. Basel: P. Schlettwein, 2001.

———. "Voices in the Liberation Struggle: Discourse and Ideology in the SWAPO Exile Media." In *Re-Examining Liberation in Namibia: Political Culture since Independence,* edited by Henning Melber, 25–34. Uppsala: Nordik Africa Institute, 2003.

Horwitz, B. Robert. *Communication and Democratic Reform in South Africa.* Cambridge: Cambridge University Press, 2001.

Houston, Gregory. "The Post-Rivonia ANC/SACP Underground." In *The Road to Democracy in South Africa, Volume 1, 1960–1970,* edited by SADET. Cape Town: Zebra Press, 2004.

Houston, Gregory, et al., eds. *The Other Side of Freedom: Stories of Hope and Loss in the South African Liberation Struggle, 1950–1994.* Cape Town, HSRC Press, 2017.

Kumar, R. *Research Methodology: A Step-By-Step Guide for Beginners.* London: Sage, 2005.

Langa, Aurélio Valente. *Memórias de um combatente da causa.* Maputo: JV Editores, 2011.

Lasswell, Harold. *Propaganda Technique in World War I.* Cambridge, MA: MIT Press, 1971.

Mbweazara, Hayes M. "'Pirate' Radio, Convergence and Reception in Zimbabwe." *Telematics and Informatics* 30, no. 3 (2013).

Laurence, J. *The Seeds of Disaster: A Guide to the Realities, Race Politics and Worldwide Propaganda Campaign of the Republic of South Africa.* London: Gollancz, 1968.

Legum, C. "Dialogue: Africa's Great Debate." *Africa Contemporary Record Special Issues Series.* London: Rex Collings, 1972.

Lekgoathi, Sekibakiba P. "The African National Congress's *Radio Freedom* and Its Audiences in Apartheid South Africa 1963–1991." *Journal of African Media Studies* 2, no. 2 (2010).

———. "The ANC's *Radio Freedom*, Its Audiences and the Struggle against Apartheid, 1963–1991." In *The Road to Democracy in South Africa*, edited by SADET. Vol. 6, 1990–1996. Pretoria: Unisa Press, 2013.

———. "Bantustan Identity, Censorship and Subversion on Northern Sotho Radio under Apartheid, 1960s–1980s." In *Radio in Africa: Publics, Cultures, Communities*, edited by Liz Gunner et al. Johannesburg: Wits University Press, 2011.

———. "Radio Freedom, Songs of Freedom and the Liberation Struggle in South Africa, 1963–1991." In *The Soundtrack of Conflict: The Role of Music in Radio Broadcasting in Wartime and in Conflict Situations*, edited by M. J. Grant and F. J. Stone-Davis. Zurich, New York: Georg Olms Verlag, 2013.

———. "'You are Listening to Radio Lebowa': Bantustan Identity, Censorship and Subversion: The African National Congress's Radio Freedom and its Audiences in Apartheid South Africa, 1963–1991." *Journal of African Media Studies* 2, no. 2 (2010).

Lenin, Vladimir L. *What Is to Be Done?* London: Panther Books, 1970.

Maaba, Brown. "The PAC's War against the State, 1960–1963" In *The Road to Democracy in South Africa*, edited by SADET. Vol. 1, 1960–1970. Cape Town: Zebra Press, 2004.

Maasdorp, H. "New Rhodesian Censorship Rule Remains Untested." *IPI Report* 25, no. 8 (August 1976).

Macmillan, Hugh. *Lusaka Years: The ANC in Exile in Zambia, 1963 to 1994.* Auckland Park: Jacana, 2013.

Magnusson, Ake. *The Voice of South Africa.* Research Report No. 35. Uppsala: Nordik Africa Institute, 1975.

Mandela, Nelson. *Long Walk to Freedom: The Autobiography of Nelson Mandela.* Randburg: Macdonald Purnell, 1994.

Manong, Stanley. *If We Must Die: An Autobiography of a Former Commander of uMkhonto we Sizwe.* Johannesburg: Nkululeko Publishers, 2015.

Manungo, Kenneth D. "The Role Peasants Played in the Zimbabwe War of Liberation with Special Emphasis on Chiweshe District." PhD diss., Department of History, Ohio University, 1991.

Martin, David, and Phyllis Johnson. *The Struggle for Zimbabwe.* Harare: Zimbabwe Publishing House, 1981.

Masiye, Andreya C. *Singing for Freedom: Zambia's Struggle for African Government.* Lusaka: Oxford University Press, 1977.

Mateus, Dalila Cabrita. *Memórias do Colonialismo e da Guerra.* Lisboa: ASA, 2006.

———. *A PIDE/DGS na guerra colonial, 1961–1974.* Lisboa: Terramar, 2004.

Matlou, V. "South Africa: Social Production, Social Deprivation and Social Emancipation." Paper presented at the CODESRIA Conference on "Another Development for Southern Africa," University of Zambia, Lusaka, September 3–7, 1979.

Mbeki, Thabo. "Domestic and Foreign Policies of New South Africa." *Perspective and Policy Options*, Carleton University, Ottawa, February 1978.

Mgadla, Themba P., and Brian Mokopakgosi. "Botswana and the Liberation Struggle of South Africa: An evolving Story of Sacrifice." In *The Road to Democracy in South Africa*, edited by SADET. Vol. 5, African Solidarity, Part 1. Pretoria: Unisa Press, 2013.

Mhanda, Dzino W. *Memories of a Freedom Fighter.* Harare: Weaver Press. 2011.

Mlambo, Alois S. "From Second World War to UDI, 1940–1965." In *Becoming Zimbabwe: A History from the Pre-Colonial Period to 2008*, edited by Brian Raftopoulos and Alois S. Mlambo. Harare: Weaver Press, 2009.

Moloi, Tshepo. *Place of Thorns: Black Political Protest in Kroonstad since 1976*. Johannesburg: Wits University Press, 2015.

Mondlane, Eduardo. *Lutar por Moçambique*. Lisboa: Sá da Costa, 1976.

Moorcraft, Paul L., and Peter McLaughlin. *The Rhodesian War: A Military History*. Mechanicsburg: Stackpole Books, 2008.

Moore, D. "The Contradictory Construction of Hegemony in Zimbabwe: Politics, Ideology and Class in the Formation of a New African State." DPhil diss., York University, 1990.

Moorman, Marissa J. "Airing the Polities of Nations: Radio in Angola." In *Radio in Africa: Politics, Cultures, Communities*, edited by Liz Gunner et al. Johannesburg: Wits University Press, 2011.

———. "Guerrilla Broadcasters and Unnerved Colonial State in Angola, 1961–1974." Paper presented at workshop on Liberation Radios in Southern Africa, Maputo, November 2017, 1–32.

———. *Intonations: A social History of Music and Nation in Luanda, Angola from 1945 to Recent Times*. Athens: Ohio University Press, 2008.

———. *Powerful Frequencies: Radio, State Power, and the Cold War in Angola, 1931–2002*. Athens: Ohio University Press, 2019.

Mosia, Lebona, Charles Riddle, and Jim Zaffiro. "From Revolutionary to Regime Radio: Three Decades of Nationalist Broadcasting in Southern Africa." *Africa Media Review* 8, no. 1 (1994): 1–24.

Moyo, Dumisani. "Contesting Mainstream Media Power: Mediating the Zimbabwe Crisis through Clandestine Radio." In *Radio in Africa: Publics, Cultures, Communities*, edited by Liz Gunner et al. Johannesburg: Wits University Press, 2011.

———. "Reincarnating Clandestine Radio in Independent Zimbabwe." *Radio Journal: International Studies in Broadcast and Audio Media* 8, no. 1 (2010): 23–36.

Mtisi, James, Munyaradzi Nyakudya, and Theresa Barnes. "War in Rhodesia, 1965–1980." In *Becoming Zimbabwe: A History from the Pre-Colonial Period to 2008*, edited by Brian Raftopoulos and Alois S. Mlambo. Harare: Weaver Press, 2009.

Müller, Martin. "What's in a Word? Problematizing Translation between Languages." *Area* 39, no. 2 (2007).

Murphy, Philip, ed. *Central Africa, Part 2: Crisis and Dissolution*. British Documents on the End of Empire, Series B, Vol. 9. London: TSO, 2005.

Mushonga, Munyaradzi. "The Formation, Organisation and Activities of the Catholic Commission for Justice and Peace in Rhodesia with Particular Reference to the Rhodesian War, 1972–1980." BA Honors diss., History Department, University of Zimbabwe, 1990.

Musoni, Francis. "Forced Resettlement, Ethnicity, and the (Un)Making of the Ndebele Identity in Buhera District, Zimbabwe." *African Studies Review* 57 (2014).

Mussanhane, Ana Bouene. *Protagonistas da Luta de Libertação Nacional*. Maputo: Marimbique, 2012.

Mutambara, Agrippa. *The Rebel in Me: A ZANLA Guerrilla Commander in the Rhodesian Bush War, 1974–1980*. Solihul: Helion & Company. 2014.

Muzorewa, Abel T. *Rise Up and Walk: An Autobiography*. London: Evans, 1979.

Ndlovu, Everette. "The Positioning of Citizen-Influenced Radio in the Battle for the Control of Minds." In *Participatory Politics and Citizen Journalism in a Networked Africa*, edited by B. Mutsvairo. New York: Palgrave Macmillan, 2016.

———. "Radio as a Recruiting Medium in Zimbabwe's Liberation Struggle." *Westminster Papers in Communication and Culture* 12, no. 2 (2017): 52–58.

Ndlovu, Sifiso M. "The ANC and the World." In *The Road to Democracy in South Africa*, edited by SADET. Vol. 1, 1960–1970. Cape Town: Zebra Press, 2004.

———. "The ANC's Diplomacy and International Relations." In *The Road to Democracy in South Africa*, edited by SADET. Vol. 2, 1970–1980. Pretoria: Unisa Press, 2006.

———. "The Geopolitics of Apartheid South Africa in the African Continent: 1948–1994." In *The Road to Democracy in South Africa*, edited by SADET. Vol. 5, African Solidarity, Part 1. Pretoria: Unisa Press, 2014.

Ndlovu, Sifiso M., and Miranda Strydom. *The Thabo Mbeki I Know*. Johannesburg: Picador Africa, 2016.

Nehwati, Francis. "The Social and Communal Background to '*Zhii*': The African Riots in Bulawayo, Southern Rhodesia in 1960." *African Affairs* 69, no. 276 (1970).

Ngculu, James. *The Honour to Serve: Recollections of an Umkhonto Soldier.* Claremont: New Afrika Books, 2010.

Nhongo-Simbanegavi, Josephine. *For Better or Worse: Women and ZANLA in Zimbabwe's Liberation Struggle.* Harare: Weaver Press, 2000.

Nkomo, Joshua. *The Story of My Life.* Harare: SAPES Books, 2001.

Nolutshungu, Sam. *South Africa in Africa: A Study of Ideology and Foreign Policy.* Manchester: Manchester University Press, 1975.

Nyamjoh, Francis. "Africans Consuming Hair, Africans Consumed by Hair." *Africa Insight* 44, no. 1 (2014).

Nyelele, Libero, and Ellen Drake. *The Raid on Gaborone: June 14, 1985: A Memorial.* Gaborone: Self-published, 1987.

Onslow, Sue. "Zimbabwe and Political Transition." London School of Economics and Political Science, March 2011, http://eprints.lse.ac.uk.

Peters, John D. *Speaking into the Air: A History of the Idea of Communication.* Chicago: University of Chicago Press, 2012.

Pfister, Roger. "Apartheid South Africa's Foreign Relations with African States, 1961–1994." PhD diss., Rhodes University, 2003.

Pfukwa, Charles. "Black September et al.: Chimurenga Songs as Historical Narrative in the Zimbabwean Liberation War." *Muziki* 5, no. 1 (2008): 30–61.

Pongweni, Alec J. C. *Songs that Won the Liberation War.* Harare: College Press, 1982.

Portelli, Alessandro. *The Order Has Been Carried Out: History, Memory, and Meaning of a Nazi Massacre in Rome.* New York: Palgrave, 2003.

Powdermaker, Hortense. *Copper Town: Changing Africa; The Human Situation on the Rhodesian Copperbelt.* New York: Harper & Row, 1962.

Preston, Matthew. "Stalemate and the Termination of Civil War: Rhodesia Reassessed." *Journal of Peace Research* 41, no. 1 (2004): 65–83.

Ranger, Terence. O. *Are We Not Also Men?: The Samkange Family and African Politics in Zimbabwe, 1920–1964.* Harare: Baobab Books, 1995.

———. *Bulawayo Burning: The Social History of a Southern African City, 1893–1960.* Harare: Weaver Press, 2010.

Rhoodie, E. *The Real Information Scandal.* Pretoria and Atlanta: Orbis, 1983.

Rivers, B. "The Role of South African Oil and of Western Oil Companies and Possibilities of Oil Embargo against South Africa." Testimony before the United Nations Special Committee Against Apartheid, December 1, 1977.

Russell, David. E. "Oral History Methodology, The Art of Interviewing." Oral History Program, University of California–Santa Barbara, n.d.

Saíde, Alda Romão Saúte. "As mulheres e a luta de libertação Nacional." In *História da Luta de Libertação Nacional*, coordinated by Joel das Neves Tembe. Vol. 1. Maputo: Ministério dos Combatentes, 2014.

Saíde, Alda Romão Saúte, and Joel das Neves Tembe. "Moçambique e a luta de libertação na África Austral" In SADC Hashim Mbita Project. *Southern African Liberation Struggles, Contemporary Documents 1960–1994*, 211–303. Vol. 2. Tanzania: Mkuki na Nyota Publishers Ltd., 2014.

Schmidt, Elizabeth. "Patriarchy, Colonialism and the Colonial State in Colonial Zimbabwe." *Signs: Journal of Women in Culture and Society* 16, no. 4 (1999).

Selby, Angus. "Commercial Farmers and the State: Interest Group Politics and Land Reform in Zimbabwe." DPhil diss., Oxford University, 2006.

Shaw, Angus. *Kandaya: Another Time, Another Place.* Harare: Baobab Books. 1993.

Sibanda, Eliakim M. *The Zimbabwe African People's Union—A Political History of Insurgency in Southern Rhodesia.* Trenton: Africa World Press. 2005.

Sithole, Jabulani. "The ANC Underground in Natal." In, *The Road to Democracy in South Africa*, edited by SADET. Vol. 2, 1970–1980. Pretoria: Unisa Press, 2006.

Sithole, Jabulani, and Sifiso Ndlovu. 'The Revival of the Labour Movement, 1970–1980." In *The Road to Democracy in South Africa*, edited by SADET. Vol. 2, 1970–1980. Pretoria: Unisa Press, 2006.

Sithole, Masipula. "Class and Factionalism in the Zimbabwe Nationalist Movement." *African Studies Review* 27, no. 1 (1984).

———. *Zimbabwe: Struggles within the Struggle*. 2nd ed. Harare: Rujeko Publishers, 1999.

Smyth, Rosaleen. "A Note on the 'Saucepan Special': The People's Radio of Central Africa." *Historical Journal of Film Radio and Television* 4, no. 2 (1984).

Souto, Amélia Neves de. *Caetano e o ocaso do «Império»: Administração e Guerra Colonial em Moçambique durante o Marcelismo (1968–1974)*. Porto: Edições Afrontamento, 2007.

Suttner, Raymond. *The ANC Underground in South Africa to 1976*. Johannesburg: Jacana Media, 2008.

Swapo. *To Be Born a Nation: The Liberation Struggle for Namibia*. London: Zed Books, 1981.

Tekere, Edgar 2-Boy Zivanai. *A Lifetime of Struggle*. Harare: SAPES Books, 2007.

Tembe, Joel das Neves, coordinator. *História da Luta de Libertação Nacional*. Vol. 1. Maputo: Ministério dos Combatentes, 2014.

Thomas, Scott. *The Diplomacy of Liberation: The Foreign Relations of the African National Congress since 1960*. London: I. B. Tauris, 1996.

Vansina, Jan. *Oral Tradition as History*. Madison: University of Wisconsin Press, 1985.

Vera, Yvonne. *Nehanda*. Harare: Baobab Books, 1993.

Wakati, David. "Radio Tanzania Dar Es Salaam." In *Making Broadcasting Useful: The African Experience*, edited by George Wedell. Manchester: Manchester University Press, 1986.

Welch, David. "Introduction: Propaganda in Historical Perspective." In *Propaganda and Mass Persuasion: A Historical Encyclopedia, 1500 to the Present*, edited by Nicholas J. Cull, David Culbert, and David Welch. Santa Barbara, Denver, and Oxford: ABC CLIO, 2003.

Wele, Patrick. *Zambia's Most Famous Dissidents: From Mushala to Luchembe*. Solwezi: PMW, 1995.

Zaffiro, James J. "Broadcasting and Political Change in Zimbabwe, 1931–1984." PhD diss., University of Wisconsin–Madison, 1984.

Index

Smith, Ian Douglas, 68, 167
soldiers, 27
Solomon Mahlangu Freedom College
(SOMAFCO), 222
Sorte grande (Great luck), 36
South African Broadcasting Corporation
(SABC), 156, 169, 171, 188, 203, 241
South African Communist Party (SACP),
203, 213
South African Indian Congress, 203
South African Student Movement
(SASM), 164, 187, 193
South African Student Organization
(SASO), 192
Southern African Development
Coordination Conference (SADCC),
155, 171, 178
Southern Rhodesia African National
Congress, 70
South West Africa, 203
South West African People's Organization
(SWAPO), 137, 204, 230, 237
Soviet Union. *See* Union of the Soviet
Socialist Republics (USSR)
Soweto, 187
spirit mediums (svikiros), 85, 87, 88, 89,
92, 93, 94, 100
Sunday News, 123, 126
Suttner, Raymond, 209
SWAPO. *See* South West African People's
Organization
Swapo Collection (Basler Afrika
Bibliographien), 7
Swedish government, 209, 215, 216
Swedish International Development
Authority (SIDA), 215, 217

Taela, 32
Tagwira, Thomas, 129
Tambaoga, Jimmy, 88, 92, 94, 102n8,
103n29
Tambo, Reginald Oliver, 202, 206, 209,
213, 216
Tanzania, 106
Tanzania Broadcasting Corporation (TBC),
141
Tanzanian government foreign policy
objectives, 23
Tanzania's External Service Radio, 23

Tasco, Brown, 241
Tawfik, Rawia, 231
TBC. *See* Tanzania Broadcasting
Corporation
technological state-crafting, 66
Tembe, Rosária, 23, 24, 25, 31
terrorist, 93
Tete, 28, 32
The Africanist, 230, 239
Thorbjorn Falldin, 216
Tichatonga, Grey, 68, 69, 70, 130
Tilburg, 220
Tiri Muvanhu/Sise Bantwini, 78, 79
Tjombe, Kaomo, 145, 148
Tlhakisetso, 174
Toboti, Waters "Bishop", 238, 240, 241
Toivo ya Toivo, Andimba, 139
Tongogara, Josiah, 130
Torre de Tombo, 43. *See also* Portuguese
National Archives of Lisbon
Total Strategy, 175
training (in broadcasting), 25
transcription of radio broadcasts, 35, 43,
47, 48, 53
transmitter(s), 100, 114, 115, 116
treason trial, 219
Tsonga, 25
Tumirai Vana Kuhondo, 76, 77
Tungwarara, Shingirai, 130
Twin Palms Radio Station, 114

Uchoane, Afonso André, 30
UDENAMO. *See* National Democratic
Union of Mozambique
UDI. *See* Unilateral Declaration of
Independence
uMkhonto we Sizwe (MK), 161, 184, 204,
213
UN. *See* United Nations General Assembly
UNAMI. *See* National African Union of
Independent Mozambique
União de Populações de Angola (Union of
Angolan People) (UPA), 45
Unilateral Declaration of Independence
(UDI), 13, 106, 110, 110–111
UNIN. *See* United Nations Institute for
Namibia
Union of the Soviet Socialist Republics
(USSR), 186, 213, 214

About the Authors

Mhoze Chikowero is associate professor of African history at the University of California, Santa Barbara. His articles on music, electrification, nationalism, and broadcasting have appeared in numerous peer-reviewed journals and edited volumes. His first book, *African Music, Power and Being in Colonial Zimbabwe* (2015), won the 2016 J. H. Kwabena Nketia Book Award. He is currently finishing two books, *The Military Entertainment Complex: Music, Media and State Making in Zimbabwe*, and *Tool of Empire, Technology of Self-Liberation: Radio Broadcasting in Colonial Zambia, Zimbabwe and Malawi*.

Cris Chinaka is a journalism veteran who spent a quarter of a century at Reuters International News Agency until his retirement. He worked as a reporter largely around southern Africa and was chief correspondent for the Reuters Zimbabwe Bureau for twenty years. Cris retired in 2015 to go into media training and consultancy, and serves on boards of several Zimbabwean media organizations. He is founding editor-in-chief of Zimbabwe's first national fact-checking platform, ZimFact.

Lloyd Hazvineyi is a doctoral fellow and assistant lecturer at the University of the Witwatersrand, Johannesburg. He is also a resident doctoral fellow at Wits University's Humanities Graduate Centre, and is a holder of a master's degree in African history from the University of Zimbabwe. His research interests include Zimbabwe's liberation war history. His PhD research explores the different relationships between nature and human communities in Southern Rhodesia, now Zimbabwe.

Robert Heinze is a researcher and lecturer at the University of Trier. He received his PhD at the University of Konstanz with a dissertation on the history of radio in the decolonization of Zambia and Namibia. He is currently working on a postdoctoral research project on urban transport in African cities. Among his published articles are "'Men Between': The Role of Zambian Broadcasters in Decolonisation" (2014) and "Fighting over Urban Space: Matatu Infrastructure and Bus Stations in Nairobi, 1960–2000" (2019). His research interests include the history of radio in southern Africa, the history of infrastructure and transport in Africa, and postcolonial urban economies.

Ali Khangela Hlongwane holds a PhD in heritage studies from the University of the Witwatersrand. He is a researcher in the History Workshop at the University of the Witwatersrand and a 2019 Institute for Creative Arts (ICA) Writing Fellow, University of Cape Town. He has published on the public histories of the 1976 uprisings, *Soweto '76 Reflections on the Liberation Struggles: Commemorating the 30th Anniversary of June 16, 1976* (2006), and *The Road to Democracy in South Africa, Volume 7: Soweto Uprisings- New Perspectives, Commemoration and Memorialisation* (2017). His recent publication coauthored with Sifiso Mxolisi Ndlovu is *Public History and Culture in South Africa: Memorialisation and Liberation Heritage Sites in Johannesburg and the Township Space* (2019). His biography of PAC veteran leader Zephania Lekoame Mothopeng will be published in 2020.

Sekibakiba Peter Lekgoathi is associate professor at the University of the Witwatersrand, Johannesburg. He holds a PhD in African history from the University of Minnesota, Twin Cities. He has published widely on Ndebele ethnicity, public radio in African languages in South Africa, the ANC's Radio Freedom, the politics of knowledge production, as well as on popular protests in rural and urban South Africa. Lekgoathi is currently completing a monograph titled *The Politics of Ndebele Ethnicity in South Africa, 1960–2010*. He has contributed to school history textbooks, and, through the History Workshop, he has been involved in facilitating oral history workshops with history teachers and students across the country. He is currently serving as a member of the Ministerial Task Team (History) of the Department of Basic Education.

Tshepo Moloi is senior lecturer at the University of the Free State, Qwaqwa Campus, where he teaches history. He obtained his PhD in history from the University of the Witwatersrand, Johannesburg. Moloi is the author of *Place of Thorns: Black Political Protest in Kroonstad since 1976*. His research interests include histories of liberation struggle in South Africa, and he has published on student and youth politics, and underground work.

Marissa J. Moorman is professor of African history and cinema and media studies at Indiana University Bloomington. Her research focuses on politics and culture in colonial and independent Angola. Moorman's work explores different media and how their uses, the practices and meanings people develop around them, and their relationship to power shift over time. She has authored two books: *Powerful Frequencies: Radio, State Power, and the Cold War in Angola, 1931–2002* (2019) and *Intonations: A Social History of Music and Nation in Luanda, Angola, 1945–Recent Times* (2008). Fellowships from ACLS, Fulbright Hays, and the SSRC have supported her research. Moorman has published on music, fashion, film, radio, and urban space. Moorman is an editor of *The Journal of African History* and on the editorial collective of *The Radical History Review*. She is an active member of the editorial board of *Africa Is a Country*, the blog that is not about Bono, famine, or Obama, where she is also a regular contributor.

Dumisani Moyo is associate professor and vice dean, academic, at the University of Johannesburg. His research interests include media policy and regulation in Africa, new and alternative media, political engagement through media in Africa, journalism in the digital era, and media and elections. Among his major work are two coauthored books: *Radio in Africa: Publics, Cultures, Communities* and *Media Policy in a Changing Southern Africa: Critical Reflections on Media Reforms in the Global Age.*

Munyaradzi Mushonga, PhD, is senior lecturer and program director for the Africa Studies Program in the Centre for Gender and Africa Studies at the University of the Free State. He previously taught history, environmental history, and cultural and heritage studies at the University of Zimbabwe and the National University of Lesotho between 1992 and 2019. He is an interdisciplinary scholar who deploys postcolonial and decolonial lenses to interrogate African nationalism, oral history, IKS, higher education, race, ethnicity, gender, and sexuality, among others.

Sifiso Mxolisi Ndlovu is professor of history at the University of South Africa, and executive director at the South African Democracy Education Trust. He has an MA in history from the University of Natal, Pietermaritzburg, and a PhD in history from the University of the Witwatersrand. He is coauthor of the book *Public History and Culture in South Africa: Memorialisation and Liberation Heritage Sites in Johannesburg and the Township Space* (2019), and editor-in-chief of *The Road to Democracy in South Africa* multi-volume series.

Munyaradzi Nyakudya is senior lecturer in the History Department at the University of Zimbabwe. He holds a PhD in history from the University of South Africa, and has published several articles and book chapters on Zimbabwe's liberation war, notably "War in Rhodesia, 1965–1980" and "Social and Economic Developments during the UDI Period." In addition, he has coedited two books, one on the Zimbabwe crisis entitled *Resilience Under Siege: The Zimbabwe Economy, Politics and Society* (2016), and the other *Victors, Victims and Villains: Women and Musical Arts in Zimbabwe* (2018) on women's contribution to the musical arts in Zimbabwe.

Alda Romão Saúte Saíde is associate professor at Pedagogic University in Maputo where she has been training undergraduate and postgraduate students in African history, economic history, and southern African history for the last twenty-four years. Saíde holds a PhD in African history from the University of Minnesota. She has also taught graduate courses as a visiting scholar at Superior Institute of Science of Education – ISCED, Luanda, Republic of Angola. Since 2001, she is acting as senior researcher of the Center of Population Studies (now known as Center of Policy Analysis – CAP) where, as a team leader, she has conducted studies on democracy and good governance and HIV and sexual reproductive health and gender. Saíde published two books on the history of education, Christian missions, and colonialism, and coauthored a book on Mozambican labor migration to South African farms. Her major research focus is on the regional history of southern Africa, looking at governance, migration, education, liberation struggles, HIV, and gender.

www.ingramcontent.com/pod-product-compliance
Lightning Source LLC
Chambersburg PA
CBHW030643270326
41929CB00007B/187